'As Liverpool's exceptional bishops, David Sheppard and Derek Worlock healed old wounds, championed great causes, and put faith into action in the city's forgotten neighbourhoods. A first-class biography of David Sheppard is long overdue, and Andrew Bradstock has provided it.'
David Alton (Lord Alton of Liverpool)

'*David Sheppard: Batting for the Poor* is an excellent biography dedicated to the life and times of outstanding English test batsman, captain and highly respected Anglican bishop, David Sheppard. David was a man of principle often facing difficult social times in ministry and sport. He lived his life in sacrificial service to others and for the glory of God. A wonderful opponent and encouraging Christian friend when the Ashes were played in true respect of cricket. An uplifting and challenging read.'
Brian Booth MBE, Australian test cricketer and captain

'This book captures the charisma of Bishop David Sheppard, who inspired a generation of young people and lives on in the influence he still has today.'
The Rt Hon. Gordon Brown, former Prime Minister

'This is a superb biography. At the end of it you feel you know not only the man, with all his strengths and frailties, but also the times in which he lived, with all their challenges.'
Stephen Chalke, cricket historian

'David Sheppard "stood out" in every sense of the term. He was unusually tall; played cricket for England; championed the disadvantaged; and turned a fiercely sectarian city into a beacon of ecumenism. This book tells us how.'
Grace Davie, Professor Emeritus, University of Exeter

'David Sheppard's life is fully deserving of this detailed, even forensic, biography. His character fully epitomized the old adage for life, "make a plan and stick to it". He was a friend to me in my private life, as well as a stalwart partner on the cricket field – we put on 124 runs together on the final winning day of the Melbourne Test in 1963!'
Ted Dexter CBE, former captain, Sussex and England

'Sheppard's life encapsulates the flavour and position of the Church of England in the contemporary world, both its flaws and successes. Bradstock has produced a rich and comprehensive biography of arguably one of the leading religious figures of the twentieth century.'
Dr Eliza Filby, author of *God and Mrs Thatcher*

'An excellent biography, well researched, well written. Bradstock explores the struggle between ambition and virtue in Sheppard's life on the cricket field, in the Church and in his family. This is fascinating not just for cricket lovers but for everyone.'
Brian Griffiths (Lord Griffiths of Fforestfach), Chairman, Centre for Enterprise, Markets and Ethics (CEME)

'Bishop David Sheppard's partnership with Archbishop Derek Worlock overcame the religious barriers as they led the fight against poverty and division in Liverpool, which has had a lasting effect and which is well documented in this publication.'
The Most Revd Malcolm McMahon OP, Archbishop of Liverpool

'David Sheppard, former England cricket captain, ought to have been Archbishop of Canterbury. He was a remarkable man, who did good wherever he went. This splendid work is the full-scale biography that we have long needed.'
Peter Oborne, author, biographer of Basil D'Oliveira and political columnist for the *Daily Mail* and *Middle East Eye*

'Men as gifted as David Sheppard don't come along all that often.
    Sitting alongside him on the Labour benches in the House of Lords, I came to learn a great deal about the complexity and compromises involved in public life. Most importantly, I learned that you couldn't get everything right – we were both wrong in supporting the Iraq War – it wasn't that we didn't discuss and even agonize over it, we simply placed our trust in the wrong facts and the wrong people. Andrew Bradstock has succeeded in illuminating these moments of doubt in the life of one of the more legitimate heroes of twentieth-century Britain.

David Sheppard continually asked awkward questions, both of himself and others, but always in the context of an unshakeable faith.

This is a book, and a life, we could all learn from.'
David Puttnam (Lord Puttnam Kt, CBE)

'I was honoured to have known and worked with David Sheppard. At least, I thought I knew him. What is clear to me from this not wholly uncritical, yet authorized, biography is that I had only the sketchiest knowledge of this remarkable man of God. And cricket. In Andrew Bradstock's almost forensic account of David Sheppard's life we see the reshaping of the evangelical Christian Church through the second half of the twentieth century, alongside the social, political, economic and cultural changes through which he strove to push and pull it into the twenty-first century. And we – I – discover a man who, although he could have been one of the greatest cricketers of all time, pursued his religious commitments to even greater heights. There is the relatively well-known sporting history (with new insights and detail from his sporting contemporaries), running alongside a little known and dramatic family saga and the stresses and strains of running a huge "business", the Liverpool diocese. His first and unbinding care was for the urban poor. And his legacy is largely for them. A fascinating read on many levels.'
Jane Reed CBE, former editor, *Woman's Own*

'By the time I was in a Christian Union in the late 1970s, David Sheppard was Bishop of Liverpool. He was no longer writing pamphlets for Scripture Union, but he still came and spoke for our CU. His was a minority voice within evangelicalism, but within it still. In our one conversation, as Labour colleagues in Parliament, I told him how deeply *Built as a City* influenced me. *Faith in the City* and *Unemployment and the Future of Work* had a huge impact on government policies. Sheppard's work, superbly surveyed in this account, reshaped church approaches to poverty. If we want an explanation for why, since 2010, the churches, uniquely, have been so effective in tackling rising food poverty, through the foodbank movement, we need look no further than this biography.'
The Rt Hon. Stephen Timms, MP

'With elegant prose and faithful reporting, Andrew Bradstock has produced an accurate portrait of the life and ministry of the David Sheppard I knew and admired. You may wish to start by dipping into Chapter 8, which encapsulates David's practical and spiritual commitment to truth and justice.'

The Rt Revd Wilfred Wood, retired Bishop of Croydon

DAVID SHEPPARD
BATTING FOR THE POOR

DAVID SHEPPARD

BATTING

FOR THE POOR

THE AUTHORIZED BIOGRAPHY
OF THE CELEBRATED
CRICKETER AND BISHOP

ANDREW BRADSTOCK

First published in Great Britain in 2019

Society for Promoting Christian Knowledge
36 Causton Street
London SW1P 4ST
www.spck.org.uk

British Library Cataloguing-in-Publication Data
A catalogue record for this book is available from the British Library

ISBN 978–0–281–08105–9
eBook ISBN 978–0–281–08104–2

Typeset by Fakenham Prepress Solutions, Fakenham, Norfolk NR21 8NL
First printed in Great Britain by TJ International
Subsequently digitally printed in Great Britain

eBook by Fakenham Prepress Solutions, Fakenham, Norfolk NR21 8NL

Produced on paper from sustainable forests

To
Canon Brian Fessey (1939–2017)
who helped so much with this book but did not live to see its
completion

and

Ella Rebecca Afonso (b. 2013)
and
Toby Russell Afonso (b. 2015)
who will also leave the world a better place than they found it

Contents

Plates

Page 7
With Michael Henshall and the first women deacons
A parting word with Pope John Paul II
In the autumn of their years

Page 8
At Bishop's Lodge
A masterclass for his grandsons
Archbishop Desmond Tutu at Sheppard's memorial stone

Foreword

During the apartheid years, it meant more than I can say to have a friend like David Sheppard.

We, the victims of that system, needed all the help we could get, and it was fantastic to have his. Even those who really did not know the difference between cricket and ping-pong took very great encouragement from his stand.

As a former captain of England, he could not be dismissed lightly, or at all. We realized that we did indeed have friends in high places.

But it took great courage. As a cricketer he sacrificed much by refusing to play against a team calling itself 'South Africa' but chosen only from its white minority.

When he later challenged the MCC over its handling of the 'D'Oliveira affair', and led a peaceful campaign to stop the 1970 tour, he lost good friends and risked his reputation.

He was often dismissed as a 'political extremist'. Yet history has vindicated his stand. His call to boycott apartheid was a major factor in its removal.

It wasn't 'politics' that drove him, of course, but his deep and vital faith. He believed that Christians should seek change in society as well as in individuals. He believed in a God who hated injustice and challenged people to combat it.

David responded to that challenge, speaking out consistently with a bias for the poor, the marginalized, the downtrodden. He used his name and influence to benefit others, to create a more just world.

His legacy can be seen not just here in South Africa but in Liverpool, the diocese he served as bishop for more than 20 years.

A biography of David Sheppard is long overdue, and I welcome the publication of this book. It faithfully recounts his career in sport and the church, but also shows what made him tick and drove him to achieve all that he did. We also meet Grace, an equally amazing person in her own right.

David and Grace were genuinely gentle people, always seeking change through persuasion, not force. My father used to say, 'Improve your argument, don't raise your voice.' By their very lives and way of doing things, David and Grace embodied that saying. What a huge privilege to have known them.

The Most Revd Desmond Tutu
Archbishop Emeritus of Cape Town

Preface

David Sheppard achieved the rare distinction of becoming a household name in two different spheres of life, cricket and the Church.

As a cricketer, he was seldom out of the news. His flair as a batsman and fielder, and natural authority as a captain, made him a favourite with spectators and the media alike. To a generation of schoolchildren, he was a *Boy's Own* hero, someone to emulate as a player and sportsman. To their elders he was also a figure to admire, though his film-star looks, and gracious demeanour stretched his appeal beyond fathers who took their sons to watch him play. It was not a sports or boys magazine for which he wrote a weekly column for 17 years, but *Woman's Own*. His life was a constant source of interest for the press, who covered not only his engagement, wedding and daughter's birth, but less glamorous activities such as his duties in the parish, his ordination and even his house moves. His eagerness to speak publicly about his faith only fuelled the public's interest in him, as did his decision to withdraw from cricket, with a glittering career in prospect, for the life of a priest. His call for a sporting boycott of South Africa later turned sections of the media against him, but they could not ignore him. He was a 'celebrity' before the term became popular.

As a bishop he remained in the public view. At first, this was a spill-over from his sporting career, but he gradually became known as a church leader with a passion to make a difference on the wider stage. His challenge to governments to prioritize the inner-city, his partnership with his Roman Catholic counterpart in Liverpool, Derek Worlock, his advocacy of the poor and discriminated against, all made him noteworthy in the eyes of the media. At a time when the church was often in the papers, he was the most instantly recognizable of its bishops, the one whose opinions the papers liked to know. He did not go looking for fame, but his role in significant national events, from the D'Oliveira affair, to the visit of Pope John Paul II, to the *Faith in the City* report, kept him constantly in the spotlight. He was centre stage in events which commentators would define as the most important in post-war church history. In Liverpool, he was also a focus, a leader and a presence, whether helping the city overcome its sectarian past, building bridges after the unrest in Toxteth, or standing up for the city and supporting its grieving communities following Hillsborough. He and Archbishop Worlock enjoyed a profile unique among the bishops of their day, perhaps of any day. Not without reason were they known as 'fish and chips', always together and never out of the paper.

*

This is the first attempt to recount Sheppard's life and assess his impact as a sportsman, campaigner and church leader. It draws on hundreds of interviews, conversations and exchanges with people who knew, worked with and played alongside him, plus his extensive archive of private papers. Sheppard wrote two accounts of his life, but like most autobiographies they are as notable for what they omit as for what they contain. I have been less selective, revealing not only the contribution he made to the church and public life, but something of its cost, both to himself and others, and the convictions and experiences that underpinned his powerful sense of vocation.

His was a full life, and this book could have been much thicker. I have included every significant event or activity in which he was involved, though each has been approached through the lens of his involvement rather than treated more broadly. Readers wishing to study issues more deeply may find the bibliography of use.

What I could not have done is written two slimmer volumes, one on Sheppard the sportsman and one on Sheppard the bishop. Cricket and the church were interwoven in his life, and must be treated as such. To separate them would result in a very one-dimensional portrayal, and I have not attempted to do that here.

I have also not treated Sheppard's faith as a discrete entity. It infused his life, including his passion to work for justice, reconciliation and the common good, and it cannot be compartmentalized. The pivotal moment in his life was his conversion at the age of 20. Over the years he broadened the interpretation of the Christian gospel he embraced on that occasion, but the moment when he 'opened his heart and mind to Christ' remains the key to understanding the whole of his life.

*

This is the 'authorized' biography in the sense that it draws on its subject's private papers, which are closed to public view. I am grateful to the custodians of these papers for granting me access to them: Jenny Sinclair, David and Grace's daughter, and Canon Godfrey Butland, the former chaplain to whom Sheppard entrusted his literary affairs.

The archive proved an indispensable resource. Its more than 60 box files contain correspondence covering every aspect of Sheppard's life and career, from his schooldays to his retirement, together with his sermons, addresses and articles, many in draft as well as final form. Quite how biographers of our contemporaries will manage in the future I do not know. Virtually every correspondence Sheppard engaged in would nowadays be conducted by email, and in many cases deleted, a fate which would probably befall other documents produced and filed digitally. Sheppard did use email and word-processing in his final years, but he was in the last generation of public figures to operate almost entirely before electronic communication became commonplace. As I pored over the thousands of paper letters and carbon-copy replies he had retained and filed, this was a fact for which I was frequently thankful.

*

This has been one of the most absorbing tasks I have undertaken. Having spent my professional life studying the churches' contribution in public life, and at times seeking to assist that contribution, it has been a privilege to examine critically one of the most prominent socially engaged church figures of the twentieth century. It has also been a joy to research his career in cricket, another of my passions. Long before I progressed to long trousers I was listening to commentary on the radio, reading about cricket and going to matches, encouraged particularly by my mother. I was just too young to have seen Sheppard play, but I do remember being given a souvenir book about the MCC tour to Australia and New Zealand in 1962–3, produced by a domestic soap manufacturer, and wondering why, on the scorecards, one player had 'Rev' in front of his name, and what it meant.

If I have another qualification for undertaking this project, it is that I never met David Sheppard. He once said that if anybody aspired to write his life story it should be somebody he did not know. I have often pondered what lay behind this request, but if his concern was to reduce the possibility of his biographer producing either a hagiography or hatchet job, I hope he would feel reassured by this effort. Since Sheppard was neither a friend nor acquaintance, I thought it appropriate to refer to him by his surname throughout, save when I am dealing with his childhood or talking about him in relation to his wife, Grace. His companion for fifty years, Grace has a crucial role in this book, with her journey from being a support to her husband, to developing a career and ministry in her own right, discussed in full.

I have tried to keep my own political and religious biases from influencing the text, but no one can write an objective history. The positioning of information, and choice of phrasing, inevitably casts a certain angle, and it will be clear that I share aspects of Sheppard's world view. However, except in the conclusion, I have avoided seeking to interpret or pontificate upon the events and opinions described. I do not believe biographers should tell readers what to think, nor what their subject might have 'really' meant or thought about a certain matter. In telling his story I have tried neither to explain nor justify Sheppard's words and actions. It is for the reader to make her or his own judgement.

Yet in writing this book I wanted to do more than chronicle a 'great life' and add to our understanding of a certain period of history. In his commitment to 'speak for those who cannot speak', as the Book of Proverbs puts it, Sheppard demonstrates that faith can be a force for good in society, an impulse to improve the lives of individuals and communities. As he learned about the human misery and hopelessness that poverty and unemployment can engender, so he was driven to challenge the underlying causes and press for remedial action. 'Batting for the poor' meant more than looking for voluntary or charitable solutions, important though they were. It meant examining the structures of society and how they might be changed, joining the political fray if necessary and engaging the powers that be. Sheppard was a latter-day prophet, not in the sense of foretelling the future, but of forth-telling how things are in the present, and proposing solutions.

He did not interpret the gospel purely in social terms, however. He never forgot its power to change people spiritually, to give them the peace of knowing themselves forgiven, accepted and loved by God. This was how he understood his conversion, and he held the need for individual transformation always in tandem with a wider understanding of his faith. In his second autobiography, *Steps along Hope Street*, he mentions two visits to Tate & Lyle factories, one in the 1950s and one in the 1980s. The first was to conduct an evangelistic mission, the second to persuade its management not to close and make its employees redundant, and both he saw as authentic expressions of the Christian gospel. His personal spiritual development remained central throughout his life. When asked as a bishop to name the priorities in his life, he placed 'inward journey with God' at the top.

*

I have been struck by the continuing relevance of Sheppard's work. For a new generation his books may be unfamiliar, yet *Bias to the Poor*, with its call to the church to reflect God's special concern for those suffering the indignity of unemployment, inadequate income, or substandard housing, has hardly been overtaken by events since its publication in 1983. His even earlier volume, *Built as a City*, with its reflections on growing a church in the inner city by building bridges, developing local leadership and rejecting models appropriate to different settings, would still be a resource and encouragement for church-planters.

Sheppard also provides an example of moral leadership. Leaders of principle are rare in any generation, so telling the story of one seemed worthwhile and instructive, not just an exercise in nostalgia. Perhaps Sheppard might continue to inspire others more earnestly to pursue righteousness, integrity and virtue in whatever their calling.

Andrew Bradstock

Acknowledgements

I would like to thank the following people who have shown extraordinary generosity in their willingness to read draft chapters, offer advice, make connections and help and encourage me in other invaluable ways. I gladly acknowledge my huge debt to each: Malcolm Alexander, the Revd Dr Malcolm Brown, Canon Godfrey Butland, Stephen Chalke, John Crathorne, the late Hubert Doggart OBE, the Very Revd Nicholas Frayling, Mgr John Furnival, Hugh Griffiths, Canon Anthony Hawley, Rosemary Hawley MBE, the Revd Dr Richard Higginson, the Revd Christopher Idle, Pat Jones CBE, Dr Michael Lambert, the Revd Dr Colin Marchant, Dr Sarah Maxwell, Douglas Miller, Roger Morris OBE, Rachel Newton, Professor Hilary Russell, Lesley Sanders, Nicholas Sharp, Jenny Sinclair, Dr Pat Starkey, Canon Dick Williams and the late Su Williams.

Many others have also shown me great kindness during the course of researching and writing this book.

Rachel Hassall, archivist at Sherborne School, went way beyond the call of duty to help me research Sheppard's time there. Elaine Thornton did a similar job at Ridley Hall, Cambridge.

Other institutions which kindly granted me access to their papers are: Sussex County Cricket Club Museum, Hove (with special thanks to Phil Barnes, Norman Epps, Richard Barrow, Jon Filby and Rob Boddie); River Christian Centre, Canning Town (Doreen McIntosh); Slinfold Cricket Club (Martyn Haines and Ian Haines); MCC (Robert Curphey and Neil Robinson); St Mary's Church, Islington (the Revd Simon Harvey); the Bishopsgate Institute (Stefan Dickers); the Francis Holland Schools Trust (Alistair Brown); Trinity Hall, Cambridge (Alexandra Browne); and the Women's Library at the LSE. I also spent the equivalent of three months in Liverpool Central Library, where David Sheppard's papers are archived. The website <cricketarchive.com> proved an invaluable resource, as did the British Newspaper Archive at the British Library.

Acknowledgements

I thank Jenny Sinclair and Dr Sarah Maxwell for letting me see family letters and other papers, and Jenny for permission to use photos from her private collection.

I am grateful to Gladstone's Library, Hawarden, for allowing me to inspect Eric James' papers, and to the Warden, the Revd Dr Peter Francis, for so kindly giving me a short fellowship at the Library in October 2017.

Colin and Mary Watts showed extraordinary generosity in arranging and hosting a group of fellow ex-Mayflower friends at their house during the summer of 2016. I thank them for this, and each of their guests for giving up a day to be there and share their memories: Rita Dennis, Bill Green, Len Howell, Pat Howell, Sylvia Latch, Frances Tilley and Jack Tilley. The Revd Peter Markby also helped me contact many other former Mayflower people.

I spent a delightful morning at the vicarage of St Mary's Church, Islington, with three parishioners who remembered David Sheppard's time there as a young curate: Barbara Quantrill, Kathleen Read and Elizabeth Salmon. My thanks to them, and to the then vicar, the Revd Simon Harvey, for arranging and hosting this get-together.

It was a privilege to receive help from the former Australian Test batsman, Brian Booth, and the distinguished Australian cricket writer and publisher, Ronald Cardwell. Both went to great lengths to help me understand the impact Sheppard made in their country, not least during his visit with MCC in 1962–3. I also greatly valued the help and advice of my friend Dr Ian Wilkinson in Melbourne. We first met while doing our post-doctoral studies at Otago in 1990 and continue to share our love of cricket across the miles.

Just as I was commencing this project *The Guardian* newspaper ran an intensive course on 'writing biography'. I thank the tutors, Jon Cook and Richard Holmes, for all they shared over those two days, and hope my fellow students have made good progress with their ventures.

Special thanks go to my hardworking copy editor, Ali Hull, for improving the text; the Editor at Large at SPCK, Tony Collins, for his faith in this book and encouragement along the way; Dawn Ingram, for proofreading the text; and Stephen Chalke who, in addition to offering expert advice on the cricket and other sections of the book, most generously provided the statistical summary of Sheppard's career.

My profound thanks also to Archbishop Desmond Tutu for so kindly providing the foreword. I am honoured that he has shown his support for the book and admiration for its subject in this way.

Many others have helped in different ways, and for reasons of space I simply list them. They know what their contribution has meant to me: the Revd Horace Busk, the Revd Dr Steve Griffiths, Dr Alana Harris, Trevor Tutu, Dr Eliza Filby, John Peart-Binns, John Reeve, the Revd Terry Drummond, Nick Jones, Terry Philpot, Patrick Francis, Peter Morris, the Revd Paul Newman, Barbara Whatley, Professor Diarmaid MacCulloch Kt, Canon Dr Jeremy Morris, the Revd Phil Jump, Professor Gerald Pillay, Sheila Hayes, the Revd Annis Fessey, Dr David Goodhew, Peter Oborne, Peter Baxter, Jean Fessey, Anthony Hannay, Sam Smart, Ian Pratt, Canon Ellen Loudon, Dr Teresa Beynon, Professor Chris Rowland, Janet Gosling, Andrew Graystone, Martin Light, Michael Bloch, Canon Paul Oestreicher, the Revd Stephen Copson, Wendy Cooper, Lord (Maurice) Glasman, Sue Doggart, Albert Ramsey, Peter Dawe, Dr Brian Stanley, the Revd Kerry Birch, Gillian Sanders, Jenny Beaven, Charles Collingwood, Stella Fletcher, the Revd David Haslam, the Revd Donald Reeves, Huw Turbervill, Theo Barclay, and the brothers at Bishop Eton Monastery, Woolton, Liverpool.

I owe a debt of a wholly different kind to a number of individuals and organizations, without whose support the research for this book would never have been possible. It is their generosity which has enabled me to carve out the necessary time and to cover the various overheads connected with the work. I am humbled by their belief in the project and my gratitude to them cannot be adequately expressed. Individual donors would not expect to be named, but I do wish to acknowledge publicly the support of the following major charitable trust donors: CCLA Investment Management; the IW Griffiths Trust; PH Holt Foundation; The Maurice and Hilda Laing Charitable Trust; Lord Leverhulme's Charitable Trust; and Garfield Weston Foundation. This support has been gathered and coordinated by a committee of dedicated people whose efforts have been unstinting. I wish to record a further debt of very deep gratitude to each. Chaired by Lord Griffiths of Fforestfach, this committee comprised: Robin Baird-Smith; Nicholas Barber CBE; Rt Hon. John Battle KCSG; the Revd Canon Godfrey Butland; Professor Martin Daunton FBA,

FRHistS; Roger Morris OBE, DL; Canon Dr Robert Reiss (Treasurer); and Jenny Sinclair.

If I have any sadness about the process of writing this book it is that my father-in-law, Brian Fessey, did not live to see its completion. With his characteristic enthusiasm Brian gave me great encouragement from the outset in both word and deed, the latter taking the form of transcribing most of the early interviews I conducted. I dedicate this book to Brian, and to my (step) grandchildren, Ella and Toby.

Last, but absolutely not least, my thanks to my wife Helen for her invaluable contribution to this book. Not only did she put up with my absences while undertaking research, and long hours in my study writing it all up, Helen transcribed the lion's share of the interviews, read each chapter in draft, and helped in other practical ways with research and administration. Having just completed writing up her PhD when I started on this journey she had a measure of empathy with my situation, but she has very much borne the heat and burden of the day with this, and simply to state my undying love and gratitude to her seems laughably insufficient. Needless to say, the experience has not made her any more well-disposed towards cricket.

1

Early life
(1929–1942)

The author of *Bias to the Poor*[1] and *The Other Britain*[2] never sought to hide his privileged origins. Born just months before the Wall Street Crash, and brought up during the resulting Great Depression of the 1930s, David Sheppard acknowledged that he was born 'on the right side of the tracks'.[3] He grew up comfortably far from the other side, the family home being in one of the nation's more affluent neighbourhoods.

*

Entries for David Stuart Sheppard in most works of reference begin 'born Reigate, 6 March 1929', suggesting a childhood spent in that delightful market town in Surrey. In fact, his family had no connection with the town. He was born there because his mother chose one of its nursing homes for her confinement as it was near to her parents' home in Charlwood. The delivery of her first child in the Charlwood house six years earlier had been long and uncomfortable. Barbara Sheppard wanted to minimize the pain this time by ensuring professional care would be on hand. It was to be another 40 years, when he was bishop of Woolwich, before David became properly acquainted with the part of Surrey in which he was born.

Married in December 1922, Barbara and her husband Stuart had made their first home in a rented flat in Beaufort Street, Chelsea. At that time Chelsea was known as the 'borough of artists'. Beaufort Street is still one

---

1 Sheppard, D. S., *Bias to the Poor*, London: Hodder & Stoughton, 1983.
2 Sheppard, D. S., *The Other Britain*, London: BBC, 1984.
3 Sheppard, D. S., *Steps along Hope Street*, London: Hodder & Stoughton, 2002, p. 7.

of its main thoroughfares, linking Fulham Road and the King's Road with Battersea Bridge. With a child on the way the following year, they had sought larger accommodation nearby, moving around the corner to a house in Mallord Street. Here, at number 10, the young family was able to spread out over three floors. Mary, who was born in September 1923, enjoyed the benefits of a nursery on the top floor and a garden with a playhouse. It was a fashionable and much sought-after street. A few doors down was a house built for the painter Augustus John, while directly opposite the Sheppards lived Mr and Mrs A. A. Milne. Their son, Christopher Robin, was three years older than Mary.

Stuart was building a career with Messrs Boyce and Evans, a firm of solicitors in Stratford Place off Oxford Street. Aged 27 at the time of his marriage, he had a promising future at the firm, which numbered several large departmental stores among its clients. He had become a partner in the firm, suitably renamed Boyce, Evans and Sheppard, by the time David was born. He had had a terrible war, enduring long periods of misery in the trenches and a cocktail of illnesses. These were severe enough to see him invalided out and shipped back to Blighty, only to be sent back to France once he was deemed to have sufficiently recovered. Though he returned home again when hostilities ceased in 1918, his health remained impaired for the rest of his life, exacerbated by his addiction to cigarettes.

*

As David would enjoy pointing out, his mother was a *Shepherd* who married a *Sheppard*. Three years younger than her husband, Barbara was the daughter of William James Affleck Shepherd, the artist better known as J. A. Shepherd (JAS). Shepherd's work regularly appeared in popular children's books and bestselling journals of the day including *Punch*, for whom he drew on a weekly basis for many years, *London Illustrated News* and *Strand Magazine*. A man of great warmth and humour, JAS had a talent for caricaturing animals and birds in delightfully comical ways. He also illustrated more serious books devoted to natural history. Such was his reputation, he was once invited by the young Walt Disney to work for him in California, an offer he declined. While Shepherd would have brought in a steady income, it was his wife Nellie who ensured the family's financial security, courtesy of the fortune made by her father, George Lewis Turner. Turner was born in the Old Kent Road, the son of a brush-maker. In a classic rags to riches saga, he loaned a friend the money to start a boot-blacking business in the early days of the industry, enjoying a generous return on his investment as the Nugget Polish Company became one of the biggest manufacturers of boot and floor polishes in the world. In the 1920s Nugget merged with its rival business, Chiswick Polish Company, to create a global brand which included the famous Cherry Blossom label.

In 1926, Barbara's parents moved from their cottage in Charlwood to the much grander Tintinhull House near Yeovil in Somerset. Built around 1630, Tintinhull had a distinguished history, and was let to the Pitt family during the eighteenth century. It had a magnificent garden created by the eminent botanist Dr S. J. M. Price around 1900. As children, Mary and David often stayed at Tintinhull, where their grandmother delighted in tending the garden and their uncle Jack, their mother's youngest brother, managed the adjacent farm. Here the London-based children could enjoy the wild outdoors. Jack, an accomplished horseman, taught them to ride, and when they were not tending the farm animals or roaming the countryside, they had pets with which to play. The family entertained a tame raven who called regularly at the back door. Milking the cows and taking the churn around the village to fill up residents' jugs was popular, as was watching carthorses pulling the plough. In cold winters they would thaw out lambs in the bottom oven of the stove and complete their revival by feeding them from bottles. A further treat was watching their grandfather, whom they affectionately called 'Pa', draw sketches of animals for them.

*

David's birth led Barbara and Stuart to look for a larger house. They took the lease on 34 Carlyle Square, almost literally in view of their existing home in Mallord Street. Here the children had a day and a night nursery, and there was accommodation for the family's cook and house parlour maid, Hannah and Lettice. The garden had a plane tree, giving anyone who touched it sooty fingers. As well as playing there, Mary and David would join with other children in the square's private gardens. They used these as an improvised cricket pitch and racetrack for their bikes. At home, a more daredevil sport involved hoisting each other up in the dumb waiter lift used to bring meals from the kitchen in the basement to the ground floor dining room.

The five and a half years between David and Mary, known affectionately in the family as 'Bill', meant they were not always close. Their relationship was not without its fights, including one over a swing which ended with David losing a tooth. As in Mallord Street, the Sheppards had their share of celebrity neighbours, among them the writer Osbert Sitwell, and the actor Dame Sybil Thorndike and her husband Lewis Casson and their family. David made friends with a girl of the same age from a titled family who, because she would break his toys, he referred to as 'my difficulty'.

The children were enrolled at the Francis Holland School. Mary was in the main school and David in the preparatory or kindergarten. Barbara and Stuart developed a culture of learning, being keen to foster a love of books in their offspring, and encouraged them to read themselves as well as reading stories to them aloud. They devoured children's books illustrated by their maternal grandfather, including the Uncle Remus tales featuring Brer Rabbit, Brer Fox and others. They also read other staples popular with their contemporaries, such as *The Wind in the Willows, The Just So Stories, Dimsie Goes to School, The Story of Little Black Sambo* and the books of Arthur Ransome. They enjoyed the Winnie the Pooh stories created by their former neighbour in Mallord Street, and the Babar the Elephant tales which Milne had helped make accessible to English readers.

In addition to vacations at Tintinhull, there were family holidays each summer at Woolacombe Bay in Devon, where the Sheppards would rent rooms. The children would play on the beach by day, and in the evenings the family would walk the coastal paths or take the car out to the moors. Mary had her own surfboard, which she was allowed to take out to the rollers under strict supervision, while David and his father would use every opportunity to play beach cricket. A high point of the day was the appearance at the kitchen door of local fishermen, bringing freshly caught crab for the cook to prepare for supper.

Less eagerly anticipated visits were those to the house of two great aunts, Grace and May, in Tunbridge Wells in Kent. Elder sisters of Stuart's father, Henry Winter Sheppard, both were in their seventies when David was small. The thought of going to see them filled both children with dread because of the exacting standard of behaviour required. For a boy still in short trousers, it was hard to be expected to sit up straight at table for the duration of a meal, then remain in that position for a further 20 minutes to let his food digest before being allowed to play in the garden. Grace was the most formidable of the two. In later life David said she reminded him of pictures of the elderly Queen Victoria, while May he remembered as 'lovely and gentle'. Grace hardly endeared herself to David by reminding him that he had a squint.

Stuart's connections meant that life for the children had its exciting moments. As a member of the Carlton Club, he ensured the family had a grandstand view of the procession to mark the Silver Jubilee of King George V and Queen Mary in May 1935. For the coronation of George VI two years later, a friend inside the Palace of Westminster got the Sheppards seats in a stand in the building's courtyard. This afforded them an outstanding view of the state procession as it snaked its way from Westminster Abbey to Buckingham Palace.

*

The extent to which David's family and upbringing helped to shape his direction in life is an open question, but an interest in cricket and practical Christianity characterized members of both the Sheppard and Shepherd clans.

Both of David's parents encouraged him to develop an interest in cricket. When he was just six or seven his father took him to Lord's and Hove to watch first-class games, experiences which sparked an early appetite for the game and its traditions. Stuart was a paid-up member of Sussex County Cricket Club. For the princely sum of 15s 6d (77½p) per year he could watch all home county games from the Members' Pavilion and take Barbara as a 'lady' guest. He also took out a 'Member's Son' membership for David, who clearly got his money's worth from his ticket. 'Watching' for David was never a passive occupation. He would start each match, in the days before shirts were printed with numbers and names, by identifying each member of the fielding side as soon as possible. He learned the names and styles of each batsman who came in and absorbed the conversation of the older and wiser spectators around him.

Sheppard said his father 'turned me into a fanatical cricket fan from a very early age'.[4] Between attending matches he eagerly read reports of county and Test matches in the daily newspaper. Another source of information and enjoyment was the cricket enthusiast's bible, *Wisden*. Published annually, this contains a wealth of statistics, biographies, score-cards and match summaries.[5] Even the winter months were not barren for the cricket *aficionados* of Carlyle Square. Not only would reports of England's quests for the Ashes in Australia appear in the papers, updates on the state of play could usually be heard each morning, through the crackle, on the wireless. Stuart made a table cricket game which the two played regularly. This comprised a roulette-style wheel with a pointer to spin to indicate the number of runs scored and how the batsman was out.

Stuart encouraged his son to play cricket from an early age. Photos in the family collection show David, aged about four, padded up and taking guard in the back garden. By the time he was eight he was in the Colts team organized by his father in the Sussex village of Slinfold, where the family had a weekend cottage. In one match against a Veterans XI, David made a creditable 23. Batting at number five, he determined this would be his preferred place in the order as his career developed.[6]

Relatives on both sides of the family encouraged the boy in his passion for the game. His maternal grandfather once gave him a drawing entitled 'Animal Spirits', depicting the Lions of England playing cricket against the Kangaroos of Australia, with two wombats as umpires. J. A. Shepherd had originally produced this for *Punch* magazine in March 1895 during a

---

4 Sheppard, D.S., 'How I Found Religion', *Woman's Own*, 11 December 1957, p. 22.

5 Sheppard took *Wisden* throughout his life, but the volumes in his collection showing the most obvious signs of use are those dating from the 1930s.

6 Sheppard never forgot his connections with Slinfold Cricket Club. He was a vice-president for more than five decades, and regularly brought teams to play there. When Sussex played the Australian tourists in 1953, he got the visitors to sign a bat for the club. In the middle of the busy 1962 season he made time to open their new pavilion.

tense Ashes series in Australia. Stuart gave his son a cricket-themed gift in childhood, a bib with picture of a teddy bear batting.

To the delight of the aspiring young batsman, there was some cricketing blood in the family, his great uncle Tom having played two first-class games in the early 1900s. This was Major Thomas Winter Sheppard, half-brother of Stuart's father, Henry. Tom also helped to instigate the annual fixture between the Royal Navy and the Army. Tom was better known for his distinguished military service, and his cricketing career was very modest. But having played at county level earned him enormous respect from his young relative. 'Is it *really* true that you played for Hampshire?' the shy lad once asked him at a family gathering.

*

David would have been the first to say that the evangelical faith he later embraced could not have been inherited. It was due solely to his own one-to-one encounter with Jesus Christ. Yet his early years were influenced by Christianity in various forms. This would have helped to shape his initial understanding of the world and lay a foundation for his subsequent personal adoption of the faith.

If David's life could be described as a 'missionary' one,[7] the nearest role model in the family was his mother's brother, George Corbyn Shepherd. A qualified doctor known to everyone as 'Boy', George served as a medical missionary in Manchuria for many years. A larger than life character, who enjoyed motor racing and in later life won the British Saloon Car Championship, Boy survived a number of harrowing episodes as a missionary. These included attacks on the family home by local brigands and imprisonment on the Russia–China border on suspicion of spying. A committed member of the Plymouth Brethren, Boy's relationship with the wider family could at times be uncomfortable. In later life, David never showed enthusiasm for his uncle's exploits, and his expression of Christianity was not one his parents would have encouraged him to embrace. Barbara and Stuart preferred a less intense version of

---

7 This is how his close friend Bishop Wilfred Wood described it in his eulogy at a memorial service for Sheppard in Southwark Cathedral; see Wood, W., *Faith for a Glad Fool*, London: New Beacon, 2010, p. 105.

Christianity. An important part of the family's week was attendance at Sunday worship in the Wren Chapel of the nearby Royal Hospital, the famous retirement home for British soldiers. The chaplain at the Hospital was a friend of Stuart's, and the family appreciated the simple services arranged for the residents, known colloquially as 'Chelsea Pensioners'. The Hospital's rituals provided an added level of interest for the children, not least one performed in the kitchen after chapel. This involved the Governor plunging his sword into the puddings to check they were satisfactory.

Stuart and Barbara were mainstream Anglicans. Both had a strong faith which sustained them through their lives. In letters he wrote to his own father from the trenches, Stuart mentions attending a service of Holy Communion with just two other comrades, and gives a detailed and enthusiastic account of a military parade service. A clergyman who knew him well once described Stuart's service to others as having been undertaken 'through God and prayer'. He added that he felt put to shame by Stuart's 'faith and the way he appealed to God'. David always remembered his father's favourite Bible passage, some verses from Joshua chapter 1: 'Be thou strong and very courageous . . . for the Lord thy God is with thee whithersoever thou goest' (KJV). David would speak fondly of his mother explaining to him as a child about putting one's trust in God.

David could count at least four Anglican clergymen among his forebears: his great-great-grandfather, Henry Winter Sheppard, who held the living of Emsworth in Hampshire for the last 55 years of the nineteenth century; another great-great-grandfather, Francis Arthur Jackson, who died tragically helping to rescue people from a fire in his parish in Yorkshire; a great-great uncle, Henry Alexander Graham Sheppard, who died in 1919 at the age of 85; and a first cousin of his father, Philip Thomas Byard Clayton. 'Tubby' Clayton was the founder of the international Christian movement dedicated to promoting reconciliation and friendship, 'Toc H'. This originated in Talbot House, a centre Clayton established in Poperinge, Belgium, during the First World War, as a place where soldiers engaged on the battlefields of Flanders could rest and recuperate.[8]

---

8 Toc H is radio signallers' shorthand for the initials TH, to which Talbot House was often shortened.

Clayton had married Stuart and Barbara and was devoted to both. He was a familiar figure to David as he was growing up. He had christened David in his church, All Hallows by the Tower, and would later have contact with both the Sheppard children. Mary worked for Clayton as a young woman, and as a teenager David would stay with him at his vicarage in Trinity Square, Tower Hill. David later said, tongue in cheek, he had 'the often embarrassing experience of going around with Tubby as his ADC. He was a wonderful story teller'![9]

It is striking that in Sheppard's ordained ministry he reflected the core principles upon which Clayton had founded his movement. These included the promotion of reconciliation, and the bringing together of disparate sections of society and social classes. Clayton had a concern for a more equal society, reflected in the welcome Talbot House gave to men and officers alike. Clayton's model of leadership had a lasting effect on his younger relative, who later acknowledged the influence of the 'great man' with his record of 'caring about other people'. 'I think that was built into me', Sheppard said in a television interview in 1969, 'this was part of my inheritance for which I am tremendously grateful'.[10]

Whatever influence Clayton may have exerted on the Sheppard home, there was an example of service to others even closer to David: his father. Stuart had played a significant role in the foundation of Toc H with Tubby, and he was actively involved in the British Legion and the League of Nations. He was also committed to improving the lot of young people, especially boys. He gave much of his free time to the Chelsea Boys' Club, which he had founded with a group of friends, following his return from the war. Operating from a basement in Lackland Place in the World's End area of Chelsea, the club provided an opportunity for boys from less well-off homes to channel their energies into sport, and experience new challenges, such as sailing on the Thames.

The club was secular in ethos, reflecting the spirit of public service not uncommon among individuals of means and some public schools at that time. Through it, Stuart introduced his son to the concept of seeking the welfare of people less privileged than oneself, if not to the question of

---

9 Private letter dated 7 May 1996: Sheppard papers (SHP), 21.2.
10 Transcript of interview with Douglas Brown for *Viewpoint*, BBC 1, broadcast 15 May 1969: SHP, 20.2.

how such divisions were maintained within society, which would trouble David. He would also have been struck by his father's total commitment to the cause, his sacrifice of numerous evenings which might otherwise have been spent in leisure at home with his family. Stuart modelled for his son a sense of responsibility. He had come from a somewhat dysfunctional family background to create a loving and stable family, build a professional career, and take on pioneering charity work and public service.

A further commitment of Stuart's was to an organization called 'Children's Folk', on whose executive committee he served. Founded in 1927, Children's Folk aimed to create a better world for children to grow up in. It called on all people of goodwill to claim for every child 'adequate education, physical, mental and spiritual; the decencies of home life; green places in which to play; and reasonable security against standing all the day idle in the market place, when schooldays are over, because no man hath hired us'.

This was a vision which Stuart and Barbara Sheppard fulfilled for their own children, underpinning it, as David always acknowledged, with 'the security of never doubting that I was loved'.[11] Home was a secure, comfortable and stimulating environment, one which any young boy could reasonably have expected to enjoy until he felt ready to leave it. Yet in David's case it was not to be. In the autumn of 1937, his father's health deteriorated rapidly, and his mother broke it to him that 'God may want Daddy' very soon. Having had one kidney removed during a previous bout of sickness, Stuart was unable to survive an attack on the other. Following two days of unconsciousness, he died on the morning of 19 November. 'God did want Daddy', as David was told by his mother shortly after. Tubby Clayton, who had been up with the family all night sharing their grief, took the funeral service the following week, committing Stuart's ashes to the crypt of All Hallows. Stuart had requested in his Will that his body be buried or cremated 'without any unnecessary gloominess or black trappings'. A less formal memorial service, by the light of a Toc H lamp and including the symbolic rites of the Toc H movement, was held the following evening at the Chelsea Boys' Club. A brief obituary notice in *The Times* mentioned Stuart's wish for any donations to go to the club.

---

11 Sheppard, *Steps along Hope Street*, p. 7.

Stuart's last words to his son were a plea to 'look after Mummy'. The boy dutifully replied that he would. He was three months short of his ninth birthday: it was a heavy responsibility for one so young to accept. Yet he clearly honoured his promise throughout his life. Already deeply devoted to his 'Mumbo', as he would sometimes call her, Stuart's death brought the two of them even closer together, a bond which remained tight until Barbara's own death in 1983 at the age of 84. David had enjoyed a close relationship with his father, yet he always maintained he could never 'recover any direct memory' of the man, only occasions when they had spent time together. These included, of course, watching cricket.

*

Stuart's death, at the age of 42, affected David, Mary and their mother deeply. It prompted Barbara, who always preferred the countryside to London, to relinquish the lease on Carlyle Square and move to the cottage in Sussex, that she and Stuart had bought as a retreat. Here at Slinfold she rebuilt her life, throwing herself into the task of making the property suitable as the new family home. She sewed every curtain, bed cover and soft furnishing herself, and created a garden overflowing with flowers and produce. The cottage's location away from the village meant that she was often on her own, but she received great comfort and support from family and friends and drew strength from the beauty of the countryside. Financially things were a little tighter. Her husband's death had cut off the family's main source of income, but Stuart had made substantial provision for his widow in his Will. He established a life interest trust to provide her with a regular income and made her a substantial bequest. Barbara's mother also helped her financially, as did her late husband's aunts, Grace and May, who provided the money for David's schooling.

Mary, by now 14, was already at boarding school in Surrey where, astonishingly, she had not been told of her father's condition until after he had died.[12] David had an unhappy term at a day school in Horsham and, shortly after his ninth birthday in March 1938, he started at

---

12 Stuart did write to Mary the week before he died informing her that he had been in bed 'with an attack of bronchitis' but that he was feeling better and hoped to be up again shortly; letter 10 November 1937.

Northcliffe House in the seaside town of Bognor Regis. In view of his recent bereavement, he was allowed to enrol for his first term as a weekly boarder, but it proved a bittersweet arrangement which only exacerbated his homesickness. While he was grateful for the opportunity to return home to his mother each weekend, he found that the wounds created by having to be parted from her were reopened on a weekly basis. As he later recalled, in the months following his father's death, he and his mother would 'set each other's tears off' each time they had to part. At home he could at least afford to let his feelings show, stirred both by the trauma of having to go away to board and the relocation of the family home from London. At school he learned to bury his feelings deep, a tactic to which he resorted at many points in his life.

At Northcliffe he developed his cricket, gaining a place in the school first XI in his second year. This was due to his bowling rather than his batting, his ambition having developed from going in at number five to emulating his idol Hedley Verity, the Yorkshire and England slow left-armer.[13] David had seen Verity at Lord's, and his attempts to imitate his hero as a member of the Northcliffe attack seemed promising. In his report for 1939, his headmaster noted that 'young Sheppard, if I am not very much mistaken, will one day cause a lot of batsmen a great deal of trouble with his left-arm slows'.[14] As things turned out, the head *was* very much mistaken, for in his entire first-class career of 230 matches, Sheppard bowled just 20 overs and took two wickets. He later said that he could 'count on one finger' the solitary good ball he bowled in his adult life, and that was one he delivered while playing for Chelmsford clergy in 1958!

Sheppard's interest in cricket continued to develop outside of school. His mother, no less a devotee of the game than her late husband, chaperoned him to first-class games. From Slinfold, the two made frequent excursions to watch matches at Hove. Among the home players

---

13 Sheppard may not have completely given up on batting while in Bognor: see John Snow's reference to Sheppard hitting a six at a prep school ground in Bognor in *Cricket Rebel*, London: Hamlyn, 1976, p. 16.

14 The headmaster, Henry (Hal) Colborne Brown, was a distant relative of the Sheppards, perhaps a factor in the choice of Northcliffe for David. In 1958 Sheppard returned to the school to dedicate a font in the chapel in memory of his former headmaster, whom he referred to as 'Bruno'.

were several whom David would play alongside just eight years later. These included George Cox Jr, Charlie Oakes and the Langridge brothers, James and John. Still rather small for his age, Sheppard felt a particular affinity for the Sussex wicketkeeper Walter Cornford, known affectionately as 'Tich' on account of being barely five feet tall.

There were also trips to London to see Test cricket at Lord's and The Oval in Kennington. Here, in August 1938, David caught one day of Len Hutton's then record Test innings of 364 for England against Australia. Barbara thoughtfully arranged family visits to her parents, by now living in another large house in the Cotswolds, to coincide with the annual cricket week at Cheltenham. This was an opportunity to see cricket almost continuously for a week and a half, and for David to witness the legendary Gloucestershire and England batsman Wally Hammond. Sheppard admired Hammond even more than Verity, and his batting style would later be compared to the great man's.

Soon after the outbreak of war, Northcliffe House school was evacuated to the Tregothnan estate near Truro in Cornwall, the historic seat of the Viscounts Falmouth. The distance and the war meant weekend trips home were no longer possible, but Barbara decided to base herself in Cornwall to be near her son. There she served the war effort by joining the Mechanised Transport Corps, a women's civilian organization providing drivers for government department personnel, ambulances and lorries. For a time, she acted as chauffeuse to the regional commandant of the Home Guard. Another assignment involved transporting the wreckage of crashed aeroplanes. She stayed in the West Country until David left Northcliffe House in 1942, and then moved to London to join her daughter, Mary, who had taken a flat there upon securing a job at the BBC.

*

David was ten-and-a-half when hostilities commenced, and he took a great interest in the war. He listened intently to the news reports on the wireless and absorbed detailed information about the Allies' warships and aircraft. Indoors he tracked the progress of events on maps, while outdoors he staged imaginary battles in the fields and woods. He also threw himself into his studies, his reports suggesting he worked hard and achieved good results across the board. In later life he paid tribute to Northcliffe and its headmaster for providing the 'two things to which every young person had a right', love and discipline. These, he argued, went together, and helped him develop as a student and a person.[15] Playing cricket, and being encouraged in this by his teachers, also aided his development.

Sheppard's application to his schoolwork paid off, and in his final year at Northcliffe he won a scholarship to Sherborne School in Dorset. Northcliffe had no particular connections with Sherborne, but Barbara would have known about the school through a branch of the family on her late husband's side, generations of which had attended there since the 1860s. At what was to be the half-way point in the war, the 13-year-old Sheppard left Cornwall to embark on the next stage of his formation. He would be thankful to Northcliffe for encouraging him to develop a diligent approach, both to his studies and his cricket. His newly discovered ambitious streak would also be a useful ally in his new, more challenging, environment.

---

15 Iden, R., 'David Sheppard's Early Days at Bognor', *Bognor Regis Local History Society Newsletter*, 53, August 2005, p. 22.

2
Sherborne
(1942–1947)

Reflecting on his time at Sherborne School in later life, Sheppard wrote that 'one way or another, I found myself programmed to achieve'.[1] In one sense this was an experience shared by many who passed through the English public-school system, one goal of which is to prepare its students for leadership. He realized he had advantages in life denied to most of those with whom he chose to work. But 'programmed to achieve' also describes his own experience at school, being singled out from his peers and fast-tracked for positions of authority. His school did not *make* David Sheppard a leader, but it recognized his potential to become one and took steps to test and nurture it.

*

The origins of Sherborne School date back to the eighth century, although the present institution owes its existence to the boy-king Edward VI. Edward established a place of learning for local boys in 1550 from what remained of the Benedictine monastery and abbey dissolved by his father, Henry VIII. Many of the school's buildings are thus survivors from the pre-Reformation period, some even dating to the twelfth century. In its early days the school provided education for only a small number of pupils, but in the latter half of the nineteenth century, it assumed its present status as a boarding school accommodating several hundred boys.

Arriving at Sherborne for the start of the Summer (or Trinity) term in May 1942, Sheppard would have found the life of the school only marginally affected by the war. Situated in rural north Dorset, it was less

---

1 Sheppard, D. S., *Steps along Hope Street*, London: Hodder & Stoughton, 2002, p. 13.

of a target than institutions in more heavily populated areas, although some of its buildings were damaged during an air raid in 1940. The boarding house chosen for Sheppard, Lyon, was equipped with purpose-built concrete shelters in the garden. On the rare occasions when a raid was anticipated, boys would take their mattresses and bedding down to these quarters and sleep in bunks. Blackout restrictions were rigorously upheld at the school, and occasionally boys would participate in 'Wings for Victory' or other similar campaigns. This involved them riding around the town on borrowed ice cream tricycles, selling savings certificates to the locals.

Sherborne's boarding houses have their own distinctive ethos and identity. So diverse and uncoordinated were these institutions in Sheppard's time that the then Headmaster, the Revd A. Ross Wallace, talked of 'some centrifugal influence' at work at Sherborne which made the place seem 'more . . . a group of seven houses than a school'.[2] In the case of Lyon House, a purpose-built Edwardian structure with spacious, high-ceilinged rooms and a beautifully laid out garden, its physical detachment from the main school buildings added to its sense of singularity. Yet the idiosyncratic character it had acquired by the time Sheppard arrived there was less a factor of its location than the all-pervading influence of its longstanding housemaster, Alexander Hamelin Trelawny-Ross.

Born in 1884, Trelawny-Ross had been housemaster of Lyon House for nearly 30 years by the time Sheppard joined its ranks. A former pupil of the school, he had spent almost his entire life from the age of 15 at Sherborne. Appointed housemaster of Lyon at the age of 30, when the house was in its infancy, Trelawny-Ross had stamped his mark on it from the start. It was known throughout the school as 'Ross's Academy'. Noted for his concern for the well-being of the 70 boys entrusted to his care, but also for a dogmatism when it came to issues he felt strongly about, Trelawny-Ross left a lasting impression on all who passed through his house. Sheppard came to remember him, with some degree of fondness, as 'the Mr Chips of Sherborne'. 'Alick was a great man, completely

---

2 Gourlay, A. B., and Gibbs, D. F., *Chief: A biography of Alexander Ross Wallace 1891–1982*, Sherborne School, Dorset: 1983, p. 67.

dedicated to his job', Sheppard wrote in his first autobiography, *Parson's Pitch*. 'He had endless time for his boys, and he has been a very good friend to me.'[3]

Trelawny-Ross's eccentricities were legion. He was implacably opposed to change, even measures which the school authorities argued were necessary to keep up with the times. He was not averse to using boys to advance his causes, on one occasion forbidding them to attend Holy Communion in the chapel as a protest against the introduction of choral services. Boys in Lyon House were forbidden items that every other house took for granted, including radios, carpets and cushions. Listening to classical music was discouraged on the grounds that it was not manly. Discipline in the house was strict, with daily inspections to ensure finger-nails, shirt-collars and study rooms were kept spotless. During 'Ginger Weeks' life would be even tougher, with 'cold water only for washing at night' and punishments for putting lights out in dormitories even a second late. Cold showers and baths in the mornings were already routine. One extraordinary Lyon tradition involved the housemaster on occasions uttering the word 'Rabbits' as he exited a dormitory last thing at night. This was a signal to the boys to leap out of bed and search for him. The pandemonium that ensued would sometimes end in a pillow fight and even damage to the dormitory.

Trelawny-Ross once wrote that he believed boys came to school to be fathered, and he practised what he preached.[4] His interest in his charges began well before they arrived at the school. Each new boy would receive a letter, or even a personal visit, from their new housemaster before their first term began.[5] Once settled into his house, each Lyon boy would find Trelawny-Ross taking a personal interest not only in his academic progress but his mental, physical and moral wellbeing as well. A selection of boys stood to benefit from Trelawny-Ross's belief that it was a housemaster's duty to spot 'likely leaders' and 'long before their responsibility begins . . . steer them unconsciously towards it'. Prefects

---

3 Sheppard, D. S., *Parson's Pitch*, London: Hodder & Stoughton, 1964, p. 21; cf. Sheppard, *Steps along Hope Street*, p. 12.

4 Trelawny-Ross, A. H., *Their Prime of Life: A public school study*, Winchester: The Wykeham Press, 1956, p. 74.

5 He stayed overnight at least once at Barbara Sheppard's home in Slinfold: letter dated 19 September; no year given: Sheppard papers (SHP), 53.4.

could be identified even when in the lower reaches of the school, he argued, and duly prepared for office.[6] What distinguished the chosen from their peers was 'character', a quality which Trelawny-Ross discerned in boys who had 'achieved in life as a result of effort and self-control'. These would understand the importance of service to others and be strong both intellectually and physically. One such was the 15-year-old David Sheppard. Trelawny-Ross considered Sheppard had character in such large measure that, in only his second year at the school, he made it known he wanted the boy to be head of house by the time he was 17. Duly 'programmed to achieve', Sheppard's challenge was to live up to his housemaster's high expectations. Whatever he thought of the challenge, it was to do him much good.

*

Sheppard's contemporaries at Sherborne remember him as a 'boy you notice'. Clever, serious and with a strong personality, he was generally popular, while preferring the company of one or two special friends. He was a hard-working pupil, who took his studies seriously and did not lark around. This application soon brought results. Within his first full year he passed the School Certificate, gaining distinctions in History, Divinity and Greek, and credits in Latin, Mathematics, English Language, English Literature and French. This success in the certificate qualified him to join the sixth form and be fast-tracked for further academic achievement. At this point he was determined to pursue his first love, History. Trelawny-Ross, however, flatly forbade it and put him in for Classics. The reason, the housemaster told Sheppard's mother, was that the History master was a communist. Nothing is known of the political affiliations of the master in question, H. H. (Herbert Henry) Brown, but he is remembered by colleagues and pupils for vices such as disliking competitive games, quoting the *Manchester Guardian* in respectful terms and being liberal-minded. Any of these would have

---

6 Trelawny-Ross, *Their Prime of Life*, p. 77. Boys who did not meet with Trelawny-Ross's approval recalled him as being vindictive, bullying and inadequate: see for example Le Mesurier, J., *A Jobbing Actor*, London: Elm Tree Books, 1984, pp. 15–16. Le Mesurier was in Lyon House in the 1920s.

been enough to equate him, in Trelawny-Ross's mind, with the worst kind of Bolshevik revolutionary.

From the Michaelmas term of 1943 until his departure from Sherborne four years later, Sheppard duly, if reluctantly, studied Classics, together with Divinity, French and English. In his five years at the school he spent just four terms learning Mathematics, and studied no natural science subject whatsoever. Despite the best efforts of his protective housemaster, Sheppard did not entirely escape H. H. Brown's subversive influence. Brown taught him English for three terms.

If Sheppard was perceived in some quarters as a paragon of virtue, he was not above standard public-school mischief. In his second year, he and his closest friend, Bill Anstice-Brown, brewed up some sloe wine using Yeast Vite tablets to accelerate the process. 'I should think it is about 90% alcoholic', Sheppard told his sister, with a possible touch of exaggeration: 'It is now bottled, and we drink bits of it from time to time.'[7]

*

Trelawny-Ross would have seen Sheppard's application to his studies vindicating his faith in the boy as a future head of house. No less important as proof of the student's character were his accomplishments in the fields of sport and the arts, and commitment to the cultural life of the school.

Music was a passion for Sheppard throughout his life, and Sherborne gave him opportunity to deepen his knowledge and understanding of it. His first encounter with music was at home, where his parents owned a gramophone and substantial record collection. School enabled him to develop as a practitioner and gain experience of performing in public. As a junior boy at Sherborne he learnt to play the piano. He became competent but felt he never quite broke through to playing with real enjoyment. By contrast he excelled at singing, winning several school prizes and being regularly chosen to perform solos and lead the school choir. This was a considerable achievement given the exacting standards required by the

---

7 Letter dated 18 October 1943: SHP, 53.4. One assumes this story is not made up to impress an older sister. In this letter Sheppard signs himself 'Dave', a diminutive regularly used within the family when he was young.

music master, Mr Francis Picton. Picton would acknowledge Sheppard's greater facility with the voice. Sometimes, having watched his pupil battle his way through a piano exercise, he would suggest that he sing the piece instead. Two years running Sheppard won the Kitson Prize for Singing, a significant musical award at the school.

Sheppard's voice did not break until the relatively late age of 16 and he led the trebles in the school choir for two years. This meant he sang solo parts during services in the school chapel, and he relished above all the opportunity to sing in Sherborne Abbey, with its acoustics so suited to the great choral music of the Church. He was also selected to perform at concerts hosted by the school's Music Society. He later reflected that the experience of singing solo at these events stood him in good stead when called upon to speak in public in adult life.

Sheppard claimed to have experienced stage fright only once in his life, and that was at Sherborne. At the end of every school year, the Music Society staged a concert in the large hall known as the Big Schoolroom. For the 1944 event Sheppard was down to sing Schubert's 'Who Is Sylvia?' and 'Where'er You Walk' by Handel. As he stood on the large open stage, bathed in a bright light and staring into complete darkness with none of the audience visible, he recalled being gripped by a blind panic. He got through the first song by holding on to a rail at the front of the dais for all he was worth and was saved from further embarrassment by his accompanist adeptly concealing the fact that he had omitted two whole lines. Sheppard never forgot the experience, even writing a piece about it in later life.[8] A recording of 'Who Is Sylvia?' was his first choice on *Desert Island Discs* in 1965, and he said he could almost feel the butterflies in his stomach as he heard its opening chords.[9] He took the experience to be a salutary reminder that he should never take public appearances for granted or expect to find them easy, whether on the stage, in the pulpit or at the crease. 'It is not obvious that there is anything in common between singing, public speaking and batting', he later wrote, 'but in fact there is a sense of ordeal about each of them which has to be overcome.'[10]

---

8 Undated paper: SHP, 21.12.
9 Transcript of *Desert Island Discs* as pre-recorded 7 September 1965.
10 Sheppard, *Parson's Pitch*, p. 19.

Every year Picton planned for one of his pupils to win a choral scholarship to King's College, Cambridge. In 1945 Sheppard was lined up for the honour. Unfortunately for Mr Picton, and the school, Sheppard decided at that point to give up his singing and piano-playing to devote more time to study and cricket. Picton was decidedly not amused, but to Sheppard's satisfaction their relationship was later repaired, and the two remained on friendly terms until Picton's death in 1958. Sheppard performed in at least one more school concert before he left Sherborne, as a member of a septet rather than as a soloist.

Sheppard expanded his horizons by joining some of the societies and discussion groups the school offered for its pupils' improvement and to occupy their spare time. One was The Interpretes, a group devoted to the study of the Classics. Presided over by the Classics master, Mr Herbert Box, members spent their time reading writers such as Aristophanes, Herodotus and Juvenal in their original languages. In his final year Sheppard became honorary secretary of the group.

Another society he was invited to join was the Duffers. This was founded in the 1890s to 'keep its members alive to all that is best in English Literature, and to do so in as happy and congenial surroundings as possible'. The headmaster took an interest in this group, which was chaired by Sheppard's English teacher, Mr R. S. Thompson. Among Sheppard's contributions to its proceedings was a paper on Jane Austen, which he delivered during the Summer term of 1947. Sheppard became honorary secretary of this society, a position which required him to summarize his own paper, in the third person, in its minute book. In a brief report for the school magazine, *The Shirburnian*, he described himself as 'an ardent "Janeite"'.

A third society to benefit from Sheppard's secretarial skills was the Chin-waggers' Club. This was a Lyon House body presided over by Trelawny-Ross. Sheppard joined the Chin-waggers in September 1945, and within a month was delivering his first paper, an assessment of Winston Churchill. Three months earlier Churchill had, to the surprise of many, lost the first post-war general election to Clement Attlee's Labour Party. Sheppard was prepared to excuse the war leader's speech during the campaign which had suggested socialism could only come about with the aid of 'some form of Gestapo'. The Club was also treated to his paper on Jane Austen.

Perhaps to compensate for the lack of science teaching he was receiving, Sheppard signed up to the Alchemists. This newly formed society served those with an interest in the 'progress of science'. Like other school bodies, the Alchemists regulated its membership, with those admitted enjoying papers by distinguished speakers on topics as diverse as 'The Atom', 'Bacteria', 'The Aerodynamics of Flying Fish', 'The Iraq Oil Pipeline' and 'The Acoustics of Buildings – or Why Gentlemen Sing in Their Baths'. Sheppard might have particularly appreciated a presentation entitled 'History: Science or Art?' When the war ended, the club extended its range of activities to include visits to industrial and chemical plants.

*

The strongest witness to Sheppard's 'character' was his contribution in the field of sport. In the records of cricket at Sherborne his name outshines all others. The standard history has a chapter entitled 'War and the Age of Sheppard 1939–1950'.[11] He also excelled at fives and squash, captaining the school at both sports in his final year.

Sheppard's prowess on the sports field in his last two years at Sherborne could hardly have been predicted when he first arrived at the age of 13. The third smallest boy in his house, and a late developer physically, he was not athletic and had no natural ball skills, as he was the first to admit. In activities where strength and coordination were required, he found the going hard. In a culture which put a premium on muscularity and athleticism he felt the humiliation keenly, a feeling which having a treble voice past the age of 16 did little to assuage. Yet it may have been this sense of embarrassment that spurred him to achieve, to decide to excel at one sport and apply himself with total dedication to mastering it. By the age of 16, he had begun to imagine himself as a cricketer and committed himself to making that a reality, whatever it took.

Three things transformed Sheppard, in the space of two years, from an average player for his house to one on the verge of selection for a first-class county. First, and vitally, he shot up in height, gaining as much as a foot as he rose to six feet and beyond. With this surge in height came

---

11 Gibbs, D. F., *A History of Cricket at Sherborne School*, undated, chapter 6, pp. 20–1.

an increase in strength and the potential to become more dominant at the batting crease. The obvious explanation for his growth was nature making up for lost time, though Sheppard always wondered what effect his housemaster's practice of inviting him to take a glass of port with him every day might have had on his physical transformation.[12]

Second, having persuaded his mother of his serious intent to improve as a player, Barbara treated her son to some coaching at Lord's during the Easter holidays of 1946. This worked wonders for his technique. It also led to his being spotted by a member of the Sussex County Cricket Club committee, who thought he showed sufficient promise to warrant the county considering him for its junior side. Sheppard was twice selected in August to open the batting for Sussex in under-18 level matches. Playing against a Yorkshire side on both occasions, he scored 50 and 52 respectively. The local press waxed lyrical about his performances, noting his 'attractive style, especially in his cutting and off-driving'. Sheppard also impressed the Sussex secretary, Billy Griffith, who wrote to the young batsman inviting him to practise with the county players the following April. Sheppard kept the letter in his pocket all winter.

The final turning point for Sheppard was the appointment at Sherborne of a new professional coach, Len Creese, and the return to the school of Michael ('Micky') Walford as a master. An Oxford Blue in both cricket and rugby, as well as an international hockey player, Walford had originally joined the staff before the war. Now back at Sherborne for Sheppard's final year, Walford soon spotted the boy's potential and took him under his wing. That the two should get together is noteworthy since, although Walford was a reputable first-class cricketer, he held no official cricketing role at the school at the time. Walford's influence on the schoolboy batsman was profound. Not only did he help him to improve his technique, he told the 17-year-old that he ought to be a first-class cricketer. Sheppard always held this to be the defining moment in his cricketing career. He maintained that until Walford uttered that remark, it had never occurred to him he might play at that level.[13] In fact he had

---

12 Sheppard's new housemaster said that he could not afford port, but the boy could keep a crate of Guinness in his study and drink a bottle a day!

13 Walford subsequently became a friend of the Sheppard family and courted David's sister Mary for a time.

tried the previous year to secure a trial with Surrey, the county of his birth, and been rebuffed. Now he resolved to make the most of the opportunities opening up at Sussex and build a career in the first-class game with them.[14]

Sheppard's debut for the Sherborne first XI in May 1946 was inauspicious. Selected to open for the first two matches of the season, he went for a duck in both innings. As the year progressed, he achieved more respectable scores, including 74 and 35 against Clifton College, 87 against Downside and 80 against the Cryptics. His aggregate of runs for the season was 492 at an average of just under 45. The extent to which the team relied on him can be seen from the fact that the next best batsman scored not a third as many runs, at an average of 19. Sheppard was clearly improving as a batsman, but he knew he would only maintain his progress by sheer hard work and application. The following winter he decided to do just that, swapping the music room for the 'Sweat House', as the gym at Lyon was called. There, in front of the mirror, he practised moving his feet in the way Walford had shown him, thousands and thousands of times. 'I sometimes missed the ball still', he would later recall, 'but my feet never went to the wrong place again.'[15]

Sheppard would often describe himself as 'no infant prodigy'. He would contrast his experience with that of other leading batsmen of his generation such as Colin Cowdrey and Peter May, both of whom were selected for their school teams while in their early teens. Sheppard saw the 13-year-old Cowdrey playing for Tonbridge School at Lord's, where he outshone the other more senior boys as both a batsman and bowler. Their paths would later cross in different ways.

*

Sheppard maintained a strict regime of cricket practice at home as well as at school. Holidays would find him undertaking disciplined batting

---

14 Sheppard had approached Surrey with a view to being considered for their Colts team, unaware that this was the Second XI and not, as he had imagined, a youth side. MCC rules at the time permitted a player to represent his county of residence if different from his county of birth, but at the start of each season he had to choose for which of the two counties he would play.

15 Address to Sherborne School on the 450th Anniversary of the Refounding of the School, 14 May 2000.

sessions, sometimes throwing a tennis ball against the coal-shed door and hitting the rebound, sometimes securing the services of his mother and sister as bowlers. While the former produced steady underarm deliveries which were potentially helpful to the cause, Mary preferred to bowl overarm, often with unpredictable results. Sheppard would also play his own full-length cricket matches in the garden, taking the part of each player on the two sides and keeping the scores in a notebook. One summer he set out to complete a full English County Championship season, with 17 counties playing one another, and himself batting for every player. Sheppard always maintained that, while he never dared count the number of hours he spent in this solitary pursuit, it taught him more about batting than he learned in any other way. If the imaginary player at the crease was of Test match standard, he would replicate that hero's stance and favourite strokes. Imitating the great players stood him in good stead as his own career developed. It taught him to concentrate at the crease. 'Trying to score a century for Hammond meant I mustn't play any silly shots', he later wrote.[16]

Most of this cricket took place at the family home in Slinfold, Sussex, where Sheppard's mother and sister returned from London to live after the war. David spent his last few holidays from school at the house, known as St Briget's. For most of the war it had been let. When David enrolled at Sherborne in 1942, Barbara moved to London to join Mary, remaining there until peace was declared. Mother and daughter rented a top-floor flat in Weymouth Street, a block or two from Broadcasting House in Langham Place.

Mary's job involved working on popular war-time programmes, including *ITMA* (*It's That Man Again*), and assisting figures such as Roy Plomley, creator of *Desert Island Discs*. Barbara continued her service with the Mechanised Transport Corps by driving ambulances at the London docks. At this time, she met and fell in love with a Polish airman named Czeslaw Matusiak, who also befriended David. On one occasion he allowed the boy to fire his revolver. Contact was lost with Czeslaw when he was posted abroad and, anxious to help his mother, David wrote to the London headquarters of the Polish Government in exile

---

16 Typed manuscript from early 1959, possibly a radio broadcast: SHP, 20.2.

enquiring about the airman's whereabouts. Eventually he was told that Czeslaw was missing, believed killed. Not knowing what to do with the letter, David hid it in a drawer. As David later recalled, when his mother eventually discovered the letter, their shared loss 'drew us close together in expressing our grief again'.[17]

Sheppard spent some of his school holidays in London, where he would often accompany his mother and sister to concerts and the theatre. Ballet was one of Barbara's passions, and some weeks she and her son would go more than once to see the Sadler's Wells company perform. While the experience helped to broaden David's musical knowledge and awareness, he also admitted later to having had a crush on the principal dancer, Margot Fonteyn. Mary, now into her twenties, would give her younger brother occasional glimpses of the life enjoyed by people in broadcasting, taking him to parties, balls and other social gatherings. Being in London made David more directly aware of the effect the war was having on daily life beyond the relatively sheltered environment of his school. Sometimes a show he was attending would be interrupted by an air-raid warning, requiring a speedy exodus to the nearest underground station. On one occasion he and his mother heard a V1 flying bomb overhead and saw the red glow of its exhaust just a few hundred feet above them. Opportunities for boys to play cricket in the school holidays were sparse during and immediately after the war, but Sheppard took part in two matches in the summer of 1945, both involving travel from London. One was for Horsham, in which he did not get to bat, and one for Sussex's Junior Martlets, his first experience of playing on the county ground at Hove.

Between the theatre-going and other social interaction he enjoyed in London, Sheppard liked to spend time on his own. He developed a love of reading, devouring everything from light schoolboy fiction through Tolstoy's *War and Peace* to the novels of his favourite author, Jane Austen. Austen was a great favourite of his mother, at whose knee he may have imbibed his love for her work. He often took the short walk from Weymouth Street to Regent's Park where, perhaps unusually for a boy in his mid-teens, he would hire a boat and row alone on the lake. The

---

17 Sheppard, *Steps along Hope Street*, p. 8.

park also offered squash courts where he could practise the other sport at which he excelled. Throughout his life, Sheppard derived great benefit from spending time on his own. This led many, including close family, to describe him as an introvert. Sheppard once told a group of clergy that he was an 'Introvert' on the Myers-Briggs Type Indicator, someone who 'finds energy in more solitary situations'.[18]

Sheppard's capacity to survive without the company of others was also in evidence at Slinfold. The combination of petrol rationing and the house's location a good way from the village meant that contact with others was infrequent. This was less a problem than an opportunity to someone with a whole season of cricket matches to get through and a coal-shed door at his disposal.

*

The start of Sheppard's final year at Sherborne, 1946–7, saw him assume the position of responsibility Trelawny-Ross had mapped out for him. The housemaster had originally hoped the two might run the house in tandem, but he retired in the summer of 1946. Being head of house brought new duties and obligations for the 17-year-old Sheppard, although having been a prefect for a year, he was already empowered to administer beatings and require junior boys to fag for him. In a regime where corporal punishment was not uncommon, Sheppard claimed to have been caned only once at Sherborne, for an impertinent remark about a prefect while he was a junior boy. As a prefect and head of house he carried out beatings on other boys. In later life he regretted that he never challenged the culture at the school and hoped that the punishments he meted out had been fair.

Another of Sheppard's duties as head of house was to write confidential reports on each term's activities for the benefit of his successors. In the first of these he observed that, with Trelawny-Ross's retirement, some of the rules and customs associated with the former housemaster had been discontinued. The change which he may have found most pleasing, given

---

18 Address during Deanery visits in Liverpool, 1996/7: SHP, 16.5.

his passion for music and Test match commentary, was that 'wirelesses are to be found in studies'.

Sheppard's final year at Sherborne saw further achievements in the fields of sport and academic study. Building on the progress he had made the year before, he turned in performances at the batting crease unsurpassed in the annals of cricket at Sherborne. He also won the school's Senior Squash trophy, finished runner-up in the Fives competition, and was appointed school captain in both sports. He received his badge as a physical training instructor.

In its summary of public schools' cricket for 1947, *Wisden* noted that Sheppard 'far outstripped the other batsmen' at Sherborne. He was 'very mature for a schoolboy cricketer', it reported.[19] Opening with 104 against The Town, Sheppard scored a total of 786 runs in 14 innings that season, at an average of 78.60. He hit four centuries, of which the highest was 141. Sheppard later maintained that the batting at Sherborne that year depended too much on himself and the batsman immediately below him in the averages, Bob Tozer. This was a remarkably modest statement, considering that Tozer scored fewer than half his own total of runs at an average of 25.50.[20]

Sheppard's performance should be put in perspective. No other Sherborne batsman playing a full season had previously posted a higher average since records began to be kept in the nineteenth century. In all English public schools' cricket for 1947, only Peter May at Charterhouse had a better average.

Sheppard's final academic attainment at Sherborne was an Exhibition to Trinity Hall, Cambridge, gained in December 1946. In this, again, his housemaster had a significant role to play. In 1945 Trelawny-Ross had written to the Senior Tutor at Trinity Hall, Charles Crawley, asking him to put the boy on his list of candidates for two years ahead. Trelawny-Ross's letter is an exemplar of how things were done at the time, and an illuminating snapshot of his opinion of his 16-year-old protégé. Sheppard should sit for a Classical Scholarship, the housemaster writes, 'and incidentally is the best schoolboy cricketer Plum Warner saw at

19 Preston, H., ed., *Wisden Cricketers' Almanack 1948*, London: Sporting Handbooks, 1948, p. 660.

20 Sheppard, *Parson's Pitch*, p. 25.

Lord's nets last holidays! I suppose he is also the most charming boy I shall have asked you to take, but completely unspoilt'.[21]

A fortnight later Trelawny-Ross provided a reference for Sheppard, saying that he could 'cordially recommend' the boy 'on the grounds of character and ability'. He again alluded, though in more discreet terms, to his prowess as a cricketer, noting that 'he should be a valuable asset to any college'. By the end of the month Crawley had written to Barbara Sheppard informing her that the college had 'provisionally accepted' her son as a candidate for entry, either in October 1947 or after his period of military service.

In August, Trelawny-Ross accompanied Sheppard to see Crawley at Trinity Hall. This was an unusually paternal gesture, even for one so used to acting *in loco parentis*. One possible explanation is that Barbara Sheppard had already invited the housemaster to become local guardian to her son in the absence of his own father. Trelawny-Ross assumed the role once he retired the following summer, and describes himself as such in a letter to Crawley dated September 1946.[22] Shortly before Sheppard was due to sit for his scholarship his new housemaster, Hugh (known as Hughie) Holmes, pressed his case further with a letter to the Master of Trinity Hall, Professor Henry Dean. David Sheppard will shortly be coming to the Hall to try for an exhibition, Holmes advised the professor, and would he find time to see the boy during his visit? Maintaining the line that a pupil with sporting potential would be worth accepting whatever his academic qualities, Holmes expressed his confidence that Dean, an Old Shirburnian and a man Holmes knew personally, would like Sheppard. 'I very much hope a place may be found for him in the college whether or not he is up to scholarship award standard', Holmes concluded.[23]

In the event Sheppard won an Exhibition in Classics on account of his academic rather than batting ability, although Crawley felt it appropriate

---

21 Letter dated 5 May 1945, Trinity Hall archive (THA). The reference to the net at Lord's suggests Sheppard was there during the Easter holidays in 1945, so during wartime, as well as in 1946, or else is a figment of Trelawny-Ross's imagination. Sir Pelham 'Plum' Warner was known as the Grand Old Man of English cricket.

22 There is a curious detail in Trelawny-Ross's annual letter to old Lyon boys for 1946. Throughout these letters he would refer to current pupils by their surnames and initials but in this letter we read that 'David Sheppard is the best bat in the school . . .'

23 Letter dated 24 November 1946: THA.

to tell him that he had only just scraped a pass. Crawley had tried to deter Sheppard from taking a paper in Greek and Roman history. In the event it proved to be his mark in this paper which secured Sheppard his award or, as Crawley put it, 'helped to get you in to the bottom of the list of Exhibitioners'. At £40 per year, an Exhibition was worth less than a full Scholarship, and Sheppard was not convinced at this stage that he wanted to read Classics. But he accepted the award without hesitation and confirmed his intent to come up to Trinity Hall after his period of national service. One immediate benefit of this award was a reduction in his academic timetable at Sherborne. This allowed him more time to read and, with the prospect of selection for Cambridge now on the horizon, practise his footwork in the Sweat House.

*

Sheppard would later have misgivings about the public-school system. He did not often visit Sherborne as an old boy.[24] Yet he always highlighted the positive aspects of his experience at the school. In an address on one return visit in 2000 he listed what he felt he owed to Sherborne:

> Loyalty to friends and the group I belonged to; the discipline of Classics – a good intellectual base; training in personal reliability; confidence and motivation – a firm base from which to move out; determination to achieve; some cricketing skills; a love of music.[25]

A striking omission from this list, although he does acknowledge it elsewhere, is learning a great deal about leadership. Sheppard was never Head of School or captain of cricket, but he was picked out early as a leader. He then found that quality fostered throughout his school career, in his house, in the choir, in literary societies and in sport. His fellow

---

24 One visit in the late 1950s is immortalized in the autobiography of Charles Collingwood, 'Brian Aldridge' in the BBC radio drama *The Archers*. Sheppard was a great hero of Collingwood's, but all Collingwood could recall about the visitor's hour-long speech was that his fly buttons were undone; *Brian and Me: An autobiography*, London: Michael O'Mara Books, 2009, pp. 192–4.

25 Address to the Old Shirburnians on the 450th Anniversary of the Refounding of the School, 13 May 2000.

pupils came to see him as a natural leader, and his readiness to assume responsibility was seen by his masters as vindication of their early belief in his potential. Hughie Holmes might have been echoing Trelawny-Ross when he remarked, in his official housemaster's reference for Trinity Hall, that Sheppard 'has a positive personality and is steadily developing his powers of leadership'. Sheppard drew upon the leadership skills he developed while at Sherborne at every stage of his adult life. He later recalled Holmes as providing a bridge for him 'into adult life in quite an important way'.[26]

In terms of helping his religious faith, the school would have encouraged Sheppard to form a strong attachment to the creeds and rituals of the Christian church and see religion as important for developing self-control and character. It would have placed less emphasis on the value of individual conversion of the kind he later experienced at Cambridge. Sheppard was taught Divinity every term, he encountered staff with a devout faith,[27] and attended chapel eight or nine times a week. Yet as he later acknowledged, his religion was 'only another activity which I switched on sometimes, and switched off just as easily'.[28] The enjoyment he derived from chapel worship was rooted largely in his love of singing and the responsibilities he was given as leader of the choir, including that of giving right expression to the words being sung.

Sheppard would later affirm that he always wanted, 'in a vague sort of way, to be on God's side' while at school, but 'of any real commitment to Christ and an idea that this should change one's real attitude to everyday life, there was nothing'.[29] Opportunities to engage in the kind of applied Christianity practised by his father and Tubby Clayton were also few. Like many public schools, Sherborne had a charitable inner-city project in London, but Sheppard appears not to have been involved with it. He did reflect later that school taught him 'the tradition of service, of doing things for others'.[30] Sacrificing one's life for others was also emphasized

---

26 Private interview, January 2005.

27 One or two Sherborne staff ran extra-curricular Bible study groups, though there is no evidence Sheppard ever attended these.

28 Sheppard, D. S., 'How I Found Religion', *Woman's Own*, 11 December 1957, p. 22.

29 Transcript of interview with Douglas Brown for *Viewpoint*, BBC 1, broadcast 15 May 1969: SHP, file 20.2.

30 Sheppard, *Parson's Pitch*, p. 46.

in school worship during Sheppard's time. 'We went to chapel every day', he was later to write, 'and religion was strongly connected with turning over pages in the book of remembrance of Old Boys of the school who were killed in the war.'[31] Sheppard once spoke of Sherborne giving him 'the security of a firm base from which I could venture across some of the dividing lines of the world'.[32] It is unlikely he thought it provided much by way of *substance* for that base, certainly the one upon which he stood for the whole of his adult life.

Sheppard would have encountered little at Sherborne by way of inspiration for the world view he was later to adopt. Alick Trelawny-Ross was hardly the only opponent of progressive opinions on the staff. The headmaster, Canon Wallace, once told the school that Attlee and other Labour ministers were traitors to their class on account of their apparent plan to abolish public schools.[33] Trelawny-Ross's successor as housemaster of Lyon, Hughie Holmes, had the most unspeakably racist views which the school magazine allowed him to share.[34] In his second autobiography, Sheppard ruefully acknowledged that his mother shared many of the assumptions about politics, race and class upon which some of his schoolmasters appeared to operate, though as an adolescent he began to push back on some of those views. In his later years at the school he engaged with political ideas and tested opinions. During the 1945 election campaign he was impressed by the local Liberal Party candidate and, to the consternation of some of the other boys, publicly declared himself to be a Liberal. A year later he took up the cause of another political party in a letter to *The Shirburnian*. Unhappy at the editors' description of the 1945 election result as a 'victory of the Left over Reaction', Sheppard reminded them that, historically, 'the Conservative Party has passed more progressive bills than any other party'. His paper to the Chin-waggers suggests he harboured an admiration for Churchill,

---

31 Sheppard, D. S., and Worlock, D., *Better Together: Christian partnership in a hurt city*, London: Hodder & Stoughton, 1988, p. 21.

32 Address to Sherborne School, 14 May 2000

33 I owe this reference to Sisman, A., *John le Carré: The biography*, London: Bloomsbury, 2015, pp. 45–6. As David Cornwell, le Carré was at Sherborne during Sheppard's last two years. Some of the masters are identifiable as characters in his novels.

34 *The Shirburnian* once published a poem by Holmes entitled 'Wogs', not one of whose 36 lines could be quoted today without causing the most extreme offence.

though one of his contemporaries in Lyon House recalls Sheppard predicting that Labour would win the 1945 election, hardly mainstream opinion at the time.

*

In addition to playing as much cricket as possible at school, Sheppard maintained his interest in the first-class game and its players. One project he worked on during this final year was the compilation of a scrapbook of the MCC tour to Australia that winter, 1946–7. Perhaps to ward off potential confiscators or borrowers he housed it within a school exercise book labelled 'D S SHEPPARD, Lyon House, Roman History Notes'.[35] It is a classic schoolboy's creation. There are photographs, press-cuttings and scorecards, along with the compiler's own neatly typed reflections on issues such as England's prospects in the Tests, the selection of the side and the merits of the tourists' captain, Wally Hammond. One newspaper photograph's caption has been impatiently amended to record the actual players depicted.

Sheppard would hardly have been the only schoolboy in England at that time closely following the fortunes of his idols down under; Len Hutton, Denis Compton, Godfrey Evans, Alec Bedser and others. Not many, however, were to find, when the next MCC party to tour Australia was chosen, their own name listed alongside those of their heroes.

---

35 This is now in the archive in the Museum at the Sussex County Cricket Club Ground, Hove.

3

National service and conversion
(1947–1950)

Like most public schoolboys with a place at university secured, Sheppard undertook his compulsory military service before going on to further study. During his last weeks at Sherborne he wrote to the senior tutor at Trinity Hall, Charles Crawley, informing him he planned to join the Army at the end of the current term. It was 'safe to assume' he would be up at Cambridge for the start of the 1949–50 academic year. He did not know the exact date that he would be called up, but he did know he had some important cricket to play in the intervening period.

*

A week after leaving school at the end of July 1947, Sheppard played his first match at Lord's. Opening the innings for Southern Schools against The Rest, he turned in respectable scores of 36 and 63. This performance earned him selection for the Public Schools team to play the Combined Services at the same ground the following week, although he was unable to score so freely against this more experienced opposition. Batting alongside Sheppard was the rising star from Charterhouse, Peter May, with whom he would later form a friendship at Cambridge. May hit centuries in both matches.

The next important step in his cricketing career awaited him the following day, his debut at first-class level. Following the invitation from Sussex the previous summer, David had joined their players for some nets that April. His performance there, and continued good run for his school, had prompted the county to select him at the first opportunity. His opening match was a county championship fixture against Leicestershire at Hastings. Like his first appearance for his school, it was not a memorable occasion. Going in at number three, he was out first ball LBW in the first innings. In the second he scored just two before being dismissed in the same manner. His first run was a gratefully received gift from a compassionate opposing captain. Despite this inauspicious start, Sheppard was selected for the next two championship games. Still unable to notch up any significant score, he declared himself 'more determined than ever to work hard' at succeeding at the first-class level.[1]

His involvement at Sussex brought him some new mentors. These included the brothers James and John Langridge and George Cox Jr, players he had watched and read about all his life. Another was the county coach, E. H. 'Patsy' Hendren, one of the most prolific batsmen of all time. Cox was a particular source of encouragement to the young Sheppard and, living in a neighbouring village, became a personal friend. Cox would pick Sheppard up in his old Morris 8, its door kept shut with the aid of a lawnmower part, for a bumpy ride over the Downs to Hove. When Sheppard was at Cambridge, he secured a coaching position for Cox with the University side.

*

Sheppard was called up for national service in October 1947. In many ways he was well prepared for it. He was used to living away from home, he knew how to survive in an all-male institution, and he had had some military experience at his school. Involvement with the cadet force was compulsory at Sherborne, and he had served as a company sergeant major in the junior Training Corps. His two years as a conscript opened new doors and taught him new lessons, as well as offering further opportunities to develop his leadership skills.

Sheppard's first posting was to the Palace Barracks in Holywood, County Down.[2] Things did not start well. He was seasick on the boat across from Liverpool, and the first four months in the barracks were largely taken up with square bashing, kit inspections and learning unquestioning obedience to orders. 'At the moment most of it repels

---

1 Typed manuscript from early 1959: Sheppard papers (SHP), 20.2.
2 These would later serve as a base for the British Army during the Troubles.

me', he wrote in his first letter home, 'but I hope it won't win me over!' Among his contemporaries was Douglas Spankie, a former classmate from Sherborne, and a young Jeremy Thorpe, future leader of the Liberal Party. Thorpe managed to get himself discharged after only two months.[3] Sheppard and some friends helped liven things up at Christmas by putting on a concert in the barrack room.

One of Sheppard's happiest memories of his time at Holywood was the warm welcome he received from the local Sandes Soldiers' Home. Similar in its aims to the Toc H movement, Sandes offers sanctuary and support to soldiers, regardless of rank, as a way of sharing the Christian faith. On his first Christmas Day, Sheppard had suffered a cut lip as a result of a freak accident while watching a soccer game. To help him recover, the head of the Sandes Home, a Miss Wilson, invited him to join her and her staff for their Christmas lunch. 'It was a simple act of friendship', Sheppard later recalled, 'which meant a great deal to me.' Sheppard later discovered that some of the staff had set themselves to pray for him, prayers which he came to believe were answered in due course.[4]

With his public-school background, Sheppard was viewed as potential officer material. Arrangements were made for him to go to the War Office Selection Board (WOSB). Here candidates were divided into groups and set tasks, such as crossing a stream with planks, rope and oil drums. Initiative and leadership were critical, rather than the success of the project. Each aspiring officer was also required to give a ten-minute talk on a topic of general interest, and be interviewed about their background, interests and reasons for wanting a commission. In making their assessment, the selection boards claimed to make much of 'leadership', 'style' and 'enthusiasm', although the decision to award a pass, fail or deferral ('deferred watch') generally turned on social class. Proficiency in sport was a bonus.[5]

---

3 I owe this reference to Bloch, M., *Jeremy Thorpe*, London: Little Brown, 2014, p. 59. There is no evidence that Thorpe and Sheppard had any subsequent contact.

4 Sheppard, D. S., *Parson's Pitch*, London: Hodder & Stoughton, 1964, p. 32. Sheppard's account of this episode begins, 'There was one touch of warmth and friendship which we found in Palace Barracks . . .'. Perhaps he felt there were few others; cf. 'A thunderflash and a Christmas dinner', *Evening Argus*, 14 December 1956, p. 7.

5 Vinen, R., *National Service: A generation in uniform 1945–1963*, London: Allen Lane, 2014, pp. 203–4, 208. I am grateful for help with this section from Douglas Miller and John Reeve.

Having passed his WOSB, Sheppard moved on to Eaton Hall in Cheshire, the officer cadet training unit for men going into the infantry. The regime was still tough, but there was a different atmosphere from that at the barracks, since Sheppard and his comrades were now officer class and afforded due respect. Again, Sheppard got off to a faltering start, being paraded before the platoon on his first day as a model of how not to dress. Later he committed the unforgiveable sin of losing his rifle, only to discover, shortly before he would have been found out and possibly demoted, that it had been borrowed by a fellow trainee and left in another room. Despite these hiccups, Sheppard was chosen as Senior Under Officer for his intake and awarded the Belt of Honour. His immediate posting after Eaton Hall was to Shorncliffe Barracks near Folkestone. From there he should have joined the West African Frontier force in Ibadan, Nigeria. He had had his jabs, and was awaiting his posting, when the Adjutant asked him whether he really wanted to go. Sheppard said he was none too keen, and the Adjutant arranged for another to be recruited. 'I was not proud of the circumstances by which I stayed in England', Sheppard later wrote.[6] So from Shorncliffe, No.390538 2/Lt D. S. Sheppard joined the First Battalion of the Royal Sussex Regiment, based at Old Park Barracks in Dover. He remained in Kent for the rest of his service.

*

Sheppard viewed his spell in the army in a positive light. 'I believe they were good years for me in many ways', he noted in his first autobiography. 'They . . . reminded me that the majority of men earn their living with their hands.'[7] After a privileged upbringing, he had faced the challenge of living and working closely with all sorts and conditions of men, and found the experience instructive. In the light of his eventual career path, this broadening of his horizons would prove invaluable. The cricketers at Sussex whom Sheppard was beginning to count as friends were also largely 'professionals', men from humbler backgrounds than his own.

6 Draft of *Steps along Hope Street*: SHP, 44.6.
7 Sheppard, *Parson's Pitch*, p. 30.

Unlike him, they relied on the wage they earned from playing sport in order to survive.[8]

It is unlikely that Sheppard's time in the forces changed his approach to faith. There was institutional religion in the army as there had been at Sherborne and Northcliffe House but, away from the discipline of enforced chapel attendance, Sheppard attended church irregularly during his two years of national service. Apart from his encounter with the staff at the Sandes' Home in Cheshire, and conversations with forces chaplains, he may have had little encouragement to think seriously about issues of faith. He told his mother he found the padre 'not particularly inspiring'.[9] He later recalled how easy it was to become 'one of the boys' and embrace the general culture of swearing and locker-room talk. Having been brought up to believe in the importance of having ideals and of trying to follow Christian values, he found this becoming increasingly difficult as he 'moved out of the well-marked grooves of life at home and at school . . . It was not that I questioned the ideals', he was later to write, 'but faced with life among men of all beliefs and none in the Army, the ideals seemed impossible.'[10]

One skill which Sheppard acquired in the army and employed throughout his life, was a military technique for making decisions. This involved writing what he called an Appreciation of the Situation which needed to be resolved, then working through four key stages; Object, Courses, Factors and Plan. When faced with crucial decisions in his life, Sheppard was to find this an invaluable method for clarifying the situation he confronted, working through the factors to be considered, sifting the various options and determining the right way forward. He would later see that a further element was needed: seeking to know the will of God through prayer or, as he put it, asking God 'to confirm what seemed to be best, or to pull me back'.[11]

---

8 Until 1962 county teams comprised professionals, men who were contracted to the club and paid for playing in the summer months, and amateurs, who were also registered but who received only expenses for playing.

9 Letter, 28 October [1947?]: SHP, 53.4.

10 Sheppard, *Parson's Pitch*, p. 46.

11 See for example Sheppard, D. S., *Steps along Hope Street*, London: Hodder & Stoughton, 2002, pp.1, 26, 96; transcript of interview with Douglas Brown for *Viewpoint*, BBC 1, broadcast 15 May 1969, SHP, 20.2.

*

Cricket, and sport generally, figured prominently during Sheppard's national service. It was a requirement that officer cadets engage in sport as part of their training, and Sheppard discovered new abilities. He developed an appetite for rugby, and once found himself 'volunteered' to box for the honour of his platoon. The army laid great store by boxing as a guide to a person's character and courage and, to his surprise, Sheppard won both his bouts in the ring.

Inevitably, Sheppard looked mainly for opportunities to play cricket. These came in a variety of forms, including evening matches in Cheshire and appearances for Shorncliffe Garrison at different grounds around Kent. Sheppard played only one representative game for the army, although he was granted generous leave in order to continue his career with Sussex. During the two seasons of his national service, he played 13 first-class and ten second XI matches for the county. Sheppard's emerging sporting career was probably the reason he never served abroad.

This opportunity to play regular cricket, and encouragement from some of the senior players at Sussex, led to a great improvement in his form. Sheppard always gave credit to George Cox for helping to develop his confidence as a batsman. He cited as pivotal one incident during a match at Eastbourne in August 1949. Cox, sensing his younger partner was struggling to make runs, told him to put his foot down the wicket and hit the ball through the covers. 'So I did', Sheppard said later. 'Something seemed to click, and I went on doing it'.[12] The change was dramatic. Sheppard not only went on to score his maiden first-class century that day, he reached 199 by close of play and completed a double hundred the following morning. Sussex awarded him his county cap during this game, and he hit big hundreds in his next two matches. He became 'hungry for runs', as he later put it.[13]

Sheppard was attracting the attention of the press. 'There's a Goliath strain in this David', quipped *The People* after his innings of 80 against Championship-contenders Middlesex at Hove. The *Daily Express*

---

12 Typed manuscript from early 1959; SHP, 20.2.
13 Sheppard, *Steps along Hope Street*, p.14.

predicted 'a Compton-like future' for the young lieutenant after that same match. Media interest in Sheppard's career and his opinions would remain lively for the rest of his life, though Sheppard often found the press frustrating. More august publications were also noticing him. The *Playfair Cricket Annual* observed, in its review of Sussex's performance in the county championship in 1949, that 'Sheppard, a beautiful back player, has a remarkable temperament for his years and should clearly go far.'[14]

Cambridge continued to be on Sheppard's mind during his national service. At the start of his second year, he wrote again to Crawley at Trinity Hall to say that he was now minded to study Law rather than Classics when he came up the following year. Sheppard wondered whether Crawley could suggest some preparatory reading he might tackle now: 'I have very little work to do here at the moment', he told him.[15] Sheppard had one further change of mind before he arrived at Cambridge. At the very last minute he decided he would read History for his first two years (Part I of the Tripos) and Law for his third (Part II).[16] In terms of a career, he would follow his father into the legal profession and join the Bar. This was the future his mother had envisioned for him, and the only one he had seriously entertained while at school. Trinity Hall was founded to provide training in Law, and it had been Sheppard's only choice of college on his application form to sit for a Cambridge Scholarship. Discharged from the army at the end of September 1949, Sheppard checked in at Trinity Hall in time for his first lecture there on 10 October. He roomed for that year with John Byron, a friend from Sherborne.

*

Sheppard's initial year at Cambridge was disappointing. Crawley pulled no punches when writing to him after the results of the first-year exams were announced in June 1950. He was not only disappointed at his

---

14 West, P., ed., *Playfair Cricket Annual 1950*, London: Playfair Books, 1950, p. 96.

15 Letter dated 5 November 1948: Trinity Hall Archive (THA).

16 Tripos is the term used at Cambridge for any examination by which an undergraduate course is assessed. A Tripos is divided into two parts, Part I being broadly based and Part II allowing the student to specialize within their chosen field. Either Part I or Part II may be two years, with the other one year.

student's overall result, a Lower Second,[17] but at the poor marks he had obtained in each of his subject papers. All were below Beta. Crawley had had higher hopes and saw no chink of light in the gloom. 'I should be less unhappy if there were some streaks of much better promise in the marks', he wrote. 'I am not complaining of your industry . . . but I know you are capable of a very much better showing.'[18]

If Sheppard feared he might lose his Exhibition, a further letter from Crawley would have put his mind at rest. 'We do not regard Class II.2 as the proper home for an Exhibitioner of the College', the senior tutor wrote, but in view of Sheppard having undertaken his national service between school and university 'and of the legitimate distractions of the past term', the governing body was prepared to continue the present arrangement for a further year. If Sheppard expected to keep his Exhibition for a third year, however, he would have to 'do a bit better in the Tripos next summer'.[19]

The 'legitimate distractions' to which Crawley referred were the numerous representative cricket matches Sheppard got involved in during his third term. He had little sympathy with these intrusions into Sheppard's life. He bluntly told him he considered his being a cricketer a 'handicap'. There was, however, another reason why Sheppard's exam results were poor. He had a passionate interest in History but no academic background, not having been allowed to study it at Sherborne. As a result, he found himself out of his depth at Cambridge from the start. His lecturers assumed a certain basic knowledge which he did not have. He was unused to the idea that an answer to a question might not be judged simply as right or wrong, as in Latin and Greek. He lacked experience in marshalling evidence and arguing a case. To try to avoid slipping too far behind, he began to skip lectures and, in the library, work through the syllabus at his own speed with the aid of the recommended

---

17 As in many other universities, Cambridge honours degrees were classified as: I (First); II.i (Upper Second); II.ii (Lower Second); and III (Third).

18 Letter dated 17 June 1950: THA. Crawley would later describe Sheppard as having 'intellectual ability much above average', which may explain some of the frustration he displays here; letter dated 3 March 1953, Ridley Hall archive.

19 Letter dated 20 June 1950: THA. The loss of his Exhibition, worth £40 per year, would not have forced Sheppard to give up his studies for financial reasons. He was also in receipt of a state maintenance grant worth around £100 annually and had declared his gross unearned annual income to be £140.

books. As his solitary, intensive sessions at Sherborne had helped him to succeed at cricket, the same determination gave him confidence in the subject he loved.

As Sheppard was to discover the following year, missing lectures and working on your own need not necessarily lead to academic disaster. A passion for cricket and an eagerness to indulge it at every opportunity, however, might. The conflict for him, and others with their sights set on a Blue[20] or even higher cricketing recognition, was that University exams took place at the end of May while the cricket season began at the end of April. That might not have been problematic had the fixture list during May been light, but the University had matches against first-class opposition lined up virtually back to back throughout the month. Having performed well in the trial matches for freshmen in April, and been duly selected for the Cambridge University First XI, Sheppard played in every available match in May, plus a three-day friendly when the University team had no fixture. In addition, he turned out for Sussex against Middlesex at Lord's at the end of May. He played a total of 24 days' cricket during that month, with precisely three days allocated for study.[21] Unlike some cricketing students who did a few hours' study first thing in the morning, Sheppard's approach was to tie up his year's work by mid April and only return to it in the week immediately before the exams, when no University matches were scheduled. It was an impressive attempt at balance, but clearly Sheppard wanted to succeed as a cricketer rather than a student.[22]

*

However Sheppard saw his priorities when he started at Cambridge, an experience in his first term brought a new one hugely to the fore. He embraced the Christian faith in a personal and life-changing

---

20 A Blue is awarded to students at Cambridge and Oxford for competing at the highest level of university sport, including in a Varsity match against the other university.

21 One match, that against Yorkshire in early May, was completely rained off, possibly allowing Sheppard time for study if he wished. The four Sundays in the month would have been free.

22 In his first autobiography Sheppard talks about cricket having 'a foremost place' in his life when he first arrived at Cambridge: Sheppard, *Parson's Pitch*, p. 48.

way, a moment he would later describe as 'my conversion to Christ'. 'Life-changing' does not exaggerate the significance of this event. In Sheppard's terms, it brought 'a new centre' to his life, and a recognition that the ideas he had about his future would need to be 'examined at a new depth'. Christianity had become 'the central fact upon which my own life turned every day', he was to write.[23] It is impossible to make sense of Sheppard's life from this point on without an appreciation of the extent to which his conversion reoriented his thinking and outlook.

That Sheppard should speak of his being 'converted' to Christ appears at first glance peculiar. His upbringing had been steeped in churchgoing. Yet he was convinced he had undergone a transformation, from a knowledge of religion that was 'very much something second-hand' to a *personal* knowledge of Jesus Christ'. Until that experience, he had not considered he needed any change of direction in terms of his understanding of God. He had been confirmed into the Church of England while at prep school. He had been encouraged to think he was on the road of faith. Rather than feel that he needed consciously to search for God, he reflected later, he had believed he 'was already on the road, and must struggle on, becoming a little more religious until one day perhaps I might arrive. The idea that I might not be on the road at all had never occurred to me.' He had taken church things for granted, he later wrote. 'I had come through the machinery of Christian training, but the secret spark of personal faith was not yet alight.'[24]

The lighting of the spark of personal faith occurred for Sheppard during a week-long evangelistic mission organized by the University's Christian Union at the end of November 1949. Sheppard would later say he would not normally have attended this kind of event, but the previous week he had met one of its organizers, John Collins, who invited him as his guest. Collins was several years older than Sheppard, studying for ordination at Ridley Hall, and had no interest in cricket. But the two

---

23 Sheppard, *Steps along Hope Street,* p.1; Sheppard, *Parson's Pitch*, p. 82.

24 Transcript of radio interview with John Ellison for *Other People's Lives*, 2 December 1971: SHP, 20.2; Sheppard, *Steps along Hope Street*, p.21; Sheppard, *Parson's Pitch*, p. 47; Sheppard, D. S., 'How I Found Religion', *Woman's Own*, 11 December 1957, p. 22.

struck up a friendship after a game of squash. Collins told Sheppard the mission would be worth his attending: 'It's quite a sight and you won't be bored.'[25]

There was certainly guaranteed to be an element of showmanship during the proceedings. The speaker, the American Presbyterian pastor Dr Donald Grey Barnhouse, had a reputation for preaching in a direct and forceful manner. Sheppard always acknowledged that Barnhouse's message was not fully to his taste, but that he needed 'a blunt and aggressive preacher' to 'jolt me into thinking'. What struck Sheppard about Barnhouse was how forcefully he rebutted the idea that being a faithful member of a church was enough to make a person acceptable to God. Human efforts to reach God were doomed to failure, and only by 'the totally unreserved love and grace of Jesus Christ can anyone be accepted'. Sheppard did not immediately warm to this proposition. As his friend from Trinity Hall, John Crathorne, recalls, Sheppard left the meeting with a scowl and the comment that, 'No one has ever called me a dirty rotten sinner like that before!' Barnhouse's talk had broken through all his '"good-as-most and better-than-some-I-can-think-of" defences'.[26]

The evangelical message Sheppard was beginning to embrace was a rejection of the form of Christianity in which he had been brought up. In believing that being a church member was not enough to earn him God's favour, or that he might not be on the road to God at all, he was turning away from his upbringing and the religion still practised by his mother and sister. In *Parson's Pitch* he acknowledged that, apart from when he was a child, conversations about religion at home had skirted around deep matters of faith. 'Christian ideas of worship and morality were impressed strongly on me as a boy', he wrote. But while the family might discuss the choir or the flowers in church, 'Christ, and the daily matter of trying to follow him, would bring a strained silence.' It should have been no surprise to him to discover that both Barbara and Mary were less than enthusiastic about his conversion and were worried about the 'strong influence' he had come under while at Cambridge.[27] Sheppard

25 Interview with the Revd John T. C. B. Collins. Collins went on to become vicar of Holy Trinity Brompton, the London church where the Alpha Course was first developed.

26 Sheppard, *Parson's Pitch*, pp. 47–8; Sheppard, *Steps along Hope Street*, p. 21.

27 Sheppard, *Parson's Pitch*, pp.46, 82–3.

and his mother were always close, and Barbara's devotion and pride in his cricketing success grew as she watched him play and followed his achievements. She also did her best to help him practically in his future ministry in the church. Sheppard believed that in his decision to become ordained and subsequent work, his mother's prayers were behind him. But he also acknowledged that his mother was 'puzzled and possibly a little anxious' on first encountering his new faith.[28] However hard she tried to comprehend what her son was getting into, it would always be a foreign world to her. Neither she nor Mary really understood his change of direction and priorities, including his decision to go into the church rather than law, yet they were both immensely proud when he later became a bishop.

After the Barnhouse meeting, Sheppard walked back with Collins from the venue, Great St Mary's Church. Later, in Collins' rooms, they discussed at length what they had heard. Anxious to help Sheppard understand the full significance of that evening's message, Collins read him some Bible verses. One was from the book of Isaiah about the suffering servant. Sheppard was familiar with this from his days singing Handel's *Messiah* in the choir at Sherborne: 'All we like sheep have gone astray. We have turned every one to his own way. And the Lord hath laid on Him the iniquity of us all' (Isaiah 53.6 KJV). Using this and other texts, Collins explained the significance of Jesus' death as understood in the evangelical circles in which he moved. Collins took a Bible and placed it on one hand, Sheppard later recalled,

This represented my sin, coming between me and God, like a cloud. When he quoted the words about the suffering servant, he placed the Bible on the other hand. Jesus on the cross, the suffering servant, took our sin on himself. He cried the sinner's cry; 'My God, my God, why have you forsaken me?' Certainly the penny dropped for me at that moment. I believed that Jesus died for me . . . that day I grasped the truth that Christian faith rests on the undeserved love of God.[29]

---

28 Sheppard, *Parson's Pitch*, p. 123.
29 Sheppard, *Steps along Hope Street,* pp. 21–2.

Sheppard described what he was embracing as 'utterly new and different'. It also pulled together 'many loose threads' that had been running through his childhood and teenage years. 'I had believed all my life at a distance . . . that God had indeed sent his Son to be the Saviour of the world,' he said from the pulpit of Great St Mary's 30 years later. 'It dawned on me then that . . . it was possible for a person, including me, to respond, to open my heart and mind to Christ.'[30] 'It is all too easy to handle holy things without consciously coming close to God at all' he once said of the texts he intoned in the school choir.[31] Now he found that the words of the Prayer Book which he had said and sung so often began to make sense for him: Jesus 'made . . . a full, perfect and sufficient sacrifice . . . for the sins of the whole world . . . I believe in the forgiveness of sins'. He now understood the sense of failure that he felt when he fell short of his own standards in the light of this divine offer of forgiveness.

One of the papers Sheppard was studying covered sixteenth-century Europe, and he recognized the doctrines that he was coming to believe, including Martin Luther's teaching on justification by faith. Luther's famous rediscovery was that God's forgiveness did not depend on a person's worthiness or their good deeds but on the grace of God. Now Sheppard began to appropriate that teaching for himself. He described the experience in terms of a response to the verse from Revelation that had inspired Holman Hunt's famous painting, *The Light of the World*. 'Behold, I stand at the door and knock. If any one hears my voice and opens the door, I will come in to sup with him and he with me' (Revelation 3.20 KJV). 'It made it very plain to me', Sheppard later wrote:

Either [Jesus] was outside the door of my life or he was inside. Though I had, so to speak, talked to him through the keyhole or on the doorstep, I knew very well that I had never sincerely asked him to enter my life and take charge of it.[32]

---

30 Sermon preached at Great St Mary's Cambridge, 1 February 1981: SHP, 24.5.
31 Sheppard, *Parson's Pitch*, p. 19.
32 Sheppard, *Steps along Hope Street*, p. 22; Sheppard, *Parson's Pitch*, pp. 49–50; Sheppard, 'How I Found Religion', p. 23.

To complete the process, Sheppard returned to his rooms and, as he later wrote, 'knelt and prayed, using my own words to "open the door" and ask Christ to enter my life, imagining him knocking at the door'. Worried that he might not keep up his new-found commitment, he also made a plea for perseverance: 'Lord, I don't know where this is going to take me, but I'm willing to go with you. Please make me willing.'[33]

*

One of the first places his new-found faith took him was to Iwerne Minster in Dorset for a Christian camp, or, more accurately, house-party. The invitation to spend part of his first university vacation in this way came from John Collins, who had been converted at Iwerne (pronounced 'Euan') six years before. Collins believed that attending a camp would help his friend deepen his commitment to the Christian faith. Only boys from the so-called top 30 public schools were invited to the Iwerne camps, which aimed to secure conversions among those who had not yet professed faith, and develop a disciplined devotional life in those who had. Cultivation of a daily 'quiet time', a period set apart for private prayer and Bible study, was an important objective of each camp. With their strong emphasis on disciplined living, hierarchical structure, dormitory-style accommodation and exclusively male ethos, the camps were designed to make those attending them feel at home.[34]

Known formally as the Varsity and Public School (VPS) Camps, the Iwerne camps were the brainchild of Anglican priest and former public school chaplain, Eric J. H. Nash, known universally as 'Bash'.[35] His camps attracted criticism from people who thought it contrary to the example of Jesus to evangelize one social class in preference to others, and the richest and most privileged class at that. However, Nash believed he had a calling to bring the gospel to the 'top' boys. These were not necessarily catered for by movements such as the Boys' Brigade and Crusaders and had 'been

---

33 Sheppard, *Steps along Hope Street*, p. 22.

34 Women, who were actually known as 'biddies', attended but in a purely supportive and largely domestic role.

35 In 2017 allegations of serious physical abuse by a former chairman of the Iwerne Trust involving boys attending camps in the 1970s became public. There is no evidence of any abuse during the years of Sheppard's involvement with the Iwerne camps.

left uninspired (and perhaps unredeemed) by their experience of public-school religion'.[36] They would probably have positions of leadership in future years, Nash argued. He saw it as important to influence those who would go on to shape the life of the church and the nation.

Sheppard was impressed with his first taste of a 'Bash camp'. He attended one every vacation for the next five years. He warmed to the Bible teaching and pastoral care and to the experience of mixing with 'ordinary young men of my own age who were sincerely trying to work out the friendship of Christ every day'.[37] One of Collins' reasons for inviting Sheppard to Iwerne was his belief that his friend had the potential to be a leader in the church, something Nash also recognized by promoting Sheppard, within a few months of meeting him, to 'officer' status and encouraging him in public speaking. Sheppard's growing fame as a cricketer was also not lost on Nash, who gloried in having a first-class batsman as part of the team. When Nash heard on one occasion that Sheppard and another England cricketer and camp regular, John Dewes, were on their way down to Iwerne, he drove to the station to pick them up himself instead of, as was his usual policy, sending a minion.[38]

Nash was a major influence on a whole generation of evangelical leaders within the Church of England, many of whom, like Sheppard, became much better known than he did.[39] In terms of Sheppard's early development as a Christian believer, the 'Bash camps' were hugely formative. For several years he was heavily involved in them and a close associate of Nash himself. Sheppard always acknowledged his debts to the man and his ministry, although he came to think there were limitations in an approach focused exclusively on the inner life, and that he should distance himself from Nash. In later life Sheppard wrote quite dismissively of his old mentor's 'elitism', his attitude to women and his single-mindedness 'to the point of ruthlessness'. 'There were several who

---

36 Ward, P., *Growing up Evangelical: Youthwork and the making of a subculture*, London: SPCK, 1996, p. 37.

37 Sheppard, *Parson's Pitch,* p. 51. Sheppard's use of the word 'ordinary' to describe the boys at the camps is telling.

38 I owe this story to Elizabeth and Gordon Bridger.

39 Other well-known church leaders influenced by Nash include John Stott, Michael Green, Dick Lucas, David Watson and Timothy Dudley-Smith.

felt they had to make a total break in order to be free from his influence', he writes with palpable sorrow.[40]

Sheppard also became unhappy, in later life, with what he called 'the dogma . . . of a wrathful God punishing an innocent Christ' in the stead of sinful humans. This teaching was at the heart of Nash's theology and had been graphically rehearsed by Donald Barnhouse in his sermon in Cambridge. A more helpful interpretation of Christ's suffering on the cross, Sheppard believed, could be found in a verse from St Paul's second letter to the Corinthians. This placed an emphasis on God initiating a process of reconciliation with humanity. Sheppard thought that this not only took away the idea of God punishing his Son but could inspire people to seek to repair divisions even when the fault lay with the other. 'From the heart, we want to make a move and become part of that healing and repair ourselves,' Sheppard once put it, 'so that we enlist willingly, in St Paul's words, in the ministry of reconciliation'.[41]

*

Sheppard found further help with understanding the new direction his life had taken among the University Christian Union. A presence in the University since the 1870s, the Cambridge Inter-Collegiate Christian Union (or CICCU, pronounced 'kick-you', for short) was a rapidly growing presence in the immediate post-war years. The Saturday night Bible study had to be held in the Union debating chamber to accommodate all wishing to attend. The ethos of CICCU was not dissimilar to that of the Iwerne camps, and there was a considerable overlap of personnel and leadership between the two entities. Members placed a strong emphasis on introducing non-Christians to the gospel. They also stressed the importance of a daily quiet time as a way of growing in the Christian life, a discipline Sheppard found helpful.[42] One Bible passage he studied was chapter eight of Paul's letter to the Romans. After reading

---

40 Sheppard, *Steps along Hope Street*, p. 23.

41 Bible study for an in-service training course for Roman Catholic clergy, Liverpool Archdiocese, October 2001; the biblical reference is 2 Corinthians 5.18–19.

42 He once wrote that he hated going out to face a busy day without having 'spent an hour alone with [Jesus] first.' 'This Is Your Way to Real Peace of Mind', *Daily Mail*, 14 November 1956, p. 8.

it for the first time he noted, 'Read it again. It's terrific!' Like Iwerne, CICCU discouraged its members from taking an interest in social or political questions, seeing this as a distraction from the core business of making new converts. For two years Sheppard was the Iwerne representative at Cambridge. He made sure that campers coming up to the university could continue the practice of meeting regularly with a more mature Christian. He took on mentoring duties himself, devoting many hours each week to the students in his care.

Sheppard threw himself fully into CICCU. He became a regular at the Saturday Bible teaching sessions, the Sunday evening sermon at Holy Trinity and smaller meetings in college. He also began attending services at St Paul's Anglican church in Hills Road, which had a heavy programme of weekday activities. He had time-consuming responsibilities on behalf of Iwerne, and was becoming active in trying to persuade his fellow students to become Christians, seeking every opportunity to talk to people about his faith. It would not have been surprising if Charles Crawley had Sheppard's religious activities in mind, as well as his cricketing ones, when writing about the 'legitimate distractions' in his life.

Several of Sheppard's contemporaries at Cambridge remember his enthusiasm to see others converted. Having had the experience of Christ forgiving his sins and coming into his life, he wanted others to have it too. The ethos among the more active members of CICCU was that 'anyone who did not have a friend to bring to a Sunday sermon felt something of a failure'.[43] One way in which Sheppard sought to evangelize was by speaking at CICCU meetings, and John Collins, who was president of the movement during one of Sheppard's years at Cambridge, recalls dozens of people going forward after hearing Sheppard preach.[44] Sheppard had been impressed that Collins, as he later put it, 'risked our friendship and told me what his Christian experience meant . . . [which] . . . brought me to a personal commitment to Jesus Christ as a person'.[45] He often used that as a model to reach others with the message. 'Risking friendship'

43 Barclay, O. R., *Whatever Happened to the Jesus Lane Lot?*, Leicester: Inter-Varsity Press, 1977, p. 116.
44 Sheppard was invited to speak at CICCU events long after he left the university.
45 Transcript of interview with Douglas Brown for *Viewpoint*, BBC1, broadcast 15 May 1969.

was right in some cases. Several of Sheppard's contemporaries from Sherborne who had gone up to Cambridge the same year felt uncomfortable when he approached and invited them to CICCU events.

In hindsight, Sheppard accepted that he had sometimes been over-enthusiastic as a seeker of the lost. 'There were times when perhaps I pressed the good news too eagerly on people who were not ready for it,' he wrote. 'I needed to learn more about respect – the need to listen and understand where others were standing.'[46] He was more upbeat about his role of placing Iwerne campers with appropriate mentors at the university, and his own contribution as a counsellor. This was a judgement at least one of those who received his advice would have supported. David Watson, who later became vicar of St Michael-le-Belfrey in York and developed a worldwide ministry, devoted a whole chapter of his autobiography to describing the positive influence Sheppard had on him as a new convert to Christianity while both were students at Cambridge.[47]

*

The non-stop cricket which preoccupied Sheppard at the end of his first year at Cambridge yielded impressive results. Playing alongside May, Dewes and the captain, Hubert Doggart, a batting line-up as formidable as any county's, Sheppard scored a total of 1,072 runs at an average of 56.42 in his 13 first-class matches for the University, with four centuries and four fifties. He marked his debut for the University, which was against Sussex, with an innings of 130 in four-and-a-half hours,[48] and three weeks later he shared in an opening stand of 343 against the West Indian touring team with his friend John Dewes. Despite suffering from a heavy cold Sheppard hit 227, batting almost the entire first day and giving no chances to the fielders. The wicket that day at the University's

---

46 Sheppard, *Steps along Hope Street*, p. 24.

47 Watson, D., *You Are My God*, London: Hodder & Stoughton, 1983, chapter 2. Watson saw Sheppard almost every week throughout one academic year, 'often for as much as three hours at a time . . .'.

48 When ribbed about the fact that this match was against his own county, Sheppard acknowledged it looked very 'dodgy' but Sussex just happened to be the first side he played against; transcript of *Desert Island Discs* as pre-recorded 7 September 1965.

home ground, Fenner's, undoubtedly favoured the batsmen,[49] but the West Indians were strong opponents whose Test side would go on to defeat England later that year. 'At no time was this cricket one would expect from undergraduates against Test match bowlers,' wrote Michael Melford in the *Daily Telegraph*. One feature of Sheppard's innings was a straight drive off the bowling of Sonny Ramadhin which hit the clock on the pavilion roof. On the third day of the match Sheppard was told by Doggart he had been invited to play against Oxford in the Varsity match at Lord's in July. His participation in this match would earn him his Blue.

This run of good form brought Sheppard recognition by the England selectors. At the end of May he was invited to play in a Test Trial match at Bradford between an 'England' XI of mainly established Test players and 'the Rest', comprising players under consideration. Doggart, May and Dewes were also called up for the match, and the four drove up from London through the night. Sheppard could only manage seven runs in his two innings, but some further good performances during the summer kept him in contention for a Test place. In a run of 14 matches between mid June and mid August he scored three centuries and eight fifties, including 158 against Sussex at Hove in which he shared in another large opening stand with Dewes. This time they put on 349, still the highest opening partnership in all first-class matches for the University. Sheppard also top-scored in the University Match against Oxford at Lord's with 93 in the first innings. On 10 August came the announcement that he had been chosen for the fourth and final Test against the West Indies at The Oval. Sheppard was something of a last-minute selection, following the withdrawal of several regular players due to injury and illness. To his surprise he found himself more nervous than happy when the telegram bearing the news arrived. Despite having scored a century the previous day against Surrey, joint winners of the County Championship that year, he felt he was not playing well, and the West Indians were proving to be a formidable side as their tour progressed. But it was a remarkable achievement for the 21-year-old undergraduate in only his first full season.

---

49 The match produced 1,324 runs for the loss of seven wickets, the highest scoring first-class match ever in terms of runs per wicket. *Wisden* described the wicket as 'almost farcically unfavourable to bowlers'.

Sheppard's nerves stayed with him into the match. He was pleased to be able to spend the first day fielding and getting used to the atmosphere before having to go into bat. England lost by an innings and 56 runs, but Sheppard acquitted himself well in a poor England performance overall. Apart from Len Hutton, who carried his bat for 202 in England's first innings of 344, no home player made a fifty, and Sheppard's 29 in two hours proved to be the highest score when England followed on. In the first innings Sheppard had reached 11 when an announcement came over the public address system that Princess Elizabeth had given birth to her second child, a daughter. Some West Indian supporters in the crowd started shouting 'Let's have a wicket for the princess', and Sheppard, in two minds how to deal with a delivery from the spinner Sonny Ramadhin, unfortunately obliged. During the match it was announced that he had been chosen to join the MCC touring party to Australia and New Zealand that coming winter.

*

There was never any doubt that the university would allow Sheppard special leave to join the tour. The question was the sort of degree he could expect to get if he did go. Crawley had earlier suggested that Sheppard make a concerted effort between October and April in order to get back on track after his disappointing first year. Could he do sufficient reading on the boat and between matches to give himself a chance of obtaining the minimum pass he would need to be able to stay on and read for an honours degree? Another factor was the University's regulations concerning residency. Sheppard would need to remain in Cambridge after the completion of his third year and make up the two terms he was about to miss. Sheppard was told he would give himself a better chance in the exam if he forewent the New Zealand leg of the tour, scheduled to last the whole of March, and sailed back from Australia at the end of February. He did not commit to this, but did agree to return by air at whatever point he could get away, to ensure he was in Cambridge for the start of the third term on 18 April 1951.

*

A question which concerned Sheppard in the wake of his conversion was whether it was right to spend so much time playing cricket. More than once he had examples of cricketers who had given up the game to serve God quoted to him.[50] But he concluded that, since Jesus 'wants his followers in the middle of every walk of life . . . it was his will for me to give some years to playing cricket'.[51] Seeing the situation this way shaped Sheppard's whole time at Cambridge. The challenge was to manage his time in order to keep up with his academic work, while creating as many opportunities as possible for cricket and the other activities to which he felt God had called him. As he boarded the boat for Australia at Tilbury on 14 September, he had no qualms about the two terms of study he was going to miss.

---

50 'I had C. T. Studd thrown at me rather hard at Cambridge', he told the Reverend Malcolm Lorimer. I am grateful to Mr Lorimer for sending me a transcript of his interview with DSS conducted on 14 July 1993.

51 Sheppard, *Parson's Pitch*, pp. 51–2.

4

Trinity Hall and Sussex
(1950–1953)

At least one member of the touring party on board the ship to Australia was optimistic about England's prospects against the old foe. 'We have great hopes of twisting the kangaroo's tail', Sheppard wrote to his former English master at Sherborne, Stanley Thompson, during a stopover in Aden, 'and I do really think that we have a much better chance than most people give us'.[1] Many had written off England's chances of success before the tour began on account of the youth and inexperience of some of the party, with some suggesting it should be cancelled because the squad was so weak. Yet Sheppard's positivity was not entirely misplaced. The 'kangaroo' did triumph in the series, but England did not return in disgrace.

*

The 1950–1 tour was the first to Australia to incorporate air travel, although the passage to and from the southern hemisphere was still undertaken by ship. Travel by sea meant the players were free of jetlag upon arrival in Australia and could get to know one another on the way out. Sheppard heeded his tutor's advice and used some of the time for study, encouraged, perhaps, by the presence of two fellow students in the party, John Warr and John Dewes. 'The three university men . . . were often to be found curled up in deck chairs with books open and notes being made', a journalist accompanying the contingent observed.[2] There was a brief stopover in Ceylon for a 'friendly' before the party arrived at

---

1 Letter dated 25 September 1950, Sherborne School archive (SSA).
2 Kay, J., *Ashes to Hassett*, Altrincham: John Sherratt & Son, 1951, p. 62.

Fremantle on 9 October, a few days ahead of their first scheduled match. Sheppard prevented the seasickness to which he was prone by staying in his cabin during rough days. On arrival in Australia, the party was surprised to find steak and eggs so widely available in the hotels. Having been starved of such fare in ration-bound Britain, they soon found themselves putting on weight.

The first match was a one-day warm-up against a Western Australia Country XI at Northam. Sheppard opened the innings, and had the distinction of scoring the first run, the first boundary and the first century of the tour. The opposition was hardly top-flight, but Sheppard impressed those who had not seen him before, including the former Australian player, Jack Fingleton. Fingleton waxed lyrical about Sheppard's 'very solid' defence and well-executed strokes.[3] As one of the squad members who needed to prove himself on the tour, Sheppard would have been gratified to see his captain, Freddie Brown, coming to greet him with hand outstretched on his return to the pavilion.

Sheppard played less top-level cricket than he might have hoped. Priority for first-class matches was given to regular Test players to help keep them match-fit, leaving the remainder playing more 'country sides' than they might have preferred. During an eight-week period at the end of the year, Sheppard played just four first-class innings. Such a lack of exposure to top-class bowling did little for his form, but the turn of the year saw a change in his fortunes, and following a 67 not out against Tasmania, and two solid innings against South Australia, he found himself picked for the Fourth Test at the Adelaide Oval in early February. His inclusion raised a few eyebrows in the press box since the batsman he was replacing, Gilbert Parkhurst, had not performed badly in previous Tests. The selectors had been impressed by Sheppard's handling of spin-bowler Jack Iverson in an earlier tour match, Iverson having been a major cause of England's undoing in the previous Test. Back home in Sussex, Barbara Sheppard sent a telegram of congratulation to her son as soon as she received the news. The local paper assured its readers that Mrs Sheppard would be listening to the radio commentary in the morning, despite there being only a slight chance

---

3 Fingleton, J. H., *Brown and Company: The tour in Australia*, London: Collins, 1951, p. 38.

that her son would be batting during its short duration. Sheppard's Sussex teammate, George Cox, also telegraphed his friend with good wishes.

Sheppard failed to settle in the first innings of the match. He nearly ran out England's top-scorer, Len Hutton, in his anxiety to score his first Test run against Australia. In the second innings, with England chasing an impossible 503 runs for victory in a day and a half, Sheppard impressed the critics by holding the fort for more than three hours to score 41. 'His steadfast innings . . . was the one consolation of the day', wrote the *Daily Telegraph* correspondent, Jim Swanton.[4] Selected for the Fifth Test at Melbourne, Sheppard did not impress, but England's victory ended a run of 14 games without success against Australia.

An overnight journey by flying boat took the party to Auckland for the New Zealand leg of the tour. This comprised two regional games and two Tests. Sheppard remained with the squad, despite his tutor's advice, and hit 75 against Otago at Dunedin, his highest first-class score of the tour. He was at the crease when his captain, Freddie Brown, hit England's winning runs in the Second Test at the Basin Reserve in Wellington.

The plan had been for the party to sail home via Marseilles. In the event Sheppard and twelve others flew back via Fiji, Honolulu, San Francisco and New York, a journey of four-and-a-half days. They eventually arrived at London Airport on 4 April, where a large crowd had turned out to greet them. Among the throng were Sheppard's mother and sister, who took him back to Slinfold. There, as Barbara told an enquiring reporter, her son went straight to bed and slept till the following afternoon.

*

As Sheppard acknowledged, in terms of his own performance the tour had not been a great success. Having been selected primarily to score runs, his average of 14.5 in his three Tests and 23 in all first-class matches was below par. A singular challenge for Sheppard had been facing the Australian fast bowlers Lindwall, Miller and Walker. All were quicker

---

4 Swanton, E. W., *Elusive Victory: With F. R. Brown's M.C.C. Team 1950–51*, London: Hodder & Stoughton, 1951, p. 207.

than any he had faced before. Sheppard had a practice of raising his bat some way off the ground when facing up to a delivery, known as a high back-lift, and Lindwall exploited this weakness by a sudden change of pace.[5] Keen to learn from this experience, Sheppard worked on his batting technique during the tour, helped by advice from Hutton. As a result, he developed the art of scoring runs on the leg side. Until then he had been, like many public schoolboys of his day, primarily an 'off-side' player.

Sheppard's record on the tour appeared to vindicate those who had criticized his inclusion. Some, however, saw his potential. The veteran commentator, Neville Cardus, thought Sheppard 'intermittently revealed a latent skill as a batsman', adding that the opportunity to play continuously against the kind of bowling he had faced in Australia 'would make a first-rate player of Sheppard'.[6] Another respected commentator, Reg Hayter, suggested that even when going through a lean spell, 'Sheppard revealed himself as a potentially class batsman'.[7] The Cricketer magazine, previewing the 1951 season, suggested that Sheppard 'will have gained a wealth of experience from the tour and should be an even better player than in 1950'.[8] Sheppard later admitted that he did not think he was quite good enough to play Test cricket at 21, although the experience had toughened him in terms of his technique and temperament. 'Learning to be calm in an arena like Melbourne where you feel the lions may be let out at any moment, is vital to becoming a successful Test cricketer', he wrote.[9]

The tour was a testing time for Sheppard's new-found faith. Since his conversion, he had enjoyed the company of like-minded people in CICCU and at Iwerne. Such fellowship had been helpful in deepening his commitment. Away from this regular Christian contact, and subject

---

5 For Lindwall's explanation of his tactics against Sheppard, see Hutton, L., *Just My Story*, London: Hutchinson, 1956, p. 83.

6 Cardus, N., *Cricket All the Year*, London: Collins, 1952, p. 130. Cardus was for many years cricket correspondent of the *Manchester Guardian*.

7 Hayter, R. J., 'MCC Team in Australia and New Zealand, 1950–1951', in Preston, N., ed., *Wisden Cricketers' Almanack 1952*, London: Sporting Handbooks, 1952, p. 791.

8 *The Cricketer Spring Annual*, 1951, p. 56.

9 Steen, R., *This Sporting Life: Cricket*, Newton Abbot: David & Charles, 1999, p. 33; Sheppard, D. S., *Parson's Pitch*, London: Hodder & Stoughton, 1964, p. 81.

to what he called the 'artificial' life of the international sportsperson, he found it challenging at times to stay on the path. 'At one stage of the tour my faith seemed to be drifting away from me,' he later wrote. 'I had been terribly busy, and had allowed my time of prayer and Bible-reading to be squeezed out.'[10] He used this period of doubt to re-examine and shore up the foundations of his beliefs. One resource he found helpful was a well-known book entitled *Who Moved the Stone?* by Frank Morison.[11] Morison argues the case for the resurrection of Jesus, having initially set out to disprove it. Sheppard considered the case for the resurrection important in shedding light on how Jesus' earliest disciples discovered new hope and courage. It confirmed their belief in Jesus' divinity, after witnessing him being put to death.

Sheppard valued the friendship of John Dewes on the tour. Dewes was a fellow CICCU member and Bash protégé, and the two shared a cabin on the boat and set aside time each day to read the Bible and pray together. Sheppard enjoyed discussing his questions about belief with Dewes, who was senior to him both in age and experience as a Christian. The two supported one another when a matter of principle arose, such as the question of playing cricket on Sunday. In the first-class game, Sundays were still largely observed as rest days in the 1950s, but the match against Ceylon on the journey out took place on a Sunday. Sheppard and Dewes made it known that they did not wish to be considered for that fixture. The former cricket correspondent of *The Times* and editor of *Wisden*, John Woodcock, has suggested that, had Sunday cricket been played in Australia at the time of the tour, both men might have turned down the invitation to join it.[12]

Sheppard and Dewes spoke at many Christian services and meetings during the tour, and Sheppard found the experience helpful in developing his faith. 'There is nothing like having to explain to another what your faith is to make you think it out for yourself', he later said.[13] The two were moved by the invitations they received to visit the homes

---

10 Sheppard, *Parson's Pitch*, pp. 81–2; 'The Bible in My Life', typescript of talk given in Australia, 1963.

11 Morison, F., *Who Moved the Stone?*, London: Faber and Faber, 1930.

12 Woodcock, J., 'Hard Edge to the Good Sheppard', *The Times*, 8 March 2005, p. 66.

13 Sheppard, *Parson's Pitch*, p. 83.

of fellow Christians, people who were complete strangers but with whom they felt a unity in the faith. 'That network of prayerful welcome and support strongly coloured my understanding of what the whole Christian church could be', Sheppard later wrote.[14] He played some squash during the tour, and helped form an MCC side to take on clubs from towns and cities the party visited. One report described him as 'the star of the team'.

As in Cambridge, Sheppard looked for opportunities to share his faith during the tour. One young reporter recalls Sheppard knocking on his cabin door on the voyage out. Upon being invited in, Sheppard asked him if he had 'yet heard the knock', by which he did not mean his own knock. Most of the meetings at which Sheppard and Dewes spoke were planned to reach the 'unchurched', particularly school pupils. Writing home to his future wife, Shirley Henderson, Dewes mentioned that most of their meetings had been 'evangelistic', some attended by several hundred young people. On one occasion in Sydney 'some 130 boys from all the big schools' listened to the two cricketers speak. 'About 40 stayed to the after-meeting', Dewes wrote, 'and each received a decision card to show them the Way, and an enclosed slip to send to David or me if they took the step.' Dewes thought his friend had grown in the faith 'very markedly' during the tour.[15]

*

Sheppard returned to Cambridge on 16 April 1951, two days before the Easter term began. He had requested a room out of college for the term, and accommodation had been found for him in Warkworth Terrace, just across the road from the University cricket ground, Fenner's. Sheppard was due to take four papers in History for his Part 1 exam at the end of May, and Crawley told him that, in preparation, he would have to do the greater part of what would be a 'rather crammed course of reading' by himself. Sheppard told the tutor that he had 'made quite a fair start

---

14 Sheppard, D. S. and Worlock, D., *Better Together: Christian partnership in a hurt city*, London: Hodder & Stoughton, 1988, pp. 23–4.
15 I am indebted to Mrs Shirley Dewes for allowing me to see extracts from her late husband's letters.

to American history in the last few days – some between Auckland and Fiji.[16]

Despite the temptation of a full fixture list, and the proximity of Fenner's to his new lodgings, Sheppard stuck faithfully to his studies throughout May. He appeared in just one University match that month, against the touring South Africans. This self-denial must have been difficult, as the previous summer he had been elected Secretary of the University team for this current season, a position that carried with it the expectation of being made captain the following year. The choice of Secretary was made by the whole team, and Sheppard was preferred above Peter May, whom he thought was a stronger candidate. As the outgoing captain, Hubert Doggart, later recalled, 'I think we thought that David was certainly more outgoing . . . he would perhaps bear the burdens of both offices [secretary and captain], together with the demands of examinations, slightly more easily than Peter.'[17]

Sheppard did cope well with the demands of the examinations he faced on his return from the tour. In his Part I papers, after no formal tuition and just six weeks' cramming, he achieved a comparable grade to the one he managed after a much longer period of study the previous year. His mark impressed his tutor. In writing to congratulate him, Crawley admitted to feeling 'almost ashamed that it should be possible to get a Second in the Tripos on such a brief period of work!' Crawley paid tribute to Sheppard's application and single-minded determination, which had once again brought him results. 'You must have organised your work very well and skilfully', Crawley wrote, 'and I am sure you will agree that the attempt was well worth while.'[18] Sheppard had indeed played a shrewd game, receiving hints from tutors regarding topics likely to come up in the exam and cramming accordingly. One tutor, who happened to be keen on cricket, told Sheppard not to spend time wading through a massive two-volume study of American history he had bought to read on the plane home from Australia. Everything he needed to know for the paper was in a more accessible work called *A Pocket History of the United States*.

16 Letters dated 9 April 1959 and 11 April 1951: Trinity Hall Archive, (THA).
17 Doggart, H., *Cricket's Bounty*, Chichester: Phillimore, 2015, p. 26, and interview with author.
18 Letter dated 16 June 1951: THA.

With exams out of the way, Sheppard threw himself wholeheartedly into cricket. His form was none the worse for his enforced absence from the crease, and in his second match he scored a hundred in both innings. In all, Sheppard played ten matches for the University, averaging just below 50. He then joined Sussex for the rest of the season. Again, his contribution was significant, and he comfortably topped the county's averages with 57. In his second outing, against the South African tourists, he delighted a crowd of 10,000 at Hove with a century containing four sixes and ten fours. In all first-class cricket that season, Sheppard totalled 2,104 runs at an average of 52.6. He was perhaps unlucky to be passed over for the Test series that summer.

*

Sheppard's third year at Cambridge was another busy and productive one. Moving back into college, he again kept the discipline of finishing his studies before the start of the cricket season. When the season did arrive, he captained the University in all its matches bar one. Church, Iwerne and Christian Union activities continued to occupy much of his time and, as a national figure, he was in demand as a speaker at Christian meetings. Apart from the occasional Prom concert or game of squash, he gave little time to recreational pursuits. His days were already full, but his former pleasures of ballet, fiction and debating were not encouraged in Iwerne and CICCU circles.

In a further change to his plans, Sheppard decided to continue reading History rather than switch to Law in his final year. This was not only because he enjoyed the subject: he thought it the ideal subject for a person who wanted a degree but had no aspiration to be a scholar. History's requirement of its students that they interpret events rather than give 'right' or 'wrong' answers rendered it, he argued, 'the hardest subject [in which] to obtain first-class honours, and the easiest simply to pass'.[19]

Sheppard's decision not to take up Law signalled a profound rethink about his future. His ambition had been to follow his late father into the

---

19 Sheppard, D. S., *Steps along Hope Street,* London: Hodder & Stoughton, 2002, p. 20.

legal profession, a course of action strongly supported by his mother. His conversion to Christ now prompted a re-evaluation of all the assumptions he had brought with him to Cambridge, including those related to his career. Now he believed that God had a purpose or 'calling' for him. In giving up Law, he was freeing up his options for the future.

Sheppard duly obtained his degree in History. Having put in a full year's work he expected a higher pass than a Lower Second in his final (Part II) exams. He had reached that grade the previous year on the strength of a few weeks' cramming and no formal tuition. His tutor suggested that, considering all his commitments, Sheppard should not be disappointed with his result. He could also have pointed out that, considering Sheppard had surrendered virtually five whole terms to cricket, he had achieved a very respectable degree on the strength of half the amount of study the majority of his peers would have done.

*

Sheppard's achievements in the 1952 cricket season, his last for Cambridge, were remarkable. In his 13 matches for the University he compiled 1,581 runs, still the highest total in a season by a player for either Cambridge or Oxford. His seven centuries that summer also remains a record for both universities, as does his total of 14 in a university career.[20] In his three seasons at Cambridge he amassed 3,545 runs, a total exceeded only by Mike Brearley, whose cricketing career at Cambridge in the 1960s spanned twice as many seasons. In the Varsity match at Lord's, Sheppard's last outing for the University, he made the first hundred for Cambridge against Oxford since the war. His innings of 239 not out at Worcester earlier in the season is still the highest by a Cambridge batsman away from Fenner's. This classic 'captain's innings', containing two sixes, 28 fours and, unusually, two fives, enabled Cambridge to reach a target of 373 runs in under five hours. Sheppard's innings was the joint highest individual score of the summer, and the best of his career. He became the standard by which later university batsmen could be

---

20 These records will almost certainly never be bettered, given that Cambridge University ceased playing a full-length first-class fixture list in 2001.

measured. In his first year at Cambridge, Brearley was described in *The Times* as 'a budding Test match batsman in the May and Sheppard class as an undergraduate'.[21]

With the University season over, Sheppard again joined Sussex, helping the county to end a hitherto disappointing season with seven victories in their last eleven matches. For the second year running he was the leading Sussex batsman. He crowned the season by topping the national first-class batting averages with an aggregate of 2,262 runs at an average of 64.62. Only two other batsmen averaged more than 60 that summer, May and Hutton. No one else averaged above 50. A further honour came when Sheppard was named one of *Wisden*'s 'Five Cricketers of the Year' in 1953. The compiler of his testimonial noted that few cricketers had achieved as much as Sheppard by the age of 23. 'Tall, and well-built, [he] looks a batsman from the moment he takes guard.'[22]

Sheppard's form earned him a recall to the England team for the final two Tests against India. At Old Trafford, where England won by an innings inside three days, he shared in an opening partnership of 78 with Hutton and took a memorable catch off the bowling of Freddie Trueman. At The Oval he scored his first century for his country. Batting virtually the whole of the first day, he hit 119, putting on 143 for the first wicket with Hutton and 118 for the second with Jack Ikin. He rounded off a memorable season by captaining Sussex to victory against the Indian tourists at Hove. Only one other county side defeated the visitors that year.

*

The autumn of 1952 saw Sheppard back in Cambridge. University regulations required students to keep nine terms in order to graduate with a Bachelor's degree, and Sheppard needed to live in Cambridge for the Michaelmas and Lent terms to make up the time he had missed touring Australia in his second year. He continued to be covered by the

---

21 Chalke, S., *Summer's Crown: The Story of Cricket's County Championship*, Bath: Fairfield Books, 2015, p. 252.

22 Smith, L., 'D. S. Sheppard' in Preston, N., ed., *Wisden Cricketers' Almanack 1953*, London: Sporting Handbooks, 1953, pp. 69–71.

maintenance and tuition grant awarded by the Ministry of Education, and the University agreed to maintain his Exhibition for this extra period.

For his two supplementary terms, Sheppard enrolled for a Certificate of Diligent Study under the tutelage of Owen Chadwick, then Dean of Trinity Hall and a university lecturer in Theology. This was a further opportunity to explore the past, and he enjoyed a stimulating six months, producing essays on church history for a scholar later to be regarded as 'one of the most remarkable men of letters of the 20th century'.[23] Sheppard considered himself 'very blessed' to have had Chadwick as his supervisor, and found their tutorials deepened his appreciation of his favourite subject. They also provided a more nuanced understanding of church history than he had imbibed from his peers and mentors at Iwerne and in CICCU: 'In supervisions with Owen I learned from his clear mind to appraise with a cooler detachment those figures of history I had regarded as heroes or villains.'[24]

Sheppard's first extra term coincided with another CICCU mission.[25] He strongly approved of the choice of John Stott as missioner. The Rector of All Souls Church, Langham Place, in the heart of London's West End, Stott would have been known to Sheppard through his involvement with the Iwerne camps in the previous decade. Stott had also been an active CICCU person while reading Theology at Cambridge in the 1940s. Each night of the mission saw the University church, Great St Mary's, full to overflowing. Sheppard attended as often as he could, taking with him, as his friend John Collins had done three years before, those he felt needed to hear Stott's message. Stott and Sheppard would later become good friends.

In addition to seeking converts through the mission, CICCU hoped that Stott's thoughtful and academic style of preaching would help to improve the reputation of evangelicals in the university. In this Sheppard thought they were successful. 'I believe that the change of tone was a very

23 Morrill, J., obituary of Owen Chadwick, *The Guardian*, 19 July 2015.
24 Letter dated 15 December 1995: Sheppard papers (SHP), 21.12; Sheppard, *Steps along Hope Street*, p. 27.
25 CICCU missions were held in three-year cycles in order to give every student an opportunity to attend.

important stage in winning respect from Christians of different schools for evangelicals', he later wrote.[26]

*

By the end of 1952, Sheppard was convinced he was called to ordained ministry within the Church of England. He had been pondering the issue since shortly after his conversion. In the autumn of 1950, he had confided to Stanley Thompson that he was not only 'thinking about' ordination but 'it is probably quite likely', albeit 'in no way decided'. He would only be satisfied with a job that allowed him to promote the Christian faith full-time, he told his former teacher, although he recognized this did not rule out other possibilities.[27] In fact he considered several possible careers following his conversion. The idea of public-school teaching was partly inspired by his experience of mentoring boys at Iwerne, and he had discussed with his tutor at Cambridge the possibility of taking a teacher's training course following graduation. At one point he considered a position at Harrow School. He was strongly attracted to the idea of staying in first-class cricket, given the opportunities it presented for sharing his faith, and reasoned that full-time Christian work did not necessarily entail becoming a man of the cloth. God wanted his followers in every walk of life. School chaplaincy and 'preaching at big meetings' were other possibilities he considered alongside ordination. But he was clear that, whatever decision he reached about his future, it should not be based solely on what he wanted. It had to reflect what he discerned to be God's calling.

In 1952, to help him discern 'God's will', he wrote an 'Appreciation of the Situation' as he had learned to do in the army. The outcome suggested that he should stay in cricket unless he felt positively that God was calling him out of it. He was open to this possibility in his prayers, and before long he was clear that God *was* 'pulling him back' from that direction.

---

26 Letter dated 26 February 1997, SHP, 21.12. Sheppard may have attended the opening night with his tutor, Owen Chadwick, who later recalled being greatly impressed with the preacher's oratory that evening: see Dudley-Smith, T., *John Stott: The Making of a Leader*, Leicester: Inter-Varsity Press, 1999, p. 340.

27 Letter to R. S. Thompson dated 25 September 1950: Sherborne School Archive (SSA).

As he described this experience a decade later, 'every circumstance of the next few months seemed to show me that each job which I could really see myself doing in the future, meant being ordained.'[28] By early 1953 he had applied to be considered for training for the ordained ministry. If accepted, he planned to return to Cambridge to study at Ridley Hall.

*

In February 1953, a month before he graduated, Sheppard attended his sister's wedding in London. In the absence of their father he performed the traditional role of giving away the bride. Mary Sheppard, now 29, had left the BBC at the end of the war and returned to the house in Slinfold with her mother. Within three years she was back in London, where several job opportunities opened up. One involved assisting Tubby Clayton to raise funds for the restoration of his church, All Hallows by the Tower, which had been badly bombed during the war. During this time Mary began dating a colleague from her BBC days, Charles Maxwell, and around the end of 1952 they announced their engagement. Maxwell was well-known as the producer of the popular comedy programme *Take It From Here*. This was the show which established the reputations of its writers, Frank Muir and Denis Norden, whom Maxwell had brought together, and which introduced to the nation the charmless fictional family, The Glums.

The wedding took place in a house in Cadogan Square, Knightsbridge, according to the rites of the Church of Scotland to which Maxwell belonged. The house was used by St Columba's while its church building in Pont Street was being rebuilt following wartime damage. The guest list included a number of well-known people of the day, including Muir and Norden and their wives and *Take It From Here* cast members Jimmy Edwards, Joy Nichols and Dick Bentley. Maxwell had no interest in cricket,[29] but his bride's connection with the game was reflected in the

---

28 Sheppard, *Parson's Pitch*, pp. 121–2.

29 Maxwell once had a job reading scripted Test Match commentary on the radio which, because he had not 'the least knowledge of, or interest in, cricket', he found 'quite a chore'; Plomley, R., *Days Seemed Longer: The Early Years of a Broadcaster*, London: Eyre Methuen, 1980, p. 127.

wedding cake, one tier of which featured iced bats, stumps and cricket balls. Mary was glad of the support of her maternal grandmother, Nellie Shepherd, now widowed, and other senior members of the family, but one sadness was her mother's reluctance to give her full blessing to the occasion. Barbara Sheppard already had reservations about the 'BBC types' she met while Mary worked at the Corporation. That Maxwell was divorced with a young child, and 13 years her daughter's senior, made her inclined to afford him, at best, a lukewarm welcome into the family. Perhaps she reflected at this time on the different routes her children were taking in life, one into the world of entertainment and its *glitterati*, the other into the no less strange and forbidding domain of the theological college and evangelical Anglicanism. For very different reasons she would have viewed both with apprehension and disappointment.

*

Subject to his application proving successful, Sheppard planned to begin training for ordination at Ridley Hall in October 1953. While waiting to know if his application was successful, Sheppard had the whole of the summer free to play cricket for Sussex. The previous autumn the Sussex committee had invited him to assume the captaincy of the side following Jim Langridge's decision tó retire. Sheppard told them he could only offer one season due to his plans to train for the church, but they confirmed his appointment and offered him their full support.[30] He was still only 24, and this would be his first, and last, full season of county cricket. Sheppard was aware that Sussex had experienced problems in the recent past over the appointment of captains. In March 1950 he had spoken at a bad-tempered AGM of the club which saw the president, the Duke of Norfolk, and committee storm out when a motion of no confidence in their treatment of a former captain, Hugh Bartlett, was passed. Sheppard was determined not simply to hold the fort during his year at the helm; he wanted to take the county to higher things. The streak of ambition that had driven him to become an England player at 21 would

---

30 Counties still preferred their captain to be an amateur unless there was no one suitable. The appointment of Langridge, a professional, had been unusual, though not unique.

not allow him to tread water as an interim captain. The coming summer was an opportunity to build upon his previous experience as captain of Cambridge and prove and develop his skills as a leader.

Under Sheppard's captaincy Sussex had one of their most successful seasons to that date. Having been thirteenth in the Championship table the previous season, they rose to finish second to the reigning champions, Surrey. Surrey went on to win the title seven seasons in a row in the 1950s, but no county ran them closer for it than Sussex in 1953. Sheppard acknowledged that his players had begun to gel as a side under Jim Langridge before he took over, but every report of the 1953 season attributed Sussex's achievement to the contribution of its captain that year.

Several Sussex players from the 1953 side described Sheppard as the best skipper they ever served under. These include Alan Oakman, Rupert Webb and Jim Parks,[31] who played under more than a dozen captains in his long career. Each recalls Sheppard's concern for team members as individuals. He would offer encouragement to a player who appeared to be struggling and make time to talk with one who had something on his mind. He would offer praise on the pitch: 'He was the first captain that I'd ever played under who applauded some good fielding', recalled Alan Oakman. 'We'd never seen that before.'[32] 'As a captain, I always said you should never shout at someone who's made nought', Sheppard once said. 'It's much more constructive to have a go at someone who's made runs, and thrown his wicket away by doing something silly.'[33] 'He had this bearing, this authority,' Rupert Webb remembers. 'He led from the front, and the whole team admired him.'[34]

Hubert Doggart, a fellow amateur who captained Sheppard at Cambridge and played under him for Sussex in 1953, considered that he led 'not only by example as a player but also with an extraordinary personal magnetism which his team found hard to resist. They might

---

31 Weaver, P. and Talbot, B., *The Longest Journey: The inside story of Sussex's championship triumph*, Stroud: Sutton Publishing, 2004, p. 38; Chalke, S., *Runs in the Memory: County Cricket in the 1950s*, Bath: Fairfield Books, 1997, p. 179, and interview with Jim Parks.

32 Test Match Special tribute to DSS, introduced by Peter Baxter, May 2005.

33 Steen, *This Sporting Life*, p. 33.

34 Chalke, S., *The Way It Was: Glimpses of English cricket's past*, Bath: Fairfield Books, 2008, p. 50.

not all have . . . appreciated his evangelical leanings but they all to a man recognized David's leadership quality.'[35] 'David Sheppard has that unusual combination of kindliness and firm authority', Jim Parks wrote. 'Without any special effort he can bring the best out of any man, and any cricketer who plays alongside him will joyfully do anything for David Sheppard.'[36] Unusually, Sheppard wrote a personal letter of thanks to each member of the team at the end of the season. When Sussex played at Horsham, he invited the whole side to dinner at his mother's home in Slinfold. 'Taking care about how other members of the team are treated is a key part of captaining a side', Sheppard was later to write. 'Drawing out the best often calls for patience and encouragement.'[37]

Sheppard's batting was a major factor in Sussex's success, and he was the most prolific run-maker for the county. On more than one occasion, he produced an innings that brought the side victory. The most dramatic example was at Leicester in June, where his 186 not out enabled Sussex to reach the challenging target of 346 in under four hours. Against Gloucestershire at Eastbourne, his 128 not out allowed Sussex to declare at 181 for one and secure a ten-wicket win. In another memorable innings at Bournemouth, he hit 22 off one over from the notoriously economical Hampshire bowler, Derek Shackleton, including three successive sixes into the same beer tent.[38] Victory in this match took Sussex to the top of the Championship table for the first time in 21 years. Sheppard hit seven centuries in the County Championship and again finished the season with 2,000 runs.

Sheppard's fielding was vital to his county's success, though in his early years at Sussex, he was once demoted from the first XI for a string of dropped catches. By adopting the approach he had taken with his batting, spending day after day with a teammate hitting him catch after catch, he acquired the confidence he lacked: 'I began to say, "Where's the ball; I want to stop it" instead of "I hope a catch won't come anywhere

35 Doggart, *Cricket's Bounty*, p. 28.

36 Parks, J., *Runs in the Sun*, London: Stanley Paul, 1961, p. 85.

37 Sheppard, *Steps along Hope Street*, p. 17.

38 Matthews, D., *On the Spot: Derek Shackleton – A Biography*, Ilfracombe: Blackberry Downs Books, 1998, pp. 93–4 and correspondence with Matthews in SHP, 21.12. Shackleton bowled more than 26,000 overs in first-class cricket and only one was more expensive than this: Chalke, *The Way It Was*, p. 51.

near me".[39] He became one of the safest close fielders in the game. His total of 43 catches in 1953 was bettered by only three other players that season.

Sheppard won acclaim for his tactical approach to the game. One feature of his captaincy was his preparedness to go for a win instead of playing safe for a draw, even if that meant taking decisions some captains would have viewed as risky. In several matches Sheppard declared the Sussex innings closed in order to set his opponents challenging targets. This policy brought Sussex some good results and a reputation for playing attractive cricket, but it could go spectacularly wrong. Against Worcestershire at Dudley, Sheppard set the home side a target of 166 in an hour and a half which they achieved with six minutes to spare. Sheppard expected opposing captains to play in the same spirit and was not averse to a little skulduggery if they failed to do so. At Leicester, a county in dire financial straits at the time, he thought the home side had batted long enough to set Sussex a target and ought to declare. He asked for the new ball when it became available but told his fast bowler, Jim Wood, not to unwrap it. He then slowly re-set his field while Wood re-marked his run-up. In a matter of seconds, the Leicestershire captain sped on to the pitch to call his batsmen in. 'I knew they couldn't afford a new ball', Sheppard told his team as he led them off.[40]

In setting fields, Sheppard consulted his bowlers and sometimes deferred to their opinion. This earned him their respect and helped to bring out their best form: 'I would talk to [Ian Thomson] every over about possible ways to attack the batsmen – and he would try them all'.[41] Les Lenham, who joined Sussex as a junior professional in 1953, recalls Sheppard's uncommon capacity, for a batsman, to understand 'how bowlers tick'. Sheppard used more senior players as sounding boards for ideas during matches. He saw no conflict between being able to make decisions as a leader and being open to advice, and thought that some of his worst mistakes were made when he failed to consult with people who could have offered him wise counsel.

39 Typed manuscript from early 1959: SHP, 20.2.

40 Chalke, *The Way It Was*, pp. 50–1.

41 'Foreword' in Barclay, J., *The Appeal of the Championship: Sussex in the Summer of 1981*, Bath: Fairfield Books, 2002, p. 11.

Sheppard's will to win could sometimes get the better of him, however. He was not above instructing his bowlers to behave in a less than sporting manner if he thought it might turn a game his way. In two successive matches in August, when the opposition had the upper hand and defeat for Sussex would have impaired their chances of the Championship, he ordered his bowlers to stop the opposing batsmen playing their normal strokes by bowling down the leg side to a predominantly leg-side field. In both matches he succeeded in averting defeat, but later felt ashamed of his tactics. He apologized to one of the opposing captains when the sides met again, a gesture one commentator attributed to the seriousness with which he took his faith.[42] Sheppard was to refer to those matches as his most unhappy memory of cricket. As captain of Cambridge the previous year he had attracted criticism in the Varsity match at Lord's. Sensing victory, he broke cricketing etiquette by allowing his fastest bowler, Cuan McCarthy, to bowl in a hostile manner at an Oxford tail-ender. McCarthy even struck the batsman on the forehead which, in the days before helmets, might have proved fatal. John Woodcock believes that Sheppard did more than passively allow McCarthy's behaviour. Sheppard later attributed Sussex's failure to win the title in 1953 in part to their not having 'a real fast bowler who could roll over the tail after we had made our usual inroads'.[43] Asked once to name his most enjoyable match, Sheppard replied, 'I think what you look for most in first-class cricket is a contest, a keen match.'[44] 'David was a hard-nosed cricketer', the Sussex batsman Ken Suttle once said, 'and he didn't like to lose.'[45]

*

To win the County Championship Sussex needed to defeat their main rivals, Surrey, in their penultimate game of the season. When the two

---

42 Gibson, A., *The Cricket Captains of England*, London: Cassell, 1979, p. 169. I am indebted for information about these matches to Hubert Doggart and Stephen Chalke. Sheppard refers to them in *Parson's Pitch*, pp. 116–7 and *Steps along Hope Street*, p. 18.

43 Woodcock, 'Hard Edge to the Good Sheppard', and interview with author; Weaver and Talbot, *The Longest Journey*, p. 37. Sheppard made this point a year earlier in his foreword to Barclay's book, p. 12.

44 Transcript of *Desert Island Discs* as pre-recorded 7 September 1965.

45 Watts, D., *Young Jim: The Jim Parks Story*, Stroud: Tempus, 2005, p. 59.

sides met earlier in the season, Sheppard scored a century and Sussex ran out winners by seven wickets. He described this as his best match for Sussex. The return had a less happy ending. Sheppard declared as soon as Sussex achieved a first innings lead, but Surrey were happy to bat out the third day knowing that a draw would be enough to earn them the title. Having come so close to winning their first title Sussex's disappointment was real, but in finishing second, they achieved their highest position since 1934. The season was a personal triumph for Sheppard, whose qualities as a leader were remarked upon by players and commentators alike. His name will be forever linked with that year in the county's history.

The same pundits and players expressed sorrow that this would be Sheppard's last full season in the first-class game. 'The church's gain is cricket's loss' was a frequent refrain. 'Never . . . can a player have left a game by his own choice when at the height of such fame', wrote the Sussex-based writer Jack Arlidge. 'David Sheppard has shown us how to play the game on the cricket field', Arlidge wrote. With remarkable prescience he added, 'Now he is to set an equally fine lead in the wider sphere of life.'[46]

---

46 Arlidge, J., 'David Is Cricketer of the Year', cutting from the *Evening Argus*, early September 1953, Sussex County Cricket Club archive, Hove.

5

Ridley Hall
(1953–1955)

David Sheppard did not doubt his decision to apply for ordination. Whenever he reached a crossroads, he made it his practice to 'walk with God'. In 'dialogue' with God, the way ahead would become clear. He took many walks while reflecting on the call to ordination, and the years he spent over the decision reflected its enormity and the sacrifice it involved. It did not mean giving up serious cricket altogether, but he would have to step back from the game he loved and at which he had striven to excel.

In rational terms, his decision to give up full-time cricket made little sense. In just seven seasons he had become one of the leading batsmen and fielders in the country. He had rewritten the university record books, represented his country, and led his county to the threshold of a historic achievement. He had sacrificed innumerable hours, and the chance of a better degree, to get to the top of the game. Now, at the age of just 24, he was bailing out.

He was also foregoing a future of enormous promise. His record to date suggested he could end his career among the all-time great batsmen,[1] and many were tipping him to be the next regular captain of England. It is not hard to understand why he 'loathed' the idea of becoming ordained when it first arose.[2] It is also not surprising that, when he attempted to work out his future using the method he had learned in the army, he 'proved to [his] own satisfaction that the best way to serve God would be to stay in cricket for some years'. Had he not felt that God was drawing

---

1 Extrapolating from the rate at which he actually made runs, had Sheppard completed a full career of, say, 1,000 innings, he would have joined the select band of batsmen – currently 16 and unlikely to increase – to have scored 40,000 runs and 100 centuries.

2 Sheppard, D. S., 'How I Found Religion', full typescript of article for *Woman's Own*, December 1957, p. 5.

him back from that direction, he might have tried to pursue it.[3] What his decision underlines is his willingness to make service to God his priority. Whatever direction he believed God to be pulling him, that was the way he must go. When he later wrote that being ordained was what he 'most wanted in the world at that time', he meant exactly what he said.[4]

*

From the moment Sheppard applied to train for ordination, there was never any doubt the Church of England would take him on. 'What a very fine asset Mr Sheppard should be!', the Secretary of the Central Advisory Council of Training for the Ministry (CACTM) told Charles Crawley, when Crawley submitted a reference early in 1953.[5] The Revd Cyril Bowles, principal of the college where Sheppard intended to undertake his training, Ridley Hall, was of a similar mind: 'I do not imagine that you have any objections to [Sheppard's] coming', Bowles wrote to Crawley. Bowles does not appear to have asked for a reference, suggesting rather that the Trinity Hall senior tutor send him 'any information that you think might be helpful in guiding his training for the ministry.'[6]

Bowles also told Sheppard he saw no impediment to his being accepted. 'I am very glad that you have been able to come to a decision about your future because you have had a very trying time over the matter', Bowles wrote, on hearing of Sheppard's decision to come to Ridley. 'You certainly have my great respect for having decided to be ordained at this stage.' Bowles even deferred to Sheppard over the timing of the selection board he would be required to sit: 'If you cannot fit in a Board now before the cricket season begins, would there be any chance of your doing so after it ends?'[7] Sheppard took a holiday in north Wales once the season ended, finally sitting his selection board on the last

---

3 Sheppard, D. S., *Steps along Hope Street*, London: Hodder & Stoughton, 2002, p. 26. One newspaper report in 1954 suggested that Sheppard had turned down 'two jobs, each worth £2,000 a year, deliberately offered to him to leave him free to play'; Warth, D., 'With a Bat and a Prayer', *Daily Mirror*, 29 June 1954, p. 7.

4 Sheppard, *Steps along Hope Street*, p. 26; cf. Sheppard, 'How I Found Religion', typescript, p. 5.

5 Letter dated 19 February 1953: Ridley Hall archive (RHA).

6 Letter dated 28 February 1953: Trinity Hall archive, (THA) and RHA.

7 Letter dated 12 February 1953: RHA.

Monday in September. By then his place at Ridley was already lined up. In fact, he had put his belongings in his room at the college three days *before* he was interviewed to assess his suitability to enrol there.

The panel examining Sheppard appears to have tested his vocation. 'The Selectors very carefully considered his case', the secretary of CACTM told George Bell, the bishop of Chichester, Sheppard's home diocese, 'and finally decided that he should be recommended for training for the ministry'. The selectors' report to Bishop Bell shows how the Church of England viewed its celebrated new recruit, and what they thought he could bring to the Church once ordained. 'An outstanding personality, with far more in him than the proverbial muscular Christian!', it began:

> In spite of all his headline successes, he is still a most attractively modest and unaffected person, largely because he regards his cricket (to use his own words) as 'a God-given gift'. His primary interest, in fact, is not cricket, but evangelism, and it is very typical of him that, during his MCC tour in Australia, he made time to speak at many religious meetings. What is equally reassuring about him is that, although he came to his faith through a primarily emotional approach, he seems more and more to be realizing the importance of the intellect and the consequent need for [thorough] theological training.[8]

Sheppard was later interviewed by Bishop Bell, who told him that he expected him to serve 'in another diocese, rather than in comfortable Chichester' once he was ordained.

*

Ridley Hall was the obvious place for an evangelical Anglican with a Cambridge background to study for the ministry. Under Bowles' leadership it had made a special point of accepting conservative evangelicals, the term Sheppard used at the time to describe himself. Among its alumni were several men Sheppard knew and respected, including

---

8 Letter dated 5 October 1953: RHA.

Eric Nash, John Stott, Timothy Dudley-Smith and John Collins. Bowles took a broad approach in his teaching and, according to Ridley Hall's historian, 'imbued generations of students with the liberal evangelical tradition which he himself had learned.'[9] Sheppard's contemporaries at Ridley included Michael Harper, who became a prominent figure in the charismatic movement in the 1960s, and Michael Alison, later a Conservative Member of Parliament.

Students at Ridley were encouraged to live as a close-knit community. All 60 were expected to eat and attend lectures together, and worship in the college chapel each morning and evening. They were also expected to serve the wider community by visiting hospitals, old people's homes and schools. Students would go in groups to take Sunday services in villages around the college, and meet the next day to discuss one another's efforts. Sheppard said he found this a painful but very useful process.[10] Open-air evangelism was a regular feature of college life, with students going to the part of the River Cam known as 'the Backs' on Sunday evenings to preach to passers-by. Sheppard had come across these meetings while at Trinity Hall. He was once spotted listening intently and asked if he was interested in what was being said. 'Very', he had replied.[11]

Sheppard would have found the ethos at Ridley Hall akin to that of CICCU and the Iwerne camps. Some students viewed activities such as going to the cinema and theatre, dancing, drinking alcohol and smoking as inappropriate. But if 'worldliness' was generally to be avoided, innocent jollity was encouraged, with students and staff regularly staging pranks and rag-style events. Sheppard took part in these, once borrowing some clothes from an aunt who lived in Cambridge to dress up in drag. The protocol for late entry was unorthodox, Bowles preferring students returning after the gate was locked to climb over the wall rather than wake the porter. Sheppard, who would regularly stay up late talking with friends outside college, became well-practised at the art.

---

9 Botting, M., *Fanning the Flame: The story of Ridley Hall, volume 3, 1951–2001*, Cambridge: Ridley Hall, 2006, p. 52.

10 Sheppard, D. S., *Parson's Pitch*, London: Hodder & Stoughton, 1964, p. 123.

11 I owe this story to Michael Griffiths.

*

Ridley wanted to push Sheppard academically. On the advice of Owen Chadwick, it registered him for Part II of the University Theological Tripos. Chadwick was confident Sheppard would be able to complete the Tripos in one year. The college also enrolled its new student on the Cambridge Ordination Certificate, the more demanding of its two ordination programmes. Sheppard was a willing party to this challenge, and keen to follow up the recommendation of his selection board that he receive some solid theological grounding. He once told Bowles he felt he 'never had a real chance to do himself justice academically' as an undergraduate.[12]

Sheppard was delighted that the Tripos offered further opportunity to study church history, and to do so under Owen Chadwick. He was initially apprehensive about the programme as a whole, however. Opening oneself up to theology as taught at the University was no small deal for a conservative evangelical. Received wisdom in CICCU and Iwerne circles was that studying academic theology could seriously threaten a person's faith. It did not assume the Bible to be the inspired word of God and took a critical approach, in both senses of the word, towards confessional claims and beliefs. Sheppard came to adopt a positive attitude to the scholarship he was required to read, and a respect for positions different from his own. He enjoyed the challenges his new discipline presented, but wanted to keep it in perspective. 'I found [theology] fascinating and important', he was later to write, 'but tried to keep firmly in my mind that all this was a background to meeting real needs of real people, and not simply some unending intellectual argument.'[13] He found the challenge of trying to bring people to faith a way of earthing what he was taught, as well as an important exercise in itself.

Meeting the real needs of real people became Sheppard's mission once he was ordained. His first encounter with the idea that a Christian should be concerned about the conditions in which people lived, as well as the state of their souls, was probably at Ridley. He had witnessed powerful

---

12 Letter dated 8 October 1953: RHA.
13 Sheppard, *Parson's Pitch*, p. 120.

role models of Christian faith in action, such as his late father and Tubby Clayton, but the circles in which he had moved since his conversion discouraged mixing faith and social concerns. The Iwerne movement and CICCU held staunchly to the view that the calling of the faithful was to convert individuals, and many of the students at Ridley shared this belief. But Sheppard heard other voices there which encouraged him to work out the social and political implications of the faith that he held.

One of these was Maurice Wiles, then chaplain at Ridley Hall. He encouraged Sheppard to read the Old Testament prophets afresh, and note they were concerned with more than foretelling the coming of Christ. Sheppard discovered how writers such as Isaiah, Jeremiah, Amos and Hosea believed in a God who sides with the poor and opposes exploitation. Wiles challenged Sheppard to relate these themes to his own context, 'to think freshly about the great issues in the world'.[14] Another who inspired Sheppard to think in broader terms about his faith was the prominent Methodist preacher, Donald Soper. Soper gave a talk at Ridley on the Church's responsibility to respond to human needs, a message which stayed with Sheppard all his life. Soper argued that people need to hear about the personal salvation that Christ offers, but that the gospel also speaks to their social conditions. Changing individuals and society were two sides of the same coin. Sheppard held on to this integrated understanding of the gospel, and acknowledged Soper had been 'one factor in leading me to believe that God wants to change both human hearts and social structures'.[15]

*

Sheppard's plans to step back from first-class cricket were not helped by cricket's reluctance to let him go. At the close of the 1953 season, he expected to do no more than spend his summer holidays playing a few games for Sussex, assuming he retained his form. He also supposed he would not be considered again for Test matches. Yet barely had the 1954

---

14 Sheppard, *Steps along Hope Street*, p. 27.

15 Sheppard, *Steps along Hope Street*, p. 27; letter dated 20 July 1994 from Sheppard to Brian Frost cited in Frost, B., *Goodwill on Fire: Donald Soper's Life and Mission*, London: Hodder & Stoughton, 1996, p. 256.

season begun than MCC were tempting him back into the game and even offering him the captaincy of his country.

Sheppard had been considered for the England captaincy while still an undergraduate at Trinity Hall. Len Hutton had told him in May 1952 that he was likely be offered the captaincy, and he hoped Sheppard would accept it. In the event, Hutton himself was appointed, even though he was a professional and the convention was that only amateurs, or 'gentlemen', were suitable to captain the national team. The reason the captaincy was being discussed again, two years later, was that the MCC tour to the West Indies the previous winter had not gone well, and Hutton was being held responsible. The strain of the situation was also making Hutton ill. He captained England in the first home Test of the summer against Pakistan, but then stood down on health grounds. The papers buzzed with the announcement that Sheppard had been made captain for the second Test in the series.

Many commentators expressed surprise. One described it 'a first-class cricket sensation'.[16] Sheppard had not been considered good enough to play for England the previous season or in the West Indies, and had decided to concentrate on his studies rather than cricket. The development prompted speculation that he was also being lined up to captain the party to Australia the coming winter. MCC's secretary, Ronnie Aird, had indeed approached Sheppard about his availability for the Australia tour, and his appointment as captain for the Test against Pakistan would make it easier for the selectors to choose him to lead that tour. Sheppard later realized that he was being used by some at MCC in a plot to remove Hutton as captain and reinstate an amateur. Aird went to 'conspiratorial lengths' to keep their discussions secret, Sheppard wrote ten years later. At even greater distance from the events, he spoke of the 'old brigade' at MCC, who thought that leadership should always be the preserve of amateurs. He described one of this group, Errol Holmes, as a 'natural backstairs intriguer'.[17]

Sheppard thought MCC were putting him in a difficult position over the Australia tour, forcing him to consider breaking his training for the

16 Wellings, E. M., 'Sheppard Is New England Captain', *Evening Standard*, 25 June 1954.
17 Sheppard, *Parson's Pitch*, p. 126; Marshall, M., *Gentlemen and Players: Conversations with Cricketers*, London: Grafton Books, 1987, p. 162.

ministry in order to make a more significant return to cricket. Captaining the tour would take him away from Ridley for almost a year, since he would have to play first-class cricket for the rest of the current 1954 season to be eligible to be selected as captain. He could have avoided this predicament, had he told MCC at the outset that he was fully committed to his studies and no longer available for Test duties. But the issue was not so clear-cut. Sheppard's openness to God's leading, and awareness of the possibilities that cricket held for communicating his faith, made him wonder whether God might want him to suspend his studies in order to captain his country abroad. He also drew a distinction between being a member of the side and *captaining* it. If the selectors asked him to captain his country, it was a matter of *duty* rather than *choice* to accept. After much thought and prayer, he told the selectors he only wished to be considered for the captaincy, not just as a player.

As speculation grew about Sheppard captaining the winter tour party, the Church tried to counter rumours that their student's commitment to the ordained ministry was beginning to weaken. These had been fuelled by Ridley announcing, when Sheppard's appointment as captain against Pakistan became known, that it was releasing him from his studies for the rest of the season.[18] Bowles feared that the Archbishop of Canterbury might be asked to account for Sheppard's and Ridley's actions. He wrote immediately to assure Geoffrey Fisher that his student remained committed to his calling. 'I am quite clear that there is no question of [Sheppard's] trifling with the idea of ordination', Bowles told the Archbishop. 'His going to Australia would be a response to an invitation to meet a particular need.' Bowles said he thought that Sheppard's six months in Australia would enlarge his experience and knowledge of the world, much as a spell in a factory would do for any ministerial student.[19]

Fisher assured Bowles that he was 'entirely happy' about Sheppard spending the rest of the season playing cricket and going to Australia as captain if invited.[20] Fisher also wrote separately to Sheppard, advising him he was right to interpret the situation 'as a direct call . . . Here is a

---

18 Ridley operated a summer term from early July to mid August, during which students were expected to be in residence.

19 Letter dated 24 June 1954: RHA.

20 Letter dated 28 June 1954: RHA.

piece of what I should regard as direct service to the wider interests of the Kingdom of God which you can render', Fisher told him. 'As I understand, there really is a crying need for someone to bring back into the higher ranks of English cricket a sort of moral decisiveness and discipline which has been slipping.' Fisher clearly detected Sheppard's potential even though the two had not then met,[21] and he lived to see the young ordinand appointed a bishop. Sheppard treasured Fisher's letter for the rest of his life, though they would later exchange sharp words.[22]

Sheppard duly led England in the Second Test at Trent Bridge, which England won, and in the drawn Third Test at Old Trafford. He also played for Sussex throughout the summer. A week before the captaincy for the tour of Australia was due to be announced, he was chosen to lead the Gentlemen against the Players at Lord's. This was a signal that he was still firmly in the selectors' sights. But the invitation to lead MCC that winter never came. The selectors reappointed Hutton as captain for the fourth and final Test against Pakistan, and for the MCC tour. They told Sheppard they felt they had been unfair in their treatment of the Yorkshireman. In line with his decision only to go to Australia as captain, Sheppard was not included in the party.

Sheppard had reason to feel badly treated by the cricketing authorities. He had not wanted to be cast in the role of a rival to Hutton, a man he counted as a friend. Much of the press coverage had been unpleasant, with some newspapers campaigning for Hutton's reinstatement and suggesting the captaincy was being determined by 'privilege' rather than 'performance'. The selectors who were opposed to Hutton had misjudged the popular mood, and Sheppard had been caught in the crossfire. 'In some ways I'm disappointed about Australia', he told his former master at Sherborne, Stanley Thompson, 'but personally I think rather glad to be out of it.' He expressed a similar view to Bowles.[23]

---

21 Curiously, Fisher was in Australia and New Zealand when Sheppard was there with MCC in 1950/1, and both would have been in the same city on several occasions; Swanton, E. W., *Elusive Victory: With F. R. Brown's MCC Team 1950–51*, London: Hodder & Stoughton, 1951, pp. 12–14, and *Swanton in Australia with MCC 1946–1975*, London: Collins, 1975, p. 57.

22 Fisher's letter, dated 28 June 1954, appears in Sheppard, *Steps along Hope Street*, p. 34, and was reproduced on the back page of the brochure for DSS's memorial service in Liverpool Cathedral, 23 May 2005.

23 Letter dated 19 July, [1954]: Sherborne School archive (SSA); letter dated 21 July [54]: RHA; cf. *Parson's Pitch*, p. 128.

*

That December, while the MCC tourists were enjoying the warmth of Canberra and Melbourne, Sheppard was trudging through the snow in Liverpool. Every year Ridley students took part in missions in different parts of the country, and in 1954, the chosen city was the one in which Sheppard would later make his mark as a bishop. Four parishes were involved, each hosting a team of around 12 students. During the day teams would knock on doors, with evenings given over to special church services, film shows, and visits to youth clubs and pubs. Meetings in private homes were arranged, and events aimed at specific groups, including teenagers, parents and young wives, were organized.

Sheppard led one of the teams. He preached at several mission services during the week and spoke at men's meetings. Not surprisingly he was a focus for the media, who enjoyed describing him 'captaining' a team of students and 'going in to bat' as a preacher. One reporter asked Sheppard why the mission was addressing the question, 'Is there any difference between Xmas and Christmas?' 'It is because Christ has been left out of Christmas and out of our lives for so long that this world is in its present state', Sheppard told him.[24]

*

'There was much to crowd into those two years', Sheppard said of his spell at Ridley.[25] This included much extra-curricular activity as well as study. In addition to representing Sussex and England, he turned out for the college cricket team, sometimes opening the bowling as well as batting. Ridley had several students interested in cricket, and Sheppard never lacked for someone to give him catching practice before a big game. He also turned out for the college rugby side at scrum half, a surprising position given his height. He maintained his commitment to Iwerne, spending part of each vacation at the camps. He also threw himself into his studies, with impressive results. As Chadwick had predicted, he

24 Murray, G., 'Cricketer Has a New "Team"', *News Chronicle*, 6 December 1954.
25 Sheppard, *Parson's Pitch*, p. 120.

passed Part II of the University Theological Tripos in one year, and in his second year, he was awarded the Cambridge Ordination Certificate. He received a distinction in the 'Doctrine I' unit of this certificate, a paper that proved a challenge for some students. 'An achievement to understand the paper, much less answer it', was a comment heard when Sheppard's result was announced.[26]

Sheppard's time at Ridley was also marked by an event which, like his conversion, was as life-changing as it was unexpected. This was his first meeting with the woman who would become his wife and soulmate, Eleanor Grace Isaac, known always as Grace. Sheppard always maintained he had given no thought to marriage before he met her, nor had any serious relationships with members of the opposite sex. There had been young women with whom he had been friendly within his CICCU and church circles, but no special girlfriend in those years.[27] He had always accepted his mother's dictum that 'people like us' did not marry until they were thirty. He would need to be well-established in a professional career before he could support a home.

His first encounter with Grace followed a request for a favour from his uncle Boy, then a general practitioner in Cambridge.[28] Boy was concerned that his daughter Ann had few friends to spend time with when she was home from her boarding school in Wales. He asked David if he knew any suitable Christian girls she might meet. Sheppard sought advice from a CICCU friend, who recommended a woman training to be a teacher at Homerton College. 'Grace Isaac's the name', the friend ended his note. Grace duly accepted Sheppard's invitation to tea. She was aware that the purpose of the visit was to introduce her to a third person, but brought along a friend as a chaperone.

Sheppard was immediately attracted to Miss Isaac, but decided against following up that first meeting. During the next few weeks contact between them was limited to occasions when they happened to be at the same event. It was some time before each made the other aware of their

---

26 Botting, *Fanning the Flame*, p. 72.

27 Sheppard, *Parson's Pitch*, p. 139.

28 The date is uncertain. Friends of Grace recall her watching Sheppard play at Eastbourne in August 1954, and being quite 'goofy' about him, but this was before they started courting and possibly before they had met.

feelings: 'We discovered later that we were both worshipping from afar, each of us thinking that we had no chance'. Eventually David invited Grace to join him for a coffee after a meeting both had attended. Again, they were accompanied, and Grace left early to avoid being locked out of her college. 'With a few crumbs like this and the occasional chance meeting we made do for nearly a year', Sheppard later said.[29] They did not begin a serious relationship until both had left Cambridge.

In the circles in which David and Grace moved, the way they conducted their courtship would not have seemed unusual. They believed God had a 'will' for their lives. Contriving an opportunity to meet would have been imposing their will rather than God's. As Sheppard later recalled, when the two of them finally got together and 'compared notes . . . we found that we had both felt strong attraction from the beginning, and both tried to discipline ourselves not to seek out the other'.[30]

The norms around courtship in CICCU circles were extremely strict, even by the standards of 1950s' Britain. Casual dating was strongly discouraged, and if a boy and girl were known to be stepping out their friends would assume they had definite plans to marry. Sheppard's reluctance to follow up his initial meeting with Grace reflected in part his awareness that he was not in a position to think seriously about marriage. Bringing a chaperone to a date would not have seemed remarkable, and CICCU's membership was sufficiently close-knit to discourage couples from getting into situations where any impropriety might occur.

CICCU members would only consider marriage to people of a similar persuasion. David and Grace played by the book in this respect, both having an evangelical understanding of the faith. As a senior Iwerne officer Sheppard would have wanted Nash's approval of his choice of partner. He plays down the significance of this in *Steps along Hope Street*, suggesting that he merely told Nash he was engaged to Grace, and casually notes Nash's comment that Grace was of 'good evangelical stock'.[31] Sheppard would have had to think twice about his relationship with Grace had Nash expressed his disapproval.[32]

---

29 Sheppard, *Parson's Pitch*, p. 140.
30 Sheppard, *Steps along Hope Street*, p. 28.
31 Sheppard, *Steps along Hope Street*, p. 28.
32 'Many an officer tremblingly brought his girlfriend or fiancée to Bash to be vetted', writes

Miss Isaac certainly had the right background. Her parents, Eleanor and Bryan, were involved in missionary work. Bryan served as deputation secretary, then general secretary of the Ruanda Mission from 1946 until 1962. An ordained Anglican priest, he had been a chaplain with the British Army on the Rhine during the war, and received the MBE for his services. In April 1945 he had experienced the liberation of the Belsen concentration camp. Eleanor, who had studied at Bible college for three years, devoted herself to bringing up Grace and her younger brother John during the war. They had been evacuated to what was then the village of Milton Keynes, where Eleanor, who suffered from asthma, would walk the five miles to the nearest shops with a pram and young daughter in tow. The family then moved to live in Haywards Heath in Sussex in 1944. The Isaacs were a well-known couple in evangelical circles, and Grace, the eldest of their four children, would have found it easy to mix with the CICCU crowd during her time at Cambridge.

There was a strong emphasis in the Isaac home on self-denial, on putting Christ and others before oneself. There was a 'Ruanda movement' within the Church of England, inspired by the major Christian revival in East Africa between the wars. Its motto was 'Not I but Christ', and members saw it as vital to be 'broken' as individuals, to root out all sinful and selfish behaviour, in order to live what they called the 'Victorious Life'. This attitude might develop an attractive spirit of humility, but could also produce 'self-effacing, shrinking, diffident men and women', critics thought.[33] Grace was discouraged from paying too much attention to her appearance, including using make-up. She later recalled 'terrible warnings from Christian speakers in the past, of the perils of spending more time at our dressing tables than on our knees'.[34]

Grace had a gift for music, which she had been inspired to develop by her parents, a passion she would share with David. From an early age she would play the piano and sing for others. At her boarding-school, Wadhurst College in Sussex, she excelled at sport as well as music, but

John Stott: Stott, 'The Counsellor and friend' in Eddison, J., ed., 'Bash': A Study in Spiritual Power, Basingstoke: Marshalls, 1983, p. 65.

33 King, J. C., The Evangelicals, London: Hodder & Stoughton, 1969, pp. 60–1; cf. St John, P., Breath of Life: The Story of the Ruanda Mission, London: Norfolk Press, 1971, pp. 119–20.

34 Sheppard, G., Pits and Pedestals: A Journey towards Self-Respect, London: Darton, Longman & Todd, 1995, p. 42.

her confidence was gradually eroded by a teacher who constantly put her down. At Homerton she was able to use her talents. In addition to training to become a nursery schoolteacher and playing a role in CICCU, she continued to study the piano and to sing. She joined a choir called 'The Blest Sirens', a name inspired by Milton. Grace qualified as a teacher in the summer of 1955, aged 20, and then returned to the family home in Haywards Heath to take up a teaching post in nearby Burgess Hill.

*

Cyril Bowles had been unequivocal in recommending Sheppard for ordination. His two years at Ridley had enabled Sheppard to show 'signs of great pastoral and evangelistic gifts as well as powers of leadership,' Bowles told the Bishop of London, William Wand. 'He is completely unspoilt by his success and his public reputation.'[35]

Sheppard was ordained by Wand in St Paul's Cathedral on Michaelmas Day, 29 September 1955. His cohort included men from both the high and low church traditions. Sheppard recalled that, while the former genuflected and crossed themselves at every possible point in the service, he and his evangelical brethren made a point of not doing so to emphasize their difference. Sheppard's abiding memory of the day is of Bishop Wand holding on to the document containing his orders, instead of allowing him to take it. Sheppard's immediate thought was that he had not done enough to permit the bishop to ordain him, but Wand was posing for the camera. Unknown to Sheppard he had agreed to allow a photographer to record the famous cricketer receiving his holy orders. The photograph appeared in most of the following day's papers, and even in the Australian press.

Sheppard now moved to Islington in north London to 'serve his title' at St Mary's Church. It proved to be a remarkably eventful period for the young curate. In a way he could not have foreseen, the experience of living and working in inner-city London profoundly challenged his ideas about leadership, evangelism and mission, as undertaken by the local church. His two years in Islington were to set the agenda for the rest of his career.

---

35 Letter dated 12 July 1955: RHA.

6

Islington
(1955–1957)

Moving to Islington took David Sheppard into very new territory. At Sherborne and Cambridge, he had mixed mostly with people like himself, those who had enjoyed a privileged upbringing and shared similar values and aspirations. National Service had broadened his horizons to a degree, but now he would be living and working in the inner city, where the majority would describe themselves as working-class and where the worlds of the public school and university were virtually unknown.

*

Islington is known today for its bars, restaurants and boutiques, but it had a far less affluent image in the years between the end of the war and its gentrification in the 1960s. Even today the borough has one of the highest child poverty rates in England, but in the first two decades after the war, it had the highest percentage of households in London without basic amenities. Around three quarters of homes lacked their own stove, sink, bath and toilet.[1] People who lived in Islington at that time remember the large number of properties in multiple occupation, the lack of community resources for young people, and the difficulties experienced by the growing number of West Indian and African people moving into the area. There was no shortage of challenges facing Sheppard as he took up his curacy in this inner-city parish in October 1955.

St Mary's was one of several evangelical Anglican churches in London which grew in influence during the post-war years.[2] Founded in the

---

1 *British History Online* http://www.british-history.ac.uk/vch/middx/vol8/pp9–19 [accessed 20 June 2017].
2 Others included All Souls Langham Place, St Helen's Bishopsgate and Emmanuel Northwood.

twelfth century, a number of church buildings have stood on the site in what is now Upper Street. When Maurice Wood was appointed as vicar in 1952, funds were being raised to erect the current church following the destruction of its eighteenth-century predecessor in the Blitz of 1940. Wood's predecessor had requested the architects to construct a space fit for the 'renaissance of evangelical worship'. During his nine years as vicar, Wood maintained this vision of raising the profile of evangelical Anglicanism, and of St Mary's church itself.

Wood enjoyed the support of two curates and a 'lady worker' at any one time, although the size of his congregation when Sheppard arrived was modest. Numbers picked up once the new church was opened in 1956, but Sheppard's growing concern was the *composition* of the congregation rather than its size. Some individuals and families from the local neighbourhood played a part in the church, but most of the worshippers were from farther afield. Many were student nurses and medics from London's teaching hospitals. The fact that Wood and his curates were Oxbridge men, and Wood's abilities as a preacher and communicator, accounted for much of the church's appeal to younger, educated people. Sheppard wanted St Mary's to connect with local people who did not see the church as 'for them'. And while Wood and the church were committed to having lay people in leadership roles, Sheppard was concerned that the lay people in question were mostly students and nurses. He accepted this approach when he first arrived at St Mary's, but over time he observed a direct connection between the practice of importing leaders from outside and the lack of impact the church was having on the neighbourhood. The kind of programmes offered by the church reflected the 'tidy, bookish' culture of the student leadership, which most local people did not share.[3] An important lesson Sheppard learnt at Islington was that working people had the same potential to be effective leaders as those with 'good' backgrounds and a university education like himself. It completely altered his approach to mission.

*

---

3 Sheppard, D. S., *Steps along Hope Street*, London: Hodder & Stoughton, 2002, p. 31.

The suggestion that Sheppard serve his title at St Mary's had come from Wood, a Ridley man who had seen distinguished service during the war as a chaplain to the Royal Navy commandos. He would have admired Sheppard's decision to relinquish the chance of further fame in order to serve the Church full-time. Wood had a reputation for seeking curates he considered to have great potential and was not afraid to appoint people he recognized as more gifted than he was if they were the best person for the job. The principal of Ridley, Cyril Bowles, encouraged Sheppard to work with Wood. Sheppard's willingness to do so showed how far he had moved since the days when chaplaincy in a public school seemed the obvious step after ordination. He told a journalist that he deliberately chose Islington in preference to what he called 'a typical West End parish'[4] and acknowledged that living in Islington would take some getting used to.

Wood and Sheppard shared a passion for evangelism. One of Sheppard's first initiatives was a weekly programme of door-knocking in the parish, inviting people to attend the church. A team would gather at Sheppard's flat in College Cross before dispersing to visit a street or block of flats. Wood encouraged his new curate to see the tower blocks then springing up around the church as providing new opportunities for evangelism. Sheppard also preached in the open air and local pubs, yet the more contact he had with local people, the more he came to believe that, if any did come to church, they would feel out of place. The culture of the church was very different from that of the local population. Nowhere did the congregation of St Mary's 'share a common life with the majority group in the district.'[5] The church needed to build relationships with local people before inviting them to take the step of attending a service: 'We needed bridges, stepping stones that would enable honest searchers to meet up with local Christians, before they would feel able to approach the institutional church.'[6]

Wood was attracted by Sheppard's fame as a cricketer and the kudos that would add to the parish. In 1953, before Sheppard even began training

---

4 Mallalieu, J. P. W., 'England's Ex-skipper Hits Out for the Church', *Illustrated*, 14 April 1956, p. 19.

5 Sheppard, D. S., and Worlock, D., *Better Together: Christian partnership in a hurt city*, London: Hodder & Stoughton, 1988, p. 25.

6 Sheppard, *Steps along Hope Street*, p. 31.

for ordination, he had involved him in a Coronation Thanksgiving Service at the nearby Arsenal Stadium. Often described, in kindly tones, as a showman, Wood saw Sheppard as a catch. His correspondence teems with gratuitous references to 'my cricketing curate, David Sheppard' and 'one of our curates, David Sheppard, the Sussex and England cricketer'. In one letter Wood mentions a street which his correspondent would know, adding that it is 'where incidentally David Sheppard one of our curates lives'. Bowles once suggested to Wood that some might think he was using Sheppard's name 'as a means of advertising Islington'.[7]

Sheppard's fame was certainly used to introduce people to faith. On one occasion a special service was organized in the town hall, at which Sheppard preached and other cricketers, including Colin Cowdrey and the great Australian batsman Sir Don Bradman, took part, and people not connected with the church attended. One comment heard after the service was 'I went to hear David Sheppard and I met with Jesus Christ'. Barbara Quantrill, a faithful member of St Mary's sixty years later, remembers her family becoming involved in the church as a result of her late husband, Tom, attending the special service. Other evangelistic meetings were held at St Mary's, but Sheppard believed they appealed mainly to people 'already on the fringe of church membership' rather than complete outsiders.[8]

*

Wood took seriously his responsibility to train his curates, although the many requests Sheppard received to give talks as a Christian sportsman took him away from the parish a good deal. There was a difficult balance for Wood to strike. He wanted Sheppard to use his fame to preach the gospel, and allowed him to accept many of the invitations he received. Yet his responsibility as vicar required him to impose a discipline on his curate's diary that had hitherto been missing. Sheppard had under-taken more than 400 speaking engagements in the five years between his conversion and ordination, years devoted principally to study: one every

---

7 Letter dated 10 February 1956: Ridley Hall archive (RHA).
8 Sheppard, *Steps along Hope Street*, p. 35.

four or five days.[9] Wood once said that, although he received requests 'almost daily' for Sheppard to speak, he 'kept him firmly tied to a pretty heavy parish routine.'[10]

Heavy it certainly was. In addition to weekly door-knocking, he made regular visits to people who were unwell or lonely, started a men's group, and led worship in the local hospital. He would often preach at Sunday and weekday services. When the need for a Sunday school was identified, Sheppard took a leading role in that. He devoted time and energy to the Islington Boys' Club attached to the church, perhaps inspired by his father's example when he was growing up. As his workload increased, Sheppard found it harder to deal with the substantial postbag he received as a nationally known sportsman and Christian. He secured professional help from a member of the church, Hilary Harman. She was ready for a move from her job at *The Times* to became Sheppard's secretary, and he paid her from his own pocket. In May 1956 Sheppard told his old tutor, Charles Crawley, he was unable to make time to return to Cambridge to receive his MA degree: 'Days are more than full but the work is very rewarding here.'[11]

Sheppard must have found it hard not to believe the Church saw him as a 'gift from God'. His path to ordination training, and sympathetic treatment during the saga of the MCC captaincy, suggested that the Church had realized the potential in having a celebrity sportsman among its ranks and would accommodate his lifestyle as far as possible. Now, as a curate, he was allowed time away from the parish to be a platform speaker, and employed a secretary. These privileges were unique for someone in his position: training for curates in the 1950s was generally rigorous and could be authoritarian. Wood did work Sheppard hard, and encouraged his ministry as a 'famous Christian' with the best of motives, but he did his curate few favours by failing to treat him the same way as his peers.

---

9 Sheppard, *Steps along Hope Street*, p. 25.

10 Letter dated 7 February 1956: RHA.

11 Letter dated 18 May 1956: Trinity Hall archive (THA). Under the system at Cambridge (and Oxford and Dublin), Sheppard was entitled to proceed to the MA once he had held his BA for two years.

*

Sheppard found his involvement with the boys' club educational. It opened his eyes to the limited opportunities available to working-class young people, and the potential of the church to help them. It introduced him to the wider circle of boys' clubs, and the mutual support and encouragement available through that network. Clubs were not there to keep young people off the streets or make them good citizens, Sheppard thought. In a piece for the London *Evening News* in April 1956, he argued that clubs had the potential 'to influence the whole way in which a boy lives and thinks.' He noted the indifference many teenagers displayed to religion and life in general. He thought this attitude was rooted in their home life; 'The idea of parents reading and playing with children, of interesting themselves in homework, of doing things together is a hazy ideal,' he told his readers. Clubs could give young people the experience of 'being accepted and wanted'. This was something St Mary's was keen to do, at a time when membership of Teddy Boy and other gangs was a rival attraction. Clubs should offer spiritual as well as physical and mental fitness, Sheppard argued. If the good news about Jesus Christ was put across simply each week, club members would 'begin to see how this Jesus can step out of the mists of ancient history and into their own daily lives.'[12]

Sheppard raised funds to improve the premises used by the boys' club, a disused church near Holloway prison. A letter to the *Daily Telegraph* brought in more than £1,000, and his friend, Godfrey Evans, the Kent and England wicketkeeper, donated £500: half his winnings on the popular television show, *Double Your Money*. Sheppard used his *Evening News* articles to advertise the appeal, and staged a fund-raising cricket match at Hove involving leading Test players. His facility for raising money using his contacts and fame was to prove a two-edged sword in future years.

*

---

12 'How Can We Tame the Teddy Boys?' and 'There's More to It than Keeping Them off the Streets', *Evening News*, [late April], 1956.

Sheppard also helped the church build bridges into the community among people at the other end of the age scale. He encouraged one housebound woman known to the congregation, Ethel Noble, to invite her neighbours in for discussion, and some became interested in the faith. Sheppard took two lessons from this small event which influenced his future work. First, that a person's home could provide a bridge where neighbours and the church could meet, and second, 'that those with great personal *needs* may also have *gifts* from which those who appear stronger may receive.'[13] Another elderly and shut-in woman who inspired Sheppard was a Mrs Withers. She had had both her legs amputated, but such was her cheerfulness, lack of self-pity and strong faith that Sheppard believed he benefited more from his visits to see her than the other way around. Sheppard and his colleagues knew that Mrs Withers prayed for them every day.[14]

Sheppard saw bridges extending from the church to the growing West Indian and Nigerian communities in Islington. Churches in the United Kingdom had a reputation for not welcoming immigrants of colour at that time, but Sheppard was heartened to see members of St Mary's embracing West Indian people who were new to the parish. He later regretted the church did not do more to reach out to black newcomers in his day, although a few years after he left St Mary's, he noted that the church had 'quite a number of overseas families' in its congregation.[15]

*

Sheppard found Wood a helpful and wise mentor. He would often learn by spending time with Wood in different situations and taking from the experience what was helpful. 'Maurice led by example,' recalls Gordon Bridger, a fellow curate with Sheppard at Islington. 'His enthusiasm for the Gospel was infectious. We were given space to work things out for ourselves, and to support one another. Maurice set the pace.' Wood required his curates to keep a record of their activities and report back to him regularly.

---

13 Sheppard, *Steps along Hope Street*, pp. 31–2 (italics original); Sheppard was still recalling the gatherings at Mrs Noble's home and the impact they made on him in his retirement.

14 Sheppard, *Parson's Pitch*, London: Hodder & Stoughton, 1964, p. 137.

15 Sheppard, *Steps along Hope Street*, p. 32; Sheppard, *Parson's Pitch*, p. 138.

Wood was generally good company, but he was going through a period of nervous exhaustion when Sheppard arrived at St Mary's. The previous year his wife Marjorie had died in tragic circumstances at the age of 29. He had married again by the time Sheppard joined his team, but was still unable to take services. Sheppard considered it an education to have been close to Wood as he fought his way back to health. He was not to know how valuable the experience of helping someone close to him endure a time of mental distress would prove to be.

*

Wood was keen on advancing the cause of evangelicalism within the Church of England, and one vehicle he used was the Islington Clerical Conference, which he chaired. Founded in 1827, the Conference gathered a large number of evangelical clergy each January to hear papers and discuss matters of mutual concern. Wood liked to take the conference on tour around the country, earning it the nickname the 'Islington circus'. In 1956 he included Sheppard's name in the programme, but the idea of a man in his mid twenties, just a few months into his first curacy, being invited to speak to older, experienced clergy, caused concern. One conference regular wrote to Cyril Bowles, suggesting this was an example of Sheppard 'being exploited pretty thoroughly' by Wood. Bowles contacted Wood's bishop, Joost de Blank, who confessed he was unaware that Sheppard 'was being publicly paraded in this way . . . I am in touch with Maurice Wood telling him to behave more wisely in the training of a young deacon', de Blank assured Bowles.[16]

Wood's explanation was that Sheppard's name appeared in error in different programmes for the conference: it should have been deleted at the proof stage. Wood said he was clear that 'a young man fresh in the Ministry ought not to speak to his elders in the Ministry'. He explained that Sheppard's main role was 'business manager' for the tour, a point made in the Conference press release. He did acknowledge that Sheppard had spoken at an event in Bristol, but that was because Wood thought the theological students attending would benefit from hearing a young

16 Correspondence dated January and February 1956: RHA.

curate reflect on his first three months in the ministry. Sheppard had also spoken at evangelistic rallies in various cities, and Wood said that Sheppard's drawing power as an English cricket captain was the main reason for involving him in this way.[17]

A less public network Sheppard joined while at Islington was Eclectics, an association of young, evangelical Anglican clergy who met regularly for discussion and fellowship. It had been initiated by John Stott, who drew inspiration from the original society of that name formed by John Newton and others in the 1780s. Membership was by invitation only, and although Sheppard was not one of the 40 originally approached by Stott in April 1955, he soon became involved. As the network grew and divided according to region, Stott invited Sheppard to chair one of the London groups. Sheppard enjoyed being part of a dynamic movement which aimed to breathe new life into the national Church, an aim many thought it fulfilled.[18] He valued the opportunity to explore his faith with other like-minded young clergy in a spirit of open enquiry. Society members shared a core belief in the authority of Scripture, but within that broke new ground in terms of the topics they discussed. Sheppard found the group's readiness to relate Christianity to social issues helpful, something Maurice Wood did not prioritize, and later joined another group Stott instigated, called 'Christian Debate'. This was formed to discuss pressing issues which, Stott argued, 'even five years ago we might have ignored.'[19] These included nuclear warfare, the family in modern society, homosexuality, the Christian citizen, divorce and remarriage, and the 'just revolution'. Sheppard found these discussions useful for shaping and expanding his thinking, and they also served as a sounding board for his early ideas about urban mission.

*

On 31 March 1956, Easter Saturday, David Sheppard and Grace Isaac announced their engagement. They had been going out together for

---

17 Letter dated 7 February 1956: RHA.
18 See, for example, Dudley-Smith, T., *John Stott: The making of a leader,* Leicester: IVP, 1999, pp. 307–8.
19 Letter of invitation from Stott to the founder members, 14 November 1958, quoted in Dudley-Smith, *John Stott*, p. 258.

four or five months, and although their working commitments and the distance between them gave them limited opportunity to meet, the relationship had developed quickly. The infrequency with which they were seen together meant the news came as a surprise to many. Some of their friends were not even aware of their relationship, let alone their plans to marry. Two school friends of Grace, who also knew her during her Cambridge days, remember the engagement coming as 'a bolt out of the blue'.

The news was also greeted with surprise at St Mary's. Grace did not visit Sheppard at weekends, and he did not mention her, even to people he knew well. One regular at the weekly door-knocking sessions, who often chatted with Sheppard in his flat before the others arrived, first learned about the relationship when the engagement was mentioned in the press. Reports and photographs appeared in many of the papers, and Grace found herself for the first time on the receiving end of journalists' questions. She mentioned the importance of her and David sharing a Christian faith, and her approval of her fiancé's decision to put the Church before his sport. She was keen to correct the impression that she had no interest in cricket.

Someone else who had not met Grace before the engagement was decided was Sheppard's sister Mary, now happily married with a one-year-old daughter, Sarah. Mary wrote to Grace from her London home, welcoming her into the family. Grace asked Mary for advice concerning her relationship with her future mother-in-law, as her meetings with Barbara so far had not gone as smoothly as she had hoped.[20] Sheppard's choice of life partner undoubtedly caused his mother deep concern. The Isaacs were different in social status, and in terms of cultural wavelength, the families could not have been farther apart. As a child, Barbara had been surrounded by creative people, satirists, comic artists and writers for *Punch* like her father. Her home life had fostered a love for beauty and the arts, which she had sought to share with her children. Mary had perpetuated the family ethos by working in entertainment, marrying a radio comedy producer and building her social life around theatre and media people. David, on the

20 Letter dated 8 March 1956.

other hand, had not only embraced a form of religion Barbara did not understand, and considered rather severe and earnest, he was now to spend the rest of his life with someone of a similar persuasion. How was she to relate to someone whose background was Christian camps and daily prayer in the home, and whose social circle was limited to people of the same outlook? Grace's family were involved in missionary work, something undertaken by Barbara's brother Boy but which she considered highly eccentric and irresponsible. If Barbara had hoped that her son's evangelicalism was just a passing phase, this underlined that it was not.

Sheppard maintains that his mother gave Grace the key to her heart from the outset.[21] This may be more wishful thinking than an accurate recalling of events. Grace and Barbara, and Sheppard himself, tried extremely hard to make the relationship work, and the two women developed a genuine affection for each other, but they never spoke each other's language. Grace says in her letter to Mary that she knows she will love Barbara, but also that she understands how it must have been 'heart-rending' for Barbara to learn of her son's relationship. Barbara's comment to the press following the announcement of the engagement is illuminating: 'She's a very nice girl indeed . . . I approve of the match as much as any mother can whose only son is getting married.'[22]

*

Sheppard was entitled to a month's holiday from late July to late August. Although he was now engaged to Grace, who felt keenly the long gaps between their meetings, he planned to spend it playing cricket for Sussex.[23] However, as happened during his time at Ridley, the England selectors had more ambitious plans for his summer.

The selectors' initial approach came in early July during the Varsity match at Lord's, which Sheppard had taken the day off to watch. There

---

21 Sheppard, *Steps along Hope Street*, p. 9.
22 'Gossip of the Day', *News of the World*, 1 April 1956, p. 6.
23 Grace writes in her letter to Mary Maxwell: 'It's hard waiting for a week before we meet – but then clergymen are always so busy . . .'; letter dated 8 March 1956. Sheppard is open about his plans in both *Parson's Pitch* (p. 146) and *Steps along Hope Street* (p. 35).

he met the chairman of selectors, Gubby Allen. On discovering that Sheppard planned to play some cricket that summer, Allen raised the possibility of his being available for the Fourth Test against Australia at Manchester at the end of that month. Sheppard expressed an interest. Allen suggested that, since he had played only two first-class matches so far that summer,[24] he help the selectors assess his suitability by squeezing in another match before his intended next outing for Sussex. Sussex duly made room for Sheppard to play in their fixture at Worcester starting on 18 July, appointing him captain for the match. Despite having driven from Portsmouth that morning, after taking a school-leavers' service the night before, he hit a solid 59 in his only innings, and was duly included in the squad for the Test.

The news of his selection provided a good story for the papers. Some recounted that Sheppard heard about his call-up from his vicar, who tiptoed out of the vestry to whisper in his ear while he was leading the hymn-singing at Sunday school.[25] The most imaginative story appeared in the *Sydney Morning Herald*. In its leader on the eve of the Test, it conjured up a picture of Sheppard putting aside his clerical collar, seizing a bat from his parish boys' club and, with the rallying cry 'England and St George' ringing in his ears, hitting a century off the Australian attack. It's a story straight from the best boys' comics, they opined in half-mocking tones.[26] Yet truth proved more than a match for fiction. Despite facing Lindwall and Miller, two of the bowlers who had caused him so much trouble six years earlier, Sheppard scored 113 in England's first and only innings. It was, *Wisden* reported, a 'chanceless century', during which Sheppard 'gave not the lightest suggestion of lack of match practice.'[27] Bradman described it as 'an innings of great value and distinction.'[28] If Sheppard's achievement in this match is not better remembered, it is because it was overshadowed by an even more remarkable feat. His

---

24 One of these had been for Sussex against the Australians at Hove in which he scored 97.
25 This detail suggests that Sheppard had returned to Islington to work on the Sunday of the Sussex versus Kent match at Hastings in which he was playing.
26 'Stratagem at Old Trafford', *Sydney Morning Herald*, 24 July 1956, p. 2.
27 Preston, N., ed., *Wisden Cricketers' Almanack 1957*, London: Sporting Handbooks, 1957, p. 260.
28 *Daily Mail*, 28 July 1956, p. 6.

teammate Jim Laker took 19 of the 20 Australian wickets, a distinction unmatched in the history of cricket.

Sheppard would later say that he considered this possibly his best match.[29] His appearance made him the first, and so far, still the only, ordained minister to play Test cricket. Nor was this lost on the Australian captain, Ian Johnson. When it looked at one point as though a divine hand was altering the weather in England's favour, Johnson gestured towards Sheppard and said, 'It's not fair. You've got a professional on your side.'[30] After play Sheppard went to the Australian dressing room to apologize for a profanity used by his teammate, Tony Lock, when bowling to Richie Benaud. Lock had become frustrated at some time-wasting tactics employed by the Australians and called Benaud a 'bastard'. The Australian couldn't bring himself to tell Sheppard he had heard worse during matches in his home country.[31]

Press interest in Sheppard's return to the big time was considerable, and none milked the occasion as well as the *Daily Sketch*. They paid for 11 boys from his parish to travel to Manchester by coach, watch the first two days' play, and stay in a hotel. The paper might have suspected a divine hand at work in their favour when Sheppard's innings spanned both their chosen days. At the end of the second day, the boys gathered up hundreds of empty bottles that had been discarded by the crowd and, under the environmentally enlightened scheme operating in those days, returned them for reuse at the rate of threepence (1.25p) a bottle. Their affection for their curate can be seen from their decision to spend some of their hard-earned cash on the gift of a writing set for him. Another group of admirers keen to acknowledge Sheppard's achievement was the student body at Ridley Hall. They sent a telegram worded 'Congratulations on batting improvement since Little Shelford', a reference to Sheppard's last appearance for the Hall team. Playing against a local club side, he had been dismissed second ball for a duck.[32]

---

29 Undated letter, Sussex County Cricket Club archive, Hove.
30 Chalke, S., *At the Heart of English Cricket: The life and memories of Geoffrey Howard*, Bath: Fairfield Books, 2001, p. 136.
31 Benaud, R., *My Spin on Cricket*, London: Hodder & Stoughton, pp. 248–9.
32 Botting, M., *Fanning the Flame: The story of Ridley Hall Cambridge, Vol. 3, 1951–2001*, Cambridge: Ridley Hall, 2006, p. 81.

Sheppard fulfilled preaching engagements at Kettering and Northampton on the Sunday of the Test, and on the Monday and Tuesday caught up with Grace. Her school year had ended on the Friday, enabling her to travel to Manchester for the last two days of the match. On the Wednesday, he needed to be in Leicester for the first of his scheduled matches for Sussex. In all he played nine matches for the county that year, averaging 36.2. His last game of the summer was the Fifth Test against Australia at The Oval, in which he made 24 and 62. Sir Don Bradman, who had observed and played against England teams over four decades, ranked the side for this match England's best ever.[33]

Sheppard's successful return to Test cricket raised the question of his availability for the MCC tour to South Africa that winter. He made it known in August that he would not join the tour, and the reason he gave to journalists was his commitment to his job. He had only been ordained a year and it was impossible to be away for the winter.[34] But he had begun to be aware of apartheid and the role that sport could play in helping to undermine it. A turning point had occurred when he met Fr Trevor Huddleston earlier that year. Huddleston was a member of the Community of the Resurrection and had just been recalled to England after working in a 'coloured' quarter of Johannesburg for 12 years. His book *Naught for Your Comfort*, exposing the situation in his adopted country, had recently been published.[35] Huddleston told Sheppard that 'nothing would shift South African opinion so much as the refusal to send an England cricket team.' Huddleston's comment 'started my commitment to trying to persuade cricketers that the age-old sportsman's defence "No religion! No politics!" is an escape from reality', Sheppard said.[36] The press began to hint that Sheppard had other reasons for not touring that winter. One interview was headlined, 'I won't play in Africa'. Another reported Sheppard had wondered whether going on the tour might give him the opportunity of 'studying the racial discrimination

---

33 Perry, R., *Keith Miller: The life of a great all-rounder*, London: Aurum Press, 2006, p. 411.

34 He had also become engaged a few months earlier though appears not to have given this as a reason.

35 Huddleston, T., *Naught for Your Comfort*, Garden City, New York: Doubleday, 1956.

36 Obituary of Trevor Huddleston, *Third Way*, May 1998. Huddleston and Sheppard met at the House of Lords after Huddleston had given a talk challenging people in sport and entertainment to boycott South Africa.

in South Africa and, from first-hand experience, forming a proper conclusion.'[37] It was another four years before he publicly announced his unwillingness to play against a South African team selected according to colour rather than ability.

*

Sheppard was attracting the interest of the media in a variety of ways. In July 1956 he took part in a programme on the BBC Home Service (the forerunner of Radio 4) about career opportunities for professional people, and later that year the BBC TV religious affairs programme *Meeting Point* twice invited him to join their panel discussions. In the autumn the *Daily Mail* invited him to write a weekly column for six months. Wood encouraged him to see this as an opportunity to share the gospel, and Sheppard duly accepted. The paper trailed the series as 'provocative', and took a whole page ad in the *TV Times* asking, 'Dare you read DAVID SHEPPARD in the Daily Mail?' His first contribution appeared under the banner 'A vital new name joins the Daily Mail – with a challenge'.

Sheppard used his initial column to recount his journey from formal Christianity to a personal relationship with Christ. His aim for the series was not to preach sermons or present theories, he said, but to share his own and other Christians' experiences. The 'other Christians' were mostly his parishioners, suitably disguised, with his stories about them given a wider application and related to a Bible passage. In December he spoke about apartheid and hinted again at why he was not in South Africa with MCC.[38] 'It was plainly impossible for me to drop my work in Islington for six months', he wrote. 'I confess, however, that I do not think I should have found it easy to play in a Test in Johannesburg when over 150 political prisoners are awaiting trial in the same city.'

Aware that he might attract criticism for taking a political stance, Sheppard argued that the South African system came under judgement from the Bible. The New Testament teaches that Christ's death removed

---

37 Samuel, J., 'Sheppard Not Going to S. Africa', *Daily Herald*, 11 August 1956.
38 Around that time he had received, and declined, a private request from MCC captain, Peter May, to fly out to South Africa as a replacement for an injured player.

not only the barrier between God and humans but between humans themselves: 'Jesus died to take away the "middle wall of partition" between us. *Apartheid* puts it back.' He described how his church in Islington was welcoming people from overseas.[39]

Despite some hiccups the series continued for the planned six months. The paper caused Sheppard embarrassment when it sent copies of his first article, embossed with a purple border, to every other clergyman in the country, without warning him they planned to do this. Sheppard disliked some of the headlines the paper added to his pieces, and their habit of deleting paragraphs without consultation. Letters the paper printed suggested readers appreciated his words, although one correspondent took over the column one week to take him to task. Sheppard has no answers to the question of why God allows human suffering and death, the critic wrote. Instead, he is 'content, rather smugly, to present his easy platitudes and pointed little anecdotes.'[40] Sheppard responded by saying that there was hope in death if one believed in resurrection, Jesus's own being 'the best attested fact in history.'[41] One criticism of his pieces by a sub-editor made a lasting impression on him: 'If I am prepared to come all the way to the commitment to God you write about, your piece might touch me', the sub-editor said. 'But, suppose for the moment I am only prepared to take some small steps in my daily life, I feel you have nothing to say to me.' 'It dawned that, while expecting readers to follow me on to Christian territory, I was not prepared to make the effort to meet them on their ground,' Sheppard later wrote.[42]

*

Sheppard devoted one of his columns to the subject of marriage. Inspired by his own forthcoming wedding, he noted the challenge of Jesus'

39 'I'd Find It Hard to Mix Cricket with Apartheid', *Daily Mail*, 28 December 1956. The biblical reference is Ephesians 2.14. This article led to an exchange of correspondence with the South African High Commission, which tried to encourage him to think differently about apartheid.

40 Bashford, D. F., 'Really, Mr Sheppard, Life's Not So Simple', *Daily Mail*, 5 April 1957.

41 'Question of Faith', *Daily Mail*, 6 April 1957.

42 Sheppard, *Steps along Hope Street*, p. 33.

teaching that marriage makes two people 'one . . . Two lives becoming one is no easy matter'.[43] Within a few months he was to discover, quite painfully, the truth of that statement for himself.

On Wednesday, 19 June 1957, David and Grace married at All Saints' Church, Lindfield. This was the church Grace attended and where she was involved in children's work. Finding a date had not been easy, given Sheppard's workload in Islington and his intention to play cricket that summer. Several people involved in the proceedings recall the ceremony being arranged hurriedly. An added complication was that Sheppard had been involved in lengthy discussions about his next posting, and taken a decision to accept it, that same month.[44]

A concern for Sheppard, when fixing the date, was the possibility of another recall to Test cricket that summer. His success the previous year had raised his hopes of selection again this year against the West Indies. As in 1956, he intended to play enough cricket to enable the selectors to assess his form, but he would also need to set aside two weeks for a honeymoon. Would he be able to fit in enough matches before the fourth and fifth Tests, scheduled respectively for late July and late August? In his second autobiography, Sheppard says that 'everything was still in the diary' for that year, 'including cricket'. In the April he had 'put in some serious practice' in preparation for the season, and 'after our honeymoon I planned to play for another month.'[45]

The wedding took place in the middle of a heatwave, although as the couple left the church around 3.30 pm there was an almighty downpour. They walked to their car under large umbrellas. The weather did not discourage several hundred well-wishers from gathering outside the church. There was also a cohort of reporters and photographers, who found plenty of inspiration for cricket-themed headlines, such as 'Too good a match to be rained off' and 'This weather's a real test!' The picturesque village church, parts of which date from the thirteenth century, was full to capacity with the couple's 260 guests, many of whom, the

---

43 'How DOES marriage hit the rocks?', *Daily Mail*, 22 February 1957. The biblical reference is Matthew 19.5–6.

44 Grace's school would not have broken up by this date. It is likely she resigned her position before her marriage: see *An Aspect of Fear: A journey from anxiety to peace*, London: Darton, Longman & Todd, 1989, p. 6.

45 Sheppard, *Steps along Hope Street*, p. 39.

press reported, sported clerical collars. The congregation of St Mary's Islington was represented by the choir, and Maurice Wood gave the address. The vicar of Lindfield, Freddie Kerr-Dineen, conducted the service.[46] Sheppard's best man was Timothy Dudley-Smith, who amused the guests at the reception at Lindfield's County Hotel with an ode he had composed the night before. Full of witty allusions to cricket, it spoke of the day being 'David's happiest match', his making 'single runs no more' and his relationship with Grace beginning with 'a glance to leg'.[47]

The happy couple then flew to Italy for their honeymoon. After a few days, Grace began to feel unwell and became completely covered in spots. Diagnosed as having a virulent form of chickenpox, she was admitted to a convent hospital in the coastal town of Rapallo, and was kept isolated in a ward below ground. In addition to suffering the misery of having their honeymoon spoiled by illness, both she and David realized that their intended date of return would need to be put back until she had fully recovered. Travel plans might be easily changed, however, but David was also committed to a tight schedule of cricket matches back in England. As Grace later put it, her husband was 'caught between his two loves of cricket and his new bride'. He offered to stay with his wife, but Grace 'pressed him to return home'.[48] She realized that, if he stayed, he would not only miss some important cricket, she would consider herself responsible for having held him back.

> In stoic fashion, I persuaded him that I could manage alone, and that he was not to worry. His first engagement was an important cricket match, and my pride would not allow anyone to think that I had prevented him from playing.[49]

Sheppard agreed, and set off for home alone.

---

46 Sheppard gives the impression in *Steps along Hope Street* (p. 30) that Wood performed the ceremony.

47 I am grateful to Timothy Dudley-Smith for giving me sight of his ode, something he denied to the press at the time! Dudley-Smith went on to become Bishop of Thetford and an internationally renowned hymn-writer.

48 Sheppard, G., *Living with Dying*, London: Darton, Longman & Todd, 2010, p. 10.

49 Sheppard, *An Aspect of Fear*, p. 4.

Grace's situation, about which she has written in some detail, was utterly desperate. She was in 'a bit of a hell hole', as she put it.[50] Her highly contagious condition meant the nurses visited her infrequently, and she had no prospect of any other callers. She was in a country she did not know and whose language she could not speak. Her only contact with the outside world, a phone on an upper floor, proved unreliable. Her high fever made her delirious. Hearing explosions outside, which were actually fireworks, she imagined there was a war on. Along the corridor was a woman whose agonized crying kept her awake day and night, while her own room had bars at the window.

A letter from David brought welcome relief, and she later discovered he had tried unsuccessfully to phone her. She wrote letters home but omitted to mention her misery and loneliness. She drew David a picture of the view from her room but left out the bars. She felt that if she gave him cause to worry about her, his attention would be diverted from his work, and she would be responsible for holding back his important ministry. Eventually she recovered and was allowed to leave, but on the train to Paris her excitement about being reunited with her husband was overshadowed by fears of crossing that unfamiliar city. When she did reach London, David met her, though hopes of a private reunion were shattered by waiting press photographers insisting they stage some kisses through the train window.

Sheppard had returned to Islington and to first-class cricket. On 13 July he played the first of three consecutive three-day matches. One of these, Gentlemen versus Players at Lord's, was traditionally a trial for the Test side. Sheppard's 50 for the Gentlemen ensured his selection for the Fourth Test at Leeds, where his 68 helped England to a comfortable victory. On the Sunday he preached at St George's Church, with Colin Cowdrey and the West Indies all-rounder Collie Smith taking part. After playing for Sussex throughout the rest of his holiday month, he ended the season by opening for England in the Fifth and final Test at The Oval. Despite playing with an inflamed tendon in his left hand, he scored 40 as England again won by an innings. Grace, not long back in the country, went up to the Leeds Test, conscious of the expectations of her as the

---

50 Sheppard, *Living with Dying*, p. 11.

new wife of a cricketer. Denying herself sufficient time to convalesce, however, did not help her condition.

Sheppard has written less about the honeymoon than Grace, but he does acknowledge, in both his autobiographies, that her experience triggered off a serious nervous illness. Just how serious became clear three months later when she collapsed at Holborn tube station. She was unable to breathe or stand, and her mind was in complete turmoil. Rescued by various 'angels', including two members of St Mary's who happened to be outside in a taxi, she was taken to a doctor. The cause of her trouble could not be immediately identified, and further tests confirmed there was 'nothing organically wrong', but she showed no signs of improvement and was admitted as a voluntary patient to the psychiatric unit of Guy's Hospital in London.

Grace's seven weeks in the clinic forced her and David to confront the reality that she could no longer function unaided outside the four walls of a room. Her dignity and self-confidence were now non-existent, and she realized she had become completely dependent on him. She also became convinced that she was a hindrance to him, and that he might want to walk away from their marriage. As she searched for clues to the cause of her condition, she found she needed to go back only as far as the barred cell in the bowels of the Italian hospital in which she had recently been incarcerated.

Sheppard was as shocked and upset by this development as his wife. He had not encountered anything like it within his own family and, like his mother and sister, he did not readily confront his emotions. Yet he appears to have coped with the situation well. Grace writes of her husband continuing to treat her 'as a rational human being, able to discuss with him some of the big decisions that were needing to be made at that time.' She also found reassuring his suggestion that, if trusting God was proving hard to maintain, she should trust *him* as one whom she could see and touch. 'His faith would have to do for both of us', Grace later wrote. 'This carried me through that crisis and I did not feel so alone and afraid.'[51]

Yet Sheppard's decision to leave his new bride in Italy was clearly a factor in her nervous disorder. Grace says that, when she insisted that

---

51 Sheppard, *Living with Dying*, p. 14; Sheppard, *An Aspect of Fear*, p. 7.

David return home, he agreed 'that there was little he could usefully do by just being there.'[52] The temptation to judge decisions taken in an earlier and very different age by later norms should always be avoided, and in Sheppard's defence, the pressures on him from the cricketing authorities back home might have been considerable. Yet given Grace's age, her inexperience of foreign travel, and the remoteness of her situation, it is difficult not to conclude that his staying in Rapallo until she was better, and travelling back with her, would have helped to alleviate her anxiety enormously. Only two weeks before, Sheppard had made a solemn vow to 'comfort her . . . and keep her, in sickness and in health'. Grace has written that her husband 'finally . . . agreed he wanted to get back'.[53] His departure might not have been entirely due to her persuasive powers.

The distinguished cricket writer John Woodcock once suggested that at times 'ambition and virtue could be seen vying for supremacy' in Sheppard.[54] Woodcock was writing about Sheppard's tactics on the field, but perhaps he faced a similar struggle over his decision to return to England without Grace. Did ambition to succeed as a cricketer and a curate overcome the more virtuous course of action? Grace recalls there was 'an imbalance in our relationship' at that time. 'He became the master and I the servant.'[55] In part this was a consequence of her decision to give up her job and become 'a support' to her husband. This was not unusual for a woman in the 1950s, but Grace also felt a contrast between her husband's status as a Test cricketer and popular public speaker, and her own 'relative uselessness' due to her condition. This feeling drew on the teaching she heard as a younger woman about putting Christ first, others next, and self last. This would influence her profoundly until she had counselling in the 1980s.

For his part, Sheppard had few role models to draw upon in terms of married men. His own father had died while he was young, and several of the men he looked up to, including Eric Nash and John Stott, had taken a conscious decision not to marry. For him, marriage involved

---

52 Sheppard, *An Aspect of Fear*, p. 4.
53 Sheppard, *An Aspect of Fear*, p. 4.
54 Woodcock, J., 'Hard Edge to the Good Sheppard', *The Times*, 8 March 2005.
55 Sheppard, G., *Pits and Pedestals: A journey towards self-respect*, London: Darton, Longman & Todd, 1995, p. 68.

facing the challenge of continuing his work as a curate, with its long and irregular hours, while adjusting to life with a partner with a serious nervous condition. For all the trauma of her collapse at Holborn station, Grace considers it was 'the beginning of a newer and more honest life' for them. It showed her 'the way back to the road towards self-respect', she said later. As David shared in the psychotherapy to which it led, he understood better the responsibilities of marriage.[56]

*

Grace had moved into Sheppard's lodgings at 67 College Cross, the top two floors of a terraced house with shared facilities. Her stay in the clinic meant that she was there only a few weeks before the move to his next job. Sheppard also spent less time in Islington after their marriage, playing cricket until the end of August and then spending two days a week at the site of his next posting.

This was at the Dockland No. 1 Settlement in Canning Town, an outreach of Malvern School.[57] Early in 1957, while giving a talk there, Sheppard had become aware that the Settlement was about to close, and he wondered if he might be called to serve there, sensing its potential to provide a ministry to the surrounding neighbourhood. As with all major changes he confronted, he had to know God's mind, but his deepening commitment to share the gospel with unchurched people made the idea worth pursuing. He needed another prayer walk to ascertain God's will, after which he approached the Bishop of Barking, Hugh Gough, to talk over possibilities. Gough, coincidentally Maurice Wood's predecessor at Islington, was a member of the Dockland Settlements Committee. He was persuaded by Sheppard's enthusiasm to take on the work and set up a new committee to assume responsibility for the Settlement. Within a few weeks the 'Bishop of Barking's Committee' had decided to take Sheppard on.

A new name for the venture, the Mayflower Family Centre, was agreed, and Sheppard was formally appointed its warden on 1 August.

---

56 Sheppard, *Pits and Pedestals*, pp. 32, 46–7, 69.
57 The Canning Town project was named 'Dockland Settlement No.1.' since there were other similar centres in London and in other cities, including Southampton and Bristol.

The intention was that he and Grace would move into the centre permanently early in 1958. He wrote that they seized the opportunity to go to the Mayflower 'with both hands'.[58] Grace, however, was trepidatious about the idea of their making their first home together in such uncharted territory. 'It seemed ludicrous', she later wrote, 'to reflect that here was I, a 22-year-old with limited experience of the world, taking up this new life among people whose ways were so different from all I had ever known.'[59]

*

Sheppard's two years at Islington had proved life changing. It had been his first taste of inner-city life, and he had learned much from the people he served, particularly those with the least opportunities. As one former church member put it, 'he wanted to be an Islingtonian'. He had seen that the church needed to ask how it could serve people, rather than inform them what it could offer. The experience raised huge questions for him, however, about the effectiveness of churches in urban settings. Why did such churches find it hard to reach the people around them? Why were they reluctant to develop local leaders? Did they believe that working-class people could *be* leaders? How could churches help young people in poorer areas, many of whom were alienated not just from 'religion' but from life itself? What *is* the mission of the church in the inner city?

Such was his agenda for the next stage of his ministry. If he had only had an inkling before of the work to which God was calling him, now he had no doubts whatsoever: 'By the time I finished in Islington, there was only one thing I wanted to do – to serve in an inner-city area.'[60]

---

58 Sheppard, *Parson's Pitch*, p. 139.
59 Sheppard, *An Aspect of Fear*, p. 9.
60 Sheppard, D. S., *Steps along Hope Street*, London: Hodder & Stoughton, 2002, p. 36.

7

Mayflower
(1958–1969)

The Canning Town into which the Sheppards moved bore many scars from the war. East London had been a prime target for enemy bombers, and more than half of Canning Town's housing stock had been destroyed. Some redevelopment had taken place since 1945, but many open bombsites and shelled-out buildings remained. With good reason did residents describe their neighbourhood as 'the big debris'.

The Settlement buildings had survived intact, however. The creation of Sir Reginald Kennedy-Cox, warden of the Settlement between the wars, their mock-Tudor façade and arrangement around an Oxbridge-style quad struck an incongruous note among the older terraced streets and modern brick houses nearby. The street the buildings occupied had been judged the worst in London by *The Times* when Malvern College first established a mission there in 1894. Sheppard thought the design of the complex conveyed 'an unspoken assumption of the superiority of middle-class culture coming to a working-class community'.[1] But it housed exactly the kind of facilities he needed, including clubrooms, an accommodation block, swimming pool, playground, office space and a chapel. For their own accommodation, the Sheppards converted part of an upstairs corridor into a modest flat.

*

The Mayflower Family Centre was officially incorporated on 6 January 1958, and Sheppard was licensed as Warden two days later. A Council

---

1 Watherston, P., *A Different Kind of Church: The Mayflower Family Centre story*, London: Marshall Pickering, 1994, p. 64.

was established to oversee the centre and serve as trustees. This was chaired first by Bishop Gough and then, following Gough's appointment as Archbishop of Sydney, a Christian solicitor, Jack Wallace. The new name was chosen not just to signify a break with the past, but to echo the pioneering spirit of the community which sailed from England to establish a new colony in North America in the 1620s. The name had 'an authentic ring of Christian adventure about it', Sheppard explained in his first newsletter to supporters.[2]

This newsletter, appropriately named 'The Log of the Mayflower' and sporting an image of the original ship, described the early months of the new venture. The first phase of a three-stage building plan, drawn up shortly after Sheppard's appointment, had been completed at a cost of £10,000. Clubs were running for children of all ages from five to the teenage years, with older people joining groups such as the Young Wives Fellowship, the Older Mothers Club and the Grandfathers Club. The nursery school, run on professional lines, had 30 on the books and a long waiting list. Uniformed organizations and 'Covenanter' groups were set up, while more than 100 regularly attended the Children's Church. The term 'Family' was important in conveying the nature of its work: 'Of course there would be groups for "youth" and groups for the "elderly",' Sheppard wrote, 'but we wanted to reach the whole family.'[3]

The financial challenges facing the new centre were spelled out in the Log. Several large charities had covered the cost of the initial renovations, but £4,500 remained to be paid to the Dockland Settlements for fixtures and fittings, and another £15,000 was needed for further improvements to the premises. The heating system in the church had broken down, necessitating the use of a clubroom for worship: a replacement would involve further costs. Grants from the Local Education Authority, Chelmsford Diocese and the Church Pastoral Aid Society were covering staff salaries, and some of the internal decoration work was being done in house. But donations of 'something over £7,000 annually', half of the total running costs of the centre, would be needed to keep the work afloat. Sheppard believed the centre 'would stand to a very large extent

---

2 'The Log of the Mayflower', Spring 1958, Bishopsgate Institute archive.
3 Sheppard, D. S., *Parson's Pitch*, London: Hodder & Stoughton, 1964, p. 174.

on small donations', but with the average male salary then around £600 per annum, and the female salary much lower, he was exercising considerable faith. He might say later that this faith was justified but securing the money to maintain the Mayflower's work proved a constant concern. It was also a source of intrigue on occasions.

*

Sheppard had three core aims for the centre; first, to help an indigenous church develop in the district, with local Christian leaders and local Christian homes. Second, he hoped to serve the district in the name of Christ, meeting some of the social and educational needs of Canning Town. Third, to provide an informal training ground for Christians, generally from other social backgrounds, who wanted to learn something about Christian work in the inner-city.[4] In the early days of his curacy, Sheppard had believed leadership needed to come from outside if a church were to be built in the inner city. Now he made establishing an indigenous, locally led church his principal aim. 'God has called us first and foremost to build a Church in Canning Town,' he wrote. 'It will only be possible to claim that this has been achieved when we have strong local leadership in all our activities and when there are Christian homes established in the district.'[5] Sheppard seldom mentioned other churches in Canning Town, nor the parish in which he was operating, St Luke's.[6] The Mayflower was never a parish church, although it had the full blessing of the diocese.

An important influence on Sheppard's thinking was Roland Allen's *Missionary Methods: St Paul's or Ours?*, first published in 1912. Allen claimed that Paul founded self-reliant churches by consciously training up local leaders, a practice Sheppard thought was now largely ignored. Sheppard found compelling Allen's argument that Paul trusted his converts to take over the leadership of a church because he believed they

---

4 Watherston, *A Different Kind of Church*, p. 46.

5 Memo to the Council, Local Committee and Staff, September 1962, p. 1: Sheppard papers (SHP), 28.4.

6 The incumbent at St Luke's was Fr Sydney Goose. St Luke's also ran a youth club, the Boyd Institute.

would be indwelt by the Holy Spirit. 'Our doctrine of the Holy Spirit will not allow us to say that there are communities where we cannot expect God to produce local leadership', Sheppard wrote in an article about Allen.[7]

Where Sheppard disagreed with Allen was over the time it would take to build a church. Allen thought St Paul's practice of establishing churches within 18 months could be copied. Sheppard argued that the apostle took it for granted that in each of his churches there would be a 'strong centre of respectable religious-minded people' to take the lead. Such people are not to be found in the modern city, he thought.[8] He preferred the advice of the missionary bishop, Stephen Neill, who thought it would take 30 years of intensive pastoral care before a Christian community could be regarded as stable.[9]

*

From the outset, Sheppard was assisted by an able and loyal team, including some who had served at the former Settlement, and new staff he appointed himself. He became known as 'Skipper', reflecting his responsibility for the overall direction of the work (and his cricketing past). Among the newer staff members were two who would be pivotal to the centre's work for the next nine years: Jean Lodge Patch, appointed in January 1958 as Girls Club Leader, and George Burton, recruited after Easter to lead the youth work. Another important staff member was secretary Hilary Harman, who had moved with Grace and David from Islington. Sheppard once described Miss Harman as the one 'upon whom the efficient running of the Centre largely depends'.[10]

Team members met regularly for prayer, Bible study and mutual support, as well as to discuss business. Sheppard always tried to reach consensus, and encouraged members to be creative and share new ideas.

---

7 'Is Local Leadership Possible?', *Christians in Industrial Areas*, no. 2, May 1967, p. 10.

8 Sheppard, D. S., *Built as a City: God and the urban world today*, London: Hodder & Stoughton, 1974, p. 285.

9 'Log', Winter 1967.

10 Sheppard, *Parson's Pitch*, p. 175. Among those who stayed on from the previous work were Douglas Minton, Margaret Fish, the chaplain David Gardner and a Miss Truscott.

Staff meetings were 'frequently lively affairs'.[11] Later the team was joined by Joan de Torre, head teacher of the nursery school, and chaplain Brian Seaman and his wife Marion. When they first arrived, Brian, Marion and their young daughters lodged in the Sheppards' flat.

The first 'Log' introduced another member of staff, 'Mrs Sheppard'. Grace was continuing to receive treatment at the time of the move, and did not settle into the Mayflower until her release from hospital at Easter. Once there, she determined to be more than 'the warden's wife', despite her condition leaving her 'too frightened' to move around the centre alone.[12] Drawing on her talents, she looked after the garden, led the music in chapel, and took Bible studies. She found that the invitation to become a full member of staff did wonders for her self-confidence and sense of dignity. Yet her misgivings about moving to the Mayflower were not far beneath the surface, especially in the early months. An electrician working at the centre asked Grace if she thought she would like living there. Staring through the wire-protected windows on to a scrapyard protected by fierce Alsatian dogs, she realized she was far from sure. Politely she said that all was well, but her hesitation was detected. She always saw that conversation as a turning point. It forced her to recognize she would have to be more honest with herself and those whose space she shared at the Mayflower.

*

As the Mayflower became known, it quickly established itself as a training ground for young Christians exploring their calling or seeking wider experience. The centre had accommodation for around 20 residents at any one time, and the rooms were seldom unoccupied. Residents were mostly aspiring professionals, recommended by their church or future employer to spend their gap year between college and employment at the centre. To broaden their experience, and pay for their keep, they were expected to find work locally, typically in a factory or at the Tate & Lyle

---

11 'Introduction' in Burton, G., *People Matter More Than Things*, London: Hodder & Stoughton, 1965, p. 12.

12 Sheppard, G., *An Aspect of Fear: A journey from anxiety to peace*, London: Darton, Longman & Todd, 1989, p. 10.

refinery in nearby Silvertown. Their roles at the centre included cooking and helping with the clubs.

Sheppard's commitment to raising indigenous leaders meant that residents played a strictly supportive role at the Mayflower. If a local person emerged with the gifts to take on a task a resident had been doing, the resident was to step back. Sheppard valued the residents, but he did not want local people to see them as role models, or aspire to adopt their values. He realized that 'young Christians from a working-class background' might be tempted to 'change themselves socially' by imitating Christians from other social groups. He feared they might harbour aspirations to move to a more middle-class area where the church might be stronger:[13] he wanted local people to stay and build an 'indigenous' church.

*

Sheppard was prepared for the long game in terms of church building and evangelism. Expecting people to make on-the-spot decisions for Christ was unrealistic, he argued, given their lack of Christian background.[14] If we want people to be interested in what we have to say, we have first to be 'patiently "building bridges" of friendship', he wrote. These bridges were not 'devices' to attract people to church but attempts to meet their needs.[15] Sheppard later said that people had been reached at the Mayflower not by 'preaching missions' but because a group of Christians was prepared to live in their area for a long time.[16] People had also become interested in the faith by seeing others from their neighbourhood become Christians.[17] He believed that among the many who came to the Mayflower were those

---

13 Memo to the Council, p. 2. Sheppard consciously used the term 'working class' to describe his Canning Town neighbours since it was the one they preferred.

14 For this reason, he was unhappy about plans for a Billy Graham campaign in the East End of London. The Mayflower supported Graham's campaigns in Manchester (1961) and at Earl's Court (1966), but Sheppard argued that Graham could not be expected to 'reap' souls in the city unless churches there had been 'sowing' beforehand; 'Log' Summer 1961; 'Log' Spring 1966; minutes of the MFC Council, 6 July 1964 (held at the River Christian Centre, Canning Town).

15 'Mission – In Industrial Areas', January 1968, p. 10.

16 'Have We Failed?', *Christians in Industrial Areas*, no. 1., February 1967, p. 3.

17 Sheppard, *Built as a City*, pp. 256–7.

whom God would lead to faith: 'We pray the Holy Spirit may show us when we should bring a particular challenge to anyone.' He cited Jesus' prayer in John 17.9: 'I am not praying for the world but for those whom Thou hast given me'.[18] He thought the hardest people to reach were those he termed 'happy pagans', who did not consider themselves in any special need. They valued what the Mayflower did for their children and others in the community, but they 'did not see the Christ we preached as being for them'.[19]

Building bridges prompted Sheppard to rethink his cultural assumptions. He saw that many of the habits he assumed all Christians were required to adopt, such as daily Bible study and devouring Christian literature, reflected the circles in which he moved. They could be obstacles to faith for people unused to reading or owning books. He also learned that avoiding activities he took to be 'worldly' and off-limits for Christians, such as dancing and drinking, limited opportunities for serious conversation in a culture where parties and pubs were common settings for social interaction. There may be aspects of local culture we dislike, he would say, but it was important not to rush to judgement. Christians must be prepared to fit into the ways of the district where God has placed them, not expect their neighbours to adapt to their way of life. 'Perhaps accepting uncritically is a necessary phase to move through before we can offer a proper critique of local attitudes', he wrote.[20]

David and Grace used their home to build bridges, having learned in Islington how private homes could provide a stepping-stone where church and community could meet. They invited local couples they knew, but who did not come to church, to meet at their flat on Thursday evenings. The numbers involved were small, but friendships developed. Evenings began with a light-hearted activity, often a card game such as 'Pit'. Serious conversation might not begin until further on, and Grace found she had to develop the habit of staying up late, since that was the time people would relax and start talking. Sheppard later encouraged those attending to join a 'searching group' to explore Christian faith

---

18 Memo to the Council, pp. 1–2.

19 Sheppard, D. S., *Steps along Hope Street*, London: Hodder & Stoughton, 2002, p. 47.

20 'Mission – In Industrial Areas', p. 8; 'De-briefing II', 1970, p. 4: SHP, 28.4; Watherston, *A Different Kind of Church*, p. 64. Sheppard, *Steps along Hope Street*, pp. 51–2.

in a more focused way. This became a regular part of the Mayflower programme, though generally Sheppard disliked its activities becoming fixed and tidy, 'when our district around us is very untidy'. There should be freedom for the Spirit to lead in new directions.

*

Teenagers were the largest cohort at the Mayflower, and its youth clubs offered a range of activities. Sheppard believed that, after a hard day at the docks, young people would rather go at their own pace than feel they had to achieve something. There was space to relax as well as opportunities to engage in woodwork, sewing, cookery, painting and a variety of sports. A sense of belonging and team spirit were fostered by encouraging members to maintain and decorate the premises. This worked well following a fire at the centre in November 1961, when club members did much of the renovation work. One group of boys, who had done considerable damage to the premises in the past, even bought wallpaper. 'There is hardly a member of the club who cannot point with pride to the part which he or she did', Sheppard told readers of the Log.[21]

Members, staff and helpers found life at the centre unpredictable and exciting. Sheppard and his team worked hard to provide a space where local people could have fun but also engage in serious conversation. But it was not all plain sailing, and the centre's open policy had its dangers. Local gangs of both sexes were a persistent challenge, and several times the Log reported damage to the premises, indiscipline and 'defiance'. The police were often called in the early days, and trouble, though sporadic, was never far away. Jealousies and tensions also occurred within groups at the centre, particularly those which operated on an 'invitation only' basis and met in staff members' homes. People leading prayers learned to do so with their eyes open, particularly when billiard balls were flying around. Sheppard was clear that the Mayflower welcomed what he called the 'rougher members', though it would bar, at least temporarily, regular troublemakers.

---

21 'Log', Summer 1962.

*

The key to the success of the clubs was the senior youth leader, George Burton. Burton worked tirelessly to attract young men and women to the centre and interest them in the Christian faith. Irish by birth but brought up in Townhead in Glasgow, his career had many ingredients to fascinate the young, including army service in India, police work in Palestine, security duties in Cyprus and a spell recruiting tribesmen to form an army for the Sultan of Muscat and Oman. Burton's background gave him an empathy with the youth of Canning Town, who also respected his having been a gang member and arrested for petty crimes.[22]

Sheppard had appointed Burton knowing full well the tensions his presence at the Mayflower would create. Burton could be moody, resentful, manipulative and often deliberately offensive, particularly towards people he thought had plummy accents and middle-class attitudes. But Sheppard recognized Burton's unique capacity to relate to club members and influence them for good. In terms of fulfilling the mission of the centre, Burton was his most important asset. 'Without him', Sheppard reflected, 'we might have developed a warm and harmonious team that ran smoothly, but cut little ice locally.'[23] Sheppard and Burton were an unlikely partnership, but they had a great affection and regard for each other. They shared a sense that God had brought them together for a particular purpose. More than once Burton threatened to resign, so keeping him on was one of Sheppard's big achievements.

Burton shared Sheppard's conviction that some from the youth clubs would be converted. He also believed in building relationships in the home, and through an initiative he called the 'Sunday Group', Burton put these beliefs into action. He drew out from the clubs those he sensed God wanted him to focus on, and invited them to meet informally in his flat. He insisted Group members attend the evening service, but otherwise made few demands on them. He understood the importance of relating to people in groups, another aspect of working-class culture Sheppard had to learn. 'George taught me that the "individualistic approach of

---

22 For an excellent account of Burton's life see Hewitt, D. and J., *George Burton: A study in contradictions*, London: Hodder & Stoughton, 1969.

23 Sheppard, *Steps along Hope Street*, p. 42.

much church life" made it impossible for many Mayflower people to believe in Christ,' Sheppard wrote.[24] In developing leaders at the centre, Burton would initially give people responsibility as groups rather than as individuals.

Sheppard took a hands-off approach to the youth clubs, recognizing the gifts others brought to that work. He provided back-up by visiting members' homes and developing friendships with their parents. In a tight-knit, quite closed community, it was no small thing for him to be so readily accepted into family homes.[25] He and the team led holidays for centre members, including weeks away on the Isle of Wight and coach excursions to the continent: Blankenberge on the Belgian coast was a favourite destination. One family camp at Bracklesham Bay featured a night exercise on the Sussex Downs organized by Sheppard's old regiment, the Royal Sussex. When flares were sent up, the local police arrived, thinking the Mayflower boys might be smugglers. Mayflower coaches were well-maintained, but their age and general condition left their occupants feeling lucky to have reached the Blackwall Tunnel, let alone Belgium. On a trip to Southend an illegally parked Mayflower coach escaped getting a ticket when the policeman heard it was 'connected with David Sheppard'.[26]

Sheppard took parties on cricketing tours around Sussex, and a match against his home village of Slinfold became a regular fixture. Mayflower teams preferred wearing jeans and boots to whites, surprising their opponents when they made a respectable score. Sheppard acknowledged that his sport was not a favourite in Canning Town, and thought he would have had more kudos at the Mayflower had he captained West Ham United instead of Cambridge and Sussex.

*

Sheppard knew that a church would only develop in Canning Town if those with the potential to lead it stayed in the neighbourhood. He

---

24 Sheppard, *Steps along Hope Street*, p. 44.

25 Interview with nine former Mayflower members hosted by Mary and Colin Watts. Bill Green's mother even asked Sheppard to tell her son the facts of life.

26 I owe this story to Stephen Timms.

disliked the popular assumption that Christians were always looking to better themselves and move to ever more prosperous neighbourhoods. When that occurred, he felt the ones who remain would 'sink a little lower' because those who might have been their leaders have left them.[27] He would often express his concern for the 'left behind', working hard to persuade those converted at the centre to remain living nearby. He publicly committed himself and Grace to staying at the Mayflower at least ten years.

Sheppard did, however, acknowledge the difficulties facing those who did choose to stay in Canning Town. Long waiting lists for council properties, little affordable private property and a high mortgage rate made moving away the only feasible option for most. 'Humanly it is impossible to find housing in our district', he told the Mayflower Council in the early 1960s. When homes did become available, they were 'truly remarkable answers to prayer'.[28] As a practical solution, the centre formed a housing association in 1962, with treasurer Mark Birchall master-minding the process. By the middle of 1963, thanks to loans from West Ham Borough Council and 'an anonymous friend', the Mayflower (East London) Housing Association had bought a house near Plaistow station and seen its first four tenants move in. A second house was acquired in 1964. Sheppard was delighted with the success of this scheme, although he was sometimes accused of not wanting people to 'go up in the world'.[29]

*

If Sheppard's celebrity as a cricketer cut little ice at the Mayflower, the media continued to believe in his appeal. In April 1958 he appeared on a new religious programme for teenagers screened by ABC Television called *The Sunday Break*. He became a regular on the show, on one occasion interviewing young people at the Mayflower. He also appeared on the husband-and-wife chat show *Rich and Rich* alongside Charlie

---

27 'The Church as a Team', a privately circulated typescript, 1963, p. 10. I am grateful to Dr John Parker for sending me a copy of this document.

28 Memo to the Council, pp. 4–5; The Church as a Team, p. 11.

29 Sheppard, *Steps along Hope Street*, p.55. Housing associations were still relatively new at the time.

Chester, Richard Attenborough and Sheila Sim. Journals frequently ran interviews with him and published features about the Mayflower, and the Sunday morning services on BBC radio were broadcast from the Mayflower during March 1966 and May 1968.

The move to the Mayflower coincided with Sheppard joining *Woman's Own* as a weekly columnist. Every week, David 'will bring you messages of comfort and help in your daily life', the editor told the magazine's six million readers. His first contribution, a double-page feature entitled 'How I found Religion', pulled no punches in describing his conversion at Cambridge and the change it had made to his life. Contradicting the sub-editor's title, Sheppard explained that although 'religion' had featured much in his childhood, he had lacked that 'secret spark of Christian faith' until the moment he understood that 'Jesus had died on the Cross to bear my sins' and could be 'a reality in my everyday life'.[30]

Sheppard wrote 500 words each week for *Woman's Own* for the next 17 years. No limitations were placed on what he could say, nor were his pieces significantly altered or censored.[31] Each week he explored a theme through a combination of real-life stories, biblical reflection and gentle sermonizing. He took seriously the suggestion made by his sub-editor at the *Daily Mail* that he try to meet his readers halfway. Describing the column as 'an evangelistic opportunity which I enjoy', he valued the expert help he received from Timothy Dudley-Smith, his best man and a former editor of *Crusade* magazine, and the broadcaster Roy Trevivian. He confronted potentially thorny topics such as sin and the need for conversion, and he shared his thoughts on dating, marriage, parenting and divorce. Sheppard wanted to be simple and not go over his readers' heads: 'This means speaking not about philosophies and this theory or that, but about Jesus Christ and what He can be in everyday life.'[32]

The magazine accepted his resolve to talk frankly about his faith. The editor once asked whether he might devote more space to story-telling than to biblical references, since his stories were good and his thoughts about different issues so reassuring. He replied that if he was being asked

---

30 *Woman's Own*, 11 December 1957, pp. 22–3.
31 To avoid a repeat of his experience with the *Daily Mail*, he secured an undertaking from *Woman's Own* that they would not alter his pieces without his consent.
32 'How Does the Church Rate?', *Woman's Own*, 23 May 1959, p. 14.

to leave God out of the column, he couldn't do it, and he never was asked.[33]

*

While at the Mayflower, Sheppard appeared on *This Is Your Life* and *Desert Island Discs*, two of the most popular BBC programmes of the day. *Desert Island Discs*, a Home Service staple since the 1940s, featured a pre-recorded interview with presenter Roy Plomley. *This Is Your Life*, which had a prime-time slot on Monday evenings, was screened live, with friends, family and colleagues of the subject contributing memories. Sheppard appeared on it in October 1960 at the age of 31. As Grace later recalled, 'there wasn't a great deal of life to present to him except the cricket and the parish'.[34] His work at St Mary's as well as the Mayflower was featured, and there was a moving moment when Flo Withers, the housebound parishioner Sheppard had befriended in Islington, spoke from her wheelchair of the young curate's visits and the cheer they had brought her. George Burton characteristically ignored his brief, saying that the Mayflower aimed to convert young people to Christ, not make them better citizens. The presenter, Eamonn Andrews, ended the show on a prescient note. 'You are still a young man', he told Sheppard. 'Who knows what greater things are to come from you?'[35]

Sheppard's choice of discs for his desert island included pieces by Schubert, Mozart and Bach; the West Ham anthem 'I'm Forever Blowing Bubbles' (which 'we sing on the terraces' and 'in coaches if we're going out'); Herman's Hermits' 'I'm into something good'; and the calypso 'Cricket, Lovely Cricket'. Asked whether his work at the Mayflower could not be done just as well by a social worker, Sheppard described it as 'very decisively Christian' in its orientation. For his luxury, he chose pen and paper 'to write a novel', and for his book a collection of Dutch artwork.[36]

---

33 Correspondence with Jane Reed CBE. Sheppard continued to write occasionally for the magazine after 1975.
34 www.bigredbook.info/david_sheppard.html.
35 *This Is Your Life* script: SHP, 59.2.
36 Transcript of *Desert Island Discs* as pre-recorded, 7 September 1965.

*

Sheppard attracted further media attention when he announced in April 1960 that he would not play cricket against the South African tourists that summer. He had harboured concerns about apartheid since 1956, but not made them explicit. Now an invitation from the Duke of Norfolk to captain his XI against the tourists at Arundel, and the possibility that Sussex would ask him to play in their match against the visitors, forced him to declare his hand. The previous month 69 black protestors had been killed by police at Sharpeville, bringing the situation in South Africa once more to public attention. Sheppard found the courage to speak out in his Bible reading for that day, Isaiah chapter 58: 'Cry aloud, spare not, lift up your voice like a trumpet; declare to my people their transgressions . . . Loose the bonds of wickedness . . . to let the oppressed go free.'[37] He became the first Test cricketer to make a stand on the issue.

As a member of the MCC Committee, Sheppard had to tread with care. MCC were hosts of the South African team, and a public declaration of his position would cause it considerable embarrassment. Sheppard consulted the President, Harry Altham, who told him not to make any announcement until his term on the Committee ended on 4 May.[38] Sheppard also sought advice from several church leaders, including his friend John Stott. Stott suggested that, rather than make a one-off announcement, Sheppard make known his decision and the reasons behind it whenever he was asked.[39] But news of his intentions leaked out, and Sheppard had to go public early. Speaking to reporters at the Mayflower on 7 April, he said he had no wish to create unpleasantness but, as a cricketer and Christian, he could not remain silent. Rebutting accusations that he was 'mixing politics with sport', Sheppard said he did not regard cricket in South Africa as a non-political game. 'There are possibly 20,000 non-white cricketers in South Africa', he said. 'Because they are non-white, they will have no opportunity of playing in a club side, in a province side or a Test match.' If Christians did not speak

---

37 Sheppard, *Steps along Hope Street*, p. 84.
38 Letter dated 19 March 1960: SHP, 15.1.
39 Letter dated 30 March 1960: SHP, 15.1.

out against apartheid, they reinforced the perception of Christianity as 'the white man's religion'. Some MCC members complained of Sheppard's actions, unaware that he had the President's permission to speak to the press.

Sheppard's work with MCC was unaffected by this turbulent spell. For several years he had sat on committees reviewing the status of the amateur in the first-class game, and he saw this through to completion. Originally he was almost a lone voice in arguing that it was unfair to treat a player who drew a salary from his county, a 'professional', differently from one who might be paid by his county to be an 'assistant secretary' or earn money from journalism or advertising, but was accorded the privileged status 'amateur'. The absurdity of the situation struck him in his Cambridge days when, after one match, an opposing captain apologized to Sheppard for the 'impertinence' of a professional member of his side who had addressed him as 'David' instead of 'Mr Sheppard', despite being a friend.[40]

By 1962, opinion within MCC had shifted, and the era of gentlemen and players ended.[41] Sheppard's other work for MCC included contributing to a report on 'the future welfare of First-Class Cricket' in 1957. This included the recommendation that a knock-out competition be given a trial, something eventually introduced in 1963. Later he proposed an 85-over limit to first innings in county matches, arguing it would make for more exciting cricket on the first two days of a match when attendances were largest.[42]

*

Grace's condition meant that she and David delayed starting a family, but the Summer 1962 'Log' announced that a daughter, Jenny, had been born to them in the March. 'For at least two people, the most important arrival at the Mayflower this year has been the smallest', Sheppard told his readers. Jenny's christening, held at the Mayflower and conducted

---

40 Sheppard, *Parson's Pitch*, pp. 165–6. The player was the Gloucestershire and England batsman, Tom Graveney.

41 Sheppard played in the last ever Gentlemen versus Players match at Lords in 1962.

42 Memorandum in the MCC archive at MCC/CRI/7/2/TEMP5.

by Grace's father, Bryan Isaac, was widely covered by the media. The papers informed their readers that, although the baby would be known as 'Jenny', her full name was Jane Katharine Stuart Sheppard.

Grace had grown in self-confidence during her pregnancy. She still made occasional visits to her consultant, and was unable to leave the house unaccompanied. But she contributed fully to activities at the centre, including leading the Girl Covenanter group which met in her home. She now understood her nervous illness to be a form of agoraphobia. She did not keep it a secret, but worked to ensure it did not affect the Mayflower's life and work. Both she and David valued the support of special friends at the centre, including Hilary Harman and one of the residents, Peter Harrison.[43]

David and Grace were keen to ensure Jenny fitted into the life of the Mayflower. She loved the buzz and noise of the centre, and there was no shortage of willing babysitters among the staff and residents. Even George Burton, who could be rude and insensitive towards Grace, delighted to entertain her daughter. Burton's flat was directly above the Sheppards', and Jenny routinely fell asleep to the sound of the pop records played by his teenage visitors. She attended the nursery school on site, going on later to nearby Hallsville Primary School. The school was close to Ronan Point, the tower block which partially collapsed in May 1968 following a gas explosion. Four people were killed, and the incident led to major changes to building regulations. In school as the building came down, Jenny and the other children were told to crouch under their desks.

*

A principle established at the Mayflower was that employees should take a few months' leave every three or four years. The Council hoped that sabbaticals would keep staff fresh and less likely to resign. Sheppard believed the challenges the Mayflower faced were more akin to those of a pioneer missionary situation overseas than regular parish work, and he

---

43 Sheppard, *An Aspect of Fear*, p. 10; Sheppard, G., *Living with Dying*, London: Darton, Longman & Todd, 2010, p. 15; correspondence with Ven. Peter Harrison.

wanted staff to be committed to the long haul. In his eleven years at the Mayflower, nine staff members stayed seven years or more.

Sheppard was due a sabbatical in 1962, for which he had plans: 'After much thought and prayer, it seemed right to make myself available for some cricket this summer and for the MCC tour to Australia and New Zealand which begins on 27 September', he told Log readers.[44] A further incentive to go to Australia was an invitation from the Archbishop of Sydney, his friend Hugh Gough, to spend time in the archdiocese when the cricket was over. He had realized, some years before, that the start of the tour would coincide with the seventh anniversary of his ordination. When a journalist suggested to him early in 1962 that he might go to Australia as captain, he gave the idea more serious consideration. Soon Fleet Street began to buzz, and when the chair of selectors, Walter Robins, heard of Sheppard's availability, he decided to act.

Sheppard's account of events suggests that, so remote was the idea of selection, he thought a message to ring back a 'Mr Robins' referred to a persistent caller to the Mayflower of that name he was in no hurry to see.[45] He put off the call but when he did ring Robins, he discovered he was not only in serious contention for a place on the tour, but the captaincy as well. 'If it's true that you are available for this tour', Sheppard recalls Robins saying, 'it's the best news I've heard for English cricket for a long time.'[46] MCC formally announced Sheppard's availability for the season and winter tour on 9 May.

It seems remarkable, from a twenty-first-century standpoint, that Sheppard should have figured in MCC's plans for the tour. Even in an age when amateurs would make known their availability to play, and counties would lay off a professional to facilitate that, to return after such a long absence was unusual. Sheppard's last Test innings had been in 1957, five years before, and he had played just ten first-class matches since. In 1961 he played no first-class cricket at all. Yet the selectors and majority of cricket writers welcomed his return to the game, even if it proved to be for one season. 'There is certainly no over-abundance of

---

44 'Log', Autumn 1962.

45 The Mayflower Council had, however, discussed the possibility of Sheppard's 'going to Australia to play cricket' in January; Council minutes 15 January 1962.

46 Sheppard, *Parson's Pitch*, pp. 188–9; Robins was also quoted in the press making this point.

class about', wrote E. W. Swanton, reflecting a widely held view.[47] The only notes of caution concerned Sheppard's fitness and his need to prove himself by scoring runs.

Behind the media excitement, the Sheppards had important issues to address. First, they had a newborn baby, who would be just six months old when the tour was due to depart. Second, since Sheppard had declared that he would not go to Australia alone, Grace would need to face the prospect of travelling to the other side of the world and back at a time when crossing the road was still a challenge. Third, the possibility of leaving the Mayflower for a year without its Skipper raised some tricky questions.

'As the summer wore on, the decision was made to make myself available for the cricket tour', Sheppard wrote.[48] He and Grace had 'gradually . . . come to the conviction that this is the right decision to make should I be selected', he told the press.[49] Grace recalls deciding to 'give it a go' and needing 'to look forward and face my fears'.[50] A crucial factor was Hilary Harman's decision to take her sabbatical and accompany Grace and Jenny. Sheppard asked supporters to pray for Grace 'for whom this is all a rather formidable adventure'.[51] He later said that, in withdrawing from the Mayflower for a year, and taking Grace and Jenny with him down under, he had 'never felt more sure of doing the right thing.'[52]

His sabbatical effectively began on 20 June when he played his first match of the season. Against an indifferent Oxford University attack, he hit 108 and 55, helping Sussex to a five-wicket win. With the exception of 95 and 60 against Northants, his scores in his next six games were more modest. A century on the first day of the Gentlemen versus Players fixture in July led to press speculation that he would be in the tour party to be named the next day. In this they were right, though their equally

47 Swanton, E. W., 'David Sheppard Decides to Make Come-back', *Daily Telegraph*, 10 May 1962.

48 Sheppard, *Steps along Hope Street*, p. 73;

49 Gomery, D., 'God – and the Man Fielding at Gully', *Daily Express*, 21 June 1962.

50 Sheppard, *Living with Dying*, p. 16; Sheppard, *An Aspect of Fear*, p. 11.

51 'Log', Autumn 1962.

52 Sheppard, *Parson's Pitch*, p. 189.

confident predictions that he would be appointed captain proved wide of the mark.

The question of the captaincy had provoked much discussion in the press and cricket's corridors of power. Sheppard, Ted Dexter and Colin Cowdrey were all believed to be in contention, though the extent to which Sheppard was seriously considered has been a matter of conjecture. Sheppard's recollection is that Robins 'virtually offered me the captaincy over the phone before the season started'. He thought Robins led him in other ways to believe the job was his, including seeking his assurance that he would not criticize the Australian government's 'White Australia' immigration policy, which effectively barred people of non-European descent from immigrating. Sheppard gave this assurance, saying that Australia's policy could not be compared to apartheid since it did not allow selection for the national side on grounds of colour.[53] Another view is that Robins strung Sheppard along about the captaincy.[54] Unlike Dexter and Cowdrey, he was not trialled as captain in the home series that summer.

In the end the lot fell upon Dexter for the tour. MCC may have wondered whether Sheppard would be able to command the full backing of the other players, given his long absence from the game. Robins made it known that he wanted a captain committed to 'brighter cricket', and able to deal with the media as cleverly as the Australian skipper, Richie Benaud. On both counts the selectors might have thought Dexter a better choice than either Cowdrey or Sheppard. Sheppard might have felt a sense of *déjà vu* at having been touted for the captaincy of an Ashes tour yet ultimately passed over. One difference from 1954 was that this time he did not hear the news officially but from the press.

Once in the squad, Sheppard was selected for the final two Tests of the summer against Pakistan. Batting at number 1, a position he had not filled at Test level for nine years, he notched up 83, 57 and 9 not out. Between the Tests he continued to play for Sussex, and in 14 matches that

---

53 Steen, R., *This Sporting Life: Cricket*, Newton Abbot: David & Charles, 1999, p. 40. Some commentators believe this issue was decisive in ruling him out of the captaincy; see Simon Wilde, *England: The Biography*, London: Simon & Schuster, 2018, pp. 240–1.

54 Synge, A., *Sins of Omission: The Story of the Test Selectors 1899–1990*, London: Pelham, 1990, pp. 136–8.

season scored 1,017 runs at 44.21. He finished eleventh in the national averages. In the field his record was less impressive, though something of his former brilliance returned in the Gentlemen versus Players match when he took a sharp chance at backward short leg to dismiss Peter Parfitt. Parfitt later told him that, when he returned to the dressing-room, his captain Fred Trueman tried to console him with the thought that 'the Reverend has more chance than most of us when he puts his hands together'. Trueman later liked to turn this quote around, joking that when the Reverend dropped a catch off his bowling, he would tell him, 'Kid yourself it's Sunday, Rev, and keep your hands together.'[55]

*

The tour was a mixed one for Sheppard. In terms of the cricket, he was selected for all eight Tests, five in Australia and three in New Zealand. His highpoint came in the Second Test at Melbourne, where his century in the second innings helped England to a seven-wicket victory. Having reached 113, he was run out going for the winning run. He was one of four batsmen to score 1,000 runs in all matches on the tour. The Third Test against New Zealand at Lancaster Park, Christchurch, in which he scored 42 and 31, was his last first-class match. But his fielding was often below par, and the number of catches he dropped troubled many who remembered him as one of the safest close fielders in the country. Some blamed the number of speaking and media engagements he took on between matches.[56]

With invaluable support from Hilary Harman, Grace managed the tour well. Sailing from Tilbury at the end of November, she, Jenny and Hilary arrived in Adelaide in time to spend Christmas with David. Grace saw David's century at Melbourne on 3 January,[57] and while he

---

55 Sheppard, *Parson's Pitch*, p. 192. Trueman and Sheppard were good friends, and Trueman had a sincere Christian faith; Waters, C., *Fred Trueman: The authorised biography*, London: Aurum Press, 2011, pp. 167, 289. I am grateful to Philip Booth for alerting me to these references.

56 See for example Wellings, E. M., *Dexter v Benaud: M.C.C. Tour Australia 1962–3*, Folkestone: Bailey Bros & Swinfen, 1963, p. 161; Fingleton, J., 'This was a cricket tour we all want to forget', *Sunday Times*, 24 February 1963. It was Wellings who first suggested to Sheppard he make himself available for the tour.

57 Jenny became unsettled as her father approached his century and Grace had to miss the hundredth run.

continued with the tour, she, Jenny and Hilary moved into rented accommodation in Killara on Sydney's Upper North Shore. While the UK was experiencing one of the coldest winters on record, and letters from home shared news of snow and frozen pipes, the trio enjoyed Sydney's hottest February since 1939. David re-joined them in mid March, immediately after the New Zealand leg of the tour, and Hilary left in the April. Grace, David and Jenny then stayed in Killara until early July, enjoying a warm welcome from the neighbourhood.[58]

Sheppard proved popular as a speaker during the tour. Cathedrals in most of the cities the party visited invited him into their pulpit, and he preached to full houses.[59] He once referred to 'vast congregations waiting breathlessly for what I had to say' during the tour, although the reasons for such anticipation could be mixed. In Adelaide three members of the congregation held a sweep on the length of his sermon, with Colin Cowdrey defeating *The Times* reporter John Woodcock and BBC commentator Brian Johnston. Suspense was maintained throughout. 'I had taken my stopwatch with me', Johnston recounted,

and there was great excitement as [Sheppard] approached the various targets. He had a habit of pausing so that it seemed as if he had finished and once I was about to pay out to John Woodcock when David suddenly went off on another tack and did another four minutes.[60]

At the service in Melbourne, the lessons were read by Cowdrey and another of Sheppard's friends, Australian batsman Brian Booth. Cowdrey and Sheppard shared times of prayer and Bible-reading during the tour.

Sheppard's capacity to draw large crowds was evident during his post-tour stay in Sydney. A youth rally in the Town Hall attracted 5,000 young people, and an evangelistic 'Sportsman's service' in Hurstville was well attended. Here he was joined again by Booth, and

---

58 I am grateful to Lesley Sanders for allowing me access to her step-mother Hilary Harman's diaries for the trip.

59 Sundays were then observed as rest days in first-class cricket.

60 Johnston, Brian (ed. Johnston, Barry), *A Delicious Slice of Johnners*, London: Virgin, 2001, p. 132.

by the Australian fast bowler, Alan Davidson. Sheppard's schedule included a fortnight of industrial rallies organized by a church in Redfern, and talks to businessmen, the Mothers' Union, school-children and university students. On Easter Day he preached at Long Bay Penitentiary in the morning and Sydney Cathedral in the evening, the latter using its chapter house as an overflow.[61] He spent time in inner-city parishes in Sydney, finding similar challenges to those in Canning Town.

*

The Sheppards returned to the Mayflower on 22 July 1963, thirteen months after David began his quest for England selection. They had stayed in contact by exchanging letters and cassette tapes, then something of a novelty, though not all the communication had been social. George Burton had found the absence of one of his two main props traumatic. He thought Sheppard being on sabbatical in a different hemisphere no reason for him to leave his senior youth leader unsupported. Burton threatened suicide when Jean Lodge Patch, whom he saw as his other prop, announced she would be leaving the Mayflower to care for her father. As he had often done in person, Sheppard encouraged Burton by letter and phone throughout his absence.

Burton enjoyed wielding power in Skipper's absence. He took the opportunity to review aspects of the centre's work and oversee improve-ments to the premises. Sheppard thought tensions might arise when he took back the reins, and shrewdly gave Burton extra powers on his return. He was appointed Deputy Warden and given oversight of every aspect of the youth work. This included the power to disband the uniformed groups he so disliked.

Shortly after his return, Sheppard tackled some questions about the Mayflower in the Log, raised by some supporters. Its 'large numbers of young people' and 'free and easy atmosphere' were leading to 'false conclusions about we stand for', Sheppard noted, and he explained

---

61 I am grateful to Brian Booth for sharing his memories of these events with me, and to Ronald Cardwell and Hugh Griffiths for helping research details of Sheppard's activities in Sydney.

that its context shaped the Mayflower's approach. Conversion to Christ in Canning Town did not mean adopting 'traditions, disciplines and behaviour' appropriate for Christians in other cultures; the centre was 'presenting Christ', not a 'new law which all must observe'. 'Unjudging friendship' was important. Respect for others 'involves putting up with standards of behaviour which would not necessarily be our own', while not abandoning our God-given ideals. People were encouraged to make 'a decisive commitment to Christ', but this would happen in God's time and as bridges of friendship were built. People were lost when they were hurried on 'before they are ready.' There was a conscious dependency 'on the wisdom and power of the Holy Spirit' who 'may call us to rethink much that we do,' Sheppard explained, but there was no 'method for our work which will always bring God's blessing.'[62]

Sheppard updated readers on numbers at the centre. More than 130 young people belonged to the groups meeting in staff members' flats, and the majority had made 'a definite profession of faith in Christ'. Since the Mayflower opened, 97 people had been confirmed, all making 'a personal commitment of themselves to Christ'. From just six regular communicants at the outset, and 20 adults in church for a special occasion, Sunday evening congregations were now between 100 and 150. Two-thirds of those attending were aged between 13 and 23. Around 520 people attended regular activities at the centre in any one week, with 300 more dropping in occasionally. More than 30 of the young people who met with George Burton and others were involved in running groups or clubs, replacing leaders imported from outside.

Particularly satisfying to Sheppard and Burton was the emergence of people with potential for leadership within the Church. These included Jim Gosling, Len Howell and Ted Lyons, all converted through the Mayflower. Encouraged by Burton and Sheppard, they enrolled on a lay reader's course. Lyons, a former gang leader, and Gosling went on to further study and ordination. Sheppard believed that developing local leadership involved overcoming 'the hurdle of self-confidence', and he did the course alongside them. Lyons, who eventually became an honorary canon of Coventry Cathedral, and Gosling, who served parishes in Essex,

---

62 'Log', Winter 1963.

Kent and Devon, both considered such careers had been unthinkable for them and their families before Burton and Sheppard planted the idea. Another of Burton's Sunday Group protégés, Bill Turner, later became senior youth leader at the Mayflower, the first local person appointed to the staff. Sheppard considered the growth in self-confidence among the Mayflower's young people, many of whom received little encouragement to achieve elsewhere, a truer measure of its success than any numerical growth.

An important step towards the establishment of an 'indigenous church' was taken in 1967 with the formation of the Mayflower Committee. Elected by and from members of the church, this was to manage all the centre's activities and make decisions in key policy areas. Hitherto these decisions had been taken by the Council, whose members represented the national denominations. Announcing this transition, Sheppard said the centre had decided to wait before setting up the Committee until there were at least twice as many Christians capable of serving on it as were needed. It was vital to prevent the situation where people remained on the committee for life, and a system of enforced retirement after three years was established.[63]

*

Spring 1964 saw the publication of Sheppard's first book, *Parson's Pitch*.[64] Begun on the voyage home from Australia, and completed in the following three months, Sheppard wanted it to reflect 'a Christian trying to work out his faith in the worlds of cricket and in ministry in East London.'[65] Stories from St Mary's and the Mayflower, and explanations of his beliefs, rubbed shoulders with anecdotes about innings he had played and cricketers he knew. In a chapter entitled 'Questions which hurt', he consciously wove together the ethical and sporting strands of the book. The questions were sporting links with South Africa, the amateur–professional distinction, and sport on Sundays.

---

63 'Log,' Spring 1967; *Christians in Industrial Areas*, 10 January 1969, p. 2.
64 Sheppard, *Parson's Pitch*.
65 Sheppard, *Steps along Hope Street*, p. 77.

The publishers invested heavily in the book. They had been pressing him to write for several years and paid an advance above average for a young new author. Their faith was rewarded, with 14,000 copies selling in the first six months. Serialization in the *Sunday Telegraph* and *Woman's Own* brought it to a wider readership, although Sheppard was disappointed that the *Telegraph* rejected his request to include the account of his conversion. Whether the book would have sold so well under its working title, 'God and the Man in the Gully', must remain conjecture.[66]

Reviews of the book were mixed. The Christian press saw its potential to reach cricket enthusiasts with the gospel, and veteran cricket writers Jim Swanton and Gerard Martineau both welcomed it. Other reviewers found the writing 'flat' and the juxtaposition of the 'religious' and 'sporting' material uneven. In an incisive review the Revd Nicholas Stacey, who knew of Sheppard's work at the Mayflower first-hand, regretted the author's failure to 'open himself up' in the way that he felt writers of autobiographies ought to be prepared to do. The inner turmoil Sheppard must have experienced at key moments in his life was either unacknowledged or treated superficially. 'There is a great deal about the pitch and very little about the parson', Stacey concluded. Sheppard had spoken in the book of the danger of hiding one's feelings, and how being open with one other 'leads to more real relationships between people.'[67]

Another bestseller from the Mayflower followed, George Burton's *People Matter More Than Things*.[68] This was a lively apologia for the author's approach to youth work. The title conveyed his conviction that winning souls for Christ must outweigh all other considerations. In his 'Introduction', Sheppard praised his colleague's 'exceptional gifts' as a leader and youth worker. Carefully choosing his words, he spoke of Burton's 'highly individual' approach to youth leadership and critical stance towards other Christian methods. He was thankful for Burton's

---

66 This may have been inspired by the title of a piece by Donald Gomery in the *Daily Express* in 1962.

67 Stacey, N., 'David Sheppard has me stumped', *Daily Herald*, 8 June 1964; Sheppard, *Parson's Pitch*, p. 30.

68 Burton, G., *People Matter More Than Things*, London: Hodder & Stoughton, 1965. Burton lived with a distrust of his own ability to write (though he had learnt to speak Arabic fluently while living in the Middle East). He relied heavily on help from others when preparing the text, including Jean Lodge Patch and Mayflower residents David Hewitt, Ian Elliott and John Parker.

'clear-sightedness which sometimes pursues our vision with a streak of ruthlessness'.[69] The book made a huge impact. Within eight months of publication it underwent its fourth printing.

The Mayflower also produced a series of booklets for young people at the request of Scripture Union. In drafting them, Sheppard drew on more than 40 hours of recorded discussion involving members of George Burton's 'Sunday Group'. Ted Lyons and Vic Mead, both talented artists involved with the group, produced high quality drawings and cartoons to accompany the text. Sheppard thought the booklets, entitled 'Arguing', 'Belonging', 'Loving' and 'Working', suitable for young people accustomed to reading the *Daily Mirror*. The London *Evening News* commended Sheppard for using 'very "with it" production techniques'.

*

In October 1965, Grace underwent surgery for ovarian cancer. She had begun to experience discomfort during a holiday with David in the summer, so when her pain increased and appendicitis was suspected, she went for exploratory tests at the London Hospital in Whitechapel Road.[70] These revealed not a burst appendix but a highly developed tumour, requiring immediate surgery. While she was under anaesthetic, David was also out of contact, driving Jenny to stay with his mother in Sussex. The surgeons had to make the decision, as a life-saving measure, to remove both the tumour and Grace's ovaries. A week later the diagnosis of cancer was confirmed, and Grace and David were told the full extent of the surgery.

For some weeks it was uncertain whether Grace would survive. Her surgeon would only give her a 50–50 chance, and she saw the other four women on her ward die from their cancers. 'There is no end to my gratitude for the gift of life', she wrote of this experience. She recalled how her husband's daily visits helped her find the courage to face her fears, and his being her 'rock' in a time of crisis.[71] Sheppard recalled feeling 'the

---

69 'Introduction', Burton, *People Matter More Than Things*, p. 13.
70 This was the hospital where she had given birth to Jenny three years before. It became the Royal London in 1990.
71 Sheppard, *Living with Dying*, p. 17; Sheppard, *An Aspect of Fear*, p. 16.

weaker partner' at the time, and 'needing to be strengthened by the patient ... I felt resigned to loss, not knowing what God was doing with us', he wrote.[72] Visits from three-year-old Jenny, sometimes sporting a nurse's outfit, stethoscope and doctor's bag, also gave Grace the will to survive.

As well as coming to terms with all that had happened, David and Grace had two profound challenges to face. One was the prospect of months of radiotherapy and convalescence, including further periods in hospital. The other was the impossibility of having further children. Five years later they considered adopting a child, but after exploring the idea with Jenny they decided not to proceed.

*

Illness hit the Mayflower a few months later when George Burton contracted what he was told was bronchial asthma. He was admitted to hospital, where doctors discovered an aggressive tumour and removed his left lung. He returned to work, but in the August, while on holiday in Switzerland, he caught pneumonia and died. He was just 51. The gap he left at the Mayflower was immense.

Sheppard was unwilling to allow all that Burton had achieved to die with him. He took on the role of youth leader himself, despite his lack of experience and the other demands on his time. He said he found leading the Mayflower's youth work 'the most demanding and emotionally exhausting task' he had ever undertaken, although it deepened his understanding of the young people he wanted to reach.[73] Burton was eventually replaced, a year later, by John Roberts, a youth worker from Birkenhead. Sheppard met Roberts at a conference and invited him to work at the Mayflower.

*

Throughout Sheppard's time at the Mayflower, a constant source of concern was finance. Expenditure significantly exceeded income in

---

72 Sheppard, D. S., and Worlock, D., *With Hope in Our Hearts,* London: Darton, Longman & Todd, 1994, p. 104.

73 Sheppard, *Steps along Hope Street,* pp. 64–5.

four of his first five years as warden. The centre often carried overdrafts of several thousand pounds, significant sums for the time.[74] The level of donations from supporters seldom met expectations, and only a quarter of the 5,000 people receiving the Log sent money. The centre stayed afloat through grants from trusts and charities, legacies, and anonymous donations, the latter usually arriving at particular moments of crisis.

Sheppard's renown accounted for much of the Mayflower's income. His personal reputation inspired many to give, and he spoke at dinners and events which generated support. He also encouraged his high-profile friends and contacts to take an interest in the centre. Among those who visited the Mayflower were Viscount Montgomery, Peter Sellers, Richard Attenborough and Cliff Richard. Sheppard received help in kind from his mother, who would spend time on her visits hand-sewing the enormous church curtains. In addition he contributed to the work himself, as the Council discovered when it insisted on knowing the source of the anonymous donations being offered to the centre.[75] Sheppard spoke regularly of God blessing the Mayflower financially, but the absence of a sustainable funding strategy had serious implications. It meant that the centre largely survived on a hand-to-mouth basis. More significantly, it undermined Sheppard's intent to establish a fully indigenous church. He worked tirelessly to develop a local leadership, but appears never to have tried to make the centre's ministry locally financed, thereby leaving problems for his successors.[76]

*

By 1968, Sheppard had fulfilled his commitment to serve ten years at the Mayflower. He and Grace planned another year-long sabbatical

---

74 On two occasions, October 1961 and October 1963, Council minutes record the overdraft as £4,000.

75 Council minutes, 4 October 1960.

76 Steve Griffiths argues that the people of Canning Town could never have raised the money needed to maintain the Mayflower's ministry (unpublished mss). I am grateful to Dr Griffiths for allowing me to draw on his research. When the Mayflower was in difficulties after he left, Sheppard wrote suggesting it sell some of its assets: letter dated 26 April 1971, SHP, 28.3.

to recharge their batteries, but in the October, he was asked by the Bishop of Southwark, Mervyn Stockwood, to become suffragan bishop of Woolwich in succession to John Robinson. The idea of a radical change of direction took hold.

Sheppard could point to progress on many fronts at the Mayflower. Christian homes had been established in the neighbourhood, and a church under local oversight was taking root. He believed God would sustain the centre once he left, comparing his situation to that of St Paul, who left the church at Ephesus he had laboured to build in the hands of local elders (Acts 20.17f). The apostle 'was sure that God was calling him to move on; therefore he believed that God would make His own provision for the work he was leaving behind.'[77]

Sheppard knew that the Mayflower was a pioneer in seeking to make an impact for Christ in the inner city. 'I sometimes have the impression that many Christians regard a work like ours as an interesting experiment on the fringe – if not "beyond the fringe" – of the Church's work', he once said.[78] He was disappointed at how few Christians were engaging with urban areas, despite the gospel's call to bring good news to the poor. As he later wrote, 'The Church's life in big cities has been marked by its inability to establish a strong, locally rooted Christian presence among the groups that society leaves without voice or power.'[79]

He saw the value of working with others who had similar concerns, creating opportunities for mutual support and sharing resources. Initiatives such as the Frontier Youth Trust (FYT) and *Christians in Industrial Areas* stemmed from his work at the Mayflower. Established in 1964, the FYT linked people who saw 'youth clubs as a sphere of Christian service.'[80] 'Frontier' reflected how members saw the nature of their mission, to reach young people 'who do not easily fit into church life' but who were 'important to God [and] valued by Him.'[81] Describing itself as a 'correspondence', *Christians in Industrial Areas* was a newsletter, founded by Sheppard with Ted Roberts and Eddie

---

77 'Log', Spring 1969.
78 'Log', Autumn 1963.
79 Sheppard, *Built as a City*, p. 11.
80 This was the title of the series of conferences which inspired FYT.
81 Speech at an event marking the Jubilee of the FYT, 18 January 1989: SHP, 16.2.

Neale. Produced on a Roneo duplicator, it provided space for evangelical Christians engaged in mission in the city, new housing estates and industry to share experiences and reflections. Many of its subscribers worked in isolation and valued the fellowship they found through its articles and correspondence.

The Sheppards also brought together a more informal group of clergy couples concerned for the church's ministry among urban communities. Calling itself 'The Eastenders', the group included Ted and Audrey Roberts, then at Bethnal Green. Like Sheppard, Roberts believed that working-class people were best equipped to lead the Church in working-class areas. He pioneered a scheme which trained local men to be priests in his own inner-city parishes.

Sheppard also learned the value of working with Christians beyond evangelical Anglicanism, including in the Catholic and Free Church traditions. Among those he counted as 'friends and allies' in east London were a Franciscan, Brother Bernard, and the Baptist minister, Colin Marchant. He found a kindred spirit in the well-known Anglo-Catholic priest, John Groser, who served for more than 40 years in the East End of London. What was important was that they 'had the heart of the matter in Christ and an openness to people and their needs.'[82]

*

Colin Marchant, who would serve in Newham for more than 50 years, wrote that Sheppard did much for east London, 'but East London did more for David Sheppard'.[83] Sheppard described his time at the Mayflower as 'like a second conversion – conversion to Christ in the city'.[84] It laid important foundations for his future work, not only by giving him an understanding of the inner city and what God was doing there, but by challenging him to consider the wider implications of the gospel. 'I was totally green politically – pietist in my Evangelical faith', Sheppard said about his first years at the Mayflower. 'Gradually I realized that loving

---

82 Sheppard, *Steps along Hope Street*, pp. 71, 78. Letter dated 28 April 1997: SHP, 5.14
83 'Remembering David Sheppard: East London 1958–1969', *Urban Bulletin*, Spring/Summer 2005, p. 8.
84 Sheppard, *Steps along Hope Street*, p. 2.

individuals would not shift some of their greatest needs unless the structures of society were attended to also.'[85]

Sheppard's political education continued in the next phase of his life, though not, at first, because of his new role within the church. As a bishop, he would often be accused of 'mixing politics with religion'. As he moved to take up his first episcopal post, he was embroiled in one of the longest and most renowned sporting controversies of all time.

---

85 'Going to the Mayflower', unpublished essay, June 1998.

8
Woolwich
(1969–1975)

Mervyn Stockwood credited an unlikely source for inspiring him to invite David Sheppard to become Bishop of Woolwich. 'For several weeks I wrestled with the problem of a successor [to John Robinson]', Stockwood wrote in the London *Evening Standard* in February 1969. 'Curiously enough, Enoch Powell was responsible for my choice, David Sheppard.' Stockwood believed that Powell's comments, in his so-called 'rivers of blood' speech about immigration the previous April, had led to racial tension in the diocese. Sheppard, he thought, could help to heal them. Sheppard had recently argued that if a whites-only South African cricket team toured the UK, race relations in south London would suffer. 'I was determined to appoint a suffragan bishop who, uncompromising on the race issue, would be a friend and pastor to all', Stockwood wrote. 'That's why my mind turned to David Sheppard.'[1]

Stockwood had known of Sheppard for a while, and they had met shortly after his appointment to Southwark in 1959. Stockwood thought then that Sheppard would make a good suffragan if a vacancy ever came up.[2] He liked to appoint people who were able and gifted and would help to put the diocese on the map, and would also have wanted to reach out to the growing evangelical constituency in his diocese. Sheppard would have struck him as having the right background, and commitment to the traditions of the church, to do that. Sheppard was a kindred spirit on inner-city deprivation, the iniquity of racism, and the

1 Stockwood, M., 'The Day I Decided: that chap should be a bishop!', *Evening Standard*, 24 February 1969, p. 11.
2 *Southwark News*, May 1975, p. 1. Sheppard's first contact with Stockwood was when the bishop had to 'tick him off' for conducting the wedding of friends in a Baptist church in Southwark diocese, Irene and John Perry.

social justice dimension of the gospel. But on one issue they would have to differ. 'Cricket was a priority in the curriculum', Stockwood said of his schooldays, '[but] I loathed the game and was bored to desperation. When I nominated David Sheppard . . . to be my Suffragan Bishop of Woolwich, I told him it was the most generous act of forgiveness in my life!'[3]

*

Sheppard followed his usual practice when faced with a big decision. There were walks with God, this time by the Firth of Forth, where the family had taken an extended holiday in lieu of their planned sabbatical. He employed the Appreciation of the Situation programme he had learned in the army and filled a notebook deliberating on this in the final weeks of 1968. He weighed up continuing at the Mayflower. Was it now God's time to move? The church there is 'a reality – if a wobbly one', he wrote. 'It could be a good moment to leave.' He considered the relative merits of the Mayflower and Woolwich in the light of his calling to be a 'popular communicator' of the Gospel. 'M has been a wonderful platform for this. I suppose that W will be more so.' He was concerned about the impact the move would have on Jenny's schooling and friendships, and reflected on his understanding of the 'visible Church'. If we believe it is 'part of Christ's church & one of His vehicles we must want to make it more effective. So some of us must sometime be prepared to work from within the Est[ablishment].'[4]

Grace was initially excited by the invitation, seeing it as recognition of David's work in east London and believing he had been clearly called. But as with the move to the Mayflower, she experienced apprehension about her new role and a feeling of unworthiness. 'I was sure that David could do the job, but equally sure that I was unsuitable', she reflected. 'I felt woefully inadequate.'[5]

---

3 Stockwood, M., *Chanctonbury Ring: An Autobiography*, London: Hodder & Stoughton, 1982, p. 11.

4 'Notebook 1968': Sheppard papers (SHP), 53.2; draft of Sheppard, D. S. *Steps along Hope Street*, London: Hodder & Stoughton, 2002: SHP, 44.6.

5 Sheppard, G., *An Aspect of Fear*, London: Darton, Longman & Todd, 1989, pp. 18–19.

There were new issues for Grace to confront this time. These included the higher public profile involved in David being a bishop, and the ceremonial aspects of the job. 'I had a dread of pomposity', she later wrote. 'Coming from an evangelical background where church worship was simple and ordinary, I found it hard to imagine being married to someone who would be dressed in scarlet and purple in the name of the Christian Church.'[6]

*

Sheppard knew where he wanted to live as Bishop of Woolwich. 'We must live in a working-class district and have continuing contact with our imm[ediate] area', he wrote in his notebook. He would 'lose his usefulness' if he were cut off from working-class life. His predecessor had occupied a six-bedroomed detached house in fashionable Blackheath. Sheppard believed he could not serve as bishop to the inner-city parishes of south-east London from such a base. He would buy his own house in the 'inner ring', in the boroughs of Southwark or Lambeth. The diocese raised objections, but eventually conceded. Sheppard later said that the job only became possible when he realized he could live in a working-class area and not Blackheath.[7] He had feared becoming a 'church bureaucrat' and losing the closeness to his neighbours he had enjoyed at the Mayflower.

The Sheppards bought 12 Asylum Road, Peckham, a four-storey terraced house set back from the road with a substantial rear garden. The former home of a doctor, it was not typical of the neighbourhood. Elsewhere in the street were derelict properties, including a large area due for demolition under what was known as slum clearance. Sheppard needed office space for himself and a secretary in addition to accommodation for the family. They moved in on 29 August 1969 after a caravan holiday on the continent. The day before, the council began digging up the road outside, so access to the house was via wooden planks across a large hole, hardly ideal for the removers. Living across the road was

---

6 Sheppard, *An Aspect of Fear*, pp. 20–1.

7 'A Most Unusual Bishop', *Woman's Own*, 18 October 1969, p. 55. The term 'inner ring' had been used by Stanley Evans to refer to an area of south London characterised by poverty.

Christopher Idle, curate of Christ Church in the Old Kent Road. Idle rang Sheppard to ask if he wanted to postpone the move. 'We're coming anyway', Sheppard replied.

*

Christ Church might have expected the Sheppards to join their number. It was close and decidedly evangelical. Instead they based themselves at their parish church, St John Chrysostom, which was firmly Anglo-Catholic.[8] Sheppard was away most Sundays on parish visits, but Grace and Jenny worshipped at St John's and Grace joined the Parochial Church Council.

Grace continued to battle with her agoraphobia. At the Mayflower, she and David had shared their lives with 30 other people around the clock. Now, with David out most of the day and Jenny at school, the new house felt empty, and her nervous condition accentuated her isolation. Every attempt to leave the house was a challenge. Eventually she found the courage to open the front door and sweep the front step, and from this humble beginning, she began to build friendships with neighbours, sometimes inviting them in for tea. A friend gave her a Morris 1100, which proved a lifeline. She always felt safer driving than she did walking, even when going to the local shops. In time she became involved in local activities, in part motivated by a need for community. She joined a group which restored a terrace of Victorian houses in Asylum Road for use by local people, and became a governor at the comprehensive school across the road from their house. On one occasion she was introduced by the chair of governors to a candidate for a teaching post as 'Mrs Bishop, the wife of the famous footballer.'

Grace excelled as a homemaker. Although she found going out difficult, she turned 12 Asylum Road into a place people loved to visit. She and David frequently hosted parties for which she did the catering. Sometimes they would mix VIPs and ordinary folk in equal measure. Invitees' names would be displayed to facilitate networking. The piano

---

8 The reasons for their choice are unclear, but they may have thought St John's more suitable for Jenny. Nor, apparently, did Sheppard think highly of the vicar of Christ Church, Eustace Davis.

was at the heart of the home, with Grace playing duets and singing with musical friends. She described these parties as among her happiest experiences, and establishing a beautiful and well-stocked garden also brought her much satisfaction.

David and Grace met with a group of friends for mutual support, valuing the opportunity to discuss issues unrelated to work in an atmosphere of trust. Among the group were other couples pioneering new Christian work, including Judy and Geoffrey Grimes and George and Pauline Hoffman. Hoffman had founded the evangelical aid agency, Tearfund, in 1968, and the Grimes ran a project in Peckham called 'Greenhouse'. This worked with young people and their families in need, most of whom were referred by the social services department. Ted and Susan Dexter also belonged to the group, though later said that they 'never felt quite comfortable . . . I suppose mine was an old fashioned "muscular" Christianity which did not involve too much soul-searching,' Dexter recalled.[9]

Jenny, now seven, was enrolled at a primary school across the Old Kent Road. Leaving her school in Canning Town had not been a wrench, as all her class moved on that year, but she did not settle easily into the new one. The school was on a large housing estate, where almost all the pupils lived. For most of her second year she was bullied by a group of girls. Grace only learned of this when the ringleader phoned the house threatening to strangle their cat. Jenny convinced her parents not to involve the school and to let her overcome it by herself. Grace's illness meant she often asked friends to take Jenny to and from school.

For Jenny's secondary education, her parents chose a local state school in preference to one of the independent schools in the area. Sheppard's mother and sister had assumed Jenny would go to Sherborne. Perhaps recalling his own experience as a child, Sheppard told an interviewer that it would 'take an earthquake' for him and Grace to send Jenny to boarding school 'because it would dislocate her from home.' The decision was consistent with Sheppard's desire to identify with their local neighbourhood, although he thought it wrong to make children 'pawns in the education game'.[10]

---

9 Correspondence with the author. Other members were Iona and Mark Birchall and Jennet and John Kidd.

10 'A Most Unusual Bishop', pp. 56, 59.

Jenny was one of two girls from her year who passed the eleven-plus, and the school she moved to was Haberdashers' Aske's Grammar School, the state school for girls in New Cross, a short bus ride away.

*

Sheppard was consecrated Bishop Suffragan of Woolwich by Archbishop Michael Ramsey in Southwark Cathedral on St Luke's Day, 18 October 1969. He was just 40 and had been ordained 14 years. He invited a wide circle of friends, and obtained permission from Ramsey for members of non-Anglican churches to receive communion. Demand for tickets was high, with readers of *Woman's Own* keen to see the columnist they read every week become a bishop. Like the announcement of Sheppard's appointment, the service was widely covered by the media. Sheppard chose a friend from Iwerne days, Michael Green, to preach. Green said Sheppard's evangelicalism should shape his ministry. An evangelical believes in conversion, in Christ's death for sinners, and in the Scriptures: 'This is your Evangelical emphasis. Do not be shy of it: do not water it down. People need it: indeed, many will look to you to provide it.' He went on to predict that Sheppard would be more radical than his predecessor, John Robinson. Robinson had become well known while at Woolwich, first for arguing in court that the novel, *Lady Chatterley's Lover*, should not be censored, and then for his own book, *Honest to God*.[11] Published in 1963, this called for a non-metaphysical understanding of God, God as 'the ground of all being' rather than an entity 'out there'. Robinson's status as an Anglican bishop made the book newsworthy, but Green saw Sheppard as more truly radical, holding as he did to 'a biblical Christianity' which challenges a person 'to the very roots of his being'.

*

Robinson was not the only reason for Southwark's fame. Stockwood wanted to bring the church alongside working people, and had drawn together a team of clergy and laypeople willing to experiment with

---

11 Robinson, J. A. T., *Honest to God*, London: SCM Press, 1963.

new ideas and practices. The diocese became known in the 1960s for promoting not only liberal expressions of the faith and radical thinking about moral questions, but innovative patterns of church life and ministry, and new approaches to liturgy, church music and church design. 'South Bank Religion', as this movement became known, kept Southwark in the public eye, something Stockwood maintained by his imaginative appointments.[12] Sheppard's media profile made him, in that sense, a natural choice for Stockwood, though he did not fit the 'South Bank' mould in his theology and more conservative views on social issues and morality. Other notable appointments Stockwood made were Eric James as vicar of Camberwell, Nicholas Stacey as Rector of Woolwich, Donald Reeves as Vicar of St Helier and Hugh Montefiore as suffragan Bishop of Kingston. James became a trusted friend of David and Grace, and an influential figure in the ministry of the church in the inner city.

*

Sheppard's media standing could hardly have been higher when Stockwood approached him. At the time he was heavily involved in a cricketing controversy which had spread from the back pages of the press to the front. The 'D'Oliveira affair', as the episode became known, was dividing not only the cricketing world but the nation. Sheppard was in the headlines almost daily.

The issue centred on the selection of the party to tour South Africa during the winter of 1968–9. The selection was made in late August 1968, following the final Test of the summer against Australia. What sparked the controversy was the initial omission from the squad of the Worcestershire all-rounder, Basil D'Oliveira. D'Oliveira's form on the previous winter tour to the West Indies had been disappointing, and his behaviour off the field had prompted criticism, but he had performed well in the summer series against Australia, and in the final Test had scored 158 under considerable pressure. Many were convinced this innings merited him a place on the tour, and his omission provoked an

---

12 Bogle, J., *South Bank Religion: The Diocese of Southwark 1959–1969*, London: Hatcham Press, 2002, p. 14.

outcry in the media. The question being asked was, had he been excluded because there were other players more deserving, or had his status as a Cape Coloured South African been a factor?

D'Oliveira had left his native South Africa in 1960 to play first-class cricket in England, an opportunity denied him under apartheid. In 1966 he was selected for the England side, and became a regular in the team. The impending tour of South Africa brought to a head the question of whether, if selected, he would be accepted in his homeland. South Africa's policy was not to allow what it called 'mixed teams' to play against its own white team at home. The selectors said that D'Oliveira had been considered solely as a batsman, and there were stronger candidates, and they had rejected the option to take him as an all-rounder in favour of including the medium-pace bowler, Tom Cartwright. But few people in the media believed D'Oliveira had been omitted for cricketing reasons: the assumption was that MCC had acted in the knowledge, or belief, that if they included D'Oliveira, the South African government would call off the tour.[13]

Sheppard thought MCC should have obtained a commitment from the South African authorities in advance that any team it selected would be accepted, raising the issue both as a member of MCC's Cricket Committee and later in print. As soon as he heard the news that D'Oliveira had been left out, he decided to find out what had happened.

Sheppard discovered that MCC had written to the South African Cricket Association (SACA) on 5 January 1968, asking for confirmation that 'no pre-conditions will be laid on the selection of the MCC team' for the tour. He also learnt that a former president of MCC, Charles Lyttelton, had met with the South African Prime Minister, B. J. Vorster, in March. Lyttelton, the tenth Viscount Cobham, told Sheppard he had asked Vorster directly whether D'Oliveira would be acceptable if selected. Vorster replied that he would not.[14] Cobham did not formally notify the MCC Committee of his conversation with Vorster. Instead, he told one

---

13 Mike Brearley was told in 2018 that the selectors *did* pick D'Oliveira but MCC exercised its power of veto and reversed the decision: Brearley, M., *On Cricket*, London: Constable, 2018, pp. 138f.

14 Steen, R., *This Sporting Life: Cricket*, Newton Abbot: David & Charles, 1999, p. 37; Sheppard, D. S., *Steps along Hope Street*, London: Hodder & Stoughton, 2002, p. 86. Cobham invited Sheppard to stay at his seat in Worcestershire: letter dated 4 September 1968: SHP, 15.2.

Committee member,[15] who then informed the secretary, Billy Griffith. Possibly only two other people at MCC, the president Arthur Gilligan and treasurer Gubby Allen, knew before the tour party was chosen of Cobham's conversation with Vorster. Allen, Gilligan and Griffith were all in the room when the selectors met to choose the party.[16]

As the saga unfolded, it became clear that MCC could have handled things better. Its official line was that it had received 'no definite reply' to its letter to SACA, although a letter from SACA dated 1 March was taken personally to Lord's by its vice-president and given to Gubby Allen. This did not give the assurance MCC requested. Allen chose not to refer the letter to the Committee, which continued to plan for the tour 'on the assumption that the selected team would be accepted by the South African Government when the time came.'[17] This assumption was based on intelligence it had received from Sir Alec Douglas-Home, the former Prime Minister who had recently served as MCC president and was still a MCC committee member. In his capacity as shadow foreign secretary, Home had also had informal discussions with Prime Minister Vorster. Home believed that D'Oliveira would be admitted to the country if selected, and advised MCC not to press for an answer to its letter. Home's line was preferred to Cobham's by those who knew of both conversations.

One further development in the story added to perceptions that MCC was politically naïve, incompetent, or both. On 16 September, Tom Cartwright withdrew from the squad, and the selectors chose D'Oliveira as his replacement. Since D'Oliveira had only been considered as a batsman, they explained their decision by saying that Cartwright's withdrawal required a rebalancing of the squad. Few were persuaded by this explanation, including Vorster. Vorster had been working behind the scenes to ensure that D'Oliveira would not be included in the squad, while appearing to allow MCC a free hand to choose whom they wanted. Now he could say that the selectors had bowed to political pressure

---

15 Sheppard believed this was George Newman: SHP, 15.2.

16 I have found helpful for this section Oborne, P., *Basil D'Oliveira: Cricket and Conspiracy – the Untold Story*, London: Sphere, 2004, and Murray, B. K. 'Politics and Cricket: The D'Oliveira Affair of 1968', *Journal of Southern African Studies*, 27:4, December 2001. MCC did not publicly admit that Gilligan, Allen and Griffith knew of Cobham's conversation with Vorster until April 1969.

17 Minutes of MCC Committee, 21 March 1968: MCC archive at MCC/SEC/1/16.

and abandoned any commitment to picking the best players. On 24 September, MCC announced the tour was off.

Sheppard had called for the tour to be cancelled a fortnight before. Writing in the *Church of England Newspaper*, he said that going to South Africa involved playing 'racialist, political cricket, against an all white team and in front of segregated crowds.' England should not tour South Africa until their sport is organized on a non-racialist basis, he said. He accepted that the selectors had been honest, if naïve, and blamed MCC for not having secured an answer from South Africa regarding D'Oliveira before the selection process began. If they had done so, and made it public, 'the political crisis could then have been separated to some degree from the selection of one man'. Sheppard described the issue as one of 'plain justice' rather than politics.[18]

Sheppard joined a group of MCC members unhappy with the Club's handling of the tour selection. Around a hundred had responded to a letter in *The Guardian* from Charles Barr,[19] and when some met in London, they decided to press for a special general meeting (SGM) of the Club. Among them were Mike Brearley, then lecturing at Newcastle University and playing half a season for Middlesex, Robin Knight, who served as secretary and the actor Peter Howell. Sheppard was glad not to be a lone voice with his concerns. As the best-known cricketer in the group, he agreed to be its chair.

The group proposed two substantive resolutions for the SGM:

[1] That the Members of MCC regret their Committee's mishandling of affairs leading up to the selection of the team for the intended tour of South Africa in 1968–1969; and

[2] That no further tours to or from South Africa be undertaken until evidence can be given of actual progress by South Africa towards non-racial cricket.

A third resolution asked that 'a Special Committee be set up to examine

18 'Why d'Oliveira should have gone', *Church of England Newspaper*, 6 September 1968, p. 6.
19 Barr also placed a notice in the personal column of *The Times*, but *The Guardian* letter appeared first and prompted the larger response.

such proposals as are submitted by the SACA towards non-racial cricket'. The group also considered asking that MCC recognize the body overseeing non-white cricket in South Africa, the Board of Control, but dropped this following advice from the Anti-Apartheid Movement. The group's supporting text again mentioned MCC's failure to obtain a definitive answer from the South African authorities about D'Oliveira's acceptability as a tourist 'without conditions'.

Six members of the group met with MCC on 12 September to discuss the SGM. Sheppard understood the meeting would be informal and involve just a few people from each side. MCC, however, planned it to follow a full meeting of the Committee, and when Sheppard and his colleagues arrived, they found 20 people seated around the Committee Room. These included Sir Alec Douglas-Home – who had flown down from Scotland especially – and the Club's solicitor, Mr A. A. Meyer. MCC wanted Sheppard to drop the idea of an SGM, and delegated Home to explain the difficulties it had faced. Sheppard stood firm on the request, which had attracted 90 signatures.

The meeting must have had a surreal quality. When Sheppard made the point about MCC not clearing D'Oliveira's acceptability in advance, Home repeatedly said, 'You can't ask the South African government hypothetical questions.' Yet Sheppard knew that Charles Cobham had done precisely that and had received a straight answer. He chose not to say so. Home also knew of Cobham's conversation at the time.

Before the meeting, the cricket writer John Arlott advised Sheppard to ask MCC to produce any correspondence which might prove or disprove any attempt to clear the apartheid issue with SACA. 'I may tell you in confidence that such correspondence does exist', Arlott told him.[20] Sheppard duly pressed the Committee, and, after much stalling, Allen said, 'Well, you may as well know that we did write . . . We never received a reply'. This showed, at best, economy with the truth.

Sheppard described the SGM, which was held at Church House, Westminster on 5 December, as the most bitter meeting he ever attended. He knew MCC were upset about facing a vote of no confidence, and that some members were losing patience with 'preaching

---

20 Letter from John Arlott, 9 September 1968: SHP, 15.2.

parsons'.[21] The official notice of the meeting from MCC contained portents. It referred to the movers of the resolutions having hidden motives, and to attacks on the selectors 'by persons so violently opposed to the domestic policies of the South African Government as to appear incapable of fair judgment'.[22] But he was unprepared for the number of personal attacks levelled at him, some from people he knew well and regarded as friends. He remembers at one point, Brearley turning in his seat as if to protect him from a physical attack. Arlott described the four-hour marathon as a 'parade of prejudice', and the distinguished lawyer Jeremy Hutchinson, whom Sheppard had asked to speak for the motions, recalled he 'had never spoken to such a large and hostile audience.'[23] One member, aware of Sheppard's new posting, said he wondered how the Bishop of Woolwich could wear his MCC tie. A voice from the gallery shouted, 'Down the back!'

Sheppard avoided personal references in his speech. He called for both sides to listen and try to understand each other. He said he was not asking MCC to judge the domestic policies of another country, but to take notice when those policies interfered with cricket. He acknowledged that everybody wanted South Africa to move towards non-racial cricket, but if playing with the country on their own terms was not changing anything, something else must be tried. He also noted the impact MCC's stance was having on community relations in the UK. Cricket acts here as a 'bridge', he said, with black and white enjoying the game together: 'This is why it was so disastrous in August that MCC's policy left the selectors in a situation where English cricket *appeared* to be bending to a racialist wind'. He again made no reference to the conversation he had had with Cobham, despite the effect it might have had on proceedings. Cobham chose not to speak, and Douglas-Home did not attend.[24]

The resolutions proposed by Sheppard and seconded by Brearley were

---

21 Robin Knight told Sheppard he had heard this from E. W. Swanton: letter, 2 November 1968, SHP, 15.2.

22 Sheppard also suspected MCC's decision to list the members of its Cricket Sub-Committee, including 'Rev D. S. Sheppard', was a dig at him, implying 'that I should have said all this earlier on'. That sub-committee, as he pointed out on the night, had nothing to do with the policy of the tour: SHP, 15.2, 15.4.

23 Williams, J., *Cricket and Race*, Oxford: Berg, 2001, p. 63; Grant, T., *Jeremy Hutchinson's Case Histories*, London: John Murray, 2015, p. 27.

24 Woodcock, J., 'MCC win on all three counts', *The Times*, 6 December 1968, p. 15.

all lost. The voting on the first was 386 to 314 among those members present, but when postal votes were added in, the defeat was much heavier – 4,357 to 1,570. The other resolutions were also defeated by a wide margin.

Sheppard always regretted the strain the episode put on his friendships. Three of his closest companions in the game, Colin Cowdrey, Peter May and Ted Dexter, firmly took the opposing side, though only May broke off their friendship for good. Sheppard was pleased to be reconciled with Dennis Silk, an MCC Committee member who made a personal attack on him at the SGM which he later regretted. Dexter encouraged their reunion. Sheppard corresponded with D'Oliveira after the tour was cancelled, and the two remained friends. 'Let's hope and pray that the future for Cricket and indeed the relationship between all men might be the better for [these events]', D'Oliveira wrote to Sheppard in the November.[25]

In his retirement, Sheppard learned from Bruce Murray, a University of the Witwatersrand professor researching the affair, that the South African government made up its mind about the tour before the selectors met. Vorster had claimed it did so only after D'Oliveira was picked to replace Cartwright, but the cabinet minutes for 27 August 1968, the day before the selectors announced their decision, state, 'MCC. *Kriekettoer 1968/69. As D'Oliveira gekies word is die toer af* – 'If D'Oliveira is chosen the tour is off.'[26]

*

Sheppard attended a course for church leaders shortly after his appointment, feeling in need of training for his new role, and realizing he knew little about the wider workings of the Church of England. The course inspired him to think critically about his performance. Each year thereafter, he set targets for the coming six or twelve months and reflected on how they were met. These related to his role in the diocese and his 'personal growth as a Christian and as a human being'. 'Reduce

---

25 Letter, 9 November 1968: SHP 15.2.
26 Sheppard, *Steps along Hope Street*, p. 89; Murray, 'Politics and Cricket: The D'Oliveira Affair of 1968', *Journal of Southern African Studies*, p. 670.

the pace, be more, do less', was a regular refrain, as was 'make time for interests and fun time with Grace and Jenny'.[27]

The admonition to 'do less' was wise. His responsibilities as a bishop included oversight of 250 clergy across 150 parishes, chairing committees, and attending civic and community events. That alone would fill his diary, but he had his weekly column for *Woman's Own*, and his involvement with initiatives such as *Christians in Industrial Areas*, Frontier Youth Trust and Eclectics. Then there were the demands of being a public figure, although he declined invitations to speak outside the diocese. And he would throw himself into causes in the world of cricket when the issue of justice demanded. He was allocated half-time assistance, but his secretary, Betty Parr, agreed to work full-time, Sheppard paying her additional salary from his own pocket. Even then she was often stretched: Sheppard received an average of 20–25 letters per day and dictated a reply to each. In the days before email, that constituted a huge workload.

Sheppard attempted what would now be called a work–life balance. The temptation to work around the clock was prevented by Miss Parr placing her phone in a soundproof box whenever she finished work, and he was conscientious about taking holidays and keeping a day off each week. He played squash for relaxation, often with the Archdeacon of Southwark, Michael Whinney, and did some cricket coaching with a local side. He broke for a meal each evening with Grace and Jenny. But his sense of calling, and feeling of obligation to meet expectations, made almost impossible demands on his time. Writing to a friend in May 1970, he confessed that, 'having been in the job still considerably less than a year I am under too much of a work load at the moment.'[28]

The long and unsocial hours he kept might have been manageable for a celibate. For a husband and father, they inevitably had repercussions. Together with the fragile state of Grace's health, and the comparative isolation of their new surroundings after the 24-hour community of the Mayflower, his routine only increased the strains on family life. During the 1970s the Sheppards realized their marriage needed serious repair.

---

27 Typed and handwritten notes: SHP, 39.3.
28 Letter to the Reverend Bob Reiss, 7 May 1970: SHP 22.2.

By the early 1980s, they had resolved the issue through counselling and spending time away together.

*

When Stockwood arranged for the Industrial Society to review the organization of the diocese, Sheppard asked them to look at his workload as a bishop. He asked how many people one person could properly supervise and was told that, in industry, the answer would be eight. 'That figure influenced all my subsequent approaches to bishoping', he later wrote.[29] To enable his clergy to have the kind of support he could not give them personally, Sheppard proposed 'joint work consultations'. This involved the pairing of priests to set goals and review their achievement together. Though used in industry, this was an innovation for the church, and it met with some resistance, but Sheppard believed it removed the isolation many clergy felt. It also helped to prevent the despair that came when they set themselves impossible goals and then 'whipped themselves for failing to achieve them'. Sheppard would later introduce this process in Liverpool.

Sheppard could not persuade Stockwood to conduct a formal review for him, but they did take a walk together once a year to talk about his work. Stockwood, Sheppard and Montefiore also went away three times a year to relax and talk about business in an unhurried manner. They met at the Surrey home of Kay Robson-Brown, the wife of a Conservative MP and a Roman Catholic. Lady Kay invited the bishops as part of her own ecumenical outreach, providing respite in a comfortable setting including the use of her swimming pool and sauna.[30] The Montefiore and Sheppard wives and children were welcomed too.

*

After the informality of the Mayflower, Sheppard needed to understand different liturgical practices and styles of churchmanship. He learned

---

29 Sheppard, *Steps along Hope Street*, p. 119.

30 I am grateful to Canon Giles Harcourt, a former chaplain to Bishop Mervyn, for alerting me to this detail; see also De-la-Noy, M., *Mervyn Stockwood: A Lonely Life*, London: Mowbray, 1996, p. 119.

from Stockwood to adapt to the custom of each church he visited. Stockwood believed that clergy should be a unifying force and not put barriers between parishioners and God. Aware that most of his churches were in the Anglo-Catholic tradition, Sheppard asked the vicar of St John's, Geoffrey Heal, to help him understand their practices. Heal and his curate, Nicholas Frayling, introduced Sheppard to the liturgical vestments he would be expected to wear in Anglo-Catholic churches. Sheppard said he was unhappy about wearing a mitre, which he thought had triumphalist, even monarchical overtones. Heal told him that if he preached at St John's without a mitre that would be the sole talking-point. No one would remember a word he had said. Sheppard later believed it was more triumphalist to insist on wearing his choice of vestment if that was alien to the people of the parish.

Sheppard learnt how to 'sing and swing', to chant the musical settings used in services and cense the altar. Censing involves swinging a metal container, known as a thurible, containing burning incense over and around the altar to venerate it. The first time he performed this ritual, he caused anxiety by circling the table repeatedly, apparently not knowing when to stop. Stockwood helped Sheppard with other liturgical actions, including making the sign of the cross. Noting his suffragan's reluctance to do this, he reassured him that the world would not fall in if he did. Stockwood gently teased Sheppard about his evangelical ways. He was once heard to say he told the Bishop of Woolwich that 'when he's giving the blessing, he's not hailing an omnibus.' Stockwood liked to choose 'Faithful shepherd, feed me' as a Communion hymn when the two were celebrating together at the cathedral.[31] Sheppard acknowledged Stockwood's role in teaching him how to be a bishop, and liked the freedom Stockwood gave him in the job, and that their relationship relied on trust.

Sheppard's encounters with churches that were not evangelical broadened his horizons. On an early pastoral visit he met a dying man who had come to faith in a high church setting. Hearing the man describe how, at elevation of the host during Mass, he 'saw vividly' what

---

31 This was known to be Stockwood's favourite hymn. Sheppard also chose it occasionally for special services. I am grateful to the Very Reverend Nicholas Frayling and Canon Roger Royle for some of the material in this chapter.

Christ had done for him on the cross, Sheppard concluded that he 'was face to face with an assurance of salvation as clear as any evangelical could wish.'[32]

*

Sheppard's half of the diocese stretched from south London to the Surrey–Sussex border,[33] and he found the mix of urban and rural brought new challenges after 14 years in the inner city. Having learned about working-class culture in his previous jobs, he now needed to understand how church people in the home counties lived and thought. Churches were often full in these areas; Sheppard worked out the percentage of the local population to be found in church in Surrey was ten times greater than in an inner-city area or outer estate.

Some of the attitudes he encountered in the leafiest parts of the diocese raised questions for him. Many who commuted to London deliberately chose to live in Surrey in order to feel they had left the city behind at the end of the day. They breathed a sigh of relief as they reached a certain point in their journey, sensing that 'London and its demands had been left behind.' Sheppard wondered how they related their faith to their work. It was as though the two operated in different worlds. People would happily give money or time to an inner-city cause, he thought, but how they behaved in their working life was more important. They needed to bring their faith to bear on their work. Members of suburban churches had an enormous influence on the kind of jobs and education that black people, or 'people from unfavourable addresses', were able to get. He wanted people in suburban parishes to reflect a 'divine bias for the losers' in their working life.[34]

The associate director of training for the diocese, Peter Selby, would invite rural or suburban congregations to consider how their assumptions

---

32 Sheppard, *Steps along Hope Street*, p. 102.

33 In Sheppard's day the episcopal area of Croydon was part of Canterbury diocese, due to the presence of two former archiepiscopal residences in the town. When Croydon transferred to Southwark in 1991, the Surrey parishes formerly in Woolwich were absorbed into this new area.

34 Sheppard, *Steps along Hope Street*, p. 101; DSS in conversation with Bryan Ellis, *Christians in Industrial Areas*, no. 448, Spring 1981, p. 16.

and way of life were factors in bringing about some of the deprivation experienced in the inner city.[35] Sheppard considered it right to speak in those terms. He thought an example was when people in more affluent and less densely populated areas put pressure on their local authority to refuse requests from inner boroughs to release land for new council housing estates. By defending their own interests in this way, they had a direct influence on forcing high densities of housing in inner London. Sheppard found resistance to arguments like these, and to attempts to discuss inequalities in the diocese.

*

Stockwood helped Sheppard build bridges with Free Church and Roman Catholic clergy in the diocese. Sheppard welcomed the opportunity to meet regularly with Roman Catholics and gained new insights into their engagement in working-class areas. He found helpful a conversation with Michael Bowen, then Bishop of Arundel and Brighton and formerly a priest in Walworth, south London, and spent a day walking with him on the South Downs. Such conversations were important staging posts in his journey to the ecumenical partnership he forged in Liverpool. He met a problem over the question of shared worship space, however. As chair of the Thamesmead Christian Council, Sheppard wanted the Catholic archbishop, Cyril Cowderoy, to join an ecumenical project in that newly built district. This involved creating a church building which several denominations would share. The archbishop insisted his people would want to have their aids to worship around them. Sheppard could not persuade him, despite having the support of a local Catholic priest.

*

Urban mission continued to be a priority for Sheppard. In 1970 he was asked to chair the Urban Ministry Project (UMP), a scheme which

---

35 Correspondence with Bishop Peter Selby. Selby was later Bishop of Kingston, then Bishop of Worcester.

trained clergy to work in tough parishes and reflect theologically on urban issues. One of its creators was Donald Reeves, a priest in the diocese. As part of their training participants spent three or four days on the streets with only a few pounds in their pocket.[36]

Sheppard also continued to co-edit *Christians in Industrial Areas*, the newsletter he founded in 1967 with Ted Roberts and Eddie Neale. In 1972, it announced a new project to provide in-service training for evangelicals in urban ministry. Its seeds had been sown at the Mayflower in the mid 1960s, when Sheppard gathered a group of clergy and laypeople to discuss evangelism among the working class. By 1970 the idea of providing training for working-class congregations had taken shape, and the Evangelical Urban Training Project (EUTP) was launched two years later. 'The training project . . . will build on a deep conviction that the gospel of Jesus Christ, when really believed and lived out by a company of Christians in areas where the Church has long been weak, is the most contemporary good news known to man', Sheppard told the *Church Times*.[37] EUTP aimed to give working people the confidence to evangelize by speaking about the experience of God in their lives.

Sheppard chaired the management committee of EUTP until he left Woolwich. Neville Black served as secretary, and Jacqueline Burgoyne, a sociology lecturer at Sheffield City College of Education, as treasurer. Burgoyne later achieved fame as a sociologist of the family before her untimely death at the age of 43. Other key figures in EUTP were Frank Deeks, a trade unionist from Dagenham, and John Hunter, whom Sheppard had contacted after reading three pieces Hunter wrote for the *Church of England Newspaper* in 1960 on 'Ministry to the Working Class'. Sheppard found Hunter's insights, as a former factory worker and priest in a working-class parish in Bootle, helpful in shaping his thinking.

When enough funds were raised, Black was appointed project officer for EUTP, continuing half-time as vicar of his parish in Everton. Black developed a distinctive programme of locally based workshops headed 'Know your church; Know your area; Know your gospel', with

---

36 Reeves, D., *The Memoirs of 'A Very Dangerous Man'*, London: Continuum, 2009, pp. 96–9. The survival exercise was known as 'the Plunge'.

37 'Evangelical urban training project', *Church Times*, 15 September 1972, p. 3.

an emphasis on learning within the group rather than written work. Sheppard believed that EUTP had significance beyond the numbers attending its courses. It created a climate in which self-confidence grew, and enabled participants 'to affirm that their own experience is as valid as that of those who have generally been accepted as the teachers and the wise in the Christian community.'[38]

*

At the Mayflower, Sheppard had built bridges with local factories and workplaces. In Southwark he welcomed opportunities to accompany chaplains from the South London Industrial Mission (SLIM) to meet with staff and board members. He encouraged managers to consider the ethical issues they confronted in their role, and formed friendships with business people who operated on principles other than the bottom line.[39] Two people who influenced Sheppard were the senior chaplain with SLIM, Peter Challen, and Cecilia Goodenough, the Assistant Diocesan Missioner. Sheppard admired Goodenough and continued to seek her advice long after he left the diocese.

Challen and Goodenough were members of the Bishop's Council for Ministry and Mission, a think tank that Robinson had brought together. Sheppard learned much from the group. Peter Selby, another of its members, said the group valued Sheppard's 'sound management, clarity of focus, pastoral care and "championing".'[40] Sheppard would fight a member's corner, sometimes with Bishop Mervyn, when the need arose.

*

Sheppard continued to promote local leadership while at Woolwich. He supported the principle behind the Southwark Ordination Course,

---

38 Foreword to Hunter, J., *A Touch of Class: Issues of Urban Mission*, Sheffield: EUTP, 1995, pp. 1–2. I have also drawn on correspondence with Canon Hunter and an interview with Canon Neville Black.

39 One such was Neil Wates, managing director of the building firm of that name. Wates's Christian commitment prevented him from trading in South Africa.

40 Correspondence with Bishop Peter Selby. I have also drawn upon correspondence with John Nicholson, a lay training officer in the diocese at the time, for sections of this chapter.

which provided training for candidates while they remained in their secular employment. He thought that ordaining working-class men without withdrawing them from their jobs was 'a sign that the Church takes seriously the idea that leadership can develop in this section of the community.' He had little patience with the argument that priests should be 'interchangeable' rather than trained to serve in specific locations. 'More than half the present clergy in the Church of England are quite incapable of ministering in urban and industrial areas,' he contended. 'No one believes that we should refuse them ordination.'[41]

He warmed to a scheme initiated by his friend, Ted Roberts, who encouraged some working-class men in his parish in Bethnal Green to consider training for ordination to serve in their own communities. Roberts' bishop, Trevor Huddleston, supported him, and Huddleston and Sheppard set up a working party to look at the scheme's wider potential. Their report, *Local Ministry in Urban and Industrial Areas*, was published in 1972, and favoured local ordained ministry. It challenged the assumption, held widely in the Church, that leaders will come from certain social and educational backgrounds and not others, arguing, 'There is indigenous leadership with intelligence and ability which cannot be easily measured by academic yardsticks.' The crucial question was not about ordination, but 'whether we believe that a locally-rooted, responsible Christian church can be established in working-class areas.'[42] Some critics thought the report, if implemented, would lead to standards of assessment for ordinands being lowered.[43]

In 1975, Sheppard and Montefiore set up a working party to consider how the diocese might respond when economic inflation forced it to employ fewer priests. Stockwood had suggested the possibility of non-stipendiary ministry, but the working party thought that, rather than opting for 'a watered down version' of full-time stipendiary ministry, the concept of 'shared ministry' should be explored. This envisaged the

---

41 Sheppard, D. S., *Built as a City*, London: Hodder & Stoughton, 1974, pp. 294, 297; cf. 250.

42 *Local Ministry in Urban and Industrial Areas*, London: Mowbray, 1972, pp. 7, 9. Huddleston was then Bishop of Stepney. See also Roberts, T., *Partners and Ministers*: London: Falcon Books, 1972. I am grateful for information from Mrs Audrey Roberts.

43 *The Place of Auxiliary Ministry, Ordained and Lay*, London: CIO, 1973; see also Simon, O., 'Ordained Local Ministry: A palliative or progressive contribution to Anglican ecclesiology?', King's College London, D.Min thesis, 2009, p. 63.

whole church, clergy and laity, being 'oriented towards ministry and mission in the world.'[44]

*

Sheppard was concerned that homelessness was on the increase in London. He petitioned Southwark council not to evict a group of squatters, and helped form a self-help community group converting abandoned properties into temporary accommodation for homeless people. He publicly expressed his regret that the council refused to discuss the massive housing problems in the borough. Sheppard argued that it was much harder for people to break out of a cycle of poverty if they lived in bad housing. Housing should be a service which is provided for all, along with a basic wage or allowance.[45] Sheppard thought the Bible offered helpful insights, and in *Built as a City*, he noted that the law of Jubilee in the Old Testament enabled land to be bought on a leasehold basis, with ownership reverting to the original owner every 50 years. This protected the poor against the effects of rich people buying up all available land; the needs of the community were put first. Sheppard advocated housing associations as a way of helping those in greatest need.[46]

*

Despite his knowledge of the apartheid system in South Africa, Sheppard was aware he knew little about the experience of black people in his own country. Canning Town was still largely a white working-class community when he left, whereas Asylum Road was 50–50 black and white. His visits to parishes revealed that some churches welcomed black people into membership. At others, black people considered themselves tolerated and not trusted with leadership roles.

---

44 'Towards Shared Ministry', April 1975: SHP, 28.10. Non-stipendiary, or unpaid, ministry later became known as self-supporting ministry.

45 Sheppard, *Built as a City*, pp. 160, 194. Sheppard appears to have been arguing for a 'basic income' while it was still a little-known idea. He developed this further in *Bias to the Poor*.

46 Sheppard, *Built as a City*, pp. 161–3; 239.

Some drifted away from mainline churches into independent black-led fellowships.

Sheppard asked Wilfred Wood, a black curate he knew, to help him understand the perspective of black people in London. The two spent a day in Wood's parish in Shepherd's Bush, west London.[47] They met with a group of black community workers, who gave a harrowing account of how they saw relations with the police. Wood helped Sheppard understand how Enoch Powell was heard within the black community. Powell was creating a climate in which black immigrants found themselves 'regarded as some kind of virus in the nation's bloodstream', Wood later put it.[48] Sheppard once described Powell's famous 'rivers of blood' speech as 'really sinister stuff . . . full of bits of half truth twisted to serve the argument.'[49] Wood made a lasting impression on Sheppard, and told him that white people needed to accept the concept of a 'proud black man'. They were wrong to believe that black people would rather be white, assuming that the world is such that it was a disadvantage to be black.[50] The lessons Sheppard learnt helped equip him for some of the challenges he would face in Liverpool.

Sheppard and Wood were involved with the Martin Luther King Fund and Foundation. Established after King's assassination in 1968, this helped black people into worthwhile work through its support of an employment agency and training scheme based in the diocese. Sheppard succeeded its founder, Canon L. John Collins, as chairman, and in 1975 he gave the Martin Luther King Memorial Lecture. He asked employers and trade unions to keep accurate statistics and pursue 'positive discrimination' to help break the vicious circle preventing black people being considered for the best jobs.[51]

---

47 In the 1980s Sheppard stayed with a priest in Southall, west London, Mano Rumalshah, to help him understand better 'the Asian presence in England'; *Steps along Hope Street*, pp. 283–4.

48 Wood, W., 'Race Relations Work in Southwark Diocese, 1969–2000' in *Report of an Independent Inquiry into Institutional Racism within the Structures of the Diocese of Southwark*, March 2000, p. 57.

49 Letter, 19 November 1968: SHP, 15.2.

50 Interview with Bishop Wilfred Wood. Sheppard, *Steps along Hope Street*, p.134. Wood later took up a parish in Southwark and, in 1985, became the first black bishop in the Church of England when he was appointed to Croydon.

51 Sheppard, D. S., *Black People and Employment: The 1975 Martin Luther King Memorial*

Sheppard supported the formation of a race relations team to work across the diocese. This was overseen by the Council for Social Aid (CSA). When one of the first appointments, a Jamaican priest, moved on, the CSA chose a young black man, Horace Parkinson, to succeed him. Parkinson's family were highly respected in the Brixton community and known for their work with a youth project at St Matthew's Church. Parkinson had recently been in prison. In 1973 he was arrested, with two others, following a fight during a fair in Brockwell Park which he was helping to break up. This became a major incident involving large numbers of police and the crowd leaving the fair. His conviction for affray, and subsequent three-year sentence, angered many in Brixton, and the campaign to 'Free the Brockwell 3' became a widespread protest about the state of police–community relations in South London. Following an appeal, his sentence was quashed, and he was immediately released.

When the CSA appointed Parkinson there was diocesan opposition. Sheppard defended the decision, believing the interviewing panel, on which he had served, was not commenting on any miscarriage of justice by its actions. It was 'part of a proper Christian belief in forgiveness and making new starts to be ready to look at him on his merits,' he said. He might also have noted Parkinson's attitude of forgiveness towards the police.[52] Sheppard would later work to build better relations between the police and the black community in Liverpool.

*

Sheppard's opposition to apartheid drew him into another high-profile campaign during his time at Woolwich. Unbowed by its experience over D'Oliveira, MCC invited South Africa to tour England in 1970. Opposition to the tour built up during 1969, and in September a coalition called 'Stop the Seventy Tour' (STST) was formed. This was

---

Lecture, London: the Martin Luther King Foundation, 1975, p. 7. Sheppard later preferred to speak of 'affirmative action' rather than 'positive discrimination'.

52 Typewritten statement: SHP, 10.11. I have also drawn on a phone conversation and correspondence with Reverend Bob Nind, who chaired CSA at the time, and Canon Richard Wheeler.

chaired by Peter Hain, then a leading Young Liberal. Some STST members had disrupted matches during a tour by an all-white South African rugby team the previous winter. Sheppard had spoken at a protest against an international match at Twickenham in December, but he opposed direct action as a tactic. He wanted the cricket tour stopped because people were 'persuaded against playing with racialist teams', not through fear of disruption at matches.[53] When STST began talking about invading pitches, and flashing mirrors into the eyes of batsmen, he formed a separate organization committed to peaceful protest.

Sheppard met with members of MCC's Council and spoke against the tour at the AGM. He challenged the Club when it announced that, although no vote was taken, the feeling of the AGM 'closely followed the majority view in this country that the tour should proceed.'[54] The Cricket Council remained committed to the tour, but in February cut its length from 28 matches to 12.[55]

Support for the tour was strong within the cricket community. In April, John Arlott announced he would not commentate on the tests if they went ahead, but few cricketers publicly said they would boycott it. Opinion was more divided among the public, and Sheppard was approached by individuals and organizations keen to identify with his non-violent stance. On 14 April he invited more than 50 senior figures from the church, trade unions, politics, business and the arts to meet at the Travellers' Club in Pall Mall. The Anti-Apartheid Movement and the South African Non-Racial Olympic Committee (SAN-ROC) were also represented. From this meeting emerged the 'Fair Cricket Campaign' (FCC), which adopted two key objectives:

i. to 'stimulate responsible bodies to make representations to the Cricket Council so that even at this late date the tour should be called off';

---

53 'Bishop Sheppard Says "Call Off 1970 Tour"', *Church Times*, 5 December 1969, p. 24. Hain was brought up in South Africa but forced to leave with his parents on account of their opposition to apartheid. He was later a Labour MP, cabinet minister and life peer.

54 Letter to Billy Griffith, 7 May 1970: SHP, 22.2.

55 By 1970 a new organization, MCC Cricket Council, known simply as the Cricket Council, had become the governing body of English cricket.

With his mother Barbara,
father Stuart and sister Mary at
St Briget's, early 1930s

An early innings

Meeting his mother for a
Sherborne 'commem', aged 13

The *Boy's Own* hero

With Mary and Barbara, 1950

Going out to bat with Len
Hutton for England against
India, Old Trafford, 1952

With George Burton, *c.* 1964

Always a serious game. With boys in Islington, mid-1950s

With Australian tourists Brian Booth and
Ian Quick, 1961

Batting in the last Gentlemen
v Players match, 1962

The inauguration of MARCEA, Liverpool Cathedral, Whit Sunday 1985. From left to right: Norwyn Denny (Methodist), Trevor Hubbard (Baptist), John Williamson (URC), Sheppard, Worlock, Douglas Rayner (Salvation Army)

As chair of the Martin Luther King Foundation, 1970s, with Grace and Wilfred Wood

With Derek Worlock and Ann Awork at the Liverpool 8 Law Centre, 1982

With Michael Henshall and the first women deacons, 1993

A parting word with Pope John
Paul II, Metropolitan Cathedral,
30 May 1982

In the autumn of their years.
Captured in Stephen Shakeshaft's
prize-winning photograph

At Bishop's Lodge a month before
retirement, September 1997

A masterclass for his grandsons,
Gilles and Stuart, May 2003

Archbishop Desmond Tutu at Sheppard's memorial stone,
Liverpool Cathedral

ii. to organize one peaceful demonstration 'which should not attempt to go inside a cricket ground'.

The group also wanted to 'celebrate good race relations in London.' The date chosen for a demonstration was 20 June, the Saturday of the Lord's Test. Sheppard, the chair of FCC, wanted this event to be clearly distinguishable from any disruptive action planned for inside the ground. The FCC met through late April and May to plan its demonstration.

The FCC attracted support from across the political spectrum. Its vice-chairmen were Labour MP, Reg Prentice, who had recently served in the Wilson government, and the former Conservative minister, Sir Edward Boyle. Betty Boothroyd, who would stand as a Labour candidate at the general election that June, was secretary. Boyle reached people unwilling to listen to someone they perceived to be on the Left, or who was from the Church. Then the *Sunday Times* leaked news of Sheppard's plans a week before the Travellers' Club meeting. A letter of invitation to that meeting had found its way to a reporter, who checked out the story with Peter Hain, who then alerted Sheppard. Hain said he welcomed the FCC and the initiative it was taking 'in the areas virtually neglected by STST'. This included lobbying MCC members.[56]

As during the D'Oliveira affair, Sheppard worried about the effect MCC's plans would have on community relations in the UK. Three of the venues chosen for the shortened tour were Kennington Oval in south London, Trent Bridge (Nottingham) and Edgbaston (Birmingham). Sheppard thought race relations would be 'very much at risk' if a white South African team played at these grounds.[57] It would crush black people's trust in assurances they received that they were 'full citizens' and 'we dislike apartheid'.[58] Sheppard was concerned that the Cricket Council had not consulted with community relations specialists about the effect of the tour, and MCC president Maurice Allom admitted to Sheppard on BBC's *Panorama* programme that he had not taken

---

56 Humphry, D., and Doust, D., 'Sheppard in Split over Boks Protest', *Sunday Times*, 5 April 1970, p. 2; letter from Hain, 4 April 1970: SHP, 22.2; Hain, P., *Don't Play with Apartheid: The Background to the Stop The Seventy Tour Campaign*, London: George Allen & Unwin, 1971, p. 186.

57 'The cricket tour and Christian conscience', *The Times*, 25 April 1970, p. 10.

58 Typescript letter to *Church of England Newspaper*, 1 June 1970: SHP, 22.3.

expert advice.[59] Sheppard invited each member of the Council to meet with community experts at a gathering hosted by Edward Boyle. He knew that the Council had been delegating decision-making to an emergency executive committee. 'Every member of the Council must be fully responsible for whether the tour goes ahead or not', he told them.[60]

On 18 May the Council announced that there would be no further Test tours involving South Africa until Test cricket was played, and tours were selected, on a multi-racial basis in that country. The move could not save the tour. By the end of the week, under heavy pressure from the government, MCC reluctantly cancelled it.[61] Other countries joined the boycott of South Africa. Its isolation from international cricket lasted until 1992, two years after the release of Nelson Mandela.

Sheppard's role in the campaign had been costly. He received criticism from friends in cricket, sections of the media and church members, including within his own diocese. Frequent themes were his lack of understanding of how things 'really are' in South Africa, his focus on one country to the exclusion of others,[62] especially Communist states, and his prioritizing of apartheid over issues nearer to home. Calls to 'keep religion and cricket apart' were routine. Some Christians commended him on his stand, while more suggested he 'keep out of politics'. Some of the mail he received was personal and abusive. Yet he could later reflect that ostracizing South Africa had been more effective in bringing about change in the country than MCC's policy of retaining links with it. Nowhere were his actions more appreciated than within South Africa itself. As Archbishop Desmond Tutu later reflected, Sheppard's status in the game meant he could not be lightly dismissed when he spoke: 'We the victims of apartheid . . . took very great encouragement. We realized we did indeed have friends in high places.'

---

59 Transcript of *Panorama*, BBC 1, 27 April 1970: SHP, 14.1.

60 Letter from FCC, 13 May 1970: SHP, 22.2.

61 A replacement series versus the Rest of the World was arranged for the summer. The RoW team comprised white South Africans and players from the West Indies, India and Pakistan.

62 Sheppard did call for a boycott of the Moscow Olympics (see below pp. 196–7) and criticized the Pakistan touring team in 1971 for following their government's line and refusing to make a humanitarian gesture during the Bangladeshi Liberation War; SHP, 22.3.

Sheppard observed that 80 per cent of his hate-mail came from the shires. He would point this out when replying to senders: 'I think it is significant that those who write angry letters to people like me over this issue generally do not live in the big cities where good race relations are an urgent issue. They have not faced at close quarters the opportunities or the difficulties of a multi-racial society.'

Most correspondents received a stock reply, but he wrote personally to Geoffrey Fisher, retired and living in rural Dorset. The former Archbishop of Canterbury took him to task for his attitude to MCC. He suggested Sheppard try talking to those with whom he disagreed. Sheppard told Fisher he had done just that, and tarred him with the brush he had used on MCC. 'I think before you condemn people for demonstrating you ought to talk very carefully with community relations officers and with black people living in this country', Sheppard wrote. 'I believe that Christians have an obligation to stand up and be counted.'[63]

When the dust had settled, Sheppard tried to get people together from the different sides of the debate. Citing the need to keep bridges of contact open, he invited 19 'cricketers and cricket lovers' to supper at Asylum Road.[64] One was Raman Subba Row, the Northamptonshire and England batsman who had been at Trinity Hall with Sheppard. Subba Row had been very active in supporting the tour.[65] Another was Peter May, who strongly opposed Sheppard over D'Oliveira and the tour. Neither May nor Subba Row attended the supper, and May's response, a terse note saying, 'I don't think we have anything to talk about', caused Sheppard much sadness. One invitee who did attend was Geoffrey Howard. As secretary of Surrey, Howard had changed his position on the tour after Sheppard arranged for a group of black sixth formers from Kennington to see him. The boys told Howard they loved watching cricket at The Oval, but if an all-white team called South Africa were playing, they would be outside, protesting.[66]

---

63 Letter to Lord Fisher of Lambeth, 20 April 1970: SHP, 22.2.
64 I am grateful to Charles Barr for sending me copies of his correspondence with DSS 1968–71.
65 Miller, D., *Raman Subba Row: Cricket Visionary*, Bath: Charlcombe Books, 2017, pp. 123–4.
66 Chalke, *At the Heart of English Cricket*, p. 207.

*

Since his days at the Mayflower, Sheppard had wanted to write a book about the Church and the inner city. He had been 'squirreling away papers' for just that purpose. In March 1971 he sent some initial ideas to friends, and over the next two years, with the help of a short sabbatical, he wrote a 160,000-word treatise. This was published in January 1974 as *Built as a City*, a title inspired by Psalm 122.3. Its subtitle was 'God and the urban world today', though not every retailer noted its religious content. One friend told Sheppard she found a copy in her local bookshop by looking under 'Constructional engineering.'

Sheppard described the book as a '"generalist's" view of the city'. Drawing on his experience in Islington, Canning Town and Peckham, he examined themes such as power and powerlessness, education and work. What kept urban people behind was not just the quality of their housing, schools or jobs, he argued, but 'an interlocking of all of these and more.' He hoped the book would encourage churches to root themselves more in working-class areas and foster local leadership. 'If we have no gospel for the city, we have no gospel', he wrote.[67] He spoke of 'the gospel of the kingdom' having both a personal and prophetic dimension. It calls people individually into a relationship with Christ, but also challenges believers to pursue God's vision for the world. Christians need to enter the public arena, 'standing up to be counted on issues of justice'.[68] Sheppard would speak often about being a 'not only . . . but also' Christian.

Sheppard found writing the book helped him pull together the multiple threads of his work. The greatest temptation in his present role, he told Canon David Edwards,

> is to feel that one's simply reacting to a hundred different demands that bear no relation to one another. It makes a lot of difference to have one's own subject and piece of work in which it's possible to put one's own stamp on what is done.[69]

---

67 Hodder & Stoughton press release, 21 January 1974.
68 Sheppard, *Built as a City*, pp. 335–8.
69 Letter 10 October 1973: SHP, 17.5.

Edwards described the book as 'a really Christian triumph'. Other Christian reviewers were positive, although Edward Norman in the *Spectator* found it wanting and in places 'rather inept'.[70] Robert Nye in *The Scotsman* described it as more important than *Honest to God*, and Anne Power, later professor of social policy at the LSE, considered it 'might well open the door and let in a breath of fresh air'.[71] One reader it impressed was Stephen Timms, then a student at Cambridge. Timms credits *Built as a City* with inspiring him to live in Newham, east London, where he was first elected to Parliament as a Labour MP in 1994. He became a Cabinet member in 2006.

*

Rumours that Sheppard was being considered for Liverpool began circulating in 1974 when Stuart Blanch, the bishop since 1966, was appointed Archbishop of York. Other names were in the frame, but Prime Minister Harold Wilson, a Liverpool MP, was determined to have Sheppard for the diocese. He claimed that he overruled the advice of his appointments secretary and the archbishops, in making the appointment. Sheppard received the official letter just after Christmas. This time there was no extended period of deliberation. 'David set himself to deciding', Grace later recalled. 'In three days, the letter of acceptance was in the post.'[72]

Grace collapsed in tears when the news was received. So did Sheppard's mother, Barbara, who dreaded him moving north. Her age and state of health meant she would not be able to travel often to see him. She and her daughter Mary were immensely proud of David's achievement, but they were disappointed the family would be living so far away. For Jenny the move was unsettling. Now 13, she was in her second year at Haberdashers' Aske's, enjoying the school and doing well academically. She would need to make a fresh start in Liverpool.

---

70 Edwards, D. L., 'The Church's Task in The Inner City', *Church Times*, 25 January 1974, p. 11; Norman, E., 'Distrait Sheppard', *The Spectator*, 26 January 1974. Edwards later became Provost of Southwark.

71 Nye, R., 'Christ in Oxford Street', *The Scotsman*, 19 January 1974; Power, A., 'A City God', *New Society*, 2 May 1974.

72 Sheppard, *An Aspect of Fear*, p. 25.

The Sheppards left Peckham in May 1975. At his farewell service in the cathedral, Sheppard struck a note of realism. The majority of working-class people still felt that the church and its gospel is not for them, he said. He felt 'mostly pessimistic' about the Christian mission in London.

> I find no help from those who only want to tell encouraging stories. Real encouragement comes from those who . . . are determined to . . . change the course of events and to offer people the chance of understanding that this living Christ can be their Deliverer and Friend in the thick of life.

In his farewell letter for the diocesan paper, *Southwark News*, he repeated the call to be partners with Christ in changing the course of events, not people who 'fit in with the way things are.' As he looked ahead to his new post, he was challenging himself as much as his hearers.

9

Liverpool
(1975–1980)

Shortly after his appointment was made public, Sheppard took the train from London to Liverpool. It was the first of many journeys between the two cities he would make in the next 30 years. He had visited the city before in a variety of capacities. As an 18 year old, he had boarded a ship for his first army posting and instantly become seasick. Six years on, he had led Sussex to a heavy defeat by Lancashire at Aigburth, his contribution being just 9 and 3. In his first term at Ridley Hall he had taken part in a week-long mission at Wavertree. The following year 500 attended a special service to hear the 'celebrity Christian'. Now he was returning as bishop, the sixth in the diocese's 95-year history. Already he knew the challenges he would face. This was a region grappling with economic decline, sectarianism and deficit of hope. He would want to discover where God was at work and how he could best serve the community, especially the poor. It was the start of a remarkable new phase in his life. Over the next 22 years, he would help bring lasting change in the region, while redefining the Church's role in the public square.

*

Sheppard had no choice about his accommodation this time. He and Grace told the Church Commissioners they thought it unnecessary for bishops to live in such expensive surroundings, but rejecting the home of his predecessors would have been a costly business. He took comfort in the knowledge that, though large and in an up-market suburb, Bishop's Lodge was a working house as well as a home. On professional advice he stationed his office at the diocesan headquarters in the city, Church House. In another change from Peckham, he had his secretary work there and not at the house. He still planned to work a lot at home and had a phone line installed connecting the diocesan HQ with Bishop's Lodge.

The Sheppards liked the house, but it only functioned because Grace was willing to be an unpaid overseer. The diocese provided staff to clean and to tend the garden, but Grace's contribution as a cook, housekeeper, and staff and property manager held it together. This was not unusual for a bishop's wife at the time. Nor was all well at the house at the start. A lack of job descriptions and management structures for the staff led to misunderstandings which Grace found difficult to navigate. Boundaries between the private and public parts of the house were also unclear. Most of the ground floor was for official use, but there was also a family room next to the kitchen, which was often commandeered as a waiting room, sometimes while it was in use. As a teenager, Jenny tolerated invasions of her space, although nervous young priests and ordinands were a particular irritation. More than one was encouraged to rethink his vocation to the backdrop of *Top of the Pops*.

Grace was happier at Bishop's Lodge than she had been at Peckham, however. The constant coming and going of people removed the sense of isolation and provided a sense of community, while help from a part-time assistant gave her time to pursue her interests. She enjoyed working with the gardeners and managing the extensive grounds. There was a heavy programme of entertaining, but she no longer did the catering and kitchen work alone, and she valued joining her husband, his chaplain and their gardener-driver for morning prayer in the chapel.

Sheppard wanted Jenny to choose her school. Gateacre Comprehensive was the nearest to their home, but St Hilda's was another possibility; a Church of England school with an ethos closer to the one she had attended in London. At 13, Jenny judged on externals, and the newer, larger and more exciting-looking comprehensive won. This may have been what her father preferred, but he later regretted putting the responsibility for making the choice on such young shoulders. The school did not stream its pupils, but Jenny found herself in a form with other children of professional parents. Conscious of being the only southerner among her 2,000 peers, she intentionally adopted a Scouse accent. Her home was another mark of difference. Its double role as a workplace could make bringing friends back awkward, although her parents made them welcome and took time to talk with them.[1] When Jenny joined a band, they practised in the chapel.

*

The Liverpool to which the Sheppards moved was a city in trouble. The port upon which its fortunes had been built no longer needed its men; in the 30 years since the war, its workforce had fallen from 25,000 to 3,000. Several factors had hastened its decline, including the advent of air travel, closer trading ties with Europe at the expense of the Empire, and the introduction of a mechanized process of loading and unloading known as containerization. Manufacturing jobs in the region had also fallen sharply. In the ten years up to Sheppard's arrival, more than 300 factories had closed with a loss of 40,000 jobs. Government policies in the 1950s and 1960s had temporarily reversed the trend, but by the late 1970s, Professor Michael Parkinson has written, 'Liverpool's manufacturing economy seemed on the verge of collapse.'[2] Total employment in Liverpool fell by 33 per cent between 1971 and 1985: nationally, the figure was 3 per cent. Experts predicted in 1984 that Liverpool's rate of economic decline threatened to make it 'the first deindustrialised city in the nation.'[3]

Sheppard thought there were two factors at work. One was the large percentage of businesses controlled by people outside the region. The other was the reputation of the city as an unsafe place to invest. 'Decisions about investment or disinvestment were made by directors with no particular interest in Liverpool or commitment to its people', he wrote in 1988. 'When this is linked with the problem of Liverpool's so-called "image", which is widely believed in business communities, the inevitable follows.'[4] He would later address both issues.

---

1 I am grateful for the help of Shelagh McNerney with this section. Jenny and Shelagh's year tutor was June Bernicoff, who later achieved fame as a participant in Channel 4's *Gogglebox*.

2 Parkinson, M., *Liverpool on the Brink*, Hermitage, Berks: Policy Journals, 1985, p. 11.

3 Parkinson, M., and Duffy, J., 'Government's Response to Inner-City Riots: The Minister for Merseyside and the Task Force', *Parliamentary Affairs*, 37:1, 1984, p. 77.

4 Sheppard, D. S., and Worlock, D., *Better Together: Christian partnership in a hurt city*, London: Hodder & Stoughton, 1988, p. 52.

*

Among the first to welcome Sheppard was the Roman Catholic Archbishop of Liverpool, George Andrew Beck, and Sheppard quickly perceived that Catholic–Protestant relations would be high on his agenda. The city had been described as 'the Belfast of England', and divisions between Catholics and Protestants had been bitter and deep-rooted. The first Orange Lodge march was held in 1819, and the situation was only aggravated by the influx of Irish people during the 1840s' potato famine, which both increased competition for jobs, and heightened tensions between the 'natives' and the incomers. A strong sense of identity developed in the two communities of Irish Catholics and Lancastrian Protestants, while different parts of the city became identified with one or other party. Separate schooling ensured children grew up having minimal contact with the 'other'. 'With such localism (fed by parochialism and physical segregation), a "them" and "us" attitude developed', writes Keith Daniel Roberts. People took solace in a strong sense of community, and so 'there was a need to protect "your" area.'[5] Violence would often break out on key dates such as St Patrick's Day and the twelfth of July.[6] Marches and processions would be broken up by the rival group, sometimes resulting in bloodshed and damage to property.[7] Liverpool had been the only constituency outside of Ireland to return an Irish Nationalist Party MP, with T. P. O'Connor serving continuously from 1885 until his death in 1929, and for 25 years after the war, the Protestant Party was the third largest party on Liverpool City Council in terms of vote share. It only disbanded in 1974, the year before Sheppard arrived. In 1967, a proposal that the Queen be invited to the consecration of the Catholic cathedral was blocked by Prime Minister Harold Wilson for fear of a 'Protestant backlash'.[8] While there was less open hostility between Protestants

---

5 Roberts, K. D., *Liverpool Sectarianism: The Rise and Demise*, Liverpool: Liverpool University Press, 2017, pp. 21–2.

6 The date when Orangemen celebrate the victory of King William of Orange over his Catholic rival, James II, at the Battle of the Boyne in 1690.

7 See, for example, Waller, P. J., *Democracy and Sectarianism: A political and social history of Liverpool 1868-1939*, Liverpool: Liverpool University Press, 1981, pp. 237–8.

8 Sheppard, D. S., *Steps along Hope Street*, London: Hodder & Stoughton, 2002, p. 164; *Daily Post*, 1 January 1998, pp. 1, 4.

and Catholics by the time Sheppard arrived, he was still advised to be cautious about 'pushing forward too quickly the promotion of Christian unity'. It was impossible to tell how close to the surface the sectarian violence and hatreds of the past still lay, he was told.[9] It would not be long before he would find out.

*

Sheppard signalled his commitment to work across church boundaries at his installation in June. The friendship that his predecessor, Stuart Blanch, had enjoyed with other church leaders must be built upon, Sheppard said, both at 'grass-roots' and 'top brass' level. Before planning 'Anglican' events, 'I hope we will ask ourselves very carefully and repeatedly why we should not plan and run these together with other Christian brothers', he told the 3,500-strong congregation. Christian reconciliation was not about ignoring points of conflict between different churches or wanting to water them down; instead, it was about getting to know one another in order to argue 'without slamming the door and living apart in our denominations . . . Let's give priority to drawing near to other groups of Christians and of other human beings', he entreated.

Sheppard spoke of another priority he had set. The Church must get involved in 'corporate life at work and in the community' if it is to help those in weaker situations. Alluding to the story of the prodigal son, or 'the waiting father', as he preferred to call it, he said church members should 'renounce the luxury of being arm-chair, elder-brother critics, keeping their hands clean of the "dirty game" of politics'.[10]

Sheppard refused to call his installation service an 'enthronement'. It had several notable features: instead of following tradition by seeking admittance to the cathedral with his bishop's crosier, Sheppard knocked on the door with the ivory mallet used by Edward VII to lay the foundation stone in 1904. He then walked 'alone and unattended'

---

9 Sheppard and Worlock, *Better Together*, p. 59.
10 *The Waiting Father* is the title of a book by Helmut Thielicke, a theologian Sheppard often quotes: Thielicke, H., *The Waiting Father: Sermons on the Parables of Jesus*, London: James Clarke, 1960 (German original, 1957). I am grateful to Richard Higginson for alerting me to this.

through the cathedral to the hymn, 'O Jesus I have promised to serve thee to the end'. There was a note of informality when he kissed Grace, Jenny and his mother Barbara during the Peace, then in a symbolic gesture, he welcomed representatives of the community as well as civic and church dignitaries. These included a grocer, a farmer, a brewery worker, a cricketer and a former domestic worker at Walton prison. Sheppard's friend Donald Swann wrote a piece for the occasion entitled 'A song in the City'. Sheppard laid great store by the charge he was given in the service to 'have a special care for the outcast and needy.'

*

Sheppard quickly put his stamp on the job. He decided not to retain the services of Pamela Edis, secretary to the two previous bishops. This caused some surprise, given her reputation and long record of faithful service. Questions were asked in diocesan synod about the decision, but Sheppard defended his right to choose his staff. Her replacements were to have a more clearly defined and limited administrative role. Another immediate change was the appointment of a domestic chaplain. Sheppard planned this while still in Peckham and had a job description prepared as early as February. The chaplain would deal with certain correspondence and with 'papers, books, journals, minutes which are sent to the bishop.' He would also handle all telephone calls at Bishop's Lodge and 'facilitate people's access to the bishop'. The job description was later expanded to include responsibility for media enquiries, processing clergy appointments and other supportive duties, but the requirement to 'read incoming and outgoing mail as often as possible' remained. Sheppard appointed his first chaplain, Alan Ripley, before the move. Ripley had served as the Liverpool diocesan youth officer and been recommended to Sheppard by John Bickersteth, the suffragan Bishop of Warrington. Sheppard invited Ripley and his wife Susan to visit him and Grace at Asylum Road.

Sheppard had seven chaplains during his time at Liverpool, each serving between three and four years. All were priests in their late twenties or early to mid thirties when appointed. Those with young families could find it a challenge to fit in with the long and sometimes unsocial hours Sheppard was accustomed to working. His final chaplain,

Paul Dawson, said that an important part of his job was simply to provide companionship to Sheppard on public occasions. 'I just need a friend with me', Sheppard said when Dawson asked him why he was required at events where he had no specific duty to fulfil. 'I was aware that simple statement came from deep within him', Dawson recalled. 'It came as quite a shock to realize that this big confident man was actually by nature quite shy and doing the public person took a lot out of him.'

*

Ripley helped Sheppard understand his new diocese. Sheppard saw similarities between Liverpool and the part of east London he knew in his Mayflower days, but beyond the city were features he had not encountered before. These included towns that had developed as major centres of industry during the nineteenth century, such as St Helens, Warrington and Wigan. They challenged some of the stereotypes he had developed in London. Owner-occupiers in these towns were not necessarily middle-class, Ripley told him. They might be miners who had been able to buy their houses. Church schools in Lancashire had a wider social mix than their counterparts in London. Sheppard thought poverty in Liverpool had more to do with unemployment than had been the case in Canning Town.[11]

He was surprised by the proportion of the population living on outer 'overspill' estates. These had mostly been established after the Second World War, and by the mid 1970s, they were housing twice as many people from the inner city as remained in the city itself. Sheppard struggled to accept that people on estates felt as marginalized as people in the inner-city. One of his priests, Michael Plunkett, tried to persuade him on this. Plunkett was a vicar on Cantril Farm, widely considered the most deprived estate in the country, and he pushed Sheppard to find an inclusive term for inner-city districts, outer estates and other areas of social deprivation. Eventually the term 'Urban Priority Areas' (UPAs) was adopted.[12] In the 1980s the Church of England found that

---

11 *Christians in Industrial Areas*, 49, Summer 1981, p. 11.

12 I have drawn here on a conversation with the Reverend Michael Plunkett. Sheppard talks about 'priority areas' within cities in *Built as a City*, e.g. pp. 229, 313, 340.

36 per cent of parishes in Liverpool diocese were UPAs. There were also more prosperous commuter areas, such as Formby and Southport.

Liverpool also differed from Woolwich in its churchmanship. In Woolwich, one parish in ten was evangelical, while the majority were in the Anglo-Catholic tradition. Liverpool had a higher proportion of evangelical parishes than any other diocese, and a mere handful were Anglo-Catholic. Liverpool's five previous bishops, from J. C. Ryle to Stuart Blanch, were all described as evangelical. Clergy in Liverpool were also more thinly spread than in London, and Sheppard found readers and other laypeople in leadership roles in many parishes. He valued their contribution. Despite the diocese having a smaller proportion of clergy to population than the south of England, 'in many ways church life is stronger than what I have known before', he once said. Laypeople had 'kept the flag flying when the Christian army has seemed very small.'[13] Sheppard welcomed the tradition of residential weekend conferences for laypeople, some of which attracted more than 300 participants. He thought they provided 'a powerful resource for an active and thoughtful laity.'[14]

Soon after the Sheppards arrived, they brought together an informal support group of 13 laypeople and clergy to meet for a meal every six weeks. The idea of resourcing themselves in this way had worked well in Peckham. Meetings had no fixed agenda and might involve playing games or watching a video as well as discussion, and the group became a 'trusted space' in which all members could air matters of concern. It became known, predictably, as the 'Baker's Dozen', and met throughout the Sheppards' years in Liverpool. David and Grace also met biannually with the bishops of 15 other dioceses in the north west and their spouses. The meetings moved around the homes of the diocesan bishops in Blackburn, Carlisle, Chester, Liverpool and Manchester, with a visit every three or four years to the Isle of Man. These were opportunities to share experience, seek advice on current issues and hear a speaker on a specific area of concern from the diocese of the host bishop.

---

13 Talk given during the centenary of the diocese, 1980: Sheppard papers (SHP), 1.8.

14 Sheppard, *Steps along Hope Street*, p. 155; *Church Times*, 21 June 1974, p. 3. Sheppard had been guest speaker at one, shortly before being named as the new bishop.

*

Sheppard anticipated his new job would be demanding. He cleared the deck of the commitments he had taken on in his previous posts. These included *Christians in Industrial Areas*, the Evangelical Urban Training Project, Frontier Youth Trust and Eclectics. Another was his weekly column for *Woman's Own*. He had faithfully turned this in for 17 years, and told the editor he was 'most reluctant' to end his contract: 'I have put off writing the letter for a long time because frankly it hurts'.[15] He would not have regretted freeing up this time, however. For a training course in 1981, he kept a log of his activities over a three-month period. This revealed he had 47 interviews or meetings with clergy and 53 with laypeople; preached 26 sermons; gave seven addresses; contributed to nine radio and television programmes and wrote two articles. He spent 174 hours on administration, 125 hours on institutional church matters, and 127 hours travelling. He took a day off every week and had 13 days' holiday. Tellingly, the section headed 'Reading' was blank, save for a reference to 'some mostly escapist reading e.g. Graham Greene'. He planned to take two reading weeks during the coming year.[16]

By the end of 1982, he was receiving 40 letters a day. 'I have a relentless post', he told one correspondent wanting to engage him on a topical issue. 'I am afraid that those letters which want to enter into a debate about great subjects in the world, have become one thing too many.' Yet he was unable to give people short measure. 'It is very difficult to do justice to the big questions that you raise in a letter – particularly when it is number 76 on the tape that I have been dictating all day!', he began a letter in 1984. He then wrote nearly 1,000 words in reply. He once said that his workload was 'self-induced' in the sense that it reflected his passion to tackle injustice. 'If you champion groups who feel no one stands by them, you cannot lightly put those commitments down.' [17]

*

---

15 Letter to Jane Reed, 15 March 1975: SHP, 31.1.
16 SHP, 29.5.
17 Correspondence: SHP, 7.6, 5.14; Sheppard, *Steps along Hope Street,* p. 198.

Sheppard had been in post a few weeks when John Bickersteth was appointed to Bath and Wells. He approved of Bickersteth's preferment but had not expected it so soon. Warrington was the only suffragan post in the diocese[18] and the vacancy enabled Sheppard to fill the post in a way that would suit his interpretation of his role. He was clear that he was called to work for the wellbeing of the city, and must not become preoccupied with 'churchy' matters. He could not do both. Advice he received while seeking a new suffragan helped him bring his thoughts together: 'If you are going to be able to have the public ministry that you should, you need a colleague who will be glad to tackle the "in-church" business of diocesan committees.'[19]

Sheppard's choice for Warrington was Michael Henshall. Henshall had been vicar of Altrincham since 1963 and served his 20 years as priest in northern dioceses. He had a reputation for getting things done and impressed Sheppard when they met, and they were to work together for the next 20 years. Their relationship was professional but also a genuine friendship. Sheppard would later say that he 'could not have asked for a more loyal and creative colleague with whom to share [his] episcopal ministry'.[20]

Henshall accepted the role that Sheppard proposed. He would take day-to-day responsibility for the diocese while Sheppard would prioritize the concerns of the city and the region. Sheppard would always steer the ship, and was not asking his suffragan to run the diocese. He would, however, allow Henshall to manage affairs his own way. As Mark Boyling, one of Sheppard's chaplains, later reflected, 'effective day to day delegation was possible because clear understanding of vision and strategy had been achieved.' Henshall's job description included the line 'to represent the Great Shepherd.' Whether any irony was intended by this is unknown.

Henshall's long experience as a parish priest, and strong roots in the north, helped him to identify with the clergy in the diocese. He would

---

18 Sheppard was also helped for eight years by an assistant bishop, Bill Flagg. Flagg had served in South America and was in Liverpool from 1978–86.

19 Sheppard, *Steps along Hope Street,* p. 161. The advice came from Prebendary Douglas Cleverley Ford.

20 Correspondence with the Very Reverend Mark Boyling.

often be their first port of call, and many valued his gifts as a pastor and encourager. Some found him willing to deal with a crisis at unsociable hours. Henshall had a similar work ethic to Sheppard, and a strong sense of personal discipline. He could be impatient with clergy he thought were not pulling their weight. 'Curates knew he would never let them down, but neither would he let them off', one obituarist reflected.[21] Many thought he earned his nickname 'Basher', but also that he administered the diocese efficiently. 'As a bishop', writes John Peart-Binns, Henshall 'combined the best professional practice of a chief executive with the pastoral attentiveness of a father-in-God who cared for clergy and laity alike.'[22]

*

Sheppard wanted to offer a 'ministry of encouragement' to his clergy in Liverpool. In his first months he and Grace visited all the vicarages in the diocese 'to try to offer support especially to those areas where the going was hardest.'[23] To ensure the wellbeing of his priests he instigated a 'three-legged stool of support'. Having seen the benefits of joint work consultations (JWCs) in Woolwich, he introduced the scheme in Liverpool. He expected all clergy to participate. Realizing that some might feel hesitant, he engaged in the first one himself. 'I needed to feel the threat the clergy will feel', he told Stuart Munns, who did the initial JWC with him. Munns was the Diocesan Missioner, and he used his business background to help Sheppard develop JWCs.

Sheppard also encouraged his clergy to have an appraisal every three years. Whereas a JWC focused on work and was conducted with a colleague, appraisals were more wide-ranging and might involve someone more distant. Sheppard developed a pattern of annual JWCs with Michael Henshall and an 'appraisal in ministry' every three years. They also had 'two-bishops' days' three times a year to discuss diocesan

21 Boyling, M., *Church Times*, 7 April 2017, p. 34.

22 Peart-Binns, J. S., *A Certain Sound: The Life of Bishop Michael Henshall*, unpublished manuscript, p. 3. I am grateful to Mr Peart-Binns for permission to draw from his research and for his assistance with this project.

23 Henderson, S., ed., *Adrift in the Eighties*, Basingstoke: Marshall Pickering, 1986, p. 54.

business. The third leg of Sheppard's stool of support was to encourage priests to have a spiritual director.

All newly ordained clergy had written terms and conditions of work. They were expected to keep two hours each day for leisure, take a regular day off each week, and have six weeks holiday a year. Having seen the benefit of sabbaticals at the Mayflower, Sheppard told clergy they should plan three months away every seven years in addition to holidays. He recognized this would not be straightforward for many, but encouraged vicars and their parochial church councils to surmount the difficulties. 'A tired clergyman is a liability to his parish, his family and himself', he wrote.[24] He also supported the idea of clergy teams, but this was often resisted by those who valued their independence. Sheppard thought team ministry could be effective in sustaining morale and maintaining continuity, particularly in difficult areas.

Sheppard promoted an inter-diocesan counselling scheme for clergy and their spouses. An initiative of the Bishop of Chester, Michael Baughen, it enabled clergy to receive professional counselling in a diocese other than their own, thus ensuring confidentiality. Sheppard also supported COMPASS,[25] an ecumenical resource for counselling that included help for marital problems. He liked to bring clergy and laypeople together to discuss marriage, and he and Grace would start the discussion by sharing challenges they had faced themselves. They had had crisis points in their own marriage and sought counselling.

Sheppard constantly felt the pressure of having the oversight of 280 clergy. He would see a priest at a moment of crisis but delegate the follow-up to others. Clergy who sought Sheppard's help valued his ministry, but others perceived that, because of the role played by his suffragan, his priests mattered less to him. This was reinforced by his not being directly contactable by phone. His predecessor, Stuart Blanch, had had an advertised phone number and was likely to answer calls himself. The Sheppards' private line was an ex-directory number, only divulged to a few, and would generally be answered by Grace. Some clergy found it hard to accept that their bishop had a role on the national

---

24 *Liverpool Diocesan News*, no. 148, April 1981, and no. 154, October 1981.
25 Counselling on Merseyside, Pastoral and Supporting Services.

and international stage, while others found it a source of pride, even if it affected his relationship with them.

This critical view of Sheppard was given prominence in an article in the local press in June 1978. The journalist (and later television presenter) Anne Robinson had sought an interview with Sheppard and been offered a date six months hence. She reproached him for having a tightly packed schedule 'planned months in advance', and went to print without an interview. Sheppard was compared unfavourably with his predecessor, who 'could be seen cycling round the city' and stopping to chat with people in the street. 'If you're not poor, black and unemployed he doesn't want to know', an anonymous vicar in 'the lusher pastures of the outer area of Liverpool' was quoted as saying.[26] Sheppard later wondered whether that might have made a good reference. He was upset by the article but clear that his 'bias to the poor' was the essence of his diocesan work. One of his closest friends, Nicholas Frayling, said that, if the price of his commitment to his ecumenical and political activities was a certain remoteness, 'he felt it was a price worth paying'. These activities 'were for him the essence of Kingdom Christianity, often at its most courageous'.[27]

*

When Archbishop Beck announced his retirement in 1975, Sheppard was consulted during the process of appointing a successor. If he put in a word for the Bishop of Portsmouth, Derek Worlock, it would have been based on a meeting they had had ten years before. Sheppard was then at the Mayflower and Worlock a priest in nearby Stepney. Their conversation, which remained in Sheppard's memory, revealed a shared concern for the inner-city. They never had the chance to develop a friendship, and Worlock went to Portsmouth shortly after.

Worlock was translated to Liverpool on 7 February 1976. He had hoped to be appointed Archbishop of Westminster and came with some reluctance. He talked of the move north as 'like a divorce'.[28] But, like

---

26 Robinson, A., 'Playing It His Way', *Liverpool Echo*, 5 June 1978.
27 The Very Reverend Nicholas Frayling, tribute at DSS memorial service, 23 May 2005.
28 Furnival, J. and Knowles, A., *Archbishop Derek Worlock: His Personal Journey*, London: Geoffrey Chapman, 1998, p. 163.

Sheppard, he would stay in Liverpool for 20 years and become, as one local journalist put it, an 'honorary Scouser'.

Worlock was to prove a formidable partner. Prior to his brief ministry in inner-city London, he had been secretary to three archbishops of Westminster. He had also been involved in the business of the Second Vatican Council, which sat between 1962 and 1965 and redefined the Catholic Church's relationship with the modern world. Worlock was secretary to the English-speaking bishops, with responsibility for gathering their bloc votes. An earlier role involved encouraging Catholic peers to support the Attlee government's social legislation in the House of Lords. He had the reputation of being an effective organizer and a person who could deliver. Sheppard described him as an 'engine room' man and an astute politician. He valued Worlock's understanding of the media and the care he took in preparing unambiguous press releases.[29] Worlock's involvement with Vatican II gave him, like Sheppard, an outward-looking vision for the Church. His concern would also be the people of his archdiocese, not just his own Catholic community.

Sheppard was Worlock's first visitor in Liverpool. Worlock recalled him appearing with a bottle of wine on his first evening in the city, a dark February night, and they soon developed a friendship. They also agreed to give a lead towards ecumenical cooperation and look for occasions when they could make that public. Like Sheppard, Worlock had been warned not to rock the boat, but he claimed good authority for working ecumenically. In sending him to Liverpool, Pope Paul VI had charged him to ensure that the city did not become 'another Belfast'. The Pope also told Worlock to make people's social and material needs a priority.[30] Sheppard and Worlock had a common agenda from the start.

They discovered that they brought complementary gifts which they were happy to share. Sheppard had begun to understand Roman Catholic traditions and social teaching while at Woolwich; now he learnt more about the church's distinctives from Worlock. Worlock asked Sheppard to explain the significance of the Scriptures in his tradition. The respect they shared for the other's beliefs, and the seriousness with which they

---

29 Sheppard, *Steps along Hope Street*, pp. 169–70.
30 Furnival and Knowles, *Archbishop Derek Worlock*, p. 170.

took their own, helped cement their unity across doctrinal divides. 'At the root of the partnership [we] experience', Sheppard later wrote, 'is not some social and political alliance which ignores theological differences, but the bond of baptism, the recognition that we are indeed brothers in Christ.' He acknowledged there were differences they had to negotiate, including over abortion and the ordination of women. But they 'shared deeply the central truths of the Gospel.'[31]

Their public friendship became a significant feature of their time in Liverpool. They were aware that they were not the first bishops in the city to work together: their predecessors, Blanch and Beck, had built bridges between their respective churches. Both had also met regularly with Free Church leaders in connection with the ecumenical mission 'Call to the North' in the late 1960s. A Liverpool Churches Ecumenical Council had been created in 1966, while further back, Archbishop Richard Downey and Bishop Albert David enjoyed a cordial relationship between the wars, as did Downey and Bishop Clifford Martin in the 1950s.[32] What made Sheppard and Worlock's relationship different was its intentionally public nature. By taking opportunities to be seen together, they consciously worked to bridge the divide between their traditions. In one sense, this was easier than it would have been for their predecessors: there was less obvious hostility between the communities in Liverpool than even a generation before. But with the Troubles in Northern Ireland continuing, ongoing sectarian sympathies in the North-West of England provided a worrying backdrop. The bishops' action required more courage than was immediately apparent and both were accused of 'treachery' by more dogmatic members of their respective churches.

In the mid-1980s, Sheppard and Worlock initiated a regular gathering of ecumenical clergy from Belfast, Glasgow and Liverpool. Calling itself

---

31 Typescript, undated: SHP, 18.5; press statement undated following Worlock's death: SHP, 30.6. Sheppard said in 1994 that he was '100% opposed to abortion on demand and its use as a contraceptive' but could not 'agree outright . . . that it is always wrong'. In *Steps along Hope Street* (p. 270) he says he 'believed that abortion was always an evil, but that there were circumstances [when it] was the lesser of evils'. When a Catholic paper publicized Sheppard's views, Worlock was pressed to denounce him. He refused to do so.

32 Williams, D., *Stuart Blanch: a life*, London: SPCK, 2001, pp. 87, 101–2; Hunter, J. G., 'A Unique Project of Mission: Forty Years on, a Personal Memoir', *Northern History*, DOI: 2018, 10.1080/0078172X.2018.1510464; *Steps along Hope Street*, p. 165; Russell, E., *Not A Dead See: Some People and Episodes in the Life of the Diocese of Liverpool 1880–1996*, Southport: Eric Russell, 1996, pp. 43–5.

the 'North West Triangle', the group met by rotation in each city for 24 hours twice a year. Their cities shared many common features. On one visit to Belfast, Sheppard saw a wall dividing Protestant and Catholic communities, and it made a lasting impression on him. He described breaking down in tears while reading a document presented at one of the meetings describing the personal cost of rejecting sectarianism.

Sheppard wanted his public witness and engagement with Worlock to have a strong spiritual base. On the first Good Friday after Worlock's arrival, he phoned him. There was no business to discuss, he said, but could they share their reflections about Christ's death 'as two disciples'? 'When I put down the phone . . . I realised the significance of our "meeting at the foot of the cross"', Worlock later wrote.[33] They made a point of meeting for reflection every subsequent Good Friday.

*

Just after her first Christmas in Liverpool, Grace made her agoraphobia publicly known. The BBC programme *Anno Domini* had approached David to do a feature on his new role. When the producer, William Nicholson, met Grace and heard about her condition, he asked her if she would be interviewed on camera. Nicholson wanted the programme to get behind the public image of 'professional religious leaders'. He felt that Grace's vulnerability would demonstrate powerfully the deep issues with which she and David were dealing.[34]

Nicholson was right: Grace's contribution was the talking point of the programme. More than 1,000 viewers wrote in, and appreciation of it was expressed for many years. 'If a bishop's wife can feel like that, then I do not feel so alone', was a typical comment Grace received.[35] Her willingness to open up owed much to the sensitivity of Nicholson and his interviewer, Peter France. In an unusual move for the time, Nicholson recorded another reel of film the same length as Grace's interview but

---

33 Sheppard and Worlock, *Better Together*, p. 61.

34 I have drawn on correspondence with William Nicholson, who later achieved fame as the writer of *Shadowlands* and other plays, screenplays and novels.

35 Sheppard, G., *An Aspect of Fear: A journey from anxiety to peace*, London: Darton, Longman & Todd, 1989.

with different material. He told Grace that he would use the substitute film if she changed her mind about the interview at any point before screening. Her decision to 'go for it', as she later put it, helped her glimpse that recovery was possible, even though it might be a long process. It was an example of 'knowing the truth, and the truth making you free'.[36] The programme was screened again the following July.

Thirteen years later Grace published a book about her struggle with agoraphobia. Entitled *An Aspect of Fear: A Journey from Anxiety to Peace*, its frankness and practical advice inspired many. Grace developed a ministry of her own in the wake of her book, with invitations to speak and appearances on BBC radio. This led to a second book, *Pits and Pedestals: A Journey Towards Self-Respect*, published in 1995. This reflected on her journey from the self-denial which characterized her childhood and adolescence, towards achieving a 'healthy balance' between humility and self-esteem.

Grace found the cathedral in Liverpool a constant challenge. She described it as 'one hell of an open space'. The thought of having to attend there often, and sit at the front, filled her with dread. Sometimes she would remove the name labels on the seats 'for her own survival'.[37] For years she survived the ordeal of public events by self-harming. Under cover of a cape bought for the purpose, she would pinch the skin on her upper arm to give her greater pain than she was already enduring.

Grace made a major contribution to public life in Liverpool, however, through her involvement with Family Service Units (FSU). Founded in Liverpool in 1948, FSU was widely respected for its work supporting families in severe difficulties, and she became chair of its Liverpool unit in 1982. Sheppard also took an interest in the work, and from 1985 until his retirement served as FSU national president. Every autumn the Sheppards opened their home and garden on behalf of the FSU. Grace also contributed to the wider Church by producing a handbook for bishops' wives. The 1980s saw a significant change in the role bishops' wives were expected to play, and the Church asked Grace to produce a

36 Sheppard, G., *Living with Dying*, London: Darton, Longman & Todd, 2010, pp. 25–6.
37 Sheppard, G., *An Aspect of Fear*, p. 26; Grace Sheppard diary, 27–28 September 1986.

practical guide.[38] Labelled the 'Jackdaw Kit', it covered a range of topics, including sensitive issues within marriage and the power relationship between spouses. 'These issues were closely worked out – with cartoons – to provide a guide for new bishops' wives as they sorted out their *modus vivendi* with or in spite of their husbands', Grace later wrote.[39]

*

Sheppard began to engage with unemployment in Merseyside as soon as he had settled in. He thought the absence of a job, or poverty wages, took away a person's dignity and rendered family life more fragile. It was a 'proper concern of the church'. In 1977, he was invited to chair the Area Board for Special Programmes of the Manpower Services Commission (MSC), a post he held for eight years. The MSC had been established in 1973 to coordinate employment and training services in the UK. Its focus on helping young people through its Youth Opportunities Programme (YOP) enthused Sheppard, and he saw that side of its work grow in Merseyside. In 1981, one in two 16-year-old school leavers in Merseyside and Cheshire went on to the YOP.[40] Sheppard had developed a good understanding of industry from his engagement with factories and active support for industrial mission while in Canning Town and Woolwich.

In 1977 the British Council of Churches produced a report on employment called *Work or What?* It argued that a new 'life ethic' was needed for an age of mass, long-term unemployment. The Protestant work ethic implied that the responsibility for finding fulfilling work lay with the individual, while those without work might be considered lazy or worthless. Now a new social purpose was required, 'rooted in the fulfilment of the potential of human beings and [built] on an understanding of our common interdependence.'[41] Sheppard welcomed

---

38 This change was partly inspired by Rosalind Runcie's decision to pursue her own career as a classical pianist while her husband was Archbishop of Canterbury.

39 These words appear in comments Grace made in the margin of a draft of *Steps along Hope Street*: Sheppard added an exclamation mark after 'husbands' in the final text (pp. 206–7): SHP, 44.6.

40 Letter dated, 14 January 1981: SHP, 11.8.

41 *Work or What? A Christian examination of the employment crisis*, London: Church Information Office, 1977, p. 41.

the report, inviting groups from management, trade unions, churches, industrial mission, local government, the black community and other networks to meet and discuss it over two weekends. He then drew on the report in a New Year message to industry in 1978. Unemployment in Merseyside was a *chronic* rather than a *cyclic* problem, he noted. He invited management and unions to consider those without work when planning their overtime for the year: 'Look seriously and soon at work sharing', he asked them. He also advocated an ethic based on the biblical idea of being 'members one of another', rather than that of 'every man for himself . . . This means powerful and highly-paid workers being willing to drop their cash standard of living, so that the more vulnerable groups can have a proper standard of living', he argued.[42] His audience might have seen this as naïve.

During the 'winter of discontent' in 1978–9, Sheppard and Worlock shared their views on the strikes affecting the country. These largely involved public sector trade unions, unhappy at the Callaghan government's imposition of a pay cap. Rubbish was left uncollected and bodies unburied. The situation was especially acute in Merseyside, where the need to lay-off staff was adding to the already high rate of unemployment. The bishops said that all who had broken the government's pay guidelines, including 'powerful groups in management and in the strongest unions', were responsible for the crisis, not only those on strike. They commended the Christian principles of concern for the poor, self-sacrifice by the strong for the sake of the weak, and a 'good society'. They repeated the call to act as 'members one of another.'[43] Sheppard lived by this principle, leading the resistance to moves by the Church Commissioners to award a pay rise to bishops twice that being sought by workers in the dispute.[44]

Sheppard later opposed calls by Conservative ministers for unemployed people to move to areas where work was more plentiful. In 1980 Prime Minister Margaret Thatcher told young people in South Wales they

---

42 'Work – or What?', typescript: SHP, 11.10. The biblical reference is Romans 12.5.
43 'A Christian Approach to the Industrial Crisis', typescript and printed leaflet, 3 February 1979: SHP, 11.3.
44 Chandler, A., *The Church of England in the Twentieth Century: The Church Commissioners and the Politics of Reform 1948-1998*, Woodbridge: Boydell Press, 2006, pp. 260-1.

ought to 'get mobile'. The Secretary of State for Employment, Norman Tebbit, famously told a party conference that his father 'got on his bike and looked for work' when he was unemployed in the 1930s. In a letter to *The Times*, Sheppard and Worlock said that, if young people did find employment elsewhere, 'the wound of this lost generation would leave a scar upon the health of the community for decades to come.' They called for the creation of more jobs in inner-city areas to provide an incentive for the adventurous to stay. They wanted opportunities for young people to train for advanced technologies, otherwise a 'vicious circle' would develop with businesses avoiding the inner-city 'because there isn't a sufficient pool of skilled labour . . . We want to say to many of the most adventurous young people, "For God's sake, stay!"'[45]

Sheppard was often challenged to say what the churches were doing about unemployment. In 1984 he helped create the Merseyside Churches' Unemployment Committee (MCUC). This monitored the effect of government policies in the region and developed 'an appropriate under-standing of work for the future.' One survey it conducted showed that church-sponsored schemes in Merseyside employed 273 full-time and 1,123 part-time workers. Jobs ranged from furniture repair to working with the elderly and on environmental projects.[46] Sheppard encountered first-hand the extent of unemployment in Liverpool when a vacancy at Church House was advertised. It was not an attractive or well-paid job, but more than 300 people applied. The development officer of MCUC, Su Williams, did a statistical analysis of the applicants, and Sheppard later used this in conversations with government ministers.

Sheppard continued to be concerned about discrimination on racial grounds in employment. In 1993 he and Wilfred Wood gave their names to a set of ten principles aimed at achieving race equality in employment.[47] The 'Wood-Sheppard Principles' largely echoed what was already required by existing legislation, but Sheppard thought 'they could put real teeth into good intentions' if backed up by 'serious monitoring'

---

45 *The Times*, 30 July 1980.

46 *Livewire*, February 1985 and May 1986; Sheppard and Worlock, *Better Together*, p. 153; I have also drawn on a conversation with Mrs Su Williams, former development officer of MCUC.

47 These were drawn up by the Churches Commission for Racial Justice and the Race Equality in Employment Project of the Ecumenical Committee for Corporate Responsibility.

within companies and supported by management. He and Wood hoped churches would encourage companies with whom they worked, or in which they invested, to have equal opportunity policies and use their principles to monitor them.

*

Sheppard's concern about unemployment prompted his first joint action with other church leaders in Liverpool. He and Worlock were already meeting regularly with the district chairman of the Methodist Church, Norwyn Denny; the Baptist regional superintendent, Trevor Hubbard; the moderator of the United Reformed Church's Mersey Province, John Williamson; and the Salvation Army's Divisional Commander, Lily Farrar. In 1976 a church leaders' group was formally established, serviced by an ecumenical officer. In 1977 the group met to discuss a government report on the 'inner areas' of major cities, which included a detailed study of Liverpool. Each church leader was invited to comment, but at Worlock's suggestion the group decided to send one agreed submission instead of separate responses. The two bishops were trusted to draft the response and submit it in the name of all the churches.

Another turning point in terms of ecumenical partnership occurred two years later. Workers at the Dunlop factory organized a protest march against a decision to close the site and make staff redundant. Worlock was asked if the churches would take part and felt confident enough to agree without consulting the others. Sheppard was committed to be at diocesan synod that day, but he left halfway through to join the others on the march. That action reflected his priorities in microcosm. 'I actually think it was very important for us that people saw that human need, like unemployment, sometimes comes before churchy things', he later wrote.[48]

The church leaders encouraged their younger members to build ecumenical bridges. Every few years they organized pilgrimages to places such as Taizé, Iona, Lindisfarne, Rome and Assisi. Some 40 or 50 would

---

48 Furnival and Knowles, *Archbishop Derek Worlock*, p. 190.

take part, along with the church leaders. The trips took a lot of time, Sheppard said, but were 'top priority'. Being together for a week meant differences could be worked through honestly by the young people and the leaders. The areas where full unity was not possible were made clear, including inter-communion. Sheppard and Worlock were committed to upholding the teachings of their churches and wanted their younger members to understand what that involved. They often spoke about the 'pain' of this division, but throughout their 20-year partnership they remained true to their own convictions and never shared communion.

Sheppard gave a high priority to the church leaders' group. He felt there was a 'high degree of trust and friendship' between its members, strong enough to stand the test of one member publicly taking an independent line on an issue, as Sheppard would do on abortion.[49] Sheppard found it helpful that the Free Church leaders stayed in office for the first ten years he and Worlock were in Liverpool. Moderators, district chairs and their equivalents generally served a fixed term of less than ten years and were then moved on. It was 'a gift of continuity we could not have organised', he said.[50] Sheppard never suggested that closer ties between Anglicans and Roman Catholics should be achieved at the cost of communion with the Free Churches. He supported proposed covenants between them and the Anglican churches: 'How can we expect to heal the rift with Rome if we are not willing to heal the rifts which are within our power to heal now?', he asked at diocesan synod in 1980.[51]

*

The completion of the Anglican Cathedral in 1978 was marked by a service of thanksgiving and dedication attended by the Queen.[52] The Palace informed Sheppard and the Dean, Edward Patey, that Her Majesty would be available for several hours after the service and would like 'to see something of church life on Merseyside.' The expectation was that

---

49 Notes for a 'study weekend', October 1980: SHP, 39.2.
50 Sheppard, *Steps along Hope Street*, p. 166.
51 Sheppard and Worlock, *Better Together*, p. 90.
52 Technically the cathedral was not quite complete at this point: see Patey, E., *My Liverpool Life*, London: Mowbray, 1983, p. 23.

this would be Anglican church life, but Sheppard wanted to highlight examples of the 'growing ecumenical trust and partnership' in the region. He suggested a focus on churches serving people in need, at home and overseas. One of the churches the Queen visited was St Mary's, Highfield Street. Sheppard later learned that this was the first time a reigning monarch had entered a Roman Catholic parish church in England since the Reformation.[53]

The cost of completing the cathedral caused Sheppard much soul-searching. It had been under construction for 74 years and was the largest in the UK and fifth largest in the world. Within his first year as bishop he had been invited to support an appeal for £460,000, a sum equivalent to £3 million four decades later. He supported a further appeal for £400,000 two years later. 'Can it be right . . . to go on building this vast place of worship [when] . . . we should put greater resources to serving the needs of the whole man,' Sheppard asked at the time of the first appeal.

He answered this in two ways. First, the question was not whether to build a great cathedral. If it were, he would vote against it. It was about keeping faith 'with other generations who have carried this great dream for seventy years.' Second, the cathedral would reflect God's greatness and help people experience that. 'Great architecture . . . helps many, whose experience of life is relentlessly urban to be aware of mystery and wonder,' Sheppard thought. Serving people in need, and worshipping in fine buildings, were not opposites. It was right to put substantial resources into making beautiful worship, since 'worship has been and is the motivator which keeps a great many people enduring when others would give up.'[54]

Sheppard made a further appeal for money when the diocese marked its centenary in 1980. This was to fund projects in deaneries and parishes, with 10 per cent going to the Anglican Province of the Southern Cone. This part of South America was linked to Liverpool through the international partnership scheme, 'Partners in Mission' (PIM). Giving proved to be slow, and the local press thought Sheppard might be the reason. The bishop is 'not pictured in the popular mind as capitalism's staunchest

---

53 Sheppard, *Steps along Hope Street*, p. 175.
54 Statement at press conference, 25 May 1976: SHP, 24.5; *Liverpool Diocesan News*, no. 91, July 1976; private letters, 8 January 1979 and 29 May 1991: SHP, 1.7, 21.14.

ally', wrote the *Echo*. He 'might have unwittingly deterred local entrepreneurs from sharing [their] capitalistic gains with him.' Sheppard thought this unlikely. He noted that many firms had given generously to the cathedral appeal.[55]

Sheppard acknowledged he was known to be concerned more for people on the shop floor than 'those who bear heavy burdens in management.' He wanted to listen to those outside the circles of power, who feel that the Church is not for them, he said. 'And I feel the strain of being a bridge person, both because I do not renounce my own background and because I also spend a lot of time, mostly privately, in the company of those who are in management.'[56] He and Worlock would later develop a pattern of regular discussions with business leaders in the region.

Sheppard saved the diocese some money during the centenary using his skills as an artist. The city was also celebrating 100 years and agreed to accept a painting of the cathedral as a gift from the diocese. Sheppard estimated £2,000 would be needed to commission a suitable work, but Michael Henshall suggested he take on the task himself. Until he was in his thirties, Sheppard had assumed the artistic talent of his maternal grandfather, J. A. Shepherd, had passed him by. With encouragement from Grace, however, he took up oil painting as a hobby, attempting at least one picture each holiday. Now he spent his post-Easter vacation producing the 'commission' for the city using a former MSC office in Leece Street as a base. This provided a fine view of the cathedral's newly completed west front from the city. He was delighted when his colleagues in the diocese agreed that his effort was suitable to be presented to the Mayor.

*

In February 1980, Sheppard spoke at General Synod in favour of a boycott of the Olympic Games to be held in Moscow that summer. His speech was widely reported, and comparisons made with his stance on apartheid South Africa. He thought the case for boycotting South Africa

---

55 Phelps, P., 'Bishop's Aid Call Falls on Deaf Ears', *Liverpool Echo*, 7 January 1981.
56 Typescript undated [1980], p. 10: SHP, 1.8.

was clearer than for the Soviet Union, since politics was so obviously part of the fabric of sporting life under apartheid. Yet the Moscow games would be used to political ends, he argued, to show Soviet Russia 'as a leader in the peaceful life of nations'.[57] A boycott of the Olympics was also the policy of the Prime Minister, Margaret Thatcher, and her government. In the event British athletes did compete. As a regular contributor to General Synod debates, he only spoke on topics in which he had a special interest and expertise, including homelessness, unemployment, taxation, racial justice, ecumenism and urban regeneration. One topic he avoided was nuclear disarmament, though he chaired the debate on the Board for Social Responsibility report *The Church and the Bomb* in 1982. This was televised and widely discussed in the media.

*

In December 1980 Sheppard was introduced to the House of Lords as a 'Lord Spiritual'. Twenty-one diocesan bishops are entitled to sit in the Lords according to seniority, with retirements creating vacancies for the next in line.[58] Sheppard chose as his 'supporters' the Bishop of Derby, Cyril Bowles, and the Bishop of Newcastle, Ronnie Bowlby. Bowles had been his principal at Ridley Hall, and Bowlby was a fellow member of a group of urban bishops which met informally.[59] He made his maiden speech in a debate on unemployment, describing the situation in Liverpool and the effect the closure of major businesses had had on local communities. He did not feel a great affinity with the House at first. 'It's a funny place', he told Hugh Montefiore in 1983.

> I sometimes feel very out of sympathy with its temper. I quite often feel that there is very little understanding of what life is like in a city

---

57 SHP, 7.11.

58 The archbishops of Canterbury and York and bishops of London, Durham and Winchester sit as of right. Since 2015, for the ensuing ten years, vacancies for the 21 other places must be filled by a female bishop, if there is one who is eligible.

59 This group had been meeting regularly, with their wives, since the late 1970s. Members included, in addition to Liverpool and Newcastle, Ripon, Lichfield, Manchester, Birmingham, Chelmsford and Stepney.

like [Liverpool]. But then that is an argument for using the opportunity to speak up.

He said, however, he found it worthwhile contributing to debates. Even if only a few peers were present, a speech could be picked up by the press or interested people in the public gallery.[60] Despite his reservations, and the relative distance of his see from London, Sheppard was one of the most regular voters on the bishops' bench. Of the 51 bishops eligible to vote during the Thatcher years, only six cast more votes than he did.[61] He hoped that all the main churches might one day be represented in the house, and later, extended this to other faiths. In retirement he nominated senior figures in the Jewish and Islamic communities for life peerages. A cartoon of Sheppard, sporting both clerical and cricketing garb, remained on the wall of the bishops' robing room until after his death.

*

As the new decade dawned, Sheppard might have thought he was getting to know his diocese. He had been in post five years and was already making his mark. The next year would bring a profound new challenge and fresh opportunities for service, healing and bridge-building.

---

60 Letter dated 11 April 1983: SHP, 7.8.
61 Partington, A., *Church and State: The Contribution of the Church of England Bishops to the House of Lords during the Thatcher Years*, Milton Keynes: Paternoster, 2006, p. 98.

10

Liverpool
(1981–1985)

The Sheppards took their first sabbatical from Liverpool in April 1981. They based themselves in London, where David spent the weekdays writing. He wanted to draw together his thinking on the gospel's 'bias to the poor'. He and Grace planned to be away for four months, but in early July, there was serious unrest in a part of inner-city Liverpool. A fortnight later, they cut short their sabbatical and returned home.

The trouble became known as the Toxteth riots. Earlier in the year there had been violent clashes between police and protestors in Brixton, south London, and events in Toxteth followed a similar pattern. Hundreds of police were injured, and 500 people arrested. Dozens of buildings were burnt to the ground and shops were looted; rioters used petrol bombs, scaffolding poles and burning milk floats. The police employed CS gas for the first time on the mainland.

Lord Scarman investigated both Brixton and Toxteth, concluding 'each was the spontaneous reaction of angry young men, most of whom were black, against what they saw as a hostile police force.' A later report by Lord Gifford spoke of a 'wholly unacceptable level of racist language and behaviour' on the part of the police. Sheppard thought another factor was a feeling of powerlessness within the community; people had no say in decisions that affected their lives.

Sheppard returned briefly to Liverpool on the third day of the trouble. Derek Worlock had kept him updated by phone and told him his absence would be noted. The two met with the Deputy Chief Constable and asked him to consider sealing off the area of the trouble that night. This advice was followed. Sheppard suggested to community leaders that they encourage people to stay indoors and keep clear of trouble. He and Worlock helped to make this happen. When the community leaders

199

needed megaphones to make themselves heard by the crowd, the bishops obtained two from the police station and got them through.

Seeking to be a calming influence, Sheppard and Worlock walked the area in subsequent weeks with local clergy and members of the community. They maintained contact with both the police and community leaders, acting as mediators when direct communication proved impossible. 'We were setting ourselves a role for the years ahead which has been at least as difficult as it has been important', they later wrote.[1] Just how difficult became clear when a second wave of rioting broke out later that month. This time police drove vehicles at high speed into crowds to disperse them, and one man died when a police van hit him. The police also suffered injuries. The bishops called for 'attitudes of reconciliation rather than revenge' on all sides: 'If better relationships are to come about, there will have to be a willingness at some time to meet and to talk.'[2]

As when he was at Woolwich, Sheppard worked to understand black issues in Liverpool. He was helped by a Passionist priest, Fr Austin Smith, and another member of the order, Fr Nicholas Postlethwaite. Both were trusted members of the Toxteth community. Sheppard called on them in his first weeks in Liverpool, surprising them by turning up at their house unannounced one evening. Sheppard was struck by Smith's assertion that the church had not been listening or 'entering into the argument' in the inner city. Smith spoke of black people's struggle to assert their human dignity, having to 'fight for equal acceptance in a world boasting equality for all.'[3]

In 1976 Sheppard wrote the introduction to the British Council of Churches' report, *The New Black Presence in Britain*. The report claimed that the 'race issue' was not a problem caused by black people. 'The basic issue concerns the nature of British society as a whole', it asserted, and 'features of that society' that pre-dated more recent immigration.[4]

---

1 Sheppard, D. S., and Worlock, D., *Better Together: Christian partnership in a hurt city*, London: Hodder & Stoughton, 1988, p. 170.

2 'Reconciliation not revenge', *Daily Post*, 13 August 1981.

3 Sheppard, D. S., *Steps along Hope Street*, London: Hodder & Stoughton, 2002, p. 212; 'Deceptively Mild', Poverty Network paper, Summer 1986, p. 5.

4 British Council of Churches' Working Party on Britain as a Multi-Racial Society, *The New Black Presence in Britain: A Christian scrutiny*, April 1976, p. 7.

Sheppard sought Smith's advice before writing the piece. Smith said the report was relevant to Liverpool and Sheppard should commend it.

Sheppard was surprised to find black people 'conspicuously absent' from mainstream life in Liverpool. Hardly any were seen working in shops or in the public sector. Most black people lived in a small area of the city known as the Granby Triangle.[5] Unlike in London, few black people in Merseyside were new to the area. The roots of the black community went back to the 1730s, making it Britain's oldest. Yet despite being an established community in the city, Sheppard noted that few black people attended church compared with London. Only three of the 220 parishes in the diocese could be described as multi-racial, and he knew of no black-led churches. In the late 1980s, he helped to create an ecumenical project aimed at enabling black people to 'find their way into the mainstream of Church life'. Churches Action for Racial Equality (CARE) also worked to build bridges with communities 'where few had known the opportunity of meeting black people'.[6]

Sheppard wanted to understand more about the police and how they coped with the pressures they faced. He spent a day at Bramshill training college in Hampshire, and he encouraged cadets to talk about their fears when confronting unpredictable situations. Senior police chiefs told him of the challenges officers faced on the beat. Shortly after the riots he was interviewed by the local police magazine, and asked to respond to the claim that, if faced with the choice, he would come down on the side of 'the people' rather than the police. 'I feel deeply for police officers doing an increasingly complex and dangerous job on behalf of us all', he replied. 'At the same time, I am called to make a special effort to stand in the shoes of those who are disadvantaged and who feel alienated from the comfortable and successful parts of our society.'[7]

Sheppard was attacked in the press for supporting the Liverpool 8 Defence Committee, formed in the wake of the riots. Sheppard understood its main role was to help people visit family members held on

---

5 Belchem, J., *Before the Windrush: Race Relations in Twentieth-century Liverpool*, Liverpool: Liverpool University Press, 2014, pp. 233–4.

6 Address to CARE AGM, 8 January 1992; Sheppard papers (SHP), 25.3; Sheppard, *Steps along Hope Street*, pp. 324–5.

7 Typescript, 'Article for *Merseybeat*', January 1982: SHP, 10.14.

remand near Warrington, but it also helped organize a march calling for the dismissal of the Chief Constable, which Sheppard acknowledged had caused controversy. Some newspapers suggested the Committee had a sinister and even violent agenda. When the British Council of Churches (BCC) made the Committee a grant of £500 through its Community and Race Relations Unit (CRRU), the press assumed local churches had arranged it.

In his autobiography, Sheppard maintains that he and other church leaders were neither consulted nor forewarned of the announcement of the grant.[8] This is an interesting form of words. Sheppard may not have been forewarned about the *announcement* of the grant, but he was aware of the grant itself. During its visit to Liverpool, the BCC team told Sheppard they would be recommending a grant, and their letter advising the Defence Committee that a grant had been agreed was copied to him. In a public statement Sheppard, Worlock and the Methodist district chairman, Norwyn Denny, said that the grant should be understood as a 'gesture of help towards those who have felt alienated from the rest of the community.' They hoped this kind of cooperation from outside would encourage the Defence Committee 'to work together for the removal of long-term mistrust, and to build more positive relationships for the future.' They affirmed their condemnation of violence and of the campaign against the Chief Constable and the police.[9]

Sheppard later acknowledged this had been an uncomfortable time. Sections of the press implied the church leaders were giving unequivocal support to the Defence Committee, and senior police officers denounced him in private and public. His clergy were deeply divided: some told him they had seen first-hand police aggression towards Toxteth people. Others had police officers in their congregation who had suffered injuries. 'There was no escaping the acute discomfort of being wedged between two sets of people, knowing that we belonged to both', he later reflected.[10]

---

8 Sheppard, *Steps along Hope Street*, p. 215.

9 Joint statement, 27 August 1981: SHP, 10.9. I am grateful for correspondence with Canon Richard Wheeler, one of the two BCC staff members who visited Liverpool prior to the award of the grant.

10 Sheppard, *Steps along Hope Street,* p. 216.

There was a positive side: Sheppard and Worlock's appearances together in Toxteth were a turning point in public perceptions of their partnership. 'There have been many occasions when I have blessed our close partnership as church leaders', Sheppard wrote with reference to Worlock and Henshall, 'never more so than at this time.'[11]

An important development was the establishment of a law centre in Liverpool 8, which aimed to provide legal and advice services to the community and improve people's contact with the police. Sheppard thought it would help the community see that the law could be a friend not a threat, and hoped it would lead to the emergence of Liverpool's first black lawyers. He raised more than £75,000 for the centre from trusts and charities, and promoted it to the Home Office, local leaders and the police. His ability to advocate for the centre was grounded in the work he did behind the scenes, building relationships with community leaders and mentoring and befriending local people.

Sheppard also wanted the centre to be managed by people elected from the community: the church leaders had no wish to control it. The centre described itself as 'a partnership of trust between the churches and the local community.' Sheppard thought its chairman, Peter Bassey, chose the right words when he thanked church leaders at its opening 'for the respect they have shown the community.'[12] When rioting broke out four years later, the centre helped communication between the Deputy Chief Constable and the community. The police again used vehicles to dispel the crowds, and Sheppard and Worlock narrowly escaped injury when a police land rover mounted the pavement and drove between a lamp post and a house. The bishops flattened themselves against a wall as a side-mirror passed beneath their faces.

*

The riots forced Merseyside up the government's agenda. Some in the Cabinet talked of leaving Liverpool to a 'managed decline' following Toxteth, while the Prime Minister, Margaret Thatcher, wanted to see

11 Handwritten memo, August 1981: SHP, 10.14.
12 CMS Annual Sermon, 1991: SHP, 16.3.

the situation for herself. She made an unannounced visit to Liverpool the following week, and with Sheppard still on sabbatical in London, Henshall accompanied Worlock to meet her.[13] Henshall spoke of the need for compassion, but Thatcher thought the term sounded condescending. Henshall explained it meant 'suffering with', a vital consideration with regard to the black community in Toxteth. Denis Thatcher, who was accompanying his wife, said, 'That's not really one of your words, is it?'[14]

The Secretary of State for the Environment, Michael Heseltine, persuaded Thatcher that he should spend three weeks in the region. He wanted to immerse himself in its problems, and felt some responsibility for Liverpool as chair of its Inner-City Partnership committee. In his view, Toxteth was a symptom. The problem 'stemmed from the long-term structural and economic decline of the city under a local leadership quite unable to rise to the challenge of events . . . We have all watched the present situation develop', he wrote shortly before his visit, 'and, for whatever reason, we have failed to find adequate solutions'.[15] He submitted a report to the Prime Minister headed, 'It took a riot', and proposed a single regional office for Merseyside, calling for greater commitment to the region from the public and private sectors.[16]

Heseltine began a number of initiatives, including recovering a tract of derelict land to host an international garden festival and creating a Tate Gallery of the North on the disused Albert Dock.[17] A Merseyside Development Corporation (MDC) was established to regenerate the dockland area, and other projects included the transformation of Cantril Farm into Stockbridge Village and development of the land around the

---

13 The account of this meeting in Sheppard, D. S., and Worlock, D., *With Hope in Our Hearts*, London: Hodder & Stoughton, 1994, has Sheppard, not Henshall, accompanying Worlock (p. 19). When Henshall raised this with both men, Sheppard faxed a handwritten reply offering a full apology for the inaccuracy. Sheppard's report in *Steps along Hope Street* is accurate (p. 216).

14 Peart-Binns, J. S., *A Certain Sound: The life of Bishop Michael Henshall*, unpublished manuscript, pp. 144–5.

15 Heseltine, M., *Life in the Jungle: My autobiography*, London: Coronet, 2000, p. 219; PRO, Heseltine departure statement, 5/8/81, PREM19/484, cited in Longino, L., 'Strategies for Change: Local Interest Groups, the Church of England, and Urban Politics in 1980s Liverpool', M. Phil thesis, University of Oxford, 2012, p. 38.

16 'It Took a Riot', 13 August 1981: www.margaretthatcher.org/document/127058 [accessed 2 August 2016].

17 Heseltine saw the garden festival as the core of his project: *Where There's a Will*, London: Hutchinson, 1987, pp. 157–9.

Anglican cathedral. A Merseyside Task Force brought together civil servants from three government departments to coordinate policy in the region. Sheppard had earlier told Heseltine that he thought an effective response to Liverpool's problems 'needs to cross the boundaries between departments.'[18] The Task Force and MDC enabled the government to bypass the local authority which it considered ineffective.

Heseltine became known as the 'Minister for Merseyside'. Sheppard claims some credit for the creation of this post, but it was Worlock who put the suggestion to the Prime Minister when he and Henshall met her in Liverpool. Whether this directly prompted the appointment is unknown. Heseltine believes the term emerged over a period of months.[19] Sheppard thought Heseltine a 'dynamic, sympathetic and impassioned advocate' for Liverpool, and was disappointed when he was moved to another post early in 1983. The Merseyside portfolio changed hands often thereafter, with junior ministers increasingly taking the role, and Sheppard felt the quick turn-around and demotion of the brief signalled the government's lessening commitment to the region. He and Worlock tried to build friendships with each new minister, though one made that difficult: 'How do I know which of you is which?', was Nicholas Ridley's warm greeting on their first visit to his office. Ridley accused the bishops of moral blackmail for suggesting their region had special needs.[20]

*

In 1982 Heseltine took 30 heads of major companies around Merseyside on a bus, hoping they would consider investing in the region. The initial response was positive, but two years later Sheppard thought there had been few outcomes from the exercise. He and Worlock invited local business leaders to a private meeting. 'Whatever happened to Michael Heseltine's bus load of businessmen?', they asked in their invitation. The

---

18 Letter, 24 July 1979: SHP, 6.7.

19 Official Number 10 record of the meeting at www.margaretthatcher.org/document/134870 [accessed 13 March 2019]; cf. Sheppard and Worlock, *Better Together*, pp. 178–9, Sheppard and Worlock, *With Hope in Our Hearts*, p. 29 and Sheppard, *Steps along Hope Street*, p. 216; author's phone conversation with Lord Heseltine.

20 Sheppard and Worlock, *With Hope in Our Hearts*, pp. 29–30.

meeting agreed that, as people on the spot, they needed to step up to their responsibility before asking outsiders to rescue them.

The group decided to meet regularly, sharing breakfast every six weeks or so until Sheppard retired. The name 'Michaelmas Group' was adopted, as their first meeting had been on Michaelmas eve, 28 September. Individuals with relevant specialist knowledge were invited, in addition to senior managers from the private, public and voluntary sectors, with both the traditional and newer business sectors in the city being represented. Michaelmas had an indirect route into government via senior officials from the Merseyside Task Force who attended. Sheppard chaired the meetings with Worlock opening the discussion, and the bishops played a pivotal role in the work of the group. As Hilary Russell comments, their presence was its 'distinctive ingredient because they were rooted in the area and identified closely with it, but were to some extent above the fray'.[21]

The Michaelmas Group did not initiate projects. It saw its role as helping 'to enable projects designed to improve the economic, commercial and social prosperity of the Region to be brought to a successful outcome'.[22] As one member put it, it inspired its members to have the confidence 'to start to think big again'.[23] The Chatham House Rule was strictly respected, enabling some very trusting conversations. Meetings enabled the bishops to put the region's case to government with more authority; group members ensured they were well-briefed, and ministers would know they were speaking for a wider community and not just the churches. Roger Morris, secretary to the group throughout its existence, considers the bishops might not have got the airtime they did from government without these connections to business: 'It was much less easy for a minister to brush them aside because they clearly were not simply speaking from a faith community perspective'.[24]

The bishops could be effective in lobbying the Prime Minister. In 1984

---

21 Russell, H., *A Faithful Presence: Working together for the common good*, London: SCM Press, 2015, p. 101.

22 'Concept and objectives' paper, July 1985: SHP, 6.12.

23 Interview with Peter and Angela Toyne.

24 Interview with Roger Morris. Morris was nominated for this role by Nicholas Barber, then Group Managing Director, Ocean Trading and Transport. I have also been grateful for a conversation with Mr Barber.

they were briefed by Michaelmas to make the case for Liverpool to be allocated one of the limited number of Freeports that the government was creating. 'Mrs Thatcher took careful notes of what we said', Sheppard said of the meeting, and that afternoon it was announced that Liverpool had been successful. Sheppard heard that a senior civil servant refused to believe the news as Liverpool was not on the recommended list.[25]

Sheppard spoke of Liverpool as a 'hurt city'. He and Worlock incorporated the term in the title of their first book, *Better Together: Christian partnership in a hurt city*. The term referred to the city's high levels of unemployment and reputation as an unsafe place to invest because of its labour disputes, sectarian past and other factors. The Michaelmas Group asked Sheppard to talk positively about the city when there was reason to do so. He said he would talk about 'enterprise city' so long as the 'hurt' dimension was not ignored. He later saw 'enterprise city' beginning to thrive as government regeneration schemes, European money, the arrival of new companies and investment to attract tourism took effect. 'As we moved into the 1990s, "Enterprise City" . . . increasingly flourished', he later wrote. 'However . . . "Hurt City" still bleeds'.[26] Sheppard was keen to support new enterprises; projects such as Blackburne House, which trains women from disadvantaged backgrounds for employment in the technical professions, was supported by Sheppard.

*

In 1983 the political landscape in Liverpool changed. The local election in May saw Labour win a majority on the city council. The new council produced an urban regeneration programme, which aimed to build 6,000 new council houses over the next three years, maintain existing stock in a better condition and make rents affordable for residents. It would create thousands of jobs. The plan set them on a collision course with the Conservative government which was re-elected the following

---

25 Sheppard, *Steps along Hope Street*, p. 255. Ships docking at Freeports are not required to pay customs duties or taxes.

26 Sheppard and Worlock, *With Hope in Our Hearts*, p. 33; Sheppard, *Steps along Hope Street*, pp. 309–10.

month. Thatcher wanted to extend home ownership, cut expenditure on public housing and give council tenants the 'right to buy'.

The council diverted funding from other sources to finance its plans, and refused to consider increasing the rates. The council, which would increasingly become dominated by the Militant Tendency, believed it was elected 'to defend existing council jobs and services, build council houses for rent . . . and refuse to cut local services or impose increases in rates and rents to compensate for Government cuts'.[27] Sheppard was encouraged that the council wanted to tackle the housing issue, regretting the government's unwillingness to consider extra funding for the city. 'Make no mistake, we are wasting the God-given resources of the nation by leaving three million on the dole and we are breeding a dangerously bitter spirit', he wrote. He thought the council's policies were 'a cry of pain' but was critical of its readiness to court confrontation with the government.[28] By producing deficit budgets the council hoped to pressure the government into giving Liverpool more money. As the government refused, the crisis in the city deepened.

Sheppard and the other church leaders issued three special calls to prayer for the city. They tried to keep the lines of communication open between the council leaders and the government as direct contact had broken down. Sheppard hosted meetings with public sector workers worried about being able to provide public services with bankruptcy looming.[29] As events reached a climax, the bishops decided to speak out.[30] In July 1985 they issued a statement regretting the council's 'apparent policy of confrontation with the Government'.[31] In October their tone hardened. The council's finances were running out and its

---

27 Parkinson, M., *Liverpool on the Brink*, Hermitage, Berks: Policy Journals, 1985, pp. 37–8. Militant describes itself as a Trotskyist movement. In the 1970s and 1980s, it was known for its tactic of encouraging its members to join and work within the Labour Party.

28 Cited in Frost, D., and North, P., *Militant Liverpool: A city on the edge*, Liverpool: Liverpool University Press, 2013, pp. 74–5.

29 Longino, 'Strategies for Change', pp. 62–3.

30 The deputy leader of the council at the time, Derek Hatton, suggests that Sheppard and Worlock were supportive of Militant's stance during its first year in office. It was only 'when things got tough, and we headed for a showdown in that second year, the bishops chose their side.' Hatton., D., *Inside Left: The story so far . . .*, London: Bloomsbury, 1988, pp. 105–6.

31 Press statement, 18 July 1985: SHP, 18.5.

employees were likely to be made redundant. In *The Times* on 1 October 1985 the bishops said they

> deplore[d] the confrontation that has to a great extent been manufactured by the Militant leadership of the city council . . . Militant's intransigence and unwillingness to engage in serious dialogue creates divisiveness and uncertainty in which the most vulnerable elements of the community suffer . . . Faced with such difficulties a great city needs to bring together all the resources which people of good will can muster. Our Christian teaching is that we are members of one another.

The paper headed the piece, 'Stand up to Liverpool's Militants'.[32]

One person who took the bishops' words to heart was the leader of the Labour Party, Neil Kinnock. Kinnock had met the bishops and shared their concerns. He had planned to make a speech at the party conference denouncing Militant's actions in Liverpool, and the bishops' article gave him extra courage. As he later told Sheppard, 'That morning, I read what you had written. And then I was filled with the spirit!'[33]

*

Sheppard opposed Militant's centralized approach to housing, wanting local communities to be involved in decisions affecting them. He feared that imposing 'new municipal housing' upon communities would necessitate dispersing families currently drawn together in mutual support.[34] He and Worlock supported two campaigns concerned with housing in the city. One was sparked by a council decision to develop Everton Park to the north of the city centre. This involved demolishing existing properties including 30 good four-bedroom houses that the community wanted to keep. The community formed the Langrove Street Action Group, which coordinated the occupation of one of the houses to prevent

---

32 *The Times*, 1 October 1985.
33 Sheppard, *Steps along Hope Street*, p.240, and author's correspondence with Lord Kinnock.
34 Letter dated 22 July 1983 to John Hamilton: SHP, 18.5.

their demolition. The group asked the team vicar, Henry Corbett, to alert Sheppard to what was happening. He and Grace joined protestors appealing to the demolition team to halt, and an injunction succeeded in stopping the process. Aware of the area's sectarian past, and with Worlock out of the country at the time, Sheppard asked a local Catholic priest, Monsignor Jim Dunne, to join him on the protest.

A longer campaign in which both Sheppard and Worlock were involved concerned an area around Eldon Street in nearby Vauxhall. Housing had been demolished in the district since the 1960s. Residents saw the need for this but wanted to maintain their community, so resisted attempts by successive local councils to rehouse them across Merseyside. A survey of residents led to the formation of a housing cooperative, which drew up plans for new homes and sheltered housing. In 1981 the nearby Tate & Lyle factory closed, and the loss of 1,700 jobs strengthened calls for the residents to be dispersed, but they saw things differently. They wanted the vacant 22-acre site to be made available for further housing. The plans went against the council's belief in central control and its dislike of housing cooperatives, and only after numerous setbacks, delays and a court case, was clearance given for what became the Eldonian village to be built on Tate & Lyle land.

Sheppard had known of the Eldonians' vision for several years, and warmed to it on two levels. First, he believed inner-city communities should stay together in order to prosper. Second, he favoured housing cooperatives, believing they enabled members to participate in planning their future homes and living circumstances. Both views were shaped by his experience at the Mayflower. He and Worlock became active supporters of the Eldonians, pleading their cause with government ministers, private sector employers and the Merseyside Task Force. Tony McGann, the mover and shaker behind the Eldonian project, and George Evans, Chief Executive of the Eldonian Housing Association, believe the bishops' role was pivotal to its success. The doors they opened, including to the Prime Minister, made the crucial difference; 'We wouldn't have even got off the starting blocks without them'.[35] Sheppard had a high

---

35 Interview with Tony McGann and George Evans. I have also drawn on an interview with Max Steinberg CBE, who played a major role in the Eldonian project. Steinberg

regard for the government minister involved, Patrick Jenkin.[36] He may have known, however, that the government's support for the Eldonians might in part have been due to its commitment to defeat Militant.

The Eldonians thanked the bishops for their help by naming two streets 'Bishop Sheppard Court' and 'Archbishop Worlock Court'. The area was strongly Catholic, and Sheppard's support showed how far ecumenical cooperation had come in recent years. A service of celebration was attended by Anglicans and Roman Catholics: 'I felt a mixture of amazement and fulfilment that we were worshipping together in [an area where] none of my predecessors would have set foot, and where joint services had been unknown', Sheppard later wrote.[37] A banner across the road read, 'Our thanks to Archbishop Derek, to Bishop David and to all our friends. WE DID IT BETTER TOGETHER.'

*

Sheppard disagreed with Militant over the appointment of a principal race adviser to the city council in 1984. The council chose a non-specialist from London, Sampson Bond, over three local candidates with relevant experience. Black leaders objected strongly to the appointment and asked Sheppard and Worlock to intervene. It was widely suspected that Bond was selected because he was a member of the Militant Tendency and would support council policy.

The bishops wanted the council to heal its relations with the black community. They chaired talks between both sides, and witnessed councillors making offers to the protestors to try to secure their support. Sheppard found it a salutary experience to see first-hand 'the tools of political power, with patronage and grant being used to promote the Militant cause.'[38] He later described Bond's appointment as 'an affront to the local black community' which 'would undo years of patient attempts

---

also worked closely with Michael Heseltine in Liverpool. Margaret Thatcher visited the Eldonian community in 1989.

36 Jenkin also respected Sheppard and Worlock. He once told them privately that 'the way your clergy and congregations are able to work together should be an inspiration to the politicians . . .': Filby, E., *God and Mrs Thatcher*, London: Biteback, 2015, p. 185.

37 Sheppard, *Steps along Hope Street*, p. 232.

38 Sheppard and Worlock, *Better Together*, p. 190.

to build better relations between black Liverpudlians and the Town Hall.'[39] He saw the episode as another example of Militant assuming it knew better than local communities.

The council's commitment to central control also damaged the voluntary sector, Sheppard thought. One example was a mission for homeless women run by Mother Teresa's order of nuns which was replaced by a council hostel. The deputy leader of the council, Derek Hatton, challenged Grace to persuade him why the Family Service Unit she chaired should not be municipalized. She succeeded, in part by highlighting the cost to the council of taking the work over.[40]

*

When Militant's control ended in March 1987, Sheppard struck a concil-iatory note. A total of 47 Labour councillors were disbarred from office, of whom 31 were non-Militant. In a press statement with Worlock and the Free Church leader, John Williamson, Sheppard acknowledged that among those departing were some 'very fine public servants who have throughout genuinely sought what they believed was in the best interests of the City.' He would have included among those the council leader, John Hamilton, who was not a Militant member. Sheppard admired Hamilton, who was a Quaker who had tried to moderate the council's policies. Sheppard thought the financial penalties the councillors had to bear (a £106k fine, to which was added £242k costs when their appeal to the House of Lords failed) was without precedent and likely to discourage people from standing for public office. He hoped that in the local elections, voters would consider candidates who 'may be willing in the difficult years ahead to cooperate across party barriers for the good of the City as a whole.'[41]

In addition to their public contributions, Sheppard and Worlock did much in private towards solving the crisis in Liverpool. In a handwritten letter to Sheppard in July 1984, John Hamilton thanked him and Worlock

---

39 'Foreword' to Liverpool Black Caucus, *The Racial Politics of Militant in Liverpool*, Liverpool and London: Merseyside Area Profile Group and The Runnymede Trust, 1986, p. 7.
40 Number 10 Briefing 841116; Sheppard, *Steps along Hope Street*, pp. 192-3.
41 Press statement 14 March 1987: SHP, 18.5.

for 'all the quiet behind-the-scenes work' they had done to that point. Hamilton told Sheppard he had not had an easy time in recent months, but 'it was the work that people like yourself were doing which sustained me.'[42] Sheppard also worked well with Alfred Stocks, a Methodist and Chief Executive of the city council during its most difficult years. He respected Stocks' professionalism and commitment to public service. The two met regularly, and Sheppard never said anything publicly about Liverpool without checking his facts with Stocks.

Sheppard always saw the wider administrative body for the region, the Merseyside County Council, in a positive light. In contrast to the city council, it was a place where consensus rather than party loyalty was valued. He spoke passionately in its defence in the face of government attempts to abolish county councils. He told the Lords that, when developments in Liverpool pointed to an urgent need for reconciliation, 'the proposed abolition of Merseyside County Council seems to me to be nothing short of a tragedy.'[43] The council enjoyed local support and Sheppard regretted its eventual demise.

*

The closer relationship developing between the Catholic and Anglican communions in Liverpool reached a high point with the visit of Pope John Paul II to the city in 1982. Worlock wanted John Paul to visit the Anglican as well as the Catholic cathedral when he came to Liverpool. It would be a powerful symbolic gesture, celebrating Liverpool's ecumenical achievement and demonstrating that the city had finally overcome sectarianism. Sheppard thought Worlock also wanted to repay his favour of making the Queen's visit in 1978 ecumenical.[44]

The visit appeared in jeopardy on several occasions. An attempt on the Pope's life, the conflict over the Falklands, and the rioting in Toxteth all raised concerns. There was also the threat of protests. Two services before the visit were disrupted by Orange Lodge members. One involved

---

42 Letter dated 27 July 1984: SHP, 6.12.
43 Hansard, Lords, Local Government (Interim Provisions) Bill, 28 June 1984, vol. 453, col. 1051; Sheppard, *Steps along Hope Street,* p. 229.
44 Sheppard, *Steps along Hope Street,* p. 175.

Archbishop Robert Runcie, who had to abandon a sermon in Liverpool Parish Church. Sheppard later met with the leader of the Lodge, the Grand Master, who voiced his fears about the Pope replacing the Queen as head of the Church of England. Sheppard worked hard to prepare people for the visit. Provoked by the opposition to it he had witnessed, he gave an unscheduled address at diocesan synod to explain his thinking. Making the visit an exclusively Roman Catholic affair would have accentuated our divisions, he said. A united service would underline what the ecumenical movement stands for, the breaking down of dividing walls between Christians. The visit did not mean the Anglican church was rushing uncritically into the arms of Rome: instead, it was about promising to work for reconciliation and a better understanding of the churches.[45]

The visit, on Whit Sunday, went off without a hitch. A million people lined the route from the airport to the Anglican cathedral, and spontaneous applause broke out from the congregation as the Pope entered the building. He shared briefly in the special Whit Sunday service before passing down Hope Street to say Mass in the Metropolitan cathedral. Impressed by the friendship he witnessed between the churches and their leaders, the Pope told Worlock he believed ecumenism to be 'not just of the intellect but also of the affections'.

In June, Liverpool cathedral invited the Orange Lodge to a special service of Evensong. Informing Sheppard of this, Dean Patey called it a 'gesture of reconciliation'. He had welcomed the low profile the Lodge had kept on Whit Sunday. 'I hope we may be credited with some impartiality (but not indifferentism) by having invited both the Pope and the Orange Order to the Cathedral in the space of three weeks!', Patey wrote.[46]

*

Patey retired a few months later. He had served 18 years, and Sheppard valued his knowledge and understanding of the city. The two shared

---

45 President's Address to synod, March 1982: SHP, 24.6. Leaked extracts from a forthcoming report of the *Anglican Roman Catholic International Commission (ARCIC)*, which talked about the Bishop of Rome becoming 'universal primate' in a reunited church, had sparked concern in some quarters.

46 Letter dated 15 June 1982: SHP, 10.12.

a common view on many issues. Sheppard was initially impressed by Patey's successor, Derrick Walters, although their relationship did not develop smoothly. Sheppard was disappointed that Walters lacked Patey's enthusiasm for ecumenical relations. He put this down to the dean being 'single-minded' in his commitment to his cathedral. Sheppard respected the fact that the cathedral was the province of the dean, but let Walters know his views about the format of large events.[47] Sheppard implies that they built a working relationship because they realized that 'a rift between bishop and dean would damage the Church'[48] but he was disappointed when Walters stopped attending bishop's staff meetings.

Walters revitalized the cathedral. Skilled at attracting grants, and networked into Downing Street, the City and the Church Commissioners, he conceived and executed what he called 'Project Rosemary'. This involved the redevelopment of the land around the cathedral, creating jobs and income. Walters built on Heseltine's original vision, overseeing the construction of a close for cathedral canons, student accommodation for the university, a women's hospital, a factory and public and private housing. At the time there was little other development in Liverpool. Walters was noted for his entrepreneurialism but some of his projects were thought to involve considerable financial risk. Sheppard once sought professional help to ensure that cathedral revenues were not being misapplied in pursuit of Project Rosemary.

Sheppard thought Walters' achievements were remarkable. The dean's commitment to regeneration and job-creation resonated with Sheppard. But the two differed profoundly in churchmanship, theology and politics. Walters was an admirer and friend of the Prime Minister and some of her cabinet. Sheppard maintained good contacts with Thatcher and her ministers but would challenge them when he thought their policies were harming the poor and unemployed. Despite their differences, Walters wrote warmly to Sheppard on his retirement in 1997:

I know that you and I have had our disagreements, but I hope you know in what high esteem I hold you. Your achievements in

---

47 One example was the memorial service for the victims of the Hillsborough disaster in 1989 (see below). Sheppard told Walters who he wanted to preach and give the blessing.
48 Sheppard, *Steps along Hope Street*, pp. 261–2.

Liverpool have justly earned high praise . . . I have valued your friendship and your care for the cathedral.

Walters acknowledged his priorities may have disappointed Sheppard but said that 'the Cathedral has been a jealous mistress!'[49]

Sheppard relished occasions to visit the cathedral, finding its music a particular source of joy. He valued the friendship of Ian Tracey, the organist for all but five of his years as bishop. The two would discuss their love of music and the format of services in which Sheppard would be involved. In preparation for services to celebrate landmarks in his career, David and Grace would sit around the piano at Bishop's Lodge with Tracey, going through pieces. Sheppard 'was really quite specific and learned on the subject', Tracey recalled. Sheppard used funding to which he had access to help choirboys in need with their education. One beneficiary of his help would later become director of music at the cathedral.

*

January 1983 saw the publication of *Bias to the Poor*.[50] It combined reflections on its author's years in the inner city with a vision for change. The premise underpinning it was bold: 'I believe that there is a divine bias to the disadvantaged, and that the Church needs to be much more faithful in reflecting it', Sheppard wrote. The disadvantaged included people in poverty in the inner city, black communities, and those facing permanent unemployment. He welcomed the multi-racial society the UK had become and called for a 'heartfelt commitment to [it] as God's best plan for us.' He saw 'flickers of hope' in the city, including people building community on outer estates and Christians staying to work out their faith within their working-class neighbourhoods. These flickers helped to keep him a believer, he said.[51]

---

49 Letter dated 24 September 1997: SHP, 27.5.

50 Sheppard, D. S., *Bias to the Poor*, London: Hodder & Stoughton, 1983. Dr John Vincent, founder of the Urban Theology Unit in Sheffield, suggested the title. He thought it better reflected the book's conclusions than Sheppard's own proposal, *The Divine Bias*.

51 Sheppard, *Bias to the Poor*, pp. 16, 101, 24, 50, 17.

Sheppard also asked how the church might respond to the divine bias, reflecting on the difficulties he had faced when shifting his priorities towards the poor. People did not expect a bishop to want to spend an equal amount of time with those outside the circles of power as with those within them, he wrote. He denied the accusation that he believed the gospel was not for the rich, or that people should feel guilty for being affluent, but he did believe Jesus spoke a different word to the rich and the poor:

> We cannot assume that both sides have equally valid positions. For the Church to hear the cry of the poor will mean losing its innocence on social and political matters . . . There will be occasions when we must get off the fence, and take sides.[52]

As with his previous books, *Bias to the Poor* sold well, with sales around 25,000. Reviewers commended Sheppard for writing from his experience; 'One is hearing the authentic voices', wrote Peter Hinchliff, and 'the very fact that a diocesan bishop of the Church of England, with an impeccably Evangelical and public school background, is willing to act as a mouthpiece for these voices is itself important.'[53] Kenneth Slack thought the value of the book had to do with *praxis*, 'the reflection on the experience of putting religious, theological and social insights to work in the actual life of our churches in the inner city.'[54] Haddon Willmer thought churches would find the book 'challenging and informative.'[55]

Not everybody was positive. A sustained critique of the book appeared the following year in a collection of essays from the think tank, the Social Affairs Unit.[56] Robert Miller, an adviser to the Institute of Economic Affairs (IEA), challenged Sheppard on his understanding of the market. Miller thought the claim that people were unemployed because the

---

52 Sheppard, *Bias to the Poor*, pp. 220–1.
53 *Theology*, July 1983.
54 *The Christian Century*, 14 September 1983.
55 *Third Way*, March 1983
56 Anderson, D., ed., *The Kindness that Kills: The churches' simplistic response to complex social issues*, London: SPCK, 1984.

market did not need their labour was a 'wholly unexamined assumption' which was unsupported by theological or economic argument. 'The truth is that the causes of unemployment are a technical matter where the Church and the Bishop have no special competence,' Miller wrote.[57] Ralph Harris, Director-General of the IEA, thought Sheppard was inconsistent. The bishop complained that the emphasis on efficiency in the free market closed down businesses in areas from which the market had departed, while defending the 'painful process of making some churches redundant in areas where the population has drastically reduced.' Sheppard's book was a 'profoundly confused and contradictory testament', Lord Harris concluded.[58]

Harris sent Sheppard a copy of the essay collection prior to publication. Sheppard disliked its tone. 'In the Gospels our Lord warns us that nothing brings God's judgment on us more than when we call our brother, "Thou fool"', he reminded Harris, and he challenged Harris and his fellow authors to spell out their commitment to the poor. 'If you disagree with the ways in which some of us suggest that we should try to help meet the needs of the poor, I believe you should make very plain what your programme is', he wrote.[59]

*

Sheppard chose the theme of poverty when the BBC invited him to give its annual Richard Dimbleby Lecture the following year. Founded to honour the distinguished broadcaster, these lectures are regarded as prestigious events. Lecturers have included Prince Philip, Prince Charles and former US president, Bill Clinton.

Sheppard highlighted the division in society between what he called 'Comfortable Britain' and 'The Other Britain'. He acknowledged that Comfortable Britain was where he was born and where most people lived, knowing it embraced the bulk of his audience. The 'Other Britain'

---

57 Miller, R., 'Unemployment: Putting Faith in the New Princes' in Anderson, *The Kindness that Kills*, pp. 74–5.

58 Harris, R., 'The Folly of Politicized Welfare' in Anderson, *The Kindness that Kills*, pp. 101, 96–7.

59 Letter dated 1 August 1984: SHP 21.12. Sheppard and Harris corresponded several times, but Sheppard struggled with Harris' tone and terminology.

was characterized by relative poverty which 'imprisons the spirit'. This was rooted in unemployment, neglected housing, poor opportunity in schooling and poor public services, which left people feeling powerless and unable to make real choices about their destiny. People in Other Britain do not compare themselves to those starving in the Third World, Sheppard argued, but to people they see around them. This leads to a sense of being excluded from 'the normal, comfortable life'. Tackling poverty should be a priority for all, especially Christians: 'If so many are imprisoned in spirit, then the whole spirit of our nation is imprisoned. We cannot leave matters as they are.' Sheppard was clear that higher levels of taxation would be needed if some of his solutions were to be effected. These included allowing everyone to remain in education or training until 18, and a government programme of public works to reduce unemployment if there were not enough jobs in the market. But he thought politicians should stop exploiting 'the grudging unwillingness of the better-off to pay taxes.' Instead they should promote paying tax as 'a way in which those who have great advantages can express being members one of another in one nation.'[60]

The lecture was seen by 4.7 million viewers, and the BBC thought it was the biggest audience for a Dimbleby Lecture since the first in 1972.[61] There had been more than 100 letters, 90 per cent approving. Several newspapers were unimpressed, however. The *Mail on Sunday* regretted that the bishop used his national pulpit in Holy Week to talk about 'the decaying inner cities and the collectivist policies he thinks would best help them . . . rather than the prospect of eternal life'. In a more reflective contribution, John Junor, the editor of the *Sunday Express* asked why millions of viewers had to have 'inflicted upon them this dreary drip droning on for 50 minutes of prime time on BBC TV'.[62]

Sheppard referred in his lecture to 'standing in the shoes' of others. Ironically, he literally did this when delivering it. Packing to travel to London, he forgot to include a pair of shoes to wear with his suit. The

---

60 *The Other Britain*, London: BBC, 1984. The published version differs in several respects from the lecture as broadcast. The point about taxation is also in Sheppard, D. S., *Built as a City: God and the Urban World Today*, London: Hodder & Stoughton, 1974, p. 40.

61 Letter from BBC, 15 June 1984: SHP, 20.3.

62 Opinion, *Mail on Sunday*, 22 April 1984; Junor, J., *Sunday Express*, 22 April 1984.

producer found three pairs the right size for him to choose from on the night. 'I felt it fitting that I should deliver this lecture on "The Other Britain" standing in someone else's shoes,' he later wrote.[63]

*

In 1983, Archbishop Runcie asked Sheppard to represent him at the inauguration of the Province of the Southern Cone. Sheppard was an obvious choice given Liverpool's links with South America through PIM, and he asked the PIM coordinator for the diocese, Mark Boyling, to accompany him.[64] The Falklands/Malvinas War had not long ended and there were long delays to enter Argentina while their visas were scrutinized. While in Argentina, they discovered one of the impacts of the conflict: a priest told them that Anglicans of British descent had been forced during the conflict to decide whether they were British or Argentinian. In Peru they linked up with Derek Worlock, who was on a separate visit, and met some Liverpool Archdiocese priests who were serving in Villa El Salvador and other shanty towns in the capital, Lima. Some of the Christian communities they visited talked positively about Liberation Theology, a topic Sheppard had discussed in *Bias to the Poor* and which would feature in the *Faith in the City* report. Sheppard declined an invitation from the UK Ambassador in Lima to play in a local cricket match, but did agree to umpire a few overs.

*

An indication of Sheppard and Worlock's reputation as symbols of unity and reconciliation was an approach they received from the Trades Union Congress (TUC) in late 1984. The TUC wanted them to be trustees of its Miners Hardship Fund. The 1984 Miners' Strike, a long-running and bitter dispute between miners and the government over the future of the coal industry, had led to the TUC receiving substantial donations to help miners' families. The Hardship Fund was established to ensure that the

---

63 Sheppard, *Steps along Hope Street*, p. 235.
64 Boyling would become Sheppard's chaplain in 1985.

money reached people in need and was not used to finance the strike. Before accepting the role of trustees, the bishops sought assurances from lawyers that the fund could not be used to support picketing.

In a press statement, the bishops said that the hardship being endured during the strike was contributing to its 'bitterness and divisions . . . The Church, as a reconciler, can never turn its back on such hardship, so we are very glad to be associated with this straightforward way of meeting human needs.' They spoke of the desirability of establishing a miners' hardship fund 'distinct from the fighting fund of a union'. This was a public acknowledgement that the union behind the strike, the National Union of Mineworkers, had a fighting fund, something from which the TUC was anxious to keep its distance.[65]

*

In 1985 Sheppard helped the churches reach a new stage in their relations. Three years before, the Merseyside Churches Ecumenical Council had set up a working party to look at new ecumenical structures. Chaired by Michael Henshall, the working party made several recommendations in its report, *Call to Partnership*. One was for a new ecumenical assembly, to be launched at Pentecost with a covenant of church leaders. Another was for the Free Churches to choose a person to form a triumvirate with the bishop and archbishop 'for the purpose of public pronouncement and witness.'

These recommendations were followed through. On Whit Sunday the church leaders signed a covenant, pledging their commitment to God and one another in their search for unity. The covenant would ensure that unity could be sustained when church leaders changed. The signing took place during services in the Catholic and Anglican cathedrals. In between, members from the different churches processed along the connecting road, Hope Street.[66] A two cathedrals' service and walk had

---

65 I have been grateful for conversations with Nicholas Jones, former labour and political correspondent at the BBC.

66 Though named after an eighteenth-century merchant, the street is seen by churches as symbolic of their desire for unity. Archbishop Beck suggested in 1967 that having the cathedrals at either end of Hope Street 'may be a piece of symbolism of greater importance

been held during visits by the Queen and the Pope. Now it became established as a Pentecost event every two years, with several thousand people taking part. Enthusiasm for the process was palpable. 'If the church leaders wanted to turn back now, we wouldn't let them,' Sheppard heard was the word on the street. The new body took the name The Merseyside and Region Churches' Ecumenical Assembly (or MARCEA). It comprised 200 members drawn from the churches and was modelled on a parliamentary debating chamber. It appointed a full-time, paid ecumenical officer, the first in the country. Its first elected 'speaker' was Alfred Stocks. Separate departments covered ecumenical affairs, social responsibility, education, ministry and international affairs.[67]

The Free Churches elected a Moderator for Merseyside, John Williamson of the United Reformed Church. Williamson began to play a public role alongside Sheppard and Worlock. The three often acted together during the crisis with the city council. Sheppard thought it an added strength to be able to say at meetings with politicians that all the mainline churches in the region were being represented.

When Dr John Newton succeeded Williamson, the triumvirate became even more significant. Newton was appointed Methodist District Chair in 1986. He was already known in church circles as the successor to Donald Soper at the West London Mission, as a former president of the Methodist Conference and as the author of studies of Susanna Wesley and Bishop Edward King. A scholar, theologian and preacher, Newton brought distinctive gifts to the ministry of the Merseyside churches. He had made the Church's need to serve the poor a priority during his time as Methodist president, and shared Sheppard and Worlock's concerns. His scholarship in church history and knowledge of Wesley's commitment to the poor endeared him to Sheppard. Worlock valued Newton's experience on the Methodist Catholic Commission and membership of the Ecumenical Society of the Blessed Virgin Mary. The leaders developed a strong friendship and would often spend time

---

than many of us have yet realized.' Sheppard captured this symbolism in the title of his second autobiography.

67 I have drawn here on conversations with Canon Michael Wolfe, Merseyside Ecumenical Officer 1982-89. In 2003 MARCEA changed its way of working and became 'Churches Together in the Merseyside Region'.

around the dinner table or while travelling to events discussing their shared beliefs and differences. They were sometimes referred to as 'The Liverpool Three'.

The churches having three leaders posed problems for the media. Newspapers could not accommodate triple authorship of pieces. Television and radio producers had difficulty editing interviews with three voices down to 20-second clips. A photograph of the three leaders was trimmed before publication to remove Williamson. Placing the Moderator between the bishops helped prevent this occurring again but was not foolproof. During one photo session the Moderator was told his car needed moving. When he went outside, on what proved to be a futile mission, the photographer snapped just the two bishops.

Call to Partnership had spoken of churches moving along a continuum from 'competition' to 'communion' through 'coexistence', 'cooperation' and 'commitment'. One senior figure thinks the churches never got beyond cooperation. In time some 15 local covenants between groups of churches were signed, and in 1983, Sheppard and Worlock opened the first of two shared Anglican–Roman Catholic churches built in their time in Merseyside. St Basil and All Saints, Widnes, was created after three years of consultation and public meetings which demonstrated unanimous support for the project. Another ecumenical project Sheppard keenly supported was the 'Fourth Dimension' charity shop in Huyton. Founded by nine local churches to raise money for a well-drilling project in Mali, it has a mission to provide 'good things at good prices for those in need of them'. Sheppard opened the shop in 1981, and it has raised more than £300,000 for Christian Aid in its first four decades of operating.[68]

Another ecumenical project Sheppard and Worlock pursued was a joint Anglican–Roman Catholic school in the diocese. Education had historically been a driver of sectarian division and they had long held a desire to see joint schools. In 1990 the possibility of a venture on the growing Croxteth Park estate in Knowsley arose, and the local priest told Sheppard how the school would benefit the community. The two

---

68 I have valued a conversation with Enid and Philip Lodge, who have been heavily involved in 'Fourth Dimension' since its inception.

dioceses liaised with the relevant authorities and property developers over several years to make it happen. When the project was completed shortly before he retired, Sheppard described it as a dream come true. The school took the name Emmaus, recalling the account in Luke's Gospel of two disciples travelling together after the resurrection and meeting an unknown stranger, the risen Jesus.

A further legacy of Sheppard's commitment to ecumenism in the field of education is Liverpool Hope University. Shortly after they arrived in Liverpool, Sheppard and Worlock were approached by the principals of the city's three higher education colleges. Notre Dame and Christ's were Roman Catholic and St Katherine's was Anglican. The colleges were in an informal federation and hoped to amalgamate in the face of government plans to close Notre Dame and St Katherine's. They believed that uniting could also serve a deeper purpose against the background of Liverpool's sectarian past. Sheppard and Worlock shared this vision, and encouraged the process towards unity. In 1976 they made what is often described as a historic journey to London to see the minister of state for further and higher education, Gordon Oakes. Oakes was MP for nearby Widnes, a native of the town, and a graduate of Liverpool University. Sheppard believes his local roots meant he understood the case for an ecumenical institute. Another theory is that Oakes allowed it only as an expedient because he thought it would not last very long.[69]

The colleges formed an ecumenical federation in 1979 as the Liverpool Institute of Higher Education (LIHE). Sheppard and Worlock described this as 'a sign of hope, a declaration of intent for the future'. They chaired its governing council alternately for two-year periods. When LIHE became a unified college in 1995, the newly appointed rector, Professor Simon Lee, proposed 'Hope' as its title. Lee worked to promote the 'deeper meaning' of the term 'whereby we believe in a better world and then do something to make it happen'.[70] Liverpool Hope is Europe's

---

69 Elford, R. J., 'From Urban Beginnings . . .' in Elford, R. J., ed., *The Foundation of Hope: Turning Dreams into Reality*, Liverpool: Liverpool University Press, 2003, p. 7.

70 Lee, S., 'Impressions of Hope' in Elford, ed., *The Foundation of Hope*, pp. 189–90. Sheppard initially supported the name 'Trinity College', but later agreed with Worlock that this was 'a facetious and secular use of "trinity"': Lee, S., 'The Big Society of SheppardWorlockism', unpublished paper, 2011, p. 1.

only ecumenical university, and one of its main buildings honours the bishops' contribution to its creation. Costing £5.34m, the Sheppard-Worlock Library was opened by Grace in 1997.

Ecumenical developments on Merseyside took place against a background of national initiatives towards unity. The Pope's visit in 1982 had been a catalyst nationally for an intensification of ecumenical relations with the Roman Catholic church, and in the same year a covenant between the Methodist, United Reformed, Moravian and Anglican churches was attempted. In 1985 an inter-church process called 'Not Strangers but Pilgrims' was launched involving all the mainstream churches, including the Roman Catholics. In 1988 Sheppard and Worlock attended a conference at Swanwick to discuss a new 'instrument' to replace the British Council of Churches. When the Council of Churches of Britain and Ireland was launched in 1990, Liverpool was the chosen venue. A service was held in the two cathedrals with a walk down Hope Street in between. Sheppard and Worlock were struck by the 'revitalized spirit' evident at Swanwick: 'The Kingdom of God had not come then and there', they later wrote, 'but a consensus was that this was the break-through for which the Churches had been waiting.'[71]

*

Sheppard and Worlock wrote three books together. The first, *Better Together*, surveyed their first ten years in Liverpool[72] and its title was inspired by the Eldonians' banner. In addition to the main co-authored text were personal insights from each author in italicized font, which enabled areas of disagreement to be identified. The story the authors told of their work for reconciliation and healing, against a background of historical sectarianism, had an impact beyond the churches. The magazine *Good Housekeeping* ran a four-page feature on the book, and the two bishops were interviewed live on the prime-time BBC chat show *Wogan*.[73]

---

71 Sheppard and Worlock, *Better Together*, p. 93.
72 Sheppard and Worlock, *Better Together*.
73 Linklater, A., 'A Holy Alliance', *Good Housekeeping*, January 1988, pp. 138–41; *Wogan*, BBC1, 11 January 1988.

Better Together was published in January 1988. The paperback edition the following year contained a 17-page Postscript. There had been developments in national life on which the bishops wanted to comment, including statements by the Prime Minister and other cabinet members suggesting there was no such thing as society, only individuals and families, and that the gospel was primarily about individual responsibility.[74] Sheppard and Worlock stressed the importance of 'community responsibility'.

A follow-up book, *With Hope in Our Hearts*, appeared in 1994. A slimmer volume, it followed the same format. This time there were italicized sections from John Newton as well as the bishops, and the title was inspired by a line in a song that has become synonymous with Liverpool FC, 'You'll Never Walk Alone'. In between, the bishops had produced a book of readings for Lent in 1990. Published by the Bible Reading Fellowship, it contained reflections on Bible passages and questions for discussion. The title, *With Christ in the Wilderness*, reflected the influence of Sheppard's mentor in Southwark, Cecilia Goodenough. Goodenough talked of 'wilderness' and 'vineyard' people in the Old Testament. The wilderness was where God would be revealed and where there were clear boundaries of right and wrong, while the vineyard depicted the settled life of the nation of Israel, where ethical decisions about justice in the community might be more complex. The premise of the book was that vineyard people need sometimes to withdraw into the wilderness to renew their clear vision of God. Lent offers an opportunity to do this. One reviewer thought it skilfully wove together 'the concerns, anxieties and delights of everyday life, the passion narratives, and broader scriptural themes.' It was 'convincingly in touch with everyday realities' and would 'nourish mind and heart.'[75]

*

Sheppard worked with other faith traditions in Liverpool. At significant moments, he and Worlock issued statements with Jewish and Muslim representatives. These included a Jewish–Christian message

---

74 Margaret Thatcher, interview with *Woman's Own*, 31 October 1987; address to the General Assembly of the Church of Scotland, 21 May 1988; Hurd, D., 'God versus Caesar?', *Church Times*, 9 September 1988, p. 12.

75 Harriot, J. F. X., *Church Times*, 9 March 1990.

denouncing election material produced by the National Front in 1976, and a Christian–Muslim statement on the (first) Gulf War in 1991. Sheppard also enjoyed good relations with the Sikh community, and in 1986 they invited him to preside and speak at a celebration of the anniversary of Guru Nanak, the founder of the faith.

Sheppard thought inter-faith relations were not the priority in Liverpool they were in other cities. There were significant, though small, other faith communities in the city, but a shortage of jobs meant there was little immigration. When Canon Michael Wolfe, the ecumenical officer, created an interfaith group after the International Garden Festival in 1984, Sheppard was happy to support it.[76] He modified his views as patterns of migration changed, and before he retired floated the idea of a Merseyside and Region Inter Faith Standing Committee.

A turning point occurred in the late 1980s when Sheppard began meeting informally with representatives from the Jewish community. The catalyst for this was a decision by the national churches to designate the 1990s a 'Decade of Evangelism'.[77] Clive Lawton, then headmaster of King David High School in Liverpool, told Sheppard how evangelism looked to a minority faith community. Lawton and Sheppard convened a Jewish–Christian group to meet privately.[78] 'We would not be polite to each other', Sheppard later wrote, so that difficult questions could be tackled. As trust built up, the group explored issues such as the policies of the state of Israel. In time a further group emerged, with members of Liverpool's Muslim community meeting with Jews and Christians.

Sheppard valued the openness in this group. 'We did not attempt to water down our beliefs', he later wrote. 'We learned together that full-blooded faith marches in step with respect for "the others" and the steps they take towards God.'[79] Sheppard spoke of the 'chunky stew of a multi-faith, multi-cultural society' in contrast to 'the melting pot, which

---

76 The Garden Festival, which attracted millions of visitors to the city, had an interfaith dimension as well as high-profile church participation.

77 Sheppard discusses the question of evangelizing Jewish people in 'Evangelism with a Good Heart', *The Expository Times*, 102:5, February 1991.

78 Regular attenders included Michael Wolfe and URC ministers Eric Allen and George Walker. Allen, a council member of the Council for Christians and Jews, was John Williamson's successor as Moderator for Mersey synod. I have valued conversations and correspondence with Reverends Wolfe and Allen.

79 Sheppard, *Steps along Hope Street*, p. 5.

assimilates all our faiths in to some inoffensive well-wishing [and] melts down the riches of religious traditions.'[80] After retirement he argued for bringing independent Muslim schools, and schools of other faiths, into the state system; 'Opening up the possibility of Muslim schools would send a strong message of inclusion to that community. Many of their young people felt disenfranchised and excluded from places of influence and power. Our message to those young people should be, "We want you as full citizens."'[81]

*

Sheppard would be involved in a major Anglican project for much of the mid 1980s. It would bring to a head his concerns for the urban poor and his disaffection with government policies on the inner cities. It would also propel him once more on to the national stage.

---

80 'Pilgrim in a Pluralist World', typescript, March 1991: SHP, 16.3.
81 Sheppard, *Steps along Hope Street*, p. 286.

11

Liverpool
(1985–1990)

Since his days in Islington, Sheppard's passion had been the inner city. Drawing on the gospels' claim that Jesus came to bring 'life in all its fulness', his vision for human flourishing had always been biased towards those in urban areas facing challenges such as poor housing, lack of employment, racial discrimination and loss of hope. In both London and Liverpool, he was committed to making the Church a more effective presence in the city. Now he was to embark on what would become the best-known project on urban issues with which he was involved, the *Faith in the City* report. He saw it as the culmination of his work, 'the personal realization of what I have lived for and worked towards for 25 years.'[1] Published in 1985, *Faith in the City* was produced by the Archbishop of Canterbury's Commission on Urban Priority Areas (ACUPA).[2]

The spark for the project was a letter from Canon Eric James in *The Times* of 27 May 1981. James had been asked by Archbishop Runcie to respond to an article by Clifford Longley, the paper's religious affairs correspondent. Longley had argued that the Church of England was in a healthy state despite predictions 15 years before that it was on the brink of crisis.[3] James thought there had been a 'policy of withdrawal' by the Church from the inner cities. Before long, there would be half as many full-time clergy in parts of south London than there were 15 years before. 'I should like myself to see the immediate appointment of an

---

1 Quoted in a typescript paper by John Rae, '"Faith in the City" – the Liverpool experience', 1988, p. 5: Sheppard papers (SHP), 12.3.

2 *Faith in the City: A Call for Action by Church and Nation. The Report of the Archbishop of Canterbury's Commission on Urban Priority Areas*, London: Church House Publishing, 1985.

3 Longley, C., 'The prophets of the press confounded', *The Times*, 25 May 1981; see James, E., *The House of My Friends: Memories and Reflections*, London: Continuum, 2003, p. 26; Sheppard, D. S., *Steps along Hope Street*, London: Hodder & Stoughton, 2002, p. 241.

Archbishop's Commission . . . called the "Staying There" Commission', James wrote. 'It would report on the church's strategy for the inner-city, and would need of course to consider the theology and spirituality of the church in the inner-city, not just finance and manpower.'[4] James was writing six weeks after the rioting in Brixton had occurred.

Runcie asked James to draw up a 'terms of reference' for a commission and suggestions for membership. Runcie wanted to involve the urban bishops' group, and James met them in June to make his case. The following day, Sheppard sent James and his fellow bishops an outline proposal for a commission, and the remit was wider than originally conceived by James. 'The questions which need to be raised are not simply about what happens in Church and society in the Inner City', Sheppard wrote. 'Deprived areas did not create their own deprivation; nor can all the answers be found within the Inner City . . . The affluent need to see that the deprivation of the poor is the reverse side of their success.'[5]

Runcie had also been thinking about the cities. He had learned first-hand of the situation in Brixton from an ecumenical delegation of local church and youth leaders, and from the Community Work Resource Unit at the British Council of Churches. During a Lords debate on the troubles in Brixton and Toxteth, he pledged the Church's determination 'not to abandon the inner city and retreat to suburbia'.[6]

The Archbishop's commission was launched on 6 July 1983. At Runcie's request, Sheppard joined as a member, playing a significant role in suggesting others, liaising with the archbishop's staff and consulting the urban bishops. Sheppard thought his greatest contribution was to suggest Sir Richard O'Brien as chair. He knew O'Brien through the Manpower Services Commission, which O'Brien had chaired until the previous year. O'Brien proved a highly effective chair, with a strong commitment to ensuring the report could not be criticized on a factual level.

---

4 Letters, *The Times*, 27 May 1981.

5 'Draft proposals concerning an inner city commission', June 1982: Eric James papers, Gladstone's Library, Hawarden.

6 Hansard, Lords, 'Brixton Disorders: The Scarman Report', 4 February 1982, cols 1413–15. I am grateful to Malcolm Brown and Richard Wheeler for help with this section.

The urban bishops were keen to involve Bishop Wilfred Wood, who was appointed vice-chair, along with Sheppard. Resource bodies and advisers were also appointed to work with the commission. These included Eric James, representing Christian Action; John Atherton for the William Temple Foundation; and Michael Eastman for the Evangelical Coalition for Urban Mission, (ECUM). ECUM had been formed in 1980 by bringing together a number of networks founded by Sheppard. These included the Frontier Youth Trust, *Christians in Industrial Areas* and the Evangelical Urban Training Project.

Sheppard wanted the commission to be ecumenical but supported the decision to keep it Anglican. 'Denominations have very different histories and organization', he later said, and 'too broad a base might "let the Church of England off the hook", when there were issues which it must face in detail.'[7] The commission was not wholly Anglican, however: two members and one adviser were from other traditions.[8]

The commission's terms of reference were

To examine the strengths, insights, problems and needs of the Church's life and mission in Urban Priority Areas and, as a result, to reflect on the challenge which God may be making to Church and Nation: and to make recommendations to appropriate bodies.

The term Urban Priority Area (UPA) was defined as including 'large Corporation estates and other areas of social deprivation' in addition to inner-city districts.

Commission members visited more than 30 cities and towns and nine inner London boroughs. As one of its advisers, John Gladwin, later wrote, it could not have done its job with integrity without gaining first-hand evidence of life in the UPAs. It also needed to test its deliberations, and the evidence submitted to it, in these areas. The visits profoundly influenced the report, Gladwin noted. Seeing the effects of

---

7 'The Ecumenical Dimension', draft paper, April 1985: SHP, 18.6; Sheppard, *Steps along Hope Street*, p. 241.

8 The non-Anglican members were Robina Rafferty, assistant director of the Catholic Housing Aid Society, and Linbert Spencer, a Salvationist and chief executive of Project Fullemploy. Michael Eastman of ECUM was a Baptist.

high unemployment levels, of poor and deteriorating housing, and of 'strained and crumbling services', upset even those on the commission familiar with UPAs.[9]

The commission summarized its observations in the introduction to its report. *Poverty* would be one word to describe what we have seen, they stated. People were not starving, as in the developing world, but 'many residents of UPAs are deprived of what the rest of society regard as the essential minimum for a decent life.' Poverty was at the root of *powerlessness*, they continued. Poor people in UPAs lacked the means and opportunity of making choices in their lives. There was a degree of *inequality* in society greater than most people would deem acceptable. *Polarization* was another way of analysing what they had witnessed, with the 'impoverished minority' becoming increasingly cut off from mainstream life. None of these categories must distract from the plain message of their observations, they concluded, that 'the nation is confronted by a *grave and fundamental injustice* in the UPAs.' The situation 'continues to deteriorate and requires urgent action', but 'no adequate response is being made by government, nation or Church'.[10] The 1977 White Paper 'Policy for the Inner Cities' contained some good proposals, but there had been no sustained effort by governments to put them into effect.[11] The commission defended the right of 'the national Church' to act as the conscience of the nation. 'It must question all economic philosophies, not least those which, when put into practice, have contributed to the blighting of whole districts, which do not offer the hope of amelioration, and which perpetuate . . . human misery and despair . . .'[12]

The report ran to 400 pages and made 61 recommendations, nearly two-thirds of which were addressed to the Church. One called for the establishment of a Church Urban Fund to strengthen the Church's presence in UPAs. Another wanted the resources of the Church redistributed between dioceses to equalize the amount parishes contributed

---

9 Gladwin, J., 'Faith in the City', *Crucible*, Jan–Mar 1986, p. 5. Gladwin was an adviser to the commission representing the Church of England Board of Social Responsibility.

10 *Faith in the City*, 'Introduction', pp. xiv–xv.

11 *Faith in the City*, Section 8.19–20, pp. 173-4.

12 *Faith in the City*, Section 9.41, p. 208.

to clergy stipends. Synod had carried a motion calling for this in 1983, as Runcie noted when launching the commission. A Commission on Black Anglican Concerns was proposed, and the report challenged the Church to be orientated towards the well-being of the whole community. Many of the recommendations to 'Government and Nation' specifically called on the government to expand existing programmes, set up enquiries or shift priorities. Encouragement was also given to the voluntary sector, small businesses, and involvement by local people at neighbourhood level in the UPAs.

The week before the report's publication, Sheppard wrote to the Prime Minister, reminding her that they had corresponded earlier about the commission and saying its work was now complete. 'The report is a very thorough piece of work', he wrote. 'There is a great deal of detailed analysis and recommendation for the Church. And we have raised public policy questions about the confusing and interlocking factors, which make urban life what it is.' Sheppard hoped that the government would regard the report as constructive and that it would have lasting value.[13]

He could hardly have been more disappointed. The report had been embargoed until Tuesday 3 December, but the Sunday before a 'senior government figure' was quoted in the press saying that parts of it were 'pure Marxist theology'.[14] The *Sunday Times* report also said the commission had called for an end to mortgage tax relief, which was 'certain to anger Mrs Thatcher'. In fact it had called for 'a major examination of the whole system of housing finance, including mortgage tax relief'.[15] The media buzzed with the story throughout the day and it was front-page news on the Monday, so Sheppard spent the whole of Monday afternoon doing interviews. The commission held its press launch as planned on the Tuesday, but the government had already

---

13 Letter to the Prime Minister, 25 November 1985: SHP, 29.8. Thatcher initiated a discussion about the work of the commission at a meeting with Sheppard in November 1984: No. 10 Briefing 841115.

14 'Church report is "Marxist"', *Sunday Times*, 1 December 1985, p. 1. Norman Tebbit has often been cited as the source of this quote, but he has always denied this (letter to the author 25 July 2018).

15 Sheppard later explained that the commission did not advocate abolishing mortgage tax relief, but 'phasing it out in favour of a more equitable way of using that huge subsidy'. This echoed the recommendation of the 1984 Rowntree inquiry into housing chaired by the Duke of Edinburgh: 'Deceptively Mild', Poverty Network paper, Summer 1986, p. 3.

given their work more profile than they could ever have imagined. Ironically Number 10 had decided a few days before that 'no attempt should be made to pre-empt the report this weekend . . . a pre-emptive strike could draw more attention to the report than it would otherwise get.' 'Kill it with kindness', the Prime Minister's private secretary David Norgrove advised her. 'A Church–Government row would keep the Report on the front pages.'[16] The report would eventually sell 50,000 copies.

Behind the scenes a more considered response was being prepared by one of the Prime Minister's advisers, Brian Griffiths. He thought the report tried to avoid a confrontation with the government, and was not condemning its policies wholesale. Nevertheless, there was running through it 'a deep hostility to government policy and the philosophy on which it is based.' Griffiths described the report as 'collectivist, determinist and Keynesian' with nothing to say to the individual family wishing to escape from poverty. A practising Anglican, Griffiths expressed concern that a Church which stressed the value and dignity of each person should play down the importance of individual effort. He thought the report was Marxist in the sense that it emphasized 'the *structure* of society being the cause of poverty' rather than individual agency. At Cabinet on 5 December the government agreed to follow Griffiths' line.[17] Margaret Thatcher later expressed her 'absolute shock' that the Church had failed to say anything to individuals and families.[18]

The government's hostility to the report should be viewed in context. Relations between the Church hierarchy and Margaret Thatcher's government had been strained since her first election victory in 1979. The service to mark the end of the Falklands War in 1982 had been an early cause of friction. The Church wanted to acknowledge the Argentinian dead and avoid a triumphalist note. The miners' strike was

---

16 Memo from Bernard Ingham, 28 November 1985, The National Archive (TNA): PREM 19/1920_2; Moore, C., *Margaret Thatcher: The authorized biography*, vol 2, London: Penguin, 2015, p. 446.

17 Memo from Brian Griffiths, 3.12.85, TNA: PREM 19/1920_1; CAB 128_81_35. Griffiths and Sheppard had met through John Stott's 'Christian debate' meetings in the 1960s. A shared Christian faith and commitment to tackling social ills, albeit by different methods, enabled them to maintain a friendship despite their differences.

18 Young, H., *One of Us: A biography of Margaret Thatcher*, London: Macmillan, 1989, p. 417.

another source of tension, with several bishops publicly criticizing the government's approach. Some leading bishops, including Sheppard, regretted Thatcher's decision to end the post-War 'Butskellite' consensus in favour of greater freedom for the market.[19] For them, community was an important biblical concept. As we have seen, Sheppard often spoke of being 'members one of another', a term of St Paul's[20] and saw the provision of services from a common purse as a manifestation of community. Thatcher put her faith in free-market economics and a scaled down welfare state. There was little common ground between the bishops and the government.

Against this backdrop, *The Times* political columnist, Ronald Butt, described *Faith in the City* as 'in many ways the high-water mark of systematic criticism of the Government's policies' by the Church of England.[21] The government might have thought that the Church had been exercising its 'duty' to question its economic philosophy for several years. With the Labour Party weakened by its election defeat in 1983, and defection of some of its leading MPs to the Social Democratic Party, the Church of England was almost the *de facto* 'loyal opposition'.[22] But whether this was due to a conscious left-ward shift by the bishops is debatable. Clifford Longley argues that one reason the churches looked increasingly left-wing in the 1980s was that the Conservative Party 'had started to move steadily to the Right' after 1979. 'Without changing its outlook, therefore, the Church leadership in Britain, of which Worlock and Sheppard were in the late 1970s representative in their political attitudes, gradually found itself in increasing opposition to the major direction of government policy.'[23]

---

19 'Butskellism' refers to the cross-party agreement in British politics that accepted nationalisation, trade unions and a generous welfare state. It is a composite of the names of two post-war Chancellors, Rab Butler (Conservative) and Hugh Gaitskell (Labour).

20 Romans 12.5.

21 'The Tension of the 1980s' in Alison, M., and Edwards, D. L., eds, *Christianity and Conservatism: Are Christianity and Conservatism Compatible?*, London: Hodder & Stoughton, 1990, p. 41.

22 Runcie was to appropriate this term in 1988: Butt, 'The Tension of the 1980s', p. 33. In the House of Lords, 61 per cent of votes cast by bishops during the 1980s were against the government, and just 27 per cent in support: Partington, *Church and State*, p. 90. Whether the bishops reflected the wider view of the church is a moot point. Cf. Davie, G., *Religion in Britain since 1945: Believing without Belonging*, Oxford: Blackwell, 1994, p. 152.

23 Longley, *The Worlock Archive*, p. 317.

Malcolm Brown and Paul Ballard suggest that the church slipped into its oppositional role 'almost by accident'. Adhering to a belief in social consensus, and acting as it had always done, it was 'not only ill-prepared for the emerging creed of Thatcherism but . . . almost inadvertently found [itself] articulating the anxieties and bewilderments of a society in turmoil'.[24] Eliza Filby thinks the Church of England's role in the formation of the welfare state in part explains its commitment to defending the post-war settlement.[25]

Thatcher once invited a group of bishops to meet her at Chequers. Sheppard was one of those invited. He intended to 'sit on his hands', but a comment the Prime Minister made about *Faith in the City* provoked him. He later recalled that the Prime Minister repeatedly interrupted his attempt to speak about the report. 'It was like being heckled', he said. 'Indeed my mouth went dry as I remembered it doing once when facing Lindwall and Miller! But I kept going.'[26]

*

Not all government ministers were critical of the report. The Energy Secretary, Peter Walker, wrote to Sheppard regretting the 'absurd outbursts' by his colleagues who he said had not read the report. 'I can only express my own gratitude to you for all you have done in this sphere and only hope it will meet with success', Walker wrote.[27] The Leader of the House, John Biffen, said the report should be treated as 'a serious contribution to studying the problems in our city centres . . . We know from the words of the Bishop of Liverpool that it is a substantial and carefully researched report by people who know a good deal about the cities'.[28] By the end of the week, the press was reporting a 'mood of contrition' among some ministers. One was quoted as saying that the report was 'well meant but misguided'.[29]

---

24 Brown, M., and Ballard, P., *The Church and Economic Life: A documentary study: 1945 to the present*, Peterborough: Epworth, 2006, p. 182.

25 Filby, *God and Mrs Thatcher*, p. 176.

26 Sheppard, *Steps along Hope Street*, p. 255.

27 Letter dated 4 December 1985: SHP, 30.1; Sheppard, *Steps along Hope Street*, p. 251.

28 Hansard, Commons, 3 December 1985, vol 88, cols.151–2. Sheppard saw this as a straight compliment, but it could be read another way; Sheppard, *Steps along Hope Street*, p. 251.

29 McKie, D., 'Ministers regret berating Church', *The Guardian*, 7 December 1985, p. 3.

The senior Conservative figure who engaged most positively with *Faith in the City* was Michael Heseltine. Shortly after he resigned as Defence Secretary in January 1986, he wrote a 19-page response to the report, and later met with six members of ACUPA. He disagreed with parts of the report and thought it 'ridiculous' to blame the government entirely for the situation, but he agreed with the commission's claim that urban areas were 'suffering from economic decline, physical decay and social disintegration'. He also agreed there were deep questions at stake: 'Damn the statistics; just go and look!', he wrote. 'Of course there are clear moral issues involved in the political challenges we face.' Heseltine told Runcie, 'Your bishops have got it all wrong. Things are much *worse* than they say!'[30]

Several critics thought the membership of the commission was politically biased. *The Times* argued that the balance of the commission was 'so clearly to the left of centre, the outcome was predictable.'[31] The cabinet minister Norman Tebbit went further, by requesting a dossier on all the members of the commission. Sheppard had a tense interview with Tebbit on Channel 4 News, where he was frustrated at Tebbit's unwillingness to discuss the content of the report. Tebbit became irritated by what he saw as a comfortably well-off man, who had benefited from an expensive private education, telling him about the hardships of those without work. Tebbit had left school at 16 and his father had been unemployed. In the hospitality room after, Tebbit told Sheppard about the dossier and read from it aloud, complaining the commission had been unbalanced and contained no one from the political right. Sheppard named members he thought fitted that bill, but Tebbit was unconvinced. Sheppard then said it was difficult to find thoughtful Christians on the right. At that point Tebbit walked out.

Sheppard immediately regretted his remark. Deeply distressed by the exchange, he stayed up late writing Tebbit an apology, and said he 'would wholly disown' his words if they had stood by themselves. They were,

---

Douglas Hurd later gave a positive account of the report: see 'Reluctant Crusader: Runcie and the State' in Platten, S., ed., *Runcie: On Reflection*, Norwich: Canterbury Press, 2002, pp. 25–7.

30 Heseltine, M., 'Faith in the City: A Step Forward', 22 March 1986: SHP, 30.1; Sheppard, *Steps along Hope Street*, p. 251.

31 'A Flawed Faith', *The Times*, 3 December 1985.

however, said within the context of 'smears' being made by the minister 'on men and women whose Christian integrity I have experienced in two years of hard and honest work.' He was disturbed that Tebbit had read out the contents of his dossier with six other people present, including references to the 'personal problems' of one commission member, but said he would welcome the opportunity to meet with Tebbit privately. Tebbit accepted Sheppard's invitation, but the *Mail on Sunday* then ran a story suggesting Sheppard had admitted both accusing Tebbit of being unchristian and saying, 'it was impossible to be a thinking Christian as well as a Right-wing Tory.'[32] Sheppard had not made either claim. He received an assurance from Tebbit that his office had not leaked the story of their backstage conversation to the press: Tebbit thought the Labour Party had been involved.

*

Despite the attention the report garnered, Sheppard was dismayed by its reception. In the January he told a friend he had hoped people's first response to it would have been, 'Is it true?' Instead there was 'a deliberate leak', a smear about it being 'Marxist theology', and a focus on just one of its recommendations (a review of housing finance) which was then distorted. Sheppard thought these responses were calculated to remove the confidence of ordinary churchgoers in the report.

Sheppard was also annoyed by suggestions the commission was politically biased. 'We very deliberately said that we should find someone from the right for the economics', Sheppard said. Professor John Pickering had been selected, and Sheppard thought two other members were 'closely in touch with the CBI [and] regarded as very straight down the centre among industrialists . . . Frankly it did not occur to us to ask about the political convictions of most members of the Commission', Sheppard wrote.

We wanted thoughtful Christians who would bring together the wide range of knowledge that is needed to understand what is going

---

32 Hartley, J., 'Why I Clashed with Tebbit – by the Bishop', *Mail on Sunday*, 22 December 1985.

on in the cities. That was the context in which I made my foolish remark to Norman Tebbit in a private discussion . . .[33]

The chapter on 'theological priorities' attracted criticism. The report lacked a solid biblical underpinning and offered no 'theology of the city', some argued.[34] A more comprehensive accusation was that the Church seemed unaware that the theological methodology which had served it through the post-war consensus 'could not seamlessly accommodate the ideological upheavals and uncertainties of the Thatcher years.'[35] Sheppard said that shaping a theology of urban mission had been a priority for the commission but that members felt they first needed to 'share common experiences' with UPA people.[36] Another member of the commission, Anthony Harvey, said it was felt that a theology of the city 'ought to come out of, rather than be imposed upon, congregations in UPAs.'[37] The commission appeared not to acknowledge this when it referenced Liberation Theology, a theology done by poor communities themselves, not others on their behalf. They ended up with 'not theology *by* the poor . . . rather an imaginative leap into what such a theology might look like', as Brown puts it.[38] The theology chapter's positive references to this theology, and parallels it suggested between aspects of Marx's teaching and the Old Testament, gave further grist to the mill of those accusing the commission of left-wing bias.

*

---

33 Letter dated 23 January 1986: SHP, 18.6. Pickering in fact declined a request to write a chapter on economics – interview.

34 See for example, Marchant, C., 'Faith in the City', *The Modern Churchman*, 28 February 1986, p. 4; Willmer, H., 'Politview I: Faith in the City', *The Modern Churchman*, 28 March 1986, p. 12. For a more positive assessment of the report's theology, see Graham, E. 'Theology in the City: Ten years after *Faith in the City*', *Bulletin of the John Rylands Library*, 78 (1), 1996, pp. 173–91.

35 Brown, M., 'Some Thoughts on Theological Method', *Unemployment and the Future of Work*, London: CCBI, 1997, p. 293.

36 Sheppard, *Steps along Hope Street*, p. 242.

37 Harvey, A., *By What Authority? The Churches and Social Concern*, London: SCM Press, 2001, p. 23.

38 Brown, M., *After the Market: Economics, Moral Agreement and the Churches' Mission*, Bern: Peter Lang, 2004, p. 39.

Faith in the City spawned several initiatives. Its call for a Committee for Black Anglican Concerns (CBAC) was heeded. CBAC's main responsibilities were to monitor the work of General Synod 'with a view to supporting efforts for racial justice' and assist dioceses 'in developing strategies for combating racial bias within the Church.'[39] The report's affirmation of church-based community and voluntary work gave fresh impetus to bodies such as The Children's Society and Barnardo's, the latter when it was looking to make its Christian tradition 'more tangible' by linking with urban churches.[40]

The most high-profile outcome was the Church Urban Fund (CUF), a recommendation advocated by Sheppard. The Fund was 'to strengthen the Church's presence and promote the Christian witness' in the UPAs, the report said. In its first five years CUF raised £18 million, with a further £18 million in its next ten years, and made grants to parishes and ecumenical projects that had never dared to dream of new ventures, Sheppard later wrote. 'As a result, they became more outward-looking into the community.'[41] The Fund's impact was often overshadowed by the political fallout from the report itself.

Behind the creation of CUF was a concern to see the resources of the church distributed more evenly. Sheppard had long been troubled about the inequity in wealth between dioceses. Some had a 'financial cushion', provided by the generosity of past Christians or 'the vagaries of history'. These dioceses could ask their parishes to give less towards clergy stipends than those without such benefits, which might not themselves be in the best position to afford a higher percentage of the stipend bill. *Faith in the City* recommended redistributing resources using a formula that took into account 'potential' giving.[42] Sheppard had seen this operating in Liverpool: in 1982, a diocesan working party he set up and co-chaired said there should be an 'element of potential' in the calculations to assess parish stipends and quotas.[43] A review

---

39 Bishops' Advisory Group on UPAs, *Staying in the City: Faith in the city ten years on*, London: Church House Publishing, 1995, p. 79. CBAC was later renamed the Committee for Minority Ethnic Anglican Concerns (CMEAC).
40 I am grateful to Stephen Hanvey for alerting me to this.
41 Sheppard, *Steps along Hope Street*, p. 259.
42 *Faith in the City*, section 7.78, p. 159.
43 'Urban Priority Areas: The Report of a Working Party set up by the Diocesan Synod of the Diocese of Liverpool', March 1982, Section 5.7.3, p. 28: SHP, 12.6.

five years later found the principle of 'quota by potential' almost universally accepted by parishes as 'a very fair method of sharing the costs of our diocese.'[44] Nationally most dioceses made the change recommended by *Faith in the City*. The increased contribution from parishes with greater potential, Sheppard noted, amounted to more than the capital sum raised for CUF because those increases were sustained every year.[45] The creation of CUF and the 'quota by potential' scheme gave the Church more credibility when pressing government to spend more on its Urban Programme, as the Church was now redistributing its resources from rich to poor, a policy it wanted the state to pursue.[46]

To ensure *Faith in the City* was followed up in his own diocese, Sheppard set up an Urban Priorities Steering Group a month before the report was published, and an ecumenical sub-group produced a report called 'Faith in OUR City' in January 1987. This responded to the report's recommendations to the nation by highlighting 'issues of special local significance.'[47] Comments on the report's recommendations were drawn from across the diocese. Sheppard and the other church leaders, and the University vice chancellor, Professor Graeme Davies, also supported the establishment of Merseyside Churches Urban Institute to have an ongoing way of addressing *Faith in the City* issues, and its activities included summer schools, courses and a series of church and society booklets. The diocese also produced some theological reflections on the report, edited by the diocesan missioner, Dr Myrtle Langley.[48] Meetings to discuss *Faith in the City* were arranged in the eight district council areas, each attended by a cross-section of the community. In one borough half the council attended, including the leader and deputy leader, and Sheppard spoke at every one. A health audit was also conducted in two Liverpool districts in collaboration with the local area health authority.[49]

---

44 'Review of Quota by Potential' – report to the Diocesan Synod, May 1987: SHP, 3.3.

45 Sheppard, *Steps along Hope Street*, p. 246.

46 *Faith in the City*, Section 7.87, p. 162. The Church of England continued this policy through its 'Renewal and Reform' programme.

47 Russell, H., ed., *Faith in OUR City*, Liverpool: Liverpool Diocesan Publishing, 1987, p. 8.

48 Langley, M., ed., *Some Theological Reflections on Faith in the City*, Liverpool: Liverpool Diocesan Publishing, 1986.

49 Black, N., 'Two Years On: The Liverpool Perspective', *Anvil*, 5 January 1988, pp. 17–18.

Sheppard created another body in Liverpool during the *Faith in the City* consultation, the Group for Urban Ministry and Leadership (GUML). This aimed to train ministerial teams in UPA parishes and develop local non-stipendiary ministry. It had a focus on people with minimal formal qualifications, echoing the programme developed by Ted Roberts during Sheppard's time at Woolwich. It also drew on a report produced by the dioceses of Liverpool and Manchester in 1982 called 'To Match the Hour'. This looked at training men with special gifts for urban ministry. The mover and shaker behind GUML was Neville Black, its first director. Black had been appointed by Sheppard as 'urban leadership adviser' in 1984 with a brief to establish the new scheme. Black had formerly led the Evangelical Urban Training Project. Under Black's leadership, GUML produced teams in some 20 UPA parishes, and 13 locally ordained ministers.

Follow-up activity to *Faith in the City* constituted 'a remarkable allocation of ecclesiastical energy', one commentator noted.[50] According to the official progress report, *Living Faith in the City*, four years after its publication every diocese had a 'link officer' for UPA matters. Most had debated the report in their synod and more than 30 had coordinating committees following it up. Some were employing urban officers. Dioceses were 'well on the way' to raising their target of £18 million for the Church Urban Fund. More than £5 million had been allocated towards the funding of more than 200 projects to strengthen communities.[51] 'In very many parishes and synods there was a really encouraging response to the report's publication', Prebendary Pat Dearnley recalls.

> The report unquestionably raised the morale of many clergy and alerted suburban congregations (and not infrequently rural ones as well) to the problems facing residents in the inner cities and outer housing estates. I was inundated with requests to visit places, and especially noteworthy were meetings I addressed in solidly 'Comfortable Britain'.

Dearnley was appointed by Runcie to coordinate the Church's response to the report.

---

50 Clark, H., *The Church under Thatcher*, London: SPCK, 1993, p. 104.
51 *Living Faith in the City: A progress report by the Archbishop of Canterbury's Advisory Group on Urban Priority Areas*, London: General Synod of the Church of England, 1990, p. viii.

Sheppard would have been encouraged. He had hoped the report would challenge 'comfortable' parishes. As he told the Chief Rabbi, Immanuel Jakobovits, he wanted people in the suburbs to regard UPA people as their neighbours. Much of the report 'is rightly aimed at suburban Christians', Sheppard wrote, 'who all too easily seem to blame those who have been left behind.'[52]

Response to the policy recommendations in the report was less encouraging. One commission member, Ruth McCurry, estimated that only one of its 23 recommendations to government and nation had been carried out within the first ten years. This contrasted with 15 of its 38 recommendations to the Church.[53] This may be unsurprising given that many recommendations looked to the state to provide solutions, but more important was the extent to which the report inspired the government to tackle the situation in the inner cities more urgently.

Brian Griffiths, an insider at No.10 at the time, recalls that the report was a huge spur to the government to do more on urban issues. While the policies it adopted to rejuvenate the inner cities were different from those proposed in the report, the government's response to the Church's call for action was wholehearted. *Faith in the City* was the 'trigger' for a raft of inner-city reforms in areas such as education, housing and law and order, Griffiths says. It was not the only catalyst for government action, but in terms of providing a 'thrust' to more intensive engagement, the report was crucial. Bishop Tom Butler, who chaired the Archbishop's Advisory Group on UPAs which coordinated the follow-up to *Faith in the City*, has noted that, while urban issues were not high on the agenda of any political party at the time the report was published, 'its effectiveness can be seen by Margaret Thatcher, after her re-election in 1987 saying, "We must do something about the inner cities."'[54] Eliza Filby has argued that the prominence given to urban poverty in the election manifestos

---

52 Letter dated 4 March 1986; SHP, 29.1. Jakobovits had written a pamphlet critical of *Faith in the City* which was commended by Margaret Thatcher.

53 McCurry, R., 'Ten Years On', in Sedgwick, P., ed., *God in the City: Essays and Reflections from the Archbishop of Canterbury's Urban Theology Group*, London: Mowbray, p. 4. See also Clark, *The Church under Thatcher*, p. 107.

54 A commitment to tackle 'the regeneration of the inner cities' was contained in the Conservative Party manifesto for the 1987 election, along with policies to address housing, jobs, social security and local government.

of all parties that year is evidence that *Faith in the City* 'fulfilled its aim of alerting both the politicians and public to the plight of the nation's cities.'[55]

*

Two major tragedies involving fans of Liverpool Football Club occurred in the 1980s. Sheppard played a leading role in the churches' response to both.

In May 1985, Liverpool played the Turin club Juventus in the final of the European Cup, at the Heysel Stadium in Brussels. An hour before kick-off, fighting broke out between rival fans, and those fleeing the fighting were crushed against a collapsing wall. A total of 39 people were killed, with a further 600 injured. Most were Juventus fans. Not all the perpetrators of violence were from Liverpool, but Sheppard felt that 'the sense of shame throughout the city was enormous . . . The whole of Liverpool had to bear the brunt of reasonable and widespread condemnation, and there was no attempt to evade responsibility,' he and Worlock wrote.[56]

The Anglican Cathedral opened a Book of Condolence, and a Mass for the dead and injured was said at the Roman Catholic cathedral two days after the tragedy. The following week Sheppard preached at a special service at the Anglican cathedral, and the theme was 'sorrow and penitence in hope of reconciliation'. Sheppard said that the name of Liverpool had been 'associated with shameful behaviour on the terraces', and people were 'coming to terms with disturbing truths about [them]selves' and finding the gospel message helpful. 'When we face ourselves', Sheppard said, 'we understand . . . that it is possible to know for ourselves the free gift of God's forgiveness, bought at a great price by Jesus Christ.' He counselled against looking for people to blame: 'One of our great strengths in Liverpool is that many have learned from some deep divisions in this city how to stand together.' At the suggestion of Derek Hatton, deputy leader of the city council, a delegation of civic

---

55 'God and Mrs Thatcher', PhD thesis, p. 129.
56 Sheppard, D. S., and Worlock, D., *Better Together: Christian partnership in a hurt city*, London: Hodder & Stoughton, 1988, pp. 246–7.

leaders travelled to Turin to express the city's sorrow, where Sheppard and Worlock took part in a Mass at the shrine of the patroness of Turin, Our Lady Consolata.

Four years after Heysel, what has become known as the Hillsborough disaster occurred. The date, 15 April 1989, is etched in the memory of everyone on Merseyside. Shortly before Liverpool and Nottingham Forest were due to kick off their FA Cup semi-final at the neutral Sheffield Wednesday ground, 96 people were crushed to death and a further 750 injured. In an attempt to ease overcrowding outside the entrance, the police match commander ordered an exit gate to be opened, and this led to an influx of supporters to an already overcrowded part of the ground. Those who died were Liverpool fans, and most were from Merseyside. The disaster seemed to affect the whole city, a diocesan report noted: 'Nearly everyone in Liverpool knew someone at the match or found that someone living near them was amongst the dead or injured.'[57]

Sheppard was on the island of Barra in the Outer Hebrides when the disaster occurred. People in Liverpool expected the churches to act together at such times and he needed to return. Worlock and Newton had gone immediately to Sheffield on the Saturday afternoon to be with the families and people who were injured, and on the way back, they discussed making Sunday evening Mass at the Catholic cathedral a special service for Hillsborough, starting at 6pm. Sheppard's absence would be noted, but there were no flights or sailings from the island that day.

Sheppard's chaplain, Stephen Bellamy, reached the coastguard at Oban by phone, and the coastguard got permission for the emergency helicopter to operate outside its normal area, to carry Sheppard to Prestwick airport near Glasgow. Sheppard arrived at Prestwick in good time, but the RAF Sea King assigned to collect him had to attend an emergency in the Lake District. Eventually, it returned. As it took to the skies, an airman brought out a detailed map of Liverpool and asked Sheppard where he would like them to land.

---

57 *The Diocese of Liverpool and the Hillsborough Disaster: A Report for the Bishop's Council*, May 1990, p. 1. The actual death toll on the day was 94: one person died a few days later and another person died more than a year later.

Sheppard landed at The King's Dock with ten minutes to spare, and was met by Bellamy and his driver, George Walker. Bellamy had brought Sheppard's robes, socks and shoes. The flight had been rough, and the drive to the cathedral was no less hair-raising: Walker was escorted by police cars with sirens blaring and blue lights flashing. After crossing red lights, overtaking lines of traffic and swerving across lanes, they reached the cathedral as the choir and clergy were about to process in. Worlock spotted Sheppard arriving and held things up while he and Bellamy threw on their robes. The service had drawn a congregation of 3,000, with a further 5,000 outside. 'Bishop David didn't have to say anything in the service', Bellamy later recalled, 'but it was so important that he was there, as the city united in grief.'[58]

In the following days Sheppard made three visits to Anfield, where the pitch was covered with flowers and the barriers with scarves. He did TV and radio interviews. On 29 April the Anglican cathedral hosted the memorial service, where the Prime Minister and representatives of the royal family joined bereaved families, club officials and players. The service enabled the nation as well as the city to come together. At Sheppard and Worlock's request, John Newton preached the sermon. The next day Sheppard led a service at Anfield as the gates were closed and the period of official mourning ended.

A year later Sheppard preached at an anniversary service at Anfield, recalling how people had expressed their feelings in the aftermath of the tragedy. There was grief, anger and perhaps also guilt at having been there and survived. 'Football terraces have always been macho places', Sheppard said. 'Men weren't expected to weep or tell each other how they were feeling.' Observing that the service was on Easter Day he spoke of his belief that 'death is not the end . . . there is greater life beyond this world.'[59]

Hillsborough had a profound effect on Sheppard. He spoke of Liverpool responding to it like 'a great family standing together'. He was impressed by the club's response. The club's manager, Kenny Dalglish, attended many of the funerals, including four in one day.

---

58 I am grateful to Dr Stephen Bellamy for sharing his memories of that day with me. He had only been in post five weeks at the time.

59 Address at Hillsborough Anniversary Service, Anfield, Easter Day 1990: SHP, 16.3.

Every funeral was attended either by Dalglish or by one of the players. Dalglish and his players also spent time with bereaved families in the counselling room at Anfield. In 1997 Sheppard wrote to the Home Secretary, Jack Straw, supporting calls for a fresh enquiry into the disaster. A TV documentary had suggested there were grounds for believing there might have been negligence by public bodies. Straw later announced an independent scrutiny. Sheppard's successor, Bishop James Jones, would in due course chair the panel supervising the disclosure of documents relating to Hillsborough. In September 2012, the Hillsborough Independent Panel concluded that no Liverpool fans were responsible in any way for the disaster. Its main cause was a 'lack of police control'.[60]

With a terrible irony, Sheppard had spoken in the House of Lords two months before Hillsborough about spectators gaining access to football grounds. During a debate on what would become the Football Spectators Act 1989, Sheppard noted the challenges facing police and clubs when large numbers of fans find themselves outside a ground once a match has begun. He also spoke of the contribution Liverpool's two clubs made to unity in the city.[61]

*

The reason Sheppard was on Barra when the Hillsborough disaster occurred was to spend time with his daughter's new in-laws. The previous autumn Jenny had married Donald Sinclair, whose family lived on Barra. She had been living in Edinburgh when she met Donald. She had left home at 18 and taken a degree in Communication Studies at Goldsmiths' College in London. After graduating, she worked at the Greater London Council (GLC) as a 'girl Friday' in the Leader's office, where her duties included supporting the work of the GLC's Parliamentary Unit. The GLC was under threat of abolition at the time and its future was being debated

---

60 Hillsborough Disaster, https://en.wikipedia.org/wiki/Hillsborough_disaster [accessed February 2019]
61 Hansard, House of Lords, 2 February 1989, cols. 1233–5. The other club is, of course, Everton.

in the Lords. Jenny's employers thought her connections could come in useful.

Meeting Donald changed her life in two ways. First, because it led to marriage and a lifelong partnership, but also because through him she came to embrace the Catholic faith. As a teenager she had been confirmed in the Anglican tradition out of a sense of duty, but after leaving home she was no longer a churchgoer. On their first Sunday together, she accompanied Donald to the evening service at his parish church, St Aloysius, Glasgow. Despite her father's ecumenism, she had never attended a Catholic Mass. The Mass that night moved her deeply and raised questions she had never considered. She continued to attend weekly. Two months later she found herself undergoing a dramatic conversion experience, and sought guidance to navigate a way forward. Donald introduced her to his friend, Fr Michael Hollings in London. Hollings was to be an important mentor for Jenny in the years ahead. By June she had decided to convert. She and Donald had realized only two days after their first meeting that they were destined to marry.

Jenny knew this would be a bombshell for her parents. In addition to learning of her conversion and decision to marry, they were apprehensive about Donald. At the time, he was running an experimental theatre group in Glasgow and they did not immediately warm to each other. Sheppard rang Hollings, who assured him Donald was 'a good man'.

Jenny and Donald decided to have a small wedding in London, with only the immediate families present. Hollings came up with a formula where three ceremonies were held on the wedding day. The main service was a nuptial Mass conducted by Hollings, assisted by Grace's father, Bryan Isaac. Only the couple received communion and Sheppard's role was as father of the bride. There had been a Mass earlier in the day, at which Donald's family received, while Jenny's family received communion at an Anglican Eucharist in a neighbouring church at which Sheppard presided. All present were moved to see Archbishop Worlock at this service, sitting quietly then coming forward for a blessing. He had cleared his diary and travelled to London to support the Sheppards. He would have recalled a similar situation from his time at Portsmouth when the Anglican bishop's daughter married a Roman Catholic.[62] Members of Jenny's extended family, not least her aunt Mary, were upset at not being included in any of these ceremonies.

As Grace, David and Donald got to know each other, a genuine friendship developed. Grace and David also accepted Jenny's becoming a Catholic. In 1993 Jenny and Donald moved to London, and the four would meet there as well as in Liverpool. A few years later would come news that brought them even closer.

*

In May 1989 Sheppard finally set foot on South African soil. He and Worlock had received an invitation from the Anglican and Roman Catholic archbishops of Cape Town, Desmond Tutu and Stephen Naidoo. Naidoo had visited the bishops in Liverpool, and wanted his own people to see how a partnership such as theirs could work. Grace accompanied her husband as a guest. Mgr John Furnival travelled as Worlock's chaplain, and Julian Filochowski, Director of the Catholic Fund for Overseas Development, was their guide.

The situation in the country was tense. The state of emergency had another year to run and Nelson Mandela was still in jail. The bishops wanted to listen more than speak. They did not want a tourist's view and stayed overnight in several townships. This enabled them to see more of black people's lives than 98 per cent of white South Africans, they were told. 'Our Churches took us across many of the barriers which divide South Africans', Sheppard later wrote.[63] He described the trip as 'one of those visits which made each of us feel we would never be quite the same again.'[64] He had been told that apartheid was crumbling, but his perception was that small changes might have occurred but 'grand

---

62 This was also resolved by having more than one service, a practice which became known as 'the Portsmouth solution': see Sheppard and Worlock, *Better Together*, p. 17.

63 Sheppard, *Steps along Hope Street*, p. 278; address to Liverpool diocesan synod, 1989: SHP, 14.3.

64 Private letter, 13 July 1989, to Bernard Palmer, editor of the *Church Times*: SHP, 14.3.

apartheid' was 'firmly in place'.[65] Staying in townships allowed people to approach them unseen by any officials monitoring their visit. Sheppard was struck by the joy he found in churches: 'The singing, the movement, unhurried worship and prayer, openness to one another feed the courage to stand up to evil'.[66]

Sheppard spoke and wrote about the visit extensively, reporting that people who wanted change had urged him to 'keep up the pressures'. In a press statement he and Worlock said that, in addition to existing pressures, 'further selective, effective and targeted measures, chosen in the diplomatic, political and economic fields, should be applied progressively by Western countries'.

The trip was life-changing for Grace. Several years before she had sought the help of a clinical psychologist for her agoraphobia, and over a period of three years, she had regained a sense of her own worth and significance. Now she experienced a major breakthrough. In one township she stayed too long in a house and became detached from the group. Her only hope of finding them lay with four men outside the house who had seen what had happened. She realized that she would have to overcome her 'pride and prejudice' in order to ask them for help. 'Almost physically, I cast [those feelings] on to the sand at my feet, disgusted with myself for giving them houseroom', she later wrote. 'At that moment my agoraphobia withered and died . . . Within the space of half an hour I had crossed the Rubicon'.[67]

*

Sheppard wanted to see the effect of the sporting boycott he had so passionately supported. The BBC commentator Christopher Martin-Jenkins suggested he meet up with the former South African captain, Ali Bacher. Bacher showed Sheppard the coaching scheme he was running in Tembisa, a township near Johannesburg. Sheppard thought this a brave attempt to give talented boys a chance to get into cricket but was

65 'Little for your comfort', *The Cricketer*, August 1989, p. 26.

66 'Keep taking an interest', *Livewire* (diocesan newsletter), August 1989.

67 'White Fear Black Hope', *Livewire*, August 1989; Sheppard, G., *Living with Dying*, London: Darton, Longman & Todd, 2010, p. 28.

disappointed to find no other townships had comparable facilities. He was not convinced the initiative would go far.[68]

Sheppard had kept up his opposition to sporting links with South Africa while in Liverpool. In 1983 he took issue with the Conservative MP, John Carlisle, who wanted MCC to send a tour party to South Africa. Writing in *The Times*, Sheppard argued that 'the pressure that the sporting boycott brings should be maintained'. MCC members rejected Carlisle's motion by more than 2,000 votes.[69] Carlisle had supported the 'rebel tour' led by Graham Gooch the previous year. In 1990 Sheppard criticized Mike Gatting for leading a second unofficial tour. He thought Bacher might have damaged his coaching scheme by helping to organize Gatting's tour.[70]

Mandela was released from prison in February 1990. 'I am thankful for President de Klerk's courage and statesmanship', Sheppard told the Lords. 'It is an astonishing step forward which we could not have imagined a year ago.'[71] The following year South African cricket came under the control of a non-racial body, and in August 1994, Sheppard watched England play South Africa for the first time since the country's readmittance to Test cricket. Anticipating the trip to The Oval, he told a friend that the match 'stands for some changes that we hardly believed could happen.'[72]

*

In preparation for the Lambeth Conference in 1988, Archbishop Runcie asked every bishop to 'bring his diocese with him'.[73] To help equip him to do this, Sheppard invited each parish to hold a 'hearing' or 'audit' on ministry and mission. Results were processed by the diocesan missioner,

---

68 'Little for your comfort', p. 26.

69 *The Times* letters, 6 July 1983; Williams, *Cricket and Race*, p. 112–3. Carlisle had had a friendlier encounter with Sheppard 25 years before when the cricketer did some coaching at his school: correspondence with the author.

70 'Gatting Was Wrong', mss of article for *Cricket Life International* dated 20 February 1990: SHP, 14.3.

71 Hansard, Lords, 'South Africa and Nelson Mandela: Policy', 12 February 1990, col. 1116.

72 Letter dated 23 June 1994: SHP, 10.6.

73 Held every ten years, the conference brings bishops from the worldwide Anglican communion together for an extended time of discussion and worship.

Myrtle Langley. Sheppard wanted to hear how parishes were 'turning outward in service to the world.' This would involve them listening to voices from outside the church. The consultation built on Sheppard's regular visits to parishes. His pattern, which he developed at Woolwich, was to arrive for a parish communion at 6.30 pm on the Sunday and leave late on the Monday evening after a day spent 'walking the parish' and visiting secular institutions as well as church groups. He found that with careful preparation, involving the parish completing a question-naire in advance, much could be achieved in that time. In his early years in Liverpool he told the diocese about his fear that becoming a bishop would take him 'out of the front line'. 'I have since realized that there are other front lines than that of the local church', he wrote. 'But it is crucial for Bishops . . . to see and hear and feel what life is like in the parishes . . . There is nothing in my work I personally am more looking forward to . . . [than] . . . these visitations.'[74]

*

Sheppard's loyalty to Liverpool was tested in June 1986 when he was invited to become the next Bishop of Oxford. 'For one brief evening, I could just see reasons why that might be God's calling', he later wrote. 'But, in the morning, the reasons had floated away, and I felt that Liverpool was still his place for me.' Nor was Grace excited by the invitation.[75]

Canterbury, however, was a different story. When Runcie announced his intention to retire in 1990, Sheppard was touted as a front-runner in the media, especially in the broadsheets and serious weeklies. Topping a poll on a Channel 4 television show, and another at General Synod, ensured he stayed in the limelight. So, what went wrong?

Sheppard's ideological differences with Margaret Thatcher are often cited as the reason he was never appointed archbishop. She took seriously her responsibility to decide the name that went to the Palace, and Sheppard had been one of her government's sternest critics. Runcie himself

---

74 *Liverpool Diocesan News*, no. 98, February 1977. By sharing the visits with his suffragan and the two archdeacons each parish received a visit every five to six years.

75 Sheppard, *Steps along Hope Street*, p. 255; Grace Sheppard diary, 16 June 1986.

thought Sheppard was 'unlikely to get preferment' under Thatcher.[76] Yet Thatcher would only have needed to decide about Sheppard once he had been nominated by the Crown Appointments Commission. It was this body which gauged the opinion of the church and the diocese of Canterbury and drew up the final list. This comprised two names, with a preference clearly stated. It was thought that Thatcher had rejected the Commission's preferred candidate on two occasions in the past but had never broken protocol and rejected both names.[77] So the question was whether the Commission included Sheppard on the list it submitted to the Prime Minister. Only then would she become involved.

The appointment system is confidential[78] and details of the process leading to the appointment of George Carey as Runcie's successor may never become public knowledge. Two factors, however, suggest Sheppard's was not one of the two names considered by the Prime Minister. The first is the testimony of Robin Catford, the Prime Minister's secretary for appointments. In his autobiography, Carey describes being given the formal invitation to become Archbishop by Catford and asking Catford directly whether he was the first or second name on the list. Catford confirmed he was the first name.[79]

Second is the account the then Labour MP Frank Field gives of a private conversation he had with Margaret Thatcher in the late 1980s. Field asked Thatcher whether she would appoint David Sheppard as archbishop if his was one of the two names on the list from the Commission, he told the Commons in April 2013. 'Her reply was immediate: "Yes, of course." I was slightly staggered by that response, so I asked why. She said, "He always tells me to my face what he thinks and we always have a good argument."'[80] Field also recounted this conver-

---

76 Carpenter, H., *Robert Runcie: The Reluctant Archbishop*, London: Hodder & Stoughton, 1996, p. 215.

77 See Filby, *God and Mrs Thatcher*, pp. 148–9. In an early draft of *Steps along Hope Street*, Sheppard claims there had been 'four occasions when Mrs Thatcher had altered the order put forward by the CAC': SHP, 44.6. In correspondence with a Church Commissioner in the 1980s he claims to know of five: letter dated 27 April 1987: SHP, 1.15.

78 Conversations with people close to the process and a 'Freedom of Information' request failed to bring any hard facts to light.

79 Carey, G., *Know the Truth: A Memoir*, London: HarperCollins, 2004, p. 109.

80 Hansard, House of Commons, 10 April 2013, 'Tributes to Baroness Thatcher', col. 1652.

sation to Sheppard, who included it in an early draft of his autobiography *Steps along Hope Street*.[81]

Assuming, as we should, both stories to be true, the only conclusion is that Sheppard's was not one of the two names proposed by the Appointments Commission to succeed Robert Runcie. Yet there is another intriguing possibility. Received wisdom is that the name on the list below Carey's was John Habgood, then Archbishop of York. Thatcher was known to dislike Habgood and to have been unlikely to pick him over Carey. However, there is very strong evidence that the appointments commission did not put Habgood on the list precisely because he stood no chance. This allows for the possibility that Sheppard was the second name, and more than one very well-informed source has suggested that a Carey-Sheppard list makes perfect sense. Another factor is that it was the turn of an evangelical to go to Canterbury, under the convention that archbishoprics broadly 'rotate' between different wings of the church. This would mean the Prime Minister had second thoughts about her earlier comment about appointing Sheppard. Catford's advice would almost certainly have been to accept Carey, whose appointment he was known to have championed.

It must also remain a matter of conjecture why Sheppard was not the preferred name. Whatever 'political' factors the selectors considered, they may have considered Sheppard was no longer an evangelical. The two important figures in the process, Robin Catford and Viscount Caldecote, were both evangelicals. Caldecote, Thatcher's choice to chair the Crown Appointments Commission, saw Sheppard opposing the evangelical lobby during debates on the Broadcasting Bill in the Lords.[82] Another factor might have been age, particularly if the church wanted an archbishop who could lead it up to and beyond the next Lambeth Conference due in 1998. Sheppard would by then have been nearly 70.

Sheppard says little in print about how he coped with the speculation and outcome. Some who were close to him suggest he was disappointed

---

81 Sheppard may have had second thoughts about publishing this account while Lady Thatcher was still alive. Field also confirmed this story in email correspondence with the author.

82 See Quicke, A., and Quicke, J., *Hidden Agendas: The politics of religious broadcasting in Britain 1987–1991*, Virginia Beach: Dominion Kings Grant, 1992, p. 18.

not to be made archbishop. In *Steps along Hope Street* he says he did not covet the position and 'was relieved when it went to another'. Grace described the possibility of going to Lambeth as a 'nightmare' when originally told that her husband might be in the frame. On the day Carey's appointment was announced, Grace records that she and David were both shocked. 'Feelings of disappointment and relief came in', Grace wrote in her diary, 'but never overwhelmed us.' Sheppard was one of the first to congratulate Carey on his appointment, and the Careys and Sheppards maintained a good friendship. Carey valued Sheppard's support when a newspaper printed a critical article about him, and Sheppard replied. Sheppard's 'affirming and affectionate words meant a lot to me at a difficult time', he later wrote.[83]

Sheppard also missed out on the bishopric of London, which was John Major's first episcopal recommendation as Prime Minister. When Graham Leonard retired in May 1991 the Bishop of Wakefield, David Hope, was appointed. Sheppard was seriously in contention and, according to well-informed sources, could well have been the other name on the list. Friends thought he was more disappointed about missing out on London than Canterbury. Grace said he had 'hoped for the job for years'.[84]

Writing to his friend and mentor Cyril Bowles a month after the London announcement, Sheppard hints at how he felt while both posts were in the offing. 'It has been a strange and extended time', he wrote,

because apart from the public side of it, things were said to me by people close to decision-making which made me realise that both Canterbury and London were possible. There have been moments when it has been impossible to keep those thoughts out of my mind.

Not being appointed produced some feelings of deflation, he continued, 'but overwhelmingly a sense of being set free for a marvellous task here.' Sheppard spoke of the support he and Grace received from friends, and how their strong faith and close relationship with God through prayer had stood them in good stead at such a distracting time.

---

83 Carey, *Know the Truth*, p. 154.
84 Grace Sheppard diary, 6 January 1991.

God has been marvellously good. On the day of the Canterbury announcement last July, I was given one of those very occasional, breath-taking moments of His presence and care which was so direct and special that I felt without question His personal caring and leading.[85]

This had happened before. During his second sabbatical in Argyll in 1988, he recaptured the 'freshness of the presence of Christ' he had enjoyed when he was converted as a student. 'That awareness of His presence was quite as alive as 39 years ago', he later recalled, 'and there was a new awareness of the very close presence of my heavenly Father, together with His insistence that he is the Father of all.'[86]

*

Sheppard continued to offer leadership in other spheres. In 1989 he was invited to chair the Central Religious Advisory Committee (CRAC). CRAC had no executive power and was strictly an advisory body on broadcasting policy to the Independent Television Commission (ITC) and the BBC. Its members were appointed by the broadcasters, not the churches. Sheppard served four years as chair, and this led to his involvement in debates about a new broadcasting bill. This was an attempt by the government to liberalize and deregulate broadcasting by promoting competition. A group of Christian broadcasters wanted evangelistic programmes to be transmitted free of censorship. They objected to CRAC's multi-faith approach to religious broadcasting and tried to get the commission abolished.

Sheppard supported the idea of religious bodies owning cable television stations and local radio stations. His concern was allowing in what he called 'cheap exploitative or trivializing forms of religion', including religious advertising. At the Committee stage of the bill in the Lords, he proposed that religious advertising cover only announcements about meetings or services. He did not want to see advertising 'present any

---

85 Letter dated 12 March 1991: SHP, 36.3.
86 Sheppard, *Steps along Hope Street*, p. 308.

matter of faith, belief, doctrine or dogma . . . or appeal for the donation of any monies to any body.'[87] In seeking to ensure that the legislation did not open the door to 'cults and extremist bodies', Sheppard found an ally in the minister responsible for the bill, David Mellor.

Sheppard wanted to keep religious programmes on the mainline channels. As he noted in the Second Reading debate, allowing religion to be available only on specialized stations would

> follow the philosophy which sees the Church as a fortress of light, calling individuals to separate themselves from the darkness of the world around. In contrast, I believe that the Incarnation, by which I believe God in the person of Jesus Christ entered into the thick of life, calls us in the direction of broadcasting not narrowcasting.[88]

In his younger days Sheppard would have had some sympathy with the views he was now challenging. In the late 1950s he hosted discussions with fellow evangelicals at the Mayflower. They wanted to make more use of religious TV and considered producing a series of documentaries through which 'it should be possible to present some very considerable teaching about Jesus Christ himself'. Sheppard had talked with the film producer, Richard Attenborough, about the idea.

*

Sheppard's years in Liverpool would soon be over, but before they were, there would be further opportunities to speak for the church and the poor in the public square. He would also be identified with two further reports which would excite public debate and attract opposition in equal measure.

---

87 Hansard, Lords, Broadcasting Bill, 5 June 1990, col.1319; 11 July 1990, col. 401. For this section I have drawn on Quicke and Quicke, *Hidden Agendas*. Sheppard was critical of this book which, he thought, was based on a 'conspiracy theory' that religious advisers to the broadcasting authorities deliberately set out to keep evangelical Christianity from radio and television: Hansard, Lords, 'Religious Broadcasting', 9 November 1992, col. 56.

88 Hansard, Lords, Broadcasting Bill, 5 June 1990, col. 1320.

12

Liverpool, retirement and death (1991–2005)

Sheppard's appointment as chair of the Church of England Board for Social Responsibility (BSR) in 1991 gave him a new base from which to contribute to public affairs. The Board existed 'to promote and coordinate the thought and action of the Church in matters affecting the lives of all in society.' He had declined the chair in 1987 due to pressure of work, but now he accepted the invitation from the new archbishop, George Carey, giving up some extracurricular duties to create the time. He saw the role as an opportunity to work out his belief that the Church is called 'to change both human hearts and social structures.'

The breadth of the work brought Sheppard new challenges. The BSR had staff and committees dealing with industrial and economic affairs, social policy, international affairs, race and community relations, ecology, and medical ethics. Sheppard was also required to engage with divorce law reform, the marketing of baby formula, the situation in former Yugoslavia, and complex issues in medical ethics including assisted dying, so he drew on the advice of specialists in areas in which he had no expertise. The BSR worked ecumenically with other mainstream churches on issues such as Sunday observance and the National Lottery. When amendments to Sunday trading laws were proposed in 1991, Sheppard told the Lords that the churches 'unitedly opposed unrestricted opening of shops on Sundays'. The proposals touched issues of family life and 'the spiritual values of the nation', and he welcomed government attempts to find a consensus.[1] The churches had strong reservations about the introduction of a national lottery, and Sheppard led a delegation of mainstream church leaders to talk to the

---

1 Hansard, Lords, 'Sunday Trading Laws', 27 November 1991, col. 1352.

government minister. Much of the research on this issue was undertaken by the Methodist Church.

The BSR project which had the biggest impact in Sheppard's time was the report of its working party on family life, overseen by the social policy committee chaired by Bishop Jim Thompson. The report, *Something to Celebrate*, discussed a range of issues touching families, parenting and relationships, drawing upon more than 1,000 submissions from individuals and churches. The report acknowledged the variety of family forms that existed, and wanted 'gay and lesbian families' to be given encouragement and to find a 'ready welcome within the whole family of God'. It called on the government to review areas of policy relating to the plight of families living in poverty and poor housing.[2]

At the request of General Synod, the report also discussed cohabitation, stating 'lifelong, monogamous marriage lies at the heart of the Church's understanding of how the love of God is made manifest in the sexual companionship of a man and a woman.' It felt that the increasing popularity of cohabitation was no reason to modify this belief. However, Christians could hold fast to the centrality of marriage but also see cohabitation as 'a step along the way towards that fuller and more complete commitment' for some. In that context, the report considered, 'the first step the Church should take is to abandon the phrase "living in sin"'. It was 'a most unhelpful way of characterising the lives of cohabitees.'[3]

There were many positive responses to the report but, to Sheppard's dismay, critics focused on this one sentence. Sections of the press suggested the Church had abandoned all opposition to cohabitation, while the *Church Times* said the report had come 'dangerously close' to 'affirming people, whatever their lifestyle.'[4] In the House of Lords, Viscount Brentford suggested the report supported 'many of the aspects of cohabitation as opposed to marriage.'[5] Sheppard thought people who

---

2 *Something to Celebrate: Valuing Families in Church and Society*, London: Church House Publishing, 1995, pp. 120, 213. I have valued a conversation with Alison Webster, secretary of the social policy committee at the time.

3 *Something to Celebrate*, pp. 115–18.

4 'Extending the family, or undermining it?', *Church Times*, 9 June 1995, p. 10.

5 Hansard, Lords, debate on the Family Law Bill, 30 November 1995, col. 761.

had not read the report would be unaware of the strong affirmation marriage received: it was not suggesting that cohabitation had equal validity with marriage. Thompson told Sheppard that the press had told him they would have covered the report the same way whether it had included a reference to 'living in sin' or not.[6]

There were calls for an emergency debate in Synod when it next met, a month after the report appeared. Sheppard was strongly against such a step, believing a hurried debate would imply the Church was panicking, driven by irresponsible and unbalanced reporting which ignored the wider report. Members needed time to read and absorb it. Privately, he admitted the balance of the report was not entirely how he would have wanted it, but when the Church appointed 'distinguished Christians' to do a piece of work, it should accept that they might say uncomfortable things. He thought the report was right not to take 'absolutist positions' but to try to speak to people 'in the messy situations in which so many find themselves.' It was important to 'meet people on their own ground'.[7]

Sheppard enjoyed steering the BSR. He valued the support and professionalism of its staff, whom he had got to know and trust and who felt supported by him. He owed a particular debt to the Secretary of the Board, David Skidmore, to whom he wrote a handwritten letter of thanks. 'These five years have been a very significant period for me in my own pilgrimage', he told Skidmore.

> I owe more than I can put into words to you for your support at so many and varied times . . . I believe that the Church is taken seriously in many arenas of the world where thoughtful people care about truth and justice. That owes a great deal to the BSR and in particular to its staff.[8]

*

---

6 Letter dated 24 July 1997: Sheppard papers (SHP), 8.10.
7 Letter dated 12 July 1995: SHP, 8.10.
8 Letter to David Skidmore dated 1 June 1996: SHP, 29.7.

In November 1992, General Synod voted to ordain women to the priesthood, a move Sheppard had long been advocating. In the early 1970s, a decade before the decision to ordain women as deacons, he had spoken of the possibility of ordaining people with ability 'whatever their social class or academic achievement – or sex – may be.'[9] He often met with women in the diocese who believed they were called to the priesthood. When a motion at General Synod in favour of ordaining women as priests was lost in 1978, he invited all the deaconesses and women in accredited lay ministry in the diocese to share their feelings with him. In 1982, he fought successfully to have the diocesan missioner, a lay woman, admitted to his staff team, and he often spoke of the gifts that God had given women being wasted. He saw the ordination of women as God's will for the Church, and rejoiced at being able to ordain 28 women to the priesthood in 1994. He was sensitive, however, to those who 'conscientiously disagreed' with the step the Church had taken, wanting them to continue seeing themselves as 'valued members of our Church', and he hoped the Church would reach out to them. He set aside time to meet with those who felt hurt by the vote, and recognized that the vote was an obstacle to unity with Roman Catholics. In *Better Together*, he and Worlock acknowledged their differences on the issue. 'True ecumenism is not helped forward by holding back from actions we deeply believe to be right', Sheppard wrote.[10]

*

Liverpool witnessed two horrific murders in the 1990s. Sheppard was deeply affected by both.

In February 1993, two ten-year-old boys abducted two-year-old James Bulger from a shopping centre in Bootle. They led him for two and a half miles to a railway line in Walton before torturing him and battering him to death. Sheppard was asked to present 'Thought for

---

9 Sheppard, D. S., *Built as a City: God and the Urban World Today*, London: Hodder & Stoughton, 1974, p. 292.

10 Sheppard, D. S., and Worlock, D., *Better Together: Christian partnership in a hurt city*, London: Hodder & Stoughton, 1988, p. 110.

the Day' on BBC's *Today* programme the day after the boys were found guilty of murder. He noted how society was becoming 'unshockable' but hoped he would always be shocked and angry at violence to a child. He raised the question of forgiveness and warned against confusing it with condoning:

> True forgiveness . . . includes a firm hostility to evil . . . Christian insight about the possibility of forgiveness includes even those boys. There's no condoning the sheer evil of what they've done. But they can be redeemed. We're not to consign them to the dustbin.

Three years later a young vicar in the diocese, Christopher Gray, was murdered outside his vicarage. He had willingly chosen to serve in a parish in an urban priority area. In a piece for the Catholic magazine, *The Tablet*, Sheppard challenged those who questioned whether clergy and their families should be asked to live in disadvantaged areas and offer a ministry at the vicarage door. It was not just in UPAs that clergy are at risk, he wrote, 'and belonging to the community brings with it sensitive understanding of people's experiences and feelings.' This 'could never be achieved by someone coming in from nine to five.'[11]

*

Sheppard and Worlock's contribution to Liverpool was acknowledged with the award of the honorary freedom of the city in 1995. Historically linked with privileged trading rights and exemption from taxes, the freedom was a way for the city council to acknowledge 'persons of distinction' who had rendered it 'eminent services'. Only 16 people had been so honoured in Liverpool since the war, including MPs Bessie Braddock and Eric Heffer, Liverpool FC manager Bob Paisley, and Messrs Lennon, McCartney, Harrison and Starkey. At the ceremony at St George's Hall, Sheppard said that he and Grace had 'become infected with the magic of Liverpool, which makes us want to write, to paint, to sing and to share in its life.' He thought the decision to honour both

---

11 Manuscript dated 19 August 1996 and notes: SHP, 16.5.

bishops was not just to keep a 'tactful balance' but to acknowledge their partnership and involvement in the whole life of the city. 'This honour is . . . a recognition that you see the Churches as comrades in arms in the life of Liverpool', he said.

Liverpool University and Liverpool Polytechnic conferred honorary degrees on Sheppard. The award from the Poly, later to become Liverpool John Moores University, was a doctorate in technology. Sheppard said this was remarkable since he could not mend a plug, but the Vice Chancellor, Peter Toyne, told him he was a 'bridge builder'. There were also degrees from the Open University and the universities of Exeter, Birmingham and Wales, and in 1990, Sheppard's *alma mater*, Trinity Hall, made him an honorary Doctor of Divinity. It had made him an honorary fellow in 1983. Grace's contribution to Liverpool and public life was also recognized: in 1992, she was awarded an honorary fellowship by Liverpool John Moores University. Worlock delayed an urgent operation in order to give the oration at the ceremony.

*

One of Sheppard's last acts while at the BSR was to help initiate a national enquiry into the future of work. He had long believed that the Church should support the principle of 'good work': it helped to give people dignity and enable families and communities to flourish. The enquiry was to be an ecumenical endeavour rather than one conducted by the BSR. The idea had been discussed for a while, including by Sheppard, and as chair of the BSR, he took it to the Council of Churches for Britain and Ireland (CCBI). Having secured the CCBI's support, its Public Affairs Secretary, Ermal Kirby, convened a 'shadow' sponsoring body, which did the groundwork for the project and drafted some terms of reference. The mainstream churches then nominated members for a formal Sponsoring Body, to be chaired by Sheppard, with Worlock representing the Roman Catholic Church. The Sponsoring Body appointed the working party, whose members were drawn from all the major denominations; and care was taken to ensure its diversity. The title of the final report, *Unemployment and the Future of Work*, brought together the two main strands of its work.[12] There had earlier been a debate about whether the enquiry should focus on just one of these.

Launching the enquiry in September 1995, Sheppard said God was concerned with both unemployment and the future of work. The churches had an obligation to consider such matters and were well placed to do so, having access to all sections of the community. They were also able to 'test the ideas currently being considered and to think of fresh possibilities.'[13] The terms of reference for the project included 'examining the changing nature and patterns of employment' and the effect these had on the well-being of all. Sheppard raised much of the funding for the enquiry.[14]

The working party travelled to all five nations, holding consultations with people in industry, trade unions, local government, the churches, industrial mission and academe. In Liverpool its members joined the Michaelmas Group for breakfast. Listening to unemployed people was an important part of each visit, and in between, the working party discussed papers drafted by the Executive Secretary, Andrew Britton. He had been Director of the National Institute of Economic and Social Research, one of the Treasury's team of 'seven wise men' advising the Chancellor. He had taken early retirement to work for the enquiry, and he compiled the final report.

The process suffered a setback after seven months when the chair of the working party, Sir Geoffrey Holland, resigned. Holland was Vice Chancellor of Exeter University and a former Permanent Secretary at the Department of Employment. He said his appointment to the Dearing Inquiry into Higher Education meant he could not continue. In fact, he had become increasingly uncomfortable about the process. He was unused to seeing a faith perspective brought to bear on economic issues and feared he might not feel completely at home with the report's conclusions. Sheppard felt let down and angry, but was more than happy with his replacement, Patrick Coldstream, who had been Director of the Council for Industry and Higher Education. Well-received by the working party, he steered the project to its conclusion.

---

12 *Unemployment and the Future of Work: An Enquiry for the Churches*, London: CCBI, 1997 (hereafter UFW).

13 'Churches look into unemployment and future of work', press release, 29 September 1995.

14 A list of funders appears on p. 203 of the report.

The report called for the creation of 'enough good work for everyone to do' and outlined eight policies most likely to achieve this aim, including tax reform to generate more jobs in the private sector; raising taxes to finance more employment in the public sector; a national minimum wage; and giving priority in the education system to basic skills for all young people. It was clear that 'one of the principal means by which the strong help the weak in our society is by paying their taxes, part of which the state uses to combat poverty.' The report called for new policy measures to be implemented in a spirit of 'justice and compassion', which was as important as the design of the policies themselves.[15] The report also looked at examples of employment projects created by Christian networks and the role of industrial mission.

Sheppard was originally sceptical about talk of full employment. In an early paper for the urban bishops, he wrote that 'we do not believe that – given any policies currently canvassed – there will be full employment in the foreseeable future.' He also argued this in *Bias to the Poor*. But the working party persuaded him that full employment was possible given the political will, and its members had decided from the start to champion it as a policy objective. Sheppard approved of their emphasis on 'good' work for all: they were not saying that 'any old dead-end job will do.'[16] Every member of the working party endorsed the report's conclusions. As one later said, 'it was an extraordinary feat to bring such a balanced and diverse ecumenical group together . . . Either it was God or David Sheppard.'[17]

The report was published on 7 April 1997, three weeks before the general election. Archbishop Carey and Cardinal Hume were both unhappy about the timing, feeling the churches would be seen to be deliberately trying to intervene in the election, and Carey tried, unsuccessfully, to delay the report.[18] The working group keenly debated the

---

15 *UFW*, pp. 9, 174.

16 'The Future of Work – The case for a Churches' Initiative' (July 1993): SHP, 11.9; Sheppard, D. S., *Bias to the Poor*, London: Hodder & Stoughton, 1983, p. 122; Sheppard, D. S., *Steps along Hope Street*, London: Hodder & Stoughton, 2002, p. 300.

17 Interview with Kumar Jacob. I have also drawn on interviews and correspondence with Andrew Britton, Patrick Coldstream, Protasia Torkington, Malcolm Brown, Bishop Michael Bourke and Lord (Clive) Brooke.

18 Brown, M., 'The Case for Anglican Social Theology Today' in Brown, M., ed., *Anglican Social Theology*, London: Church House Publishing, 2014, p. 13.

question of when to release it. John Cole, former political editor at the BBC and the URC representative on the working party, warned that the media would have got tired of the issues the report was raising, if publication was delayed until after the election. Working party members also felt the unemployed people they had met expected their experiences would feed into the election debate.

The political parties were aware of the enquiry. In its early stages Sheppard discussed with David Hunt, Secretary of State for Employment, the possibility of his Department seconding someone to service the project. In October 1995 Sheppard wrote to the leader of the opposition, Tony Blair, advising him the enquiry was beginning. As the election approached, Sheppard corresponded with David Blunkett, the Shadow Employment Secretary, and told him he hoped the report would help change the climate of opinion about employment in the longer term.[19]

Gordon Brown, soon to be Chancellor of the Exchequer, welcomed the report enthusiastically.[20] Sheppard met with Brown, who spoke at a conference in London on the report, and said he was greatly heartened to hear Brown say he regarded unemployment as the greatest scourge of the country and making 'enough good work for everyone' would be his top priority. 'Of course it is another matter for him to deliver', Sheppard wrote, 'but I believe we owe him our prayers and support in every way we can.'[21] Brown and other ministers met with the Sponsoring Group during 1997.

The report was not influenced by conversations Sheppard had with Labour politicians. As its author, Andrew Britton, has said, it was careful to say that 'none of the political parties has put forward a programme which seriously tackles the central questions we raise about unemployment and the future of work'. Yet similarities can be found between some of the report's conclusions and the 'New Deal' policy

---

19 Letter to David Blunkett, 11 February 1997; SHP, 11.9.

20 The *Daily Telegraph* noted that Brown used the word 'church' ten times at a Labour Party press conference on the day of the report's publication: Paul Goodman, 'Socialism at last', 9 April 1997, p. 22.

21 Letter dated 17 September 1997; SHP, 11.9. Brown described Sheppard as one of his heroes in his autobiography, and saw him as an important advocate 'of the need to build a more socially just United Kingdom'; Brown, G., *My Life, Our Times*, London: The Bodley Head, 2017, p. 425, and correspondence with the author.

introduced by Labour within a year of taking office. Labour's policy aimed to reduce unemployment by providing training, and offered a tax rebate to employers taking on people who had been out of work for more than two years, to be funded initially by a one-off windfall tax on the privatized utility companies. The New Deal originated before the churches' enquiry began, yet reports of the enquiry's work filtered through to senior members of the shadow cabinet.[22] They took an interest in what the report would say, and were able to steal a march on the government with a press release when it was published. The report was also leaked to the *Observer* before its publication. The *Observer* made it its lead story and main leader article.[23]

The new Labour government saw the churches as allies in their quest for full employment. It believed the churches' work to change the culture of employers and to encourage them to take on additional staff, would assist its aim of ensuring a job-creating economy. It also welcomed the churches' role in raising the sights of young people. Enquiry members told government it was keen to discuss the role of the churches 'as partners in the delivery of the New Deal'. 'We seem to be pursuing the same goals which is very encouraging', one senior minister told Sheppard in November 1997.[24]

The report was not given the oxygen of publicity that *Faith in the City* had enjoyed as a result of government disapproval. Prime Minister John Major said he regretted the churches had intervened during an election campaign with a report that could provide ammunition for the government's opponents, but it was left to Sheppard's nemeses in the press to offer a more strident political critique. In the *Daily Mail* the Catholic writer William Oddie launched a highly personal attack on Sheppard. Acknowledging his own Christian faith, Oddie described Sheppard as 'a smug and arrogant Old-Left prelate'. Although the report had been written by Britton, the *Daily Express* accused Sheppard of failing to understand economic realities. In a different key, Philip Bassett in the

---

22 Clive Brooke, a member of the enquiry who was close to Blair and Brown, kept them in touch with the direction of travel of the report.

23 Wintour, P., '"Obsessed by the middle classes"'; 'Parties founder on churches' rock'; *The Observer*, 16 March 1997.

24 Various correspondence and briefing notes, July–November 1997: SHP, 11.9.

Financial Times thought it likely most independent economic commentators would agree the study had a sound economic base and had 'done its numbers and its work properly'. The churches' intervention 'importantly reinserts the moral dimension in the arguments', Bassett wrote. *The Guardian* commended the churches for showing how unemployment could be cut: this was 'the manifesto no mainstream party would dare publish', it said. The *Economist* thought the report's key proposals 'merit further consideration'.[25]

Some academics thought the report was light on theology.[26] Both Coldstream and Britton acknowledged that the working party had struggled on this score, though there was clear intent to write the report from a 'distinctively Christian point of view'. Britton said the report never allowed 'economics and Christianity to lose contact with each other'.[27] Malcolm Brown, a member of the shadow sponsoring group, feared that the absence of a 'thoroughgoing theological case' for its proposals would leave the report open to the sort of criticism *Faith in the City* had attracted. Brown concluded that the churches 'got away with it this time', but future reports would need to be different. The absence of a 'distinctively Christian approach to economics' meant that the report could have been written by an economist of a different hue and been just as much 'the voice of the churches'.[28] Brown contributed an appendix on theological method to the report and co-edited a collection of essays reflecting theologically on it.

Unemployment and the Future of Work owed an enormous amount to Sheppard. He was not involved with the running of the enquiry or the writing of the report, but he was the principal driver. If it did not

---

25 Oddie, W., 'How dare this smug bishop tell me I am not a real Christian', *Daily Mail*, April 1997, p. 10; 'Opinion', *Daily Express*, 9 April 1997, p. 14; Bassett, P., 'Wise man gives credence to jobs report by churches', *Financial Times*, 9 April 1997; Bellos, A., 'Faith, hope . . . and workers' rights', *The Guardian*, 9 April 1997, p. 12; 'Divines Opine', *The Economist*, 10 April 1997.

26 See, for example, Biggar, N., 'Where there's a will', *Third Way*, May 1997, pp. 9–10; Forrester, D. B., 'Theological Comments on *Unemployment and the Future of Work*', in Brown, M., and Sedgwick, P., eds, *Putting Theology to Work: A Theological Symposium on 'Unemployment and the Future of Work'*, London and Manchester: CCBI and William Temple Foundation, 1998, p. 56.

27 Coldstream, P., 'A Report for the Churches', in Brown and Sedgwick, *Putting Theology to Work*, p. 7; Britton, A., 'A Distinctively Christian Report' in Brown and Sedgwick, *Putting Theology to Work*, p. 13.

28 Brown, M., 'How Can We Do Theology in Public Today?' in Brown and Sedgwick, *Putting Theology to Work*, pp. 24, 32, 30.

have the lasting effect on popular opinion or policy he hoped it would, this was partly because, as Britton was later to say, 'by the time it was published unemployment was falling and anxiety about the future of work was somewhat reduced.' But as Britton also maintains, the report did contribute to the debate about unemployment, by insisting it was a problem that could and should be solved. It showed again the Church's capacity to contribute to public debate with an expert report grounded in the experience of the people whose concerns it sought to address.

*

Worlock did not see the project through to its completion. On 8 February 1996, after living with cancer for four years, he died aged 76. Grace's own experience of the disease had drawn her closer to Worlock in his final years. She and David were a great support to Worlock at that time: 'They were truly friends in need', wrote Worlock's biographers, 'and in their presence he could sound off some of his irritations in a way that he felt had to be disguised from others, especially his own priests.'[29] They attended a Mass at Worlock's hospital bed the day before he died. During the peace he was able to exchange the greeting with them. It was effectively a goodbye.

On the night before Worlock's funeral, Sheppard spoke at the vigil Mass as the cathedral congregation gathered to receive their archbishop's body. The next day, at Worlock's request, David and Grace led the coffin from the high altar to the chapel of repose. Worlock's family came behind. On the day of his funeral Worlock should have been at Buckingham Palace to be formally admitted by the Queen as a member of the Order of the Companions of Honour.

Sheppard himself had come close to death in 1994. Three days after an operation to replace a hip he suffered a pulmonary embolism, a blood clot moving to the lungs. He was in intensive care for several days, and at one point the surgeon told Grace that her husband had 'put a toe over the touchline.' Sheppard needed a stick during his recovery, as Worlock had

29 Furnival J., and Knowles, A., *Archbishop Derek Worlock: His personal journey*, London: Geoffrey Chapman, 1998, p. 247.

done during his illness. A contemplative study of the two men leaning on their sticks by the Liverpool photographer Stephen Shakeshaft won a 'Picture of the Century' award at the National Portrait Gallery in London. The autumnal setting was powerfully symbolic.

*

Sheppard lost other close colleagues within a 12-month period. In 1995 John Newton retired and moved to Bristol. His nine years in the region had seen the churches' leaders become more obviously a team of three rather than two. Newton was replaced as Free Church Moderator by the Baptist Superintendent, Keith Hobbs. Then in 1996, after 20 years of working together, Sheppard's suffragan Michael Henshall announced his retirement. Henshall had wanted Sheppard to retire first, so he could help the new bishop to settle before retiring himself and leaving the bishop free to appoint his own suffragan. But Sheppard decided to stay another year, possibly to see *Unemployment and the Future of Work* through to its completion.

Sheppard thought about appointing an older suffragan to replace Henshall. The new man might retire within a few years, allowing Sheppard's successor to make his own appointment. In the event, however, he appointed the person he considered the best candidate for the job, John Packer, Archdeacon of West Cumberland. He had served as a priest in inner-city Sheffield, and was responsible in Cumbria for the industrial towns of Workington, Whitehaven and Maryport which had known very high levels of unemployment. Packer would only work alongside Sheppard for a year, but the two established a good relationship, and the bishop gave a lot of time and encouragement to his new colleague. Sheppard also worked well with Worlock's successor, Archbishop Patrick Kelly, though the two did not overlap long enough to allow the kind of friendship he had enjoyed with Worlock to develop.

*

Sheppard was involved in two industrial disputes in his final years in Liverpool. In 1989, the frozen food manufacturer Bird's Eye announced the closure of its factory in Kirkby with the loss of 1,000 jobs. Sheppard, Worlock and Newton concluded that the management's decision could not be reversed and put their energy into persuading the company to leave a useful legacy in the region. Local churches, however, held a vigil at the factory gates, met with management and unions, and published a joint statement urging management to reconsider its decision. Some clergy joined the picket at the factory and signed strongly worded statements. A breakdown in communication between the church leaders and their members meant that on the day Sheppard announced the deal that had been secured from the management, a local priest appeared on television to say that the church opposed the company's closure. Sheppard was far from amused.

Sheppard played a different role in a conflict involving the Mersey Docks and Harbour Company (MDHC), the sub-contractor Torside, and their workforce. Known as the Liverpool Dockers' Dispute, this lasted from 1995 until 1998. Worlock was by then seriously ill, but Sheppard and other church leaders, including the URC Moderator, Graham Cook, and the Roman Catholic Bishop, John Rawsthorne, had separate discussions over three days with the parties involved, including the leaders of the strike and the head of the MDHC. These talks ensured the parties kept working for solutions at a time when negotiations were often breaking down. All sides agreed to accept independent mediation put in place by the churches, though in the end this was not taken up. The Michaelmas Group had expressed concern at the damage the strike could do to the 'improved image' of Liverpool, while Sheppard was frustrated that 'two worlds with wholly different philosophies were unable to engage with each other' and that the dispute ended with the dockers feeling resentment.[30]

*

In January 1997 Sheppard told clergy of his intention to retire that October. The press announcement brought a flurry of requests for

---

30 Letter to MDHC dated 23 October 1995; Sheppard, *Steps along Hope Street*, p. 313. I have also drawn on correspondence with Randell Moll, senior chaplain with Mission in the Economy, which brokered the talks Sheppard hosted.

interviews, with interest coming from the national broadsheets, television news programmes, and the Jimmy Young show on Radio 2. He and Grace had bought a house in the Wirral in anticipation, as their 22 years in the north had convinced them it was where they belonged. Jenny had suggested they look at West Kirby, a favourite retreat on their days off, close to their friends across the Mersey yet not in the Liverpool diocese. 'We had our backs to Liverpool', Grace later put it.[31]

The couple planned meticulously for retirement. Their way of life would now be very different from any they had known before; no longer would they be living in a public building, with a team of staff and densely packed diaries. They listed their expectations for the first six months. Grace expected David 'to take an equal share of the chores', and hoped he would 'put gardening high on the agenda.' She was keen that they 'find a balance between public & private that suits me as well as him.' Sheppard planned to take up spiritual exercises, to master the computer, and become 'a worshipper in a pew'. He drew up a list of books to read, with theology and meditative works in the early morning and 'cricket and novels' for other times. Events to attend at Clwyd Theatr Cymru were listed. The first expectation for himself was 'find a pattern of life which shows much more spontaneity – but is not all formless.'[32] As with all important changes in his life, he wanted to discern God's plans. He recalled the Old Testament story of Elijah's encounter with God on Mount Horeb,[33] wondering whether he had been listening to God's 'still small voice', what it might be saying to him, and how he should respond.

Gardening did feature on Sheppard's agenda. A generous gift from the diocese enabled him and Grace to lay out their garden to their own design, and Sheppard threw himself into tending the lawns, hedges and sweet peas. He and Grace also joined the St Peter's Singers in nearby Heswall; Grace had sung in the Cathedral Singers during the years in Liverpool. Sheppard had not been in a choir since his days at Sherborne, but rediscovering the joy of singing was a high point in his retirement.

---

31 Sheppard, G., *Living with Dying*, London: Darton, Longman & Todd, 2010, p. 33.

32 SHP, 64.1. He had taken up spiritual exercises during a sabbatical in 1988 using the writings of the Scottish Jesuit, Gerard Hughes.

33 I Kings 19.11–13.

Sheppard loved being within earshot of the Dee. He developed the habit of 'prayer-walks' along the shore early each morning. Their new neighbours and parish church made them welcome, but initially the Sheppards wondered whether they would fit into a suburban community. The main interests in West Kirby seemed to be golf, bridge and sailing, none of which they shared. They hoped their love of painting would provide a link, however. One neighbour teased them by apologizing for not being black, poor or unemployed. The Sheppards might have recalled some of their early musings about retirement. In 1985 Grace recorded a conversation she and David had had in the car. 'D would like London and inner-city talk', she wrote. 'He would feel uncomfortable . . . out of sorts with a middle-class community . . .'[34]

*

Grace wondered where they would find a new 'buzz' to replace the 'big public arena'. One answer soon emerged. In the autumn Sheppard was invited to accept a life peerage, and the announcement was made in the New Year's Honours List in January.

Sheppard described this as a major surprise, but he might have expected some recognition for his work. Worlock's citation for admittance as a Companion of Honour was 'for services to the Roman Catholic Church and to the community in Liverpool'.[35] Sheppard had made no less a contribution to Liverpool, and his service to his church included 28 years as a bishop, involvement with various public bodies, and work at the Mayflower. He had also had a notable career as a cricketer and anti-apartheid campaigner. The 'surprise' element of Sheppard's honour lay in the fact that he was the first diocesan bishop to receive a life peerage since the introduction of the rank in 1958.[36]

Sheppard was introduced into the Lords on 28 April 1998, six months after he had left it as a bishop. His decision to sit as a Labour peer caused

---

34 Grace Sheppard diary, 30 July 1985.

35 It is unlikely that Worlock was ever considered for a peerage, given that the Roman Catholic Church forbids its priests to be members of secular legislative bodies.

36 Only two have been ennobled since: Richard Harries (Oxford) in 2006 and Richard Chartres (London) in 2017.

little surprise among those who knew him. He and Grace had joined the Labour Party shortly before their retirement, and Sheppard thought it was natural to ask if he could sit on their benches. It did, however, surprise others, and it was felt he was breaking precedent by taking sides: serving bishops sat on the bishops' bench, but no pattern existed for retired ones. Former archbishops chose to sit as crossbenchers when ennobled.[37]

Another unusual twist was that Sheppard chose as one of his 'supporters' a peer from an opposing party, his friend Colin Cowdrey, who had been ennobled the previous year and sat as a Conservative. Sheppard's other supporter was Archbishop Runcie, thus acknowledging his connections with both the Church and cricket. He incorporated his adopted city into his title, becoming Baron Sheppard of Liverpool, of West Kirby in the County of Merseyside.

Sheppard had carefully avoided direct involvement in party politics while in Woolwich and Liverpool, although Grace said that she and David had been Labour supporters all their lives.[38] Sheppard said he 'would certainly accept the label of Christian socialism – which doesn't always mean commitment to one particular programme'. He once told an interviewer he adopted 'a socialist stance' on most issues in *Bias to the Poor*.[39] In 1992 he declined an invitation to join the Commission on Social Justice, initiated by the leader of the Opposition, John Smith. Although the commission would be independent of the Labour Party and organized by the Institute for Public Policy Research (IPPR), Sheppard said he thought the connection between the IPPR and the Labour Party 'will seem strong, not least by Government Ministers with whom I will have to continue to deal.'[40] He was then chair of the BSR. In January

---

37 Ministers of other churches had taken party whips. Donald Soper, a Methodist, sat as a Labour peer, and the Church of Scotland minister and founder of the Iona community, George MacLeod, was the first Green Party peer.

38 Interview with Eliza Filby, 27 July 2006. I am grateful to Dr Filby for granting me access to her manuscript of this conversation.

39 Private letter dated 1 March 1983. Henderson, S., ed., *Adrift in the Eighties*, Basingstoke: Marshall Pickering, 1986, p. 55. Terry Philpot, 'First bat for the inner city', *Community Care*, 27 January 1983. Sheppard never joined the Christian Socialist Movement which, in 1986, became affiliated to the Labour Party: correspondence with Peter Dawe.

40 Letter dated 16 December 1992; SHP, 8.11. The commission was also known by the name of its chair, Sir Gordon Borrie.

1981, when the Social Democratic Party was coming into being, he had declined an invitation to be included in a list of non-political figures who supported the initiative, the 'Group of 100'.

Sheppard was known to many senior Labour figures before *Unemployment and the Future of Work*, and the enquiry raised his profile with them. The new Prime Minister, Tony Blair, was an admirer of *Faith in the City*,[41] and Sheppard's efforts to bridge the sectarian divide in Liverpool were of a piece with his own commitments in Northern Ireland. Sheppard made his first speech in the Lords during a debate on Northern Ireland. He used the opportunity to congratulate Blair and others who had 'persevered in the peace process'.[42]

Sheppard described himself as 'New Labour', and was a faithful supporter of the party line in the Lords, even over the invasion of Iraq. His friend and fellow Labour peer, David Puttnam, recalls him agonizing over the issue but believing the government must have had compelling information it was not making public.[43] Grace was opposed to the invasion, and was less inclined towards New Labour than her husband. 'David . . . always said that I was more radical than he was,' she once remarked.[44] Her diaries suggest she had a sneaking admiration for Derek Hatton, the Militant deputy leader of Liverpool City Council, for whom her husband had rather less time.

Sheppard retained an admiration for Blair to the last.[45] Bishop John Packer recalls Sheppard being thrilled on the night of the 1997 general election which New Labour won. He had invited some friends to watch the results rather than his neighbours, most of whom he thought would be Conservatives. Sheppard told Packer that, returning to the Lords as a life peer, he at last felt free to say the sort of things he had wanted to say there for years.

---

41 Blair, T., 'Battle for Britain', *The Guardian*, 29 January 1996, p. 11; Chapman, M. D., *Blair's Britain: A Christian Critique*, London: Darton, Longman & Todd, 2005, p. 13.

42 Hansard, Lords, Northern Ireland (Elections) Bill, 6 May 1998, col. 625. Sheppard's was not a 'maiden' speech: as he remarked, he had made that 18 years before.

43 Correspondence and phone conversation with Lord Puttnam. There is no evidence available to show Sheppard voting against the party whip, although Puttnam recalls him making a few abstentions and 'well-chosen rebellions'. Sheppard thought the first war in the Gulf had a 'just cause'.

44 Grace Sheppard interview with Eliza Filby, 27 July 2006.

45 Transcript of a private interview, March 2005.

Sheppard had six years in the Lords. He committed to attending every other week, staying one or two nights in a friend's flat near Holland Park. He would also spend evenings with his old friend Mike Brearley. He found the Lords Library an agreeable place to work, and welcomed the opportunity to meet up with bishops with whom he would otherwise have lost contact. In the chamber, he limited himself to speaking on issues in which he had a particular interest, including race relations, higher education, homelessness, the New Deal, and welfare support. In all he made 34 contributions. His last was in December 2003 when he was receiving hospital treatment, and he used the opportunity to praise the quality of nurses in the NHS.[46]

*

Sheppard's trips to London acquired an extra dimension shortly after his admission to the House. Jenny and Donald had moved from Scotland to the capital in 1993, and in September 1998 Jenny gave birth to a son, Stuart. A second son, Gilles, was born in June 2000. In naming them, Jenny and Donald honoured their sons' maternal grandfather. Stuart was Sheppard's middle name, and Gilles' second name was David. Sheppard delighted in being a grandfather and valued the opportunity to see the children afforded by his trips to the Lords. Jenny and Donald lived not far from his digs in Holland Park. 'Playing on the floor, or going to the park, with these little boys is a bonus to every visit to London,' he wrote.[47] Grace also relished grandparenthood and would sometimes travel with David to see the boys. Stuart, Gilles and their parents made regular visits to the Wirral.

But in the midst of life the Sheppards were in death. Within weeks of Stuart's baptism, Grace's father, Bryan Isaac, died at the age of 89. The previous month Sheppard had lost his brother-in-law, Charles Maxwell, his sister Mary's husband. Maxwell had become Chief Producer of Light Entertainment at Radio 4, commissioning programmes such as *I'm Sorry, I'll Read That Again*. Then in May 1999, Jo Maxwell, the wife of

---

46 Hansard, Lords, 'Address in Reply to Her Majesty's Most Gracious Speech', 1 December 2003, col. 625.

47 Sheppard, *Steps along Hope Street,* p. 331.

Sheppard's nephew, Jamie, died of cervical cancer at the age of 40. Jamie was one of the country's leading PR consultants, and set up a charity to make his late wife's illness a thing of the past.[48]

*

Since the early 1980s Sheppard had received spiritual direction from Canon Frank Wright, whom he described as a 'soul friend'. Wright was experiencing poor health at the time of Sheppard's retirement and the two agreed Sheppard should seek a new spiritual director. A fellow bishop recommended Canon Brian McConnell, then vicar of Altrincham. The two men clicked, and McConnell worked with Sheppard throughout his retirement.[49]

Sheppard looked to McConnell to help him find rhythm and balance in his new phase of life. He wanted to prevent his retirement from drifting into 'another whirl of commitments' through his involvement with the Lords and accepting invitations to speak and preach. McConnell's tradition was Celtic spirituality, and he encouraged Sheppard to explore new approaches to intercessory prayer. He talked of prayer involving an 'organic relationship with the creation and with the people for whom we pray, so that they pick up vibrations from our prayer'. Sheppard had always been disciplined about praying for individual people. Every night throughout their marriage he and Grace prayed for friends, using the hundreds of Christmas cards they received as *aides memoire*. This was also their practice at morning prayer in the chapel. He would also talk of being 'driven to his knees' as a bishop by some of the challenges he faced, which ranged from whether to give public support to the Liverpool 8 Defence Committee to 'the criticism of some of the suburban parishes.'[50] In retirement he jealously guarded the early morning as a period for 'stillness'. This included time for spiritual exercises, reading, worship and his morning walk, with its time for prayer.

---

48 See www.jostrust.org.uk.
49 I draw here on an interview with Canon McConnell, and Sheppard's correspondence at SHP, 64.1.
50 Transcript of David and Grace Sheppard interview with Dr Mathew Guest, 26 August 2003, p. 18: SHP, 54.5.

Sheppard welcomed opportunities to preach and preside at the Eucharist. With a licence to officiate from the Bishop of Chester, he could celebrate communion at his church and others in the diocese. He was made an assistant bishop in the diocese and was delighted to be asked to take confirmations and share in ordinations. He valued having more time to prepare his sermons than when he was a serving bishop, but set himself a limit of 20 public speaking engagements a year and discussed his schedule with McConnell. 'Finding the best rhythm as a bishop in retirement involves "shortening my stride" – taking on fewer commitments', he wrote.[51] He enjoyed being able to sit with Grace in the local congregation each Sunday, a rare experience when he had been a bishop.

*

Nor was cricket forgotten. Sheppard relished the opportunities retirement afforded to watch more matches. Old Trafford was only an hour away, and trips to his sister in Sussex gave him a base to see his old county play at home. In 2001 Sussex made him club president for a two-year term, and he delighted in watching matches at Horsham, Arundel and Hove. He liked to walk around the ground, chatting with members and admirers who remembered his past innings. In 2003 he celebrated the club winning the County Championship for the first time.[52]

*

One item on Sheppard's list of projects was 'write a book'. This became his second autobiography, *Steps along Hope Street,* published by Hodders in 2002. Its subtitle was 'My Life in Cricket, the Church and the Inner City'. It took him three years to write, and ranged over his whole life, omitting some of the cricketing memories included in his earlier volume, *Parson's Pitch.*[53] He spoke of the development of his faith, his priorities as a bishop, and the background to projects in which he had been involved.

---

51 Sheppard, *Steps along Hope Street,* p. 334.
52 After his death Grace was made a vice-president of the club.
53 Sheppard, D. S., *Parson's Pitch*, London: Hodder & Stoughton, 1964.

Half the book was devoted to his time in Liverpool. He found the writing 'stretching and fulfilling', and it also had a devotional dimension. 'When I come to a new chapter or theme', he reflected in 2001, 'I keep a still time attempting to recapture what was passing between me and God in that context. It is a powerful spiritual exercise.'[54]

Reviewers were unclear about the book's intended audience. Robin Marlar, who played alongside Sheppard for Cambridge and Sussex, thought Sheppard could have reached a wider audience by including more cricket.[55] The *Yorkshire Post* thought the book tried to cater for too many tastes. 'It's . . . as much political and sociological as ecclesiastical – and cricketing too', wrote its reviewer. 'The many ingredients make it a heavy pudding and the pudding is too filling.'[56] In a telling review in the *Independent Catholic News*, Eileen French suggested that it was difficult to engage with most of the book 'unless you are male, a cricketer, have evangelical inclinations or are politically pink.'

Sheppard had been urged to say more about Grace while he was drafting the book. 'She is obviously an important influence in your life', a friend told him, but 'is still to me a shadowy figure. Ill from time to time, giving her opinion on occasions . . . but not a rounded figure.' Sheppard writes movingly of how Grace's breakdown helped to bring them closer together in the early years of their marriage, but her ovarian cancer, which brought her close to death and resulted in her being unable to conceive again, is barely mentioned. The debilitating agoraphobia with which she lived for many years gets only passing references. Sheppard says that living alongside Grace as she met the challenge of her condition enabled him to learn 'that part of being truly human meant acknowledging feelings'.[57] But he had struggled since childhood with articulating his emotions, and was unable to share these feelings in print.

Sheppard thought he would write a better book if he had a richer understanding of the times through which he had lived. He approached the distinguished economic historian Martin Daunton, who gave him

---

54 Memo dated 1 March 2001: SHP, 64.1.
55 Marlar, R., 'Bookmark', *The Cricketer*, October 2002, p. 69.
56 Brown, M., 'Bishop who looked beyond the boundaries', *Yorkshire Post*, 14 November 2002.
57 Sheppard, *Steps along Hope Street*, p. 152.

some guided reading and supervision.[58] Between March 1998 and January 2001, Sheppard wrote essays on a variety of themes including immigration, Thatcherism, sexual politics in the 1960s, urban poverty and his work at the Mayflower. Daunton read and commented on each in detail. Sheppard was delighted to be studying history again, 45 years after his sessions at Ridley Hall with Owen Chadwick.

*

The autobiography ends on a troubling, yet optimistic, note. While he was drafting the chapters on Liverpool in early 2001, Sheppard suffered pains in his abdomen and a series of dizzy spells. His GP referred him to a consultant, and tests revealed cancer of the bowel. Surgery in April was followed by 24 weeks of chemotherapy.[59] While her husband was in hospital, there were so many calls to the house that Grace decided to record updating messages on the answerphone greeting. She thought that most people would want a news bulletin rather than a conversation, and this saved her having to take each call. Messages of goodwill left by family and friends were later played and relayed to David.

For the remainder of 2001 Sheppard felt well. He ate normally and retained his weight. Tiredness curtailed his early morning devotions, though he and Grace continued their early morning prayer together. McConnell assured him that five minutes of prayer done well was better than 30 minutes not done well. In the autumn Sheppard led a series of Bible studies on 'ministry and discipleship' at a three-day residential on the Wirral for priests in the Catholic archdiocese. Sheppard went each day on his way to Clatterbridge Hospital for his chemotherapy. His input was warmly received, but the event reminded him of the distance still to go to achieve full Christian unity. 'I came home bubbling after my first clergy gathering for a long time', he wrote at the time. 'In the middle of such a warm welcome and occasion, I was taken by surprise and hurt more than I can remember by having to stand back from

---

58 Daunton would later be appointed Master of Trinity Hall, Sheppard's *alma mater*.
59 I draw for this section on Grace's book, *Living with Dying*, and Sheppard's correspondence at the time.

receiving the bread and wine.'[60] In November he resumed attending the Lords.

*

When Sheppard submitted the manuscript of his book the following April, he could sign off on an upbeat note. The scan at the completion of his chemotherapy had given the all-clear. But by the time the book appeared in October, an ultrasound had shown lesions on his liver. A heavy round of launch events preoccupied him for a while, but a major operation was necessary in the December. A quarter of his liver was removed.

There was further disappointment in 2003. In May a scan showed that his bowel and liver were clear but that the cancer had spread to his lungs. More chemotherapy was prescribed, this time intravenously through a catheter known as a Hickman Line. When the cancer spots grew, Sheppard was fitted with a syringe driver which administered strong drugs via a line into his chest. In the October the intravenous catheter was removed.

There were sad developments in the wider family. In March, Grace's mother, Eleanor Isaac, died aged 92. She had moved to a nursing home on the Wirral for her final years, enabling Grace and David to visit her twice a week. Then, in the June, Sheppard's nephew Jamie Maxwell died at the age of 46. Jamie had been diagnosed with a brain tumour just two weeks before. Having lost their mother four years previously, Jamie's three young children were now orphaned. Despite his own illness, Sheppard travelled to London's Charing Cross Hospital to support the family in Jamie's final hours. He stayed with his nephew in his hospital room throughout the night he died. The following day he went to Sussex to comfort his sister Mary, Jamie's mother, who had lost her son shortly before her eightieth birthday. Sheppard conducted Jamie's funeral.

Sheppard showed great resilience through his ordeal. He continued his daily walks by the Dee and undertook other modest exercise, doing

---

60 Memo, 18 October 2001: SHP, 64.1. I am grateful to Fr Kevin Kelly for sending me the text of Sheppard's Bible studies. As Kelly says, this episode speaks volumes about Sheppard's ecumenical commitment (email 12 November 2016).

something in the garden most days. His years of playing cricket and squash had left him physically strong. His appetite remained good and he and Grace kept up their daily devotions and Bible reading. In Holy Week he gave talks on the seven words from the cross and did some events to launch the paperback version of *Steps along Hope Street*. He undertook further travel, taking part in the thanksgiving service for his close friend, Jim Thompson, in Wells Cathedral. Thompson had died in the September, shortly after retiring as Bishop of Bath and Wells.[61] By this time Sheppard had two fistula bags attached, yet in the December, he amazed everybody by returning to the Lords. Shortly after, *The Times* criticized his poor voting record for the year 2002–3. The paper later apologized, noting that his availability to vote that year had been 'greatly restricted by serious illness.'[62] He continued to attend the House into 2004.

*

Sheppard had faced the possibility of this being his final illness. After his first diagnosis his reaction was, 'I've got to die of something'. Later he and Grace discussed more openly the implications of death and dying. By the summer of 2004 they had to acknowledge it was time to ask for a prognosis. Jenny suggested they see Sheppard's surgeon, Carol Makin, together. Makin said he would see out Christmas and a month or two of the following year, and her prognosis proved to be exact. It was an extremely difficult time, but knowing the facts had many positive outcomes and enabled the family to talk and plan properly.

In October 2004, Sheppard preached at the 'Pause for Hope' service in Liverpool cathedral. This is an annual service for people living with cancer and their families. He spoke directly from his own experience. 'The grace of God, undeserved as it is, is the greatest resource we have', he said.

It enables us to accept what otherwise we find unacceptable. Acceptance is not the same thing as resignation. Being resigned to

---

61 Sheppard and Thompson had known each other since both worked in east London in the 1960s.
62 *The Times*, 1 March 2004 and 17 March 2004.

something means that we give up the fight. Acceptance is much more positive. It is active and can change our whole approach.

Sheppard mentioned the lessons he had learned as a patient, including how to be gracious in receiving from others, including his carers, friends and neighbours who gave support. He and Grace had particularly valued friends appearing with soups and casseroles just at times when they were most needed. He paid tribute to all who worked in the health service and the hospice, including cleaners, porters and 'maintenance engineers who keep the machines working', as well as the nurses, doctors and surgeons.

*

Cricket helped Sheppard cope with his final months. In his last year Jenny and Grace installed satellite TV to enable him to watch matches from around the world. It proved a marvellous diversion. 'I never thought I would bless the game so much', Grace said in their 2004 Christmas letter to friends. Towards the end of the year, four of Sheppard's former Sussex teammates made a special trip to see him. The time he spent reminiscing with Rupert Webb, Ken Suttle, Jim Parks and Alan Oakman made this one of his most enjoyable visits.[63]

*

After Christmas, Grace and Jenny began planning a party to celebrate Grace's seventieth birthday. It was to be on Saturday 5 March, the day between her and David's birthdays, and he would be 76. He was now unable to climb the stairs, and a hospital bed was set up for him in the downstairs sunroom, with the TV so that he could watch the cricket. He knew his time was short and he wanted to die at home. Grace said she could easily cancel the party, but David wanted her to go ahead.

Sheppard remained in good spirits to the end. He told Mike Brearley, a few weeks before he died, he had had 'half a good night.' Most people might have emphasized the other half of the good night, Brearley

---

63 Interview with Rupert Webb: Webb initiated the visit; cf. Sheppard, *Living with Dying*, p. 68.

thought.[64] Grace told another close friend after Carol Makin's prognosis, 'Our glass is always half-full rather than half empty.' David Puttnam recalls Sheppard's complete lack of self-pity, and the concern he and Grace showed to spare visitors any embarrassment because of his colostomy bag. There were moments when his situation, and the effect of the drugs, took him to a point of deep despair, but all who saw him in his final days recall his dignity in facing death.

In his last media interview, he said he was afraid of some of the process of dying, which is unknown, but not of death itself, 'because I believe in a living Lord, who has risen from the dead, and that is part of his promise to those who trust him.' The three-and-a-half years he and Grace had been living with his cancer were 'the best years of our life together', he noted.[65] Grace recalls that, as 5 March approached, 'all hope of David's earthly life continuing much longer had given way to a new kind of hope: that he would die peacefully and be able to reach his goal of being with us at the party.'[66]

Grace described the day of the party as one 'when joy and sorrow mingled into a creative force.' Guests could move between the kitchen-dining room, where there was food and drink and a friend playing the piano, and the sunroom, where they could sit quietly or pray with David. All acknowledged it was time to say goodbye, and occasionally Sheppard would recognize a face and whisper their name. 'He clearly knew what was happening though his strength was ebbing away', Grace later wrote. Their grandsons Stuart and Gilles, now aged six and four, were aware of what was happening and included in the day. Grace was reminded of 'Christ, our model [who] the night before he died . . . had supper with his friends.' When the last of the guests had gone, Grace and Jenny sat holding his hands either side of the bed, supported by the wisdom of a Macmillan nurse. Both were aware independently of the moment his spirit left his body.

*

---

64 Brearley, M., *On Cricket*, London: Constable, 2018, p. 152.
65 Replayed on BBC Radio Merseyside Daybreak Sunday magazine programme, 6 March 2005.
66 Sheppard, *Living with Dying*, p. 84.

The family received more than 1,000 letters and cards in the days that followed. Many who wrote shared personal stories and memories of Sheppard. The funeral service was held at their parish church, St Bridget's, on 17 March. Michael Henshall gave the address, with Mike Brearley and Sheppard's surgeon, Carol Makin, providing remembrances. There was an ecumenical dimension, with Archbishop Patrick Kelly and Grace's spiritual director, Mgr John McManus, leading prayers. Sheppard's body was cremated at Landican Cemetery and Crematorium, Birkenhead, and in September, his ashes were interred in the cathedral under a stone slab in the floor engraved with his name and dates.

Three thousand people gathered for the memorial service in Liverpool Cathedral on 23 May. Grace and Jenny were keen to include some powerful imagery as well as words and music. Two young men, a local cricketer and a friend from the L'Arche Community, brought in Sheppard's bat and ordination Bible and placed them at the front. At the end of the proceedings, balloons fell on to the worshippers as they had at Sheppard's retirement service. Different facets of Sheppard's career were represented by those giving addresses, and speakers included Johnny Barclay, a former captain of Sussex; the Labour peer, David Puttnam; Dr John Newton; and the Very Revd Nicholas Frayling, a close friend and colleague of Sheppard's in both Southwark and Liverpool.[67] Jenny spoke for the family, and Sheppard's niece, Sarah Maxwell, sang John Rutter's 'Gaelic Blessing' which begins, 'Deep peace of the running wave to you'. Frayling read a message from Archbishop Desmond Tutu.

Grace and Jenny shrewdly asked a layperson, Sir Mark Hedley, to preach the sermon. Hedley was Chancellor of the Diocese and a High Court Judge. Sheppard had greatly admired him for having moved into Everton as a young lawyer and staying, with his family, despite achieving success in his professional career.[68] Memorial services were also held at Hove cricket ground, the Mayflower, Sherborne School and other places associated with Sheppard.

*

67 Some who attended remarked that no mention was made of Sheppard's time in Islington, nor of Maurice Wood, who was in the congregation.

68 Sheppard, *Steps along Hope Street*, p. 323.

Before his health deteriorated, Sheppard planned to free up time for Grace to write. When not in London he would do all the chores for a period of several months. In the event, the need to care for her husband left her no time to write a further book during his lifetime, but Grace did later produce a moving account of David's illness and death and her role as his carer. This was published in 2010 under the title *Living with Dying*. Like her earlier books, it contained a powerful mix of humour, brutal honesty, and spiritual reflection, as well as practical guidance for others in similar circumstances.

With a tragic irony, soon after the book was published, Grace herself died of cancer. She had first noticed signs of a breast tumour in 2006. Surgery and radiotherapy followed, and when completing the book, it appeared she had overcome the illness for the second time. In the summer of 2010, however, she was found to have developed multiple secondary tumours, and she died on 11 November. She was 75, the age her husband had been at his death. Like David, her last engagement was to give a moving address at the cathedral service for people living with cancer.

*

Sheppard was an inveterate note-maker. Ideas, plans, hopes, tasks, all were committed to paper. The process of making a decision involved filling pages, even whole notebooks, with reflections on the stages he had learned in the army. Possibly the last notes he ever made appear on a sheet headed '1 Dec 04'.[69] The handwriting is shaky, and there are only random words such as 'bedridden', 'can't travel', 'a project' and 'death'. The last words could serve as an epitaph for his and Grace's final years together: 'To-day – do it now'.

---

69 SHP, 64.1.

13

Conclusion

'Mr Sheppard don't hold with going up in the world', someone at the Mayflower once said. It brought him up with a start. It was a comment on his practice of encouraging people to stay in their neighbourhood after their conversion, not move to a 'nicer' area if they could. Too often people who had leadership potential left their community poorer when they moved away, Sheppard thought. He wanted them to stay, and companies to create jobs to make that possible. He spoke of the 'left behind', those caught in a downward spiral as the more 'adventurous' in their community moved away, and investment in the neighbourhood diminished. 'It's never been an answer to the problems of big cities to try to take all the people out of the heart of the city . . . to try and say there are jobs over there if you'll get up and go,' he once said.[1] But the Mayflower comment made it appear that he opposed social mobility, and made him 'think furiously' about what he 'did hold with'.

What Sheppard held with was a belief in building community, and he would often quote St Paul's dictum about all being 'members one of another'.[2] He thought this spoke of placing the well-being of others over self-interest, of wanting the best for your neighbour as well as for yourself. 'Perhaps when you make decisions about where you want to live, your neighbours' needs should go into the scales as well as your family's needs,' he would say. This was the essence of the commandment 'to love your neighbour as yourself,' he and Worlock wrote. 'The desire inside a Christian must be about the common good.'[3] This conviction

---

1 BBC Radio 4, *Any Questions?*, broadcast 29 October 1982.

2 Romans 12.5.

3 Sheppard, D. S., *Steps along Hope Street*, London: Hodder & Stoughton, 2002, p. 55; cf. Sheppard, D. S., *Built as a City: God and the Urban World Today*, London: Hodder &

drove Sheppard throughout his life in the Church. He was passionate to see communities stay together and thrive, so the Eldonians' commitment to resist dispersal spoke to his deepest instincts. He asked leaders in business and the trade unions not to allow one set of workers to prosper at the expense of another, and supported the principle of the better-off helping the needier through a common purse. His vision for Liverpool was to see the city and all who lived there flourish.

It is against this background that his talk of 'two Britains' and 'a bias to the poor' should be understood. Sheppard thought there was 'Comfortable Britain' and the 'Other Britain'. The difference could be seen in terms of availability of jobs, living standards, wealth and access to opportunities. The Other Britain was characterized by poverty, which robbed people of the power to make choices. It imprisoned their spirit and took away their dignity. But it was a loss to the *whole* of society. Comfortable Britain needed to see the social, economic and industrial problems in the Other Britain as their problems as well. Their actions could make a difference: being members one of another meant making sacrifices, exercising restraint in the interests of others. It meant sharing as well as creating wealth. Questions of justice and equality came into play, and at times, these were on a 'collision course' with freedom.[4]

Sheppard's hopes for change rested with Comfortable Britain, so he appealed to them to act, to mount a 'wholehearted war on poverty' and unite the country. 'I make no apology for attempting . . . to persuade you to stand in the shoes of people in the Other Britain', he told the audience for his Dimbleby Lecture in 1984.[5] *Faith in the City* was a challenge to 'comfortable' parishes to see Urban Priority Area people as their neighbours. *Unemployment and the Future of Work* argued that 'change . . . will not be possible without some sacrifice on the part of those who are better off'.[6] More than any of his contemporaries, Eliza Filby writes, Sheppard understood that 'if Thatcherite individualism was to be countered, the

Stoughton, 1974, p. 222; Sheppard, D. S. and Worlock, D., *Better Together: Christian Partnership in a Hurt City*, London: Penguin, 1989, p. 305.

4 *The Other Britain*, London: BBC, 1984, pp. 4, 7, 9, 11; *Better Together*, p. 217.

5 *The Other Britain*, p. 4.

6 *Unemployment and the Future of Work*, London: CCBI, 1997, endorsement, back cover.

chief battleground was not Parliament, nor was it in places such as Toxteth, but Tory-voting middle-class constituencies – crucially those areas where the Church still has some influence.'[7]

Sheppard thought a change on the part of the rich would benefit both the poor and the rich themselves. St Paul's statement is a call to work for unity, he wrote, 'with the better off caring for the poorer – and knowing that they had much to receive from them.'[8] There was much to be gained from a culture based on reciprocity. 'Hunger in my stomach is my physical problem', he once said, quoting Nikolai Berdyaev, '"hunger in my brother's stomach is my spiritual problem". So it is a spiritual sickness when the front ranks march away, ignoring those who have fallen right back or who have collapsed by the roadside.'[9]

This was orthodox Christianity, he thought. He acknowledged that 'bias to the poor' sounded like a statement of political preference, but it sprang from Christian doctrines: Jesus' teaching on the kingdom of God was about right relationships and serving 'the others'. The incarnation was Jesus becoming poor for the sake of humanity.[10] The cross was the supreme symbol of self-sacrifice, standing 'for the exact opposite of the "free-for-all", "smash-and-grab" approach to life. It is why the demands of the individual have to be measured within the good of society as a whole.'[11]

Sheppard would also employ St Paul's depiction of the body as a symbol of unity. 'The Christian model of a society is that of a body', he wrote in *Built as a City*. 'Each part has a different function. Its achievements are cooperative achievements. Each part is valued . . . If one organ suffers, they all suffer together. If one flourishes, they all flourish together.'[12] People can be members one of another in their neighbourhood, their church and in society, he thought.[13] 'St Paul's picture of the body . . . is

---

7 Filby, E., *God and Mrs Thatcher*, London: Biteback, 2015, p. 178.

8 Sheppard, *Steps along Hope Street*, p. 259.

9 Debrabant Lecture, La Sainte Union College, Southampton, 10 May 1989, p. 7. This was one of many lectures and sermons Sheppard and Worlock delivered jointly, speaking alternately: Sheppard papers (SHP), 20.1.

10 Sheppard, D. S., *Bias to the Poor*, London: Hodder & Stoughton, 1983, p. 10; Sheppard, *Steps along Hope Street*, pp. 22–3; 2 Corinthians 8.9.

11 'A Christian Approach to the Industrial Crisis', 3 February 1979; SHP, 11.3.

12 Sheppard, *Built as a City*, p. 183. The reference is I Corinthians chapter 12.

13 Sheppard, *Built as a City*, pp. 170, 40, 183; Sheppard, *Bias to the Poor*, p. 177; cf. *BT*, pp. 60, 237.

very relevant to a great city,' he told the Lords in 1985. 'Is one weak, then all are weak.' It also challenged rich nations about their responsibility to the developing world.[14] He saw taxation as a way in which the rich could make sacrifices for the poor and express their 'being members one of another in one nation.' When told that the cost of implementing the recommendations in *Faith in the City* would be four pence in the pound in income tax, he thought this did not seem 'a terrifying figure'. 'If we could start to reverse 150 years of decay in the cities and disadvantage by only 4p in the £, we'd be pretty lucky,' he said.[15] Rather than pay large numbers of people the dole so they could go away and do nothing, all the jobs that needed doing in the community could be funded from the taxes of those 'lucky enough to have . . . demanding and well paid jobs . . . that is the way to a more co-operative society.' Unemployed people would then start paying tax themselves and 'increase the whole level of economic activity.'[16]

All this was far removed from the orthodoxy of the 1980s. Margaret Thatcher believed that welfare should be provided by the voluntary sector, with the statutory services 'underpinning where necessary'. Individuals should take responsibility for themselves and, through charity, the needs of others. Sheppard actively supported charities, and *Faith in the City* proposed measures to encourage the voluntary sector. Yet in terms of carrying the *main load* of caring for the neediest, Sheppard thought this should be the whole community. It expressed 'an important moral principle' and was 'an earnest of the community's acceptance that its weakest members are valued and not judged.' Taxation was a greater example of belonging to one body than charitable giving. Taxation was 'indiscriminate', whereas charity was 'dictated by preferences and prejudices'.[17]

Like most of his fellow bishops, Sheppard chose not to engage with the government on its own terms. He would sometimes explicitly state

---

14 Hansard, Lords, 'Local Government Bill', 15 April 1985, col.486; 'Third World Starvation', 27 March 1985, col. 1085; cf. Partington, *Church and State*, pp. 230–1.

15 'Deceptively Mild', Poverty Network paper, Summer 1986, p. 2. Sheppard is unspecific here but presumably only the recommendations to government and nation were costed.

16 *Any Questions?* 29 October 1982; 'The Other Britain', p. 13.

17 Filby, L., 'God and Mrs Thatcher: Religion and Politics in 1980s Britain', PhD thesis, University of Warwick, 2010, pp. 78–80; Hansard, Lords, 'Expenditure Cuts and The Public Services', 8 April 1981, col. 547–8.

his opposition to 'New Right' thinking, particularly its belief that the wealthiest should be helped to get wealthier so that the rest will also get richer: 'Economic growth in an increasingly unequal society does not eliminate poverty, but recreates it in new forms,' he argued.[18] He challenged the New Right's scepticism about talk of 'community . . . They see it as anti-modern . . . only making sense if all its members have freely consented to join . . . What Jesus had to say about the Kingdom of God directly challenges this.'[19] A community's responsibility to look after its weakest members was a strongly biblical idea, he thought. Christian ethics are not primarily about personal responsibility and helping others through charity, as some government ministers liked to argue. He thought they set up a false opposition by pitting this against a role for the state. 'We strongly believe and preach the personal responsibility of individuals,' he and Worlock wrote. 'At the same time we emphasise that New Testament Christianity is not about individuals standing on their own two feet. It is also about being members one of another, about bearing one another's burdens.'[20]

*

Sheppard acknowledged that he spoke from within Comfortable Britain. He was sometimes told he was working out his feelings of guilt at having been given a privileged start.[21] In fact he personified the 'conversion' within Comfortable Britain he was calling for, though he would never have said that. His background could have led him to a well-paid career in law, or a living in a leafy parish or the chaplaincy of a public school. Yet from his days as a curate he had devoted himself to working with the Other Britain and promoting its cause. He admitted he was criticizing his own, but was driven to act by the indignation he felt at the 'sick human relationships which poverty spawns . . . the sheer waste of God-given talent'.[22]

18 Debrabant Lecture, p. 19.
19 Debrabant Lecture, p. 8.
20 Sheppard, D. S., and Worlock, D., *With Hope in Our Hearts*, London: Darton, Longman & Todd, 1994, p. 55
21 Sheppard, *Bias to the Poor*, p. 16.
22 *The Other Britain*, pp. 6–7.

His talent was to use the openings and opportunities made possible by his background for the benefit of others. His involvement with the Eldonian community in central Liverpool was a good example. As their leaders affirm, it was Sheppard and Worlock who enabled their case to reach the powers that be. 'A little community in Liverpool would never have got the ear of Thatcher and her ministers', Tony McGann and George Evans have said. 'It was the two bishops who opened those doors for us.' Other campaigns in Liverpool were significantly advanced by the bishops' access to corridors of power. As Libby Longino points out, simply by virtue of having a similar educational background to many politicians on the national level, Sheppard 'had an easier time accessing politicians' calendars. Not only would he have known the procedure for requesting an appointment, but he also could frame the request in familiar language.'[23]

Sheppard was once described as 'a son of the establishment – a critical one, perhaps, but no threat to it.'[24] This was intended as a criticism, but Sheppard consciously chose to operate within the system he knew to help others. His access to high places was also aided by his cricketing past: for several politicians, he would have been a 'schoolboy hero' whom they would want to meet on that level alone.[25] Any who still followed cricket might encounter him in the members' area at Lord's or another ground. Sheppard once began a letter to a senior Conservative politician with the words, 'On that rainy afternoon at Trent Bridge last summer we talked about Liverpool', continuing with a request for a meeting.[26] Sheppard's celebrity also helped him fundraise for the campaigns he supported.

Sheppard's status as a bishop was also important in gaining him entrée to the highest levels. He accepted, as Archbishop William Temple a generation earlier had implicitly assumed, that the Church had a

---

23 Longino, L., 'Strategies for Change: Local Interest Groups, the Church of England, and Urban Politics in 1980s Liverpool', M.Phil thesis, University of Oxford, 2012, pp. 25, 22. The groups Longino studied were the Langrove Street Action Group, the Eldonians and the Liverpool 8 Law Centre.

24 Leech, K., 'Seen through class, darkly', *Church Times*, 10 January 2003, p. 16.

25 The Liverpool businessman and Michaelmas Group member, Ken Medlock OBE, knew Sheppard for many years as a bishop but said he 'couldn't see him other than in whites'.

26 Letter dated 21 June 1991: SHP, 20.1.

place at the 'top table'.[27] He acknowledged that cultivating relationships with those in power, and working behind the scenes, should not be the Church's main way of operating, but sometimes the 'discreet word' was the right way.[28] But sitting at the 'top table' did not mean taking a 'top down' approach, however. He and Worlock spoke of following the 'way of the Servant' and rejecting a love of status and pulling rank. In working with communities, they would act as advocates and representatives but not usurp local leaders. They wanted 'to interpret one to the other, but always as communicators rather than negotiators.'[29] A leader of the Langrove Street Action Group recalled that Sheppard put himself at the service of the group: 'I've got the name and the position', he said, 'but we'll do it together'. The community always felt 'that we were together as colleagues and comrades', Jane Corbett has said, 'rather than, "Oh, he's coming in to sort it, what do we do now?"'[30]

Yet there was something of the 'patrician Anglican' about Sheppard, as his identification with Temple's position would suggest. Sheppard shared many of Temple's convictions, including the dignity of each human person, interdependence, sacrifice in the interest of others, and the common good. Temple talked of people being 'members one of another'.[31] But Temple also valued the established status of the Church of England, and the opportunity that afforded it to influence society, and Sheppard followed suit. He would talk of a 'national church', with a right to act as 'the conscience of the nation'. He thought the Church's presence in every community, through the parish system, gave it the duty and authority to speak for those without a public voice. But it was more a voice *for* the poor than *of* the poor. The Church might hope to empower the poor when it spoke on their behalf, but it saw itself, not the poor, as the agent of change.

This is clear from both *Faith in the City* and *Unemployment and the Future of Work*. Both addressed the root causes of poverty, and drew upon

---

27 'Shedding the Light of the Gospel', paper for the BSR, 11 October 1991: SHP, 16.3 and 29.7.
28 Sheppard, *Bias to the Poor*, p. 220.
29 *Better Together*, pp. 135, 227; cf. Sheppard and Worlock, *With Hope in Our Hearts*, p. 19.
30 In 2002 Jane Corbett was elected as a Labour councillor for the area.
31 Suggate, A. M., 'The Temple Tradition' in Brown, M., ed., *Anglican Social Theology*, London: Church House Publishing, 2014, p. 60. Temple also initiated an enquiry into unemployment and played a conciliatory role in industrial disputes.

the first-hand experiences of people on the margins. But neither included marginalized people in their working groups. They spoke of the poor and unemployed as 'them' not 'us'.[32] They called for action by Church and government, not the poor and unemployed themselves. Sheppard's own line was similar. He could describe himself as one who knew the reality of poverty in Britain. He could articulate the authentic voice of the poor. He would work to keep poor communities together and help develop their leaders. But he saw the improvement of their situation lying in the hands of others, not in their own; hence his appeals to 'Comfortable Britain' to share their wealth and use their position within society to make a difference. When the question of church support for broad-based organizing, also known as community organizing, was raised in the 1990s, Sheppard, Worlock and Newton commissioned a working party to explore the issue. They initially gave their support, as individuals, to this form of organizing in Merseyside, but later found they were unable to reach a common position with its supporters in the churches.

One difference between Temple and Sheppard was Sheppard's greater readiness to offer specific policy proposals in support of his vision. Temple operated in a time when politicians and church leaders tended to speak the same language, and this enabled him to offer principles to guide policy choices, his 'middle axioms'.[33] Sheppard thought this approach would achieve little when the government no longer valued a welfare state and even doubted there was such a thing as society. 'In many ways I'd rather stick to general principles', he said at the time of his Dimbleby Lecture, 'though what then happens is that you are preaching 10 feet above . . . contradiction.' Taking a bias to the poor did not mean adopting a particular party-political stance, he wrote later. 'But I do not believe we can simply preach generally [sic] principles . . . there are times when we have to get off the fence about particular issues.'[34]

---

32 See, for example, *Faith in the City*, p. xv; *Unemployment and the Future of Work*, p. 178; cf. Graham, E., 'The Ecclesiology of *Unemployment and the Future of Work*' in Brown and Sedgwick, *Putting Theology to Work*, pp. 40–7.

33 Broadly speaking, middle axioms operate between general statements of the ethical demands of the gospel, and the decisions that have to be made in concrete situations. Temple cautiously offers a 'suggested programme' of action as an appendix to *Christianity and Social Order* (Harmondsworth: Penguin, 1942), but thinks this less likely to command support among Christians than his general principles.

34 Heald, T., 'No.1 who looks after the others', *Daily Telegraph*, 16 April 1984, p. 15; letter

*

Sheppard did not always see theology as the starting point for the projects he promoted, and the reports he helped to produce were often criticized on that point. But the foundation of his commitment to tackle poverty, poor housing, racism and other ills, was his understanding of the gospel and the character of God. As he broadened his perception of concepts such as the 'kingdom' or 'reign' of God, so he applied his faith to social and economic questions. At Cambridge, he understood the kingdom largely in spiritual terms: it required people to be 'born again' to enter its gates. By the time he was at Woolwich he thought the gospel was also about lifting up one's horizons 'to what God wants the world to be like, and what He wants us to be like as His responsible partners.' 'God loves things like mercy, justice and truth, and hates things like greed and oppression,' he would later write. Justice in scripture (Hebrew, *tsedeq*) is 'not the same as fairness, as though everyone started from the same line . . . *Tsedeq* topples over on behalf of those in direst need'.[35]

Sheppard's interpretation of the kingdom as both personal and political is important. He always believed that people needed to respond to the love of Christ individually, as he had done as a student, but he came to see salvation having a communal dimension as well. Making the gospel 'relevant' in an Urban Priority Area required changing that area, whereas among students at Cambridge it might have a more direct impact.

He spoke of himself as a 'not only but also' person.[36] A turning point had come in the late 1960s when he encountered the idea that evil could be found in systems and structures as well as individuals. But while he saw no tension between a 'social' and 'personal' interpretation of the gospel, for some of his evangelical friends this was a dilution of its message. His one-time mentor Eric Nash wanted him to use his influence to 'preach the gospel to the nation' rather than involve himself in the 'social gospel'. A friend from his Cambridge days told him that trying

---

dated 31 October 1991: SHP 21.14; cf. Filby, 'God and Mrs Thatcher', PhD thesis, pp. 131–2. Heald describes Temple as a 'hero' of Sheppard's.

35 Sheppard, *Built as a City*, pp. 337–8; Sheppard, *Bias to the Poor*, pp. 18, 71–2; cf. Sheppard, *Steps along Hope Street*, pp. 146–7.

36 Sheppard, *Steps along Hope Street*, pp. 145–6, 172; Sheppard, *Bias to the Poor*, pp. 17, 158.

to stop the 1970 South African tour had 'nothing to do with the Gospel, which the Lord saved you in order to preach.'[37]

Whether Sheppard remained an 'evangelical' is a moot point. The question may not have troubled him. He disliked labels, considering them misleading: 'They sought to squeeze everyone into one or other opposing camp', he thought, 'when the faith of many Christians had been enriched from different sources.'[38] They posed a threat to unity within the Church. Clearly the narrower description 'conservative evangelical', which he once embraced, became less meaningful during his years as a bishop. He continued to hold that the Bible must always have a 'controlling authority' for Christians. Core evangelical tenets such as Christ's death atoning for the sins of the world, the bodily resurrection of Christ, and the Spirit's presence in the lives of Christians, remained central to his faith. But while he held fast to these, as he told an interviewer shortly before his retirement, 'if we're true to Jesus, I think there should be much more about the kingdom of God. It isn't just about need, or the worshipping community. It is about a church that is called to be a servant – the church in the world.' He was clear that evangelism must not become a hidden motive for offering service to the poor.[39]

Sheppard's views on women and gay people in the church set him apart from a mainstream evangelical position. From his days at Woolwich onwards, he advocated the ordination of women, and he made a point of involving women in leadership and policy making at the Mayflower. He also supported the ministry of women as bishops, 30 years before that became a reality in the Church of England. 'I do believe that it is the Will of God for women to be able to test their deeply held sense of vocation to the priesthood – and the episcopate – in the same way that a man should do', he wrote in 1983.[40]

He publicly endorsed the Church's line on gay clergy, but deviated occasionally from it in practice. In 1991 the House of Bishops came

---

37 Sheppard, *Steps along Hope Street*, p. 23; letter 29 October 1970; SHP: 15.7.

38 Sheppard, *Steps along Hope Street*, p. 71.

39 Sheppard, *Steps along Hope Street*, pp. 24, 208; 'Unbeaten Stand: Matthew Bishop talks to the Rt Revd David Sheppard', *Third Way*, September 1997, p. 19; 'Evangelism with a Good Heart', *The Expository Times*, 102:5, February 1991, p. 132.

40 Letter dated 22 December 1983: SHP, 4.14.

down against permitting clergy 'to enter into sexually active homophile relationships.' The bishops affirmed the biblical ideal of 'lifelong, monogamous, heterosexual union as the setting intended by God for the proper development of men and women as sexual beings.'[41] Sheppard said he stood firmly by the bishops' report, yet in a letter to the Board for Social Responsibility in the early stages of the process, he said that he had, 'on a very small number of occasions ordained someone knowing that he had a partner – not knowing precisely what their practice was.' It would not be helpful for such men to 'come out' in the current climate, he added, though this meant 'asking people to live in a discreet way, with the obvious limitations and difficulties which that still makes for them.'[42] In a sermon in 1992, he said he wanted 'homosexual men and women' to be accepted in church congregations. 'We need to know each other much better and learn to talk as Christians about different experiences and insights,' he said.[43]

Sheppard seldom made his views on same-sex relationships public, however. As he told his friend Jim Thompson in 1979, it was 'a matter of deciding which issues one is going to stick one's neck out about . . . My neck is exposed on a number of issues which I intend to try to see through for many years,' he wrote.

> I genuinely believe that there is a danger that a subject like this would be used by many of the more orthodox Christians as a reason for not listening to things that I believe I am meant to say about some of the other great human issues.[44]

One conservative aspect of his faith he retained all his life was the observance of Sunday as a special day. Since his conversion he had valued Sundays as a time for worship, reading and slowing the pace of his hectic life. First-class cricket was rarely played on Sundays in the 1950s and 1960s, and Sheppard campaigned vigorously against any change to the

---

41 *Issues in Human Sexuality*, London: Church House Publishing, 1991, sections 5.17, 2.29.
42 Letter dated 7 September 1987: SHP, 4.9.
43 'This Is My Son, the Beloved', sermon preached in the cathedral on Mothering Sunday, 29 March 1992: SHP, 16.3.
44 Letter dated 16 November 1979: SHP, 8.22.

rule. Sunday cricket would deny people with a conscience like his from getting involved in the game, as well as forcing ground staff, caterers and others to work on Sundays. It was not a case of wanting to impose his views on others, he said: the rhythm of one day's rest in seven would benefit all. He promoted these views throughout his life. He opposed the introduction of Sunday league cricket when it was first mooted, writing to all the counties to encourage them not to support it. When Test match cricket on Sundays was proposed in 1980, he wrote to MCC asking that play be avoided in the morning, as was then the case with the Sunday league, and he continued to lobby the cricket authorities against further encroachment into Sundays into the 1990s. At the Board for Social Responsibility he campaigned against unrestricted shopping on Sundays.

Sheppard always affirmed his debt to the evangelical tradition and was happy to be associated with it. In May 1993 he spoke at the Anglican Evangelical Assembly, and a few months earlier told the House of Lords that the word 'evangelical' meant 'a great deal in positive and important ways' to him.[45] In 1990 he wrote to an author about her book on moving away from conservative evangelicalism. 'Like you', Sheppard wrote, 'I would not now be seen as "true blue" by conservative evangelicals. I still hope that at the heart of my ministry is what the word evangelical should stand for: the Gospel of *Grace*.'[46]

He once said he believed he had become more biblical, not less, through taking up issues such as housing, race and education: 'God as Creator is concerned about the whole quality of men's lives, not just with personal conversion, important though that is.'[47] As Sheppard approached retirement, the Labour politician Roy Hattersley astutely observed that 'you can take the bishop out of the evangelical movement, but you cannot take the evangelical movement out of the bishop.'[48]

Sheppard left an important legacy to the evangelical movement. Until he raised the issue of urban ministry in the 1960s, few evangelicals had seen its importance. His work at the Mayflower with George Burton, Jean Lodge Patch and others encouraged many churches to engage with young

---

45 Hansard, Lords, 'Religious Broadcasting', 9 November 1992, col. 56.
46 Letter dated 12 September 1990: SHP, 36.3.
47 Interview with Aidan Whittington, *The Sign*, [early 1970s], p. 67.
48 'Turbulent Priest', *The Guardian*, 10 March 1997, p. 6.

people in urban areas.[49] The Frontier Youth Trust, which Sheppard helped to create, developed this work further.[50] He also pioneered inner-city ministry more generally among evangelicals, including through the Evangelical Urban Training Project, which in 1999 became 'Unlock'.[51] At the first national conference of Eclectics in 1966, Ted Roberts spoke on 'Evangelism in Industrial Parishes'. 'It was quite something in those days to have [such a topic] exposed on an evangelical platform', recalled John Hunter. 'There were still those who questioned if the subject was "sound". Its presence indicated the influence of David Sheppard behind the scenes.'[52] From this event emerged *Christians in Industrial Areas*, which further encouraged evangelical interest in the inner-city. Two leading studies of Anglican evangelicalism in the twentieth century have noted Sheppard's pioneering role in promoting a concern for urban issues and social action in that tradition.[53] Ken Leech described Sheppard as representing 'a new breed of radical evangelical whose theology is deeply rooted in the Bible.'[54] Social action became an integral part of evangelical witness in the twenty-first century.

*

Sheppard moved beyond his past in another important regard. In his youth he encountered negative views about Roman Catholics, both from his mother and at university. As he later recalled, his evangelical peers at Cambridge did not consider Roman Catholics to be 'real Christians'.[55]

---

49 For more on this see Ward, P., *Growing up Evangelical: Youth work and the making of a subculture*, London: SPCK, 1996, chapter 3, pp. 63–79.

50 The FYT still operates from a base in east London: www.fyt.org.uk.

51 www.unlock-urban.org.uk

52 Hunter, J., *A Touch of Class: Issues of Urban Mission*, Sheffield: EUTP, 1995, p. 18.

53 Hylson-Smith, K., *Evangelicals in the Church of England 1734–1984*, Edinburgh: T & T Clark, 1989, p. 319; Atherstone, A., and Maiden, J., 'Anglican Evangelicalism in the Twentieth Century: Identities and Contexts' in Atherstone, A., and Maiden, J., eds, *Evangelicalism and the Church of England in the Twentieth Century: Reform, Resistance and Renewal*, Woodbridge: Boydell Press, 2014, p. 23. See also Bebbington, D., *Evangelicalism in Modern Britain: A History from the 1730s to the 1980s*, London: Unwin Hyman, 1989, p. 265.

54 Leech, K., 'Turbulent Priests', *Marxism Today*, February 1986, p. 13. Leech was a Christian socialist with a long ministry among poor communities in the East End of London. He would later say that Sheppard represented 'the best of the Anglican reformist tradition'; 'Seen through class, darkly'.

55 Sheppard, *Steps along Hope Street*, pp. 9, 24.

It was not until he encountered Roman Catholic priests and laypeople in Canning Town and south London that his understanding and appreciation of the tradition deepened. Mervyn Stockwood encouraged him to work across ecclesiastical boundaries, and through involvement with the Thamesmead Christian Council and other projects, his attitude to ecumenical endeavour transformed. By the time he was appointed to Liverpool, he was ready to work closely with his Roman Catholic opposite number, Archbishop Derek Worlock.[56]

The Sheppard–Worlock partnership was often referred to as the 'Mersey miracle'.[57] This may have been an overstatement, since they were not the first bishops in the city to work together: there were precedents in the region of cooperation by church leaders. But their working together at a particular moment in the region's history, and in such a deliberate and public way, was hugely significant. It had a lasting effect, not only on relations between the region's religious communities and civic bodies, but on the wellbeing of Liverpool and Merseyside more generally.

They took risks by appearing together. Hostility between their churches was thawing, but old suspicions were not far below the surface, and both were seen as traitors by sections in their communities. It did not take much to spark a protest, but by patient example and conscious effort, they brought the remaining barriers down and changed the culture for good. They made the idea of churches working together the 'new normal', and gave permission for ecumenical ventures to be tried at local level. They also made it harder for those on the extremes in their traditions to gain a foothold. It is interesting that it took two 'outsiders' to provide the catalyst for this change, but it is a measure of their achievement that, after nearly two centuries of bitter sectarian division in the city, they could say towards the end of their time that 'people in Liverpool have come to expect the Churches to act together.'[58] To some extent they were responding to, as well as changing, the mood of the city[59] but their time

---

56 Sheppard's transition was against the background of a closer 'drawing together' of evangelicals and Roman Catholics following Vatican II; Hylson-Smith, *Evangelicals in the Church of England*, pp. 343–4.

57 The term could also refer to the bishops' partnership with the Free Churches in the region.

58 Sheppard and Worlock, *With Hope in Our Hearts*, p. 9.

59 See Roberts, K. D., *Liverpool Sectarianism: The Rise and Demise*, Liverpool: Liverpool University Press, 2017, p. 178. Roberts also argues that the growth of religious

together saw a massive shift in culture, which history will rightly judge as their ongoing legacy to a once-divided city.

The two bishops' partnership was close. They or their staff were in touch almost daily, they worked their diaries together, and spoke at length together at least once a week. 'If we have not had good time alone together during the week, we need an hour on the telephone on Sunday night, just to catch up with the issues which involve us together at the moment', Sheppard once said.[60] They would consult together before either spoke on an issue, or took an initiative, which they looked to the other to support. 'They were very sensitive to issues that the other would find difficult', Keith Cawdron, a former Diocesan Secretary, has said, 'which meant the other almost had a veto on what one of them was doing.' They would liaise about how they should dress for each event after one occasion when one turned up in a suit and the other his cassock.

Some thought the bishops showed greater loyalty to one another than to their own communions. 'The Archbishop is for ever being photographed with his Anglican twin, David Sheppard, but never with his own auxiliary bishops', noted Simon Lee and Peter Stanford. 'He is delighted to write a book, *Better Together*, with Bishop Sheppard, but does not give his fellow Catholic bishops a higher profile by writing with them.'[61] During the process which created Liverpool Hope University, the governors and staff of the Anglican college involved looked to Michael Henshall to defend their interests, not Sheppard, 'who was thought to be too close to Archbishop Worlock.'[62] Sheppard once stood apart from his fellow bishops by refusing to support an ecumenical pilgrimage because Worlock could not endorse it. Sheppard was clear, however, that his duty was to the one who prayed that his followers 'may all be one', so the world would believe God had sent him. 'It's easy to allow ecumenical partnership a place in our diaries when all the demands of our Church

---

'indifference' had more to do with the disappearance of sectarianism in Liverpool than the efforts of the two bishops (pp. 179–85).

60 'One Church – One World: Breaking down the barriers'; the CMS Annual Sermon, 1991: SHP, 16.3.

61 Lee, S., and Stanford, P., *Believing Bishops*, London: Faber and Faber, 1990, p. 106.

62 Peart-Binns, J. S., *A Certain Sound: The Life of Bishop Michael Henshall*, unpublished manuscript, p. 113.

have been met', he said. 'But if it is a matter of obedience to Christ, it needs to be given a quite different priority.'[63]

Sheppard was loyal to the teachings and practice of his Church, and with the exception of ordaining a small number of gay clergy in relationships, he appears never to have acted against Church policy. When asked by priests for permission to admit children to communion before confirmation, he cited decisions made centrally by the Church. We belong to a 'corporate body', he would say, and change should be sought by building a sufficient consensus for it within the church. The ordination of women was a case in point. 'If I can't carry people with me', he told a priest in the 1980s, 'I do not do the Church good by going ahead on my own . . . This is the way that schism in the Church takes place.'[64] When he first began promoting the idea of local ordained ministry in urban areas, he was 'very hesitant to take steps forward' because he did not want to 'act out of step with the Church at large . . . I want to carry more people with me if we are going to do this', he said.[65] 'He would not put his head above the parapet unless his fellow bishops were willing to do so', the Chancellor of the Diocese, Mark Hedley, recalls. 'He was quite good at saying, "Please don't ask me, because I shall have to say 'No'."'

*

The bishops' partnership was based on a genuine friendship. They would watch football together and share the occasional holiday with Grace and Worlock's chaplain, John Furnival. 'Shop-window ecumenism doesn't require that', commented Bishop Vincent Malone, a close colleague of Worlock's. Sheppard described their friendship as a 'relationship in Christ'. 'Their trust in one another was such that they frequently spoke and acted on each other's behalf', Maria Power has remarked.[66] 'I could recognize what David thought before he thought it', Worlock once said.[67]

---

63 'One Church – One World: Breaking down the barriers'. The reference is to John 17.21.

64 Letter dated 30 November 1982: SHP, 1.14.

65 Conversation with Bryan Ellis in *Christians in Industrial Areas*, 49, Summer 1981, p. 18.

66 Power, M., 'Reconciling State and Society? The Practice of the Common Good in the Partnership of Bishop David Sheppard and Archbishop Derek Worlock', *Journal of Religious History*, 40:4, December 2016, p. 547.

67 Linklater, A., 'A Holy Alliance', *Good Housekeeping*, January 1988, p. 140.

Worlock described their partnership as an example of where 'one plus one adds up to more than two.' They did not duplicate each other, but speaking together, as they often did in public, said more than if they were to be given separate slots.[68]

Grace's role in the partnership was also significant. She had a personal rather than formal approach, which helped the bishops drop their guard and communicate more openly. Her dislike of airs and graces, and experience of vulnerability, compelled her to look for the authentic in others. She 'combined a deep faith with a sharp sense of humour, some would say mischief, and well-honed powers of observation', an admirer once remarked. Perhaps she understood her husband and Worlock better than they understood each other or themselves.[69] She was a vital factor in making it possible for two bishops from different traditions to forge such a strong bond of trust, and his friendship with David and Grace became for Worlock a sense of family.

The bishops also developed friendships with the Free Church leaders, especially John Newton. Their concern to involve these leaders was genuine, and something of this can be glimpsed in Sheppard's 'Thank you' letter to Pope John Paul following his visit in 1982. Seven of the nine substantive paragraphs refer to the role of the Free Churches in the life of the city.[70] The bishops' collaboration across strongly held doctrinal differences required a determined commitment, and they often spoke of the 'pain of separation'. The Sheppard–Worlock partnership inspired ecumenical activity beyond the United Kingdom. Dame Mary Tanner, former European President of the World Council of Churches, recalls a major gathering of Anglican and Catholic bishops in Canada in 2000, where their work was often mentioned as an example of 'what was possible now on the way to full visible unity.' A follow-up publication spoke of the 'outstanding and symbolic partnership' developed between Worlock, Sheppard and the Free Church Moderator for Merseyside, most noticeably, John Newton.[71]

---

68 *Symbols of Hope*, BBC Radio 4, 6 December 1987.

69 Service sheet, thanksgiving service for Grace Sheppard, Liverpool cathedral, 7 May 2011, p. 4.

70 Letter to His Holiness Pope John Paul II, 29 July 1982: SHP, 5.11.

71 The reference is to *One in Christ*, 39:1, Jan 2004.

*

The bishops' role in promoting Merseyside's interests was significant, and they were clear that they had a duty to act in this way. 'It would have been a betrayal of our responsibilities *not* to apply Gospel principles to the needs and injustices afflicting those we have been called to serve in the challenging and stressful years we have been together in Liverpool,' they wrote.[72] Their role during the 1980s, when the city council was at loggerheads with central government, was crucial. They helped support the political process by keeping channels of dialogue open between the city, the government and other agencies, and with the region's MPs unable to speak with a single voice, the bishops served as advocates for the region. When sections of the media attacked Liverpool and its people, the bishops were quick to reply with letters, articles and interviews. When politicians suggested unemployed people in Merseyside leave and look for work elsewhere, the bishops called for real investment in the region. Their access to grassroots opinion through the parishes, and their networks into the business, voluntary and other sectors in the city, enabled them to be authentic spokespeople on behalf of the region.

Their initiative in setting up the Michaelmas Group was also important in encouraging business leaders to think positively about the region. Behind the scenes, the bishops worked to save jobs and keep businesses from leaving, using their position to meet with government ministers and company chairs. They would talk to the parties in industrial disputes to seek a mutually beneficial resolution, and their efforts earned them respect and trust at the highest levels, as their award of the freedom of the city and other honours from local institutions attest. They also won the affection of residents in their adopted city, and people outside the church saw their partnership as relevant to them. Some thought they were 'the only champions they had'. 'Ecumenism?', one dock worker is reputed to have said when asked what that meant to him. 'I suppose it means those bishops fighting to keep our jobs.'[73]

---

72 Sheppard and Worlock, *With Hope in Our Hearts*, p. 19.
73 Linklater, 'A Holy Alliance', p. 141.

'I cannot think of any other city in this country which would think of producing a bishop to speak in the name of the community', the government minister, Michael Portillo, said on a visit to Liverpool in the early 1990s.[74] The BBC Merseyside radio presenter, Roger Phillips, thinks the bishops were probably the only people who could have calmed things down after the troubles in Toxteth. Seeing them walking the streets, talking and listening to all who were affected, 'I really understood for the first time ever what a community leader was', Phillips says.[75] Grace Davie thinks Liverpool was unique in being a place 'where everybody knew who the bishops were and everybody, in a manner of speaking, had a relationship to them.'

A former chief executive of the city council, Peter Bounds, thought a combination of factors peculiar to Liverpool in the 1980s put it in a place 'where the need for some healing and pastoral care and support was evident, creating an opportunity for the church to be influential.' These factors included a dysfunctional political system, widespread poverty and tragedies such as Heysel and Hillsborough. Sheppard and Worlock's genius was to see the role for the churches and follow it through.

Future historians may reduce the bishops to a footnote. Their contribution to the restoration of Merseyside's fortunes was often behind the scenes, yet it was significant and lasting. Max Steinberg has been at the heart of Liverpool's regeneration over the past 30 years, and he sees Sheppard's role as pivotal in changing perceptions of the city and region, particularly among potential investors. 'Despite some very challenging circumstances', Steinberg says,

> the fact that we had figures like David Sheppard who could and would intervene . . . contributed to that building of confidence that allowed things to happen. This in turn meant that when, for example, a private company considered the city, it saw that there was something to invest in here, something to build on.

---

74 Sheppard and Worlock, *With Hope in Our Hearts*, p. 16.
75 www.youtube.com/watch?v=1AsTozmT4V8&t=106s

Sheppard's legacy, Steinberg concludes, is the fact that 'without his interventions, without his counsel, without his calm words, without his willingness sometimes to bang the table – as he sometimes could – some of the conditions for the renaissance that has come about would not have happened.'

Roger Phillips, who has had his finger on Liverpool's pulse for several decades, thinks Sheppard and Worlock helped to give the city the confidence to apply to become European City of Culture in 1997. This would have been unthinkable even ten years before, yet Liverpool achieved that status in 2008.

The bishops would admit that, despite their interventions, factories closed, riots broke out and the Militants on the city council pursued their agenda. Yet as Andro Linklater points out,

> the fact that they did intervene, not simply by preaching from the pulpit, but by lobbying businessmen and politicians in their offices, and by talking to policemen and rioters in the streets, had a crucial effect. From each side of the fissures which threatened to split the city apart, they were perceived as a positive force for unity.[76]

'You may have failed', a priest once told Sheppard after an attempt to stop a factory closure had been unsuccessful, 'but it has meant a lot to people who are suffering that you have stood with them and been seen to fail with them.'[77] Perhaps the taxi-driver delivering David Puttnam to Sheppard's memorial service summed up the kind of change the bishops helped to effect in Liverpool. 'We stopped feeling sorry for ourselves', he said.[78]

*

A price Sheppard paid for his commitment to the city was a perception that he neglected his diocese as a result. Many clergy accepted his decision

---

76 Linklater, 'A Holy Alliance', p. 141.
77 Sheppard, *Steps along Hope Street*, p. 227.
78 David Puttnam, tribute, David Sheppard memorial service, 23 May 2005.

to focus on healing a 'hurt' city. It was a source of pride that their bishop had a national profile. Others regretted the apparent remoteness of their diocesan. 'Priests in Liverpool can see their bishop any time they like', ran one rather cutting joke, 'they just have to turn on their television.' Yet Sheppard did not neglect to visit his parishes, nor was he unavailable to priests in trouble.[79] Diary commitments might mean that he could only see a priest late at night, but he would give them his full attention when they were together. His tendency to pass on the follow-up process would sometimes be misunderstood. 'I never knew him to miss any of his obligations', one priest who worked with him closely for many years recalls. 'He did not off-load what he should be doing on to other people. But he knew how to delegate properly.' Some thought he was better at arranging the provision of pastoral care than providing it himself, yet hundreds of people, lay and ordained, would attest to the support, advice and consolation Sheppard gave them in times of distress. With hindsight, however, one example was deeply troubling. He once allowed a priest, convicted of indecent assault on a male under 16, to remain in post, believing a miscarriage of justice had occurred.[80] Such a response would later be considered unthinkable.

Occasionally his commitment to wider issues made it hard for him to connect with local parish life. Shortly after returning from South Africa he took a confirmation service, devoting his sermon to the situation he had witnessed on his trip. Many who attended expressed their disappointment about the service, noting the absence of any text for the candidates, and little acknowledgement of their journey to faith. When the parish priest wrote to inform him of this feeling, Sheppard gave a robust defence of his action.

Some thought Sheppard's never having been a parish priest affected his approach to the diocese, that he lacked an instinctive feel for the parishes and their clergy. His suggestion that clergy take regular holidays and sabbaticals was seen as unrealistic. In many cases, it was almost impossible for clergy to get cover, and leaving a house empty in some areas was unwise. On one occasion he asked a parish priest to spend

---

79 See, for example, Sheppard, *Steps along Hope Street*, pp. 157–60, 203.
80 See the Independent Inquiry into Child Sexual Abuse report on the Anglican Church, 1 July 2019, pp. 16–19.

a day at Bishop's Lodge answering his phone while he was away. The number of initiatives that he told clergy were of 'paramount importance' caused concern in some quarters. Clergy might feel they had not been consulted sufficiently. When two inner-city deaneries needed reorganization, parishes heard of their impending closure on television rather than from the bishop. Sheppard faced a rebellion, and the deaneries produced a better plan themselves.[81]

There could be an autocratic side to Sheppard. Several former colleagues recalled moments when he would demand something be done immediately and become irritated at any delay or objection. His sense of being driven, and being bound by his diary, meant that he sometimes ran on a short fuse. He could be sharp and domineering on occasions: expecting a discussion, a priest might find himself being talked to instead. Sheppard's sense of knowing what needed to be done, and when it was right to close a debate, could also sometimes be seen as an unwillingness to listen. He once side-lined a canon of the cathedral, David Hutton, following a disagreement over how best to provide training for clergy. The action weighed heavily on his mind, and it led to disaffection among several clergy in the diocese. When a young curate, Peter Forster, accepted an academic post before his three-year term was complete, Sheppard told him to withdraw his acceptance. Forster said church law was on his side, to which Sheppard replied that, in an episcopal church, it was bishops who made decisions. In such situations, however, Sheppard would not bear a grudge. While others resented Forster for standing firm and taking the job, Sheppard put it all in the past. When Forster was later appointed Bishop of Chester, and Sheppard went to live in his diocese, the two enjoyed a good and easy relationship.

Sheppard's record in recommending clergy for preferment was often noted, however. During his 22 years as bishop only one priest from Liverpool was appointed to a bishopric, and that was due entirely to the intervention of the Archbishop of York, Stuart Blanch.[82] At the Mayflower, Sheppard had been keen to see local leaders develop and grow. It was part of his understanding of leadership. In Liverpool it appeared to

---

81 Hoare, R., 'Brief Sketch of David Sheppard's Life and Formation (2) 1975–2005', 2013, p. 2.5; accessible via www.togetherforthecommongood.co.uk/conference/t4cg-conference-sessions.html.

82 This was the appointment of Gordon Bates to be Bishop of Whitby in 1983.

be different. Critics thought that perhaps he had not got to know his clergy well enough to assess their potential for promotion, or would not make the time to complete the necessary profiles and commendations. Others thought he found it difficult to affirm others, particularly fellow Anglicans who might later be a threat to him. A kinder view was that he liked priests to commit to the long term in their parishes and would be reluctant to move those doing a good job. Yet while he discouraged potential leaders from leaving their location, he would move on when he felt a calling to do so. He left Woolwich after six years, and would almost certainly have gone to London, York or Canterbury after a few years in Liverpool had those possibilities become real.

*

Sheppard's commitment to his diocese, the city, the wider church and to public life, set him enormous challenges in terms of organization, time management and prioritization. At the Mayflower he was known for being reliant on his diary. Thinking ahead was even more important as a bishop, so every aspect of his life was meticulously planned, often 18 months in advance. Colleagues teased him for being a 'diary freak', but it was the only way he could cope with the demands on his time. He set two days aside each spring to plan the following year's programme with Grace, Michael Henshall and their secretaries. The first entries would be holidays, six weeks each year. He regarded this family time as sacrosanct and essential to prevent burnout. Next would be two reading weeks: he and Grace treated these as retreats, and might spend them at a religious house. Next came quiet days, then the 'two-bishops' days' with Henshall to discuss diocesan business. The weekly phone conversation with Worlock would also go in. 'Catch-up' days were another essential, one every six weeks or so: opportunities to complete tasks for which time was running out. Other meetings and commitments were all entered and colour-coded. Sheppard told a fellow bishop that compartmentalizing the various aspects of his life and ministry was key to the way he worked. He tried to steer clear of the 'dinner circuit', and kept a check on the number of committees he joined. When lending his name to a cause or campaign, he would ask to be excused meetings.

The former Chief Rabbi, Jonathan Sacks, once asked Sheppard to explain his diary-making process. How could he be so busy yet always in control? Sacks found their conversation life-changing. He decided to adopt the same principles, and sent his personal assistant to Sheppard's office to learn more of the detail. He encouraged his rabbis to follow Sheppard's method. Sacks found Sheppard's approach to organizing time spiritual. 'It sounds very managerial', he once reflected, 'but in Judaism we think God's greatest gift to us is life. And life equals time. And unlike money, time lost can never be recovered. So I found this really life-transforming. Absolutely and totally life transforming.'

Whenever he could, Sheppard took time off for an evening meal with Grace and, until she left home, Jenny. He would always take a siesta after lunch. This enabled him to cope with his early starts and late finishes, and he stuck to it, even when travelling. When he was at Church House in London, he would ask for a room with two chairs to be set aside. He also aimed to stop work at 9.00 pm each evening. This proved hard to keep, and he would often see clergy or others with urgent business late in the evening. It was a constant struggle to keep up with correspondence and paperwork, and while monitoring his use of time for a training course in 1981, he regretted not keeping abreast of a 'relentless post'. This was despite increasing the number of three-hour desk sessions he put into the diary from four to five per week.[83] He would habitually begin replies to non-urgent correspondence with an apology for not having written sooner, and personal quiet days might be lost if the diary was overfull.

His diary allowed him to work with ruthless efficiency, however. Having allocated time for each appointment, he could give it his full attention, and he often liked to say he had given 'unhurried time' to someone. But his rigid planning left no scope for flexibility, even in extreme cases. A colleague once travelled from Liverpool to see him in Peckham, arriving two hours later than Sheppard expected. The two had got their wires crossed. Sheppard said he could not see the visitor, who trekked back home after a fruitless trip.

There was a price to pay for his heavy workload. He would keep religiously to his breaks and days off. He would always switch off on

83 'Study Weekend, October 1980', typewritten sheets, p. 8: SHP, 24.2.

holiday and spend time painting, cooking and reading novels. But he often let work creep into family time at home, despite his best intentions. Lodgers at the house in the 1980s recall Sheppard routinely rising at 5.00 am for two hours' reading and writing before breakfast. He was then drafting *Bias to the Poor*. In a moment of self-reflection in his autobiography, he recalls the effect his behaviour had on Grace at that time: 'I knew that her misgivings were not just about the details of time given to the home', he writes,

> but also at a deep level about my whole attitude. Work commitments sometimes built up to such a degree that personal and family issues were left until we were both tired – often after 11 pm or even days later. That had to change.[84]

He thought 'some modest adjustments to the timetable would be a sign', but even these proved difficult. Grace's diary in 1985 records his early starts and late returns. 'D got up at 5.00 am. Home at 10.30 pm. It's a *very* long day. I don't care for it.' 'D got up at 6.00 am to do letters & stopped for this afternoon & started again tonight. He work [sic] through the night till he's done.' Having sat down with guests for 'cocoa & a chat . . . at about 10.15 pm D apologized that he had to depart to make some 'phone calls. These calls lasted till about 11.45 pm . . . D must be chasing his tail as the 'phone has just rung (11.55 pm).' Plans for a holiday had just been 'scuppered', Grace noted, 'because of finding a date for the Church leaders to meet.' 'That's what ecumenism means to me', she added sardonically. 'Is it right that personal, marriage, time to ourselves, should be regarded as being more dispensable relatively than other engagements . . . Overall, we don't allow this to happen too much: I must be fair. But finding a date in June 1986 becoming a major difficulty . . . does seem ominous. Like, what other threats are lurking?'[85] Grace once said of David's dependence on his diary that she liked order, 'but not when it drives you into next year, before I've started to live today.'[86]

---

84 Sheppard, *Steps along Hope Street,* p. 207.
85 Grace Sheppard diaries, 1985, *passim*.
86 Transcript of David and Grace Sheppard interview with Dr Mathew Guest, 26 August 2003, p. 22.

Sheppard prioritized his time under enormous pressure. He was driven by an overwhelming sense of vocation, one Grace shared. Their profound trust in God shaped every aspect of their lives, including their big decisions. They did not give up their autonomy, and they knew all their qualities, gifts and weaknesses were called to the task. But decisions were subject to prayerful discernment together. Dialogue with their Lord was the bedrock of their routine at the beginning and end of every day. On issues such as whether David should play cricket in Australia, or become a bishop, it was through this process of trust between them, in relationship with God, that the right way forward would become clear. Sheppard's use of the passive voice in his autobiography captures this precisely. 'The decision was made to make myself available for the cricket tour', 'the decision to accept [the offer of Woolwich] was made.'[87] After his first sabbatical for nearly 20 years, Sheppard wrote that, 'together we decided that I would work at my book during normal working hours from 9 am to 6 pm, Monday to Friday.'[88]

Sheppard's character played into this decision-making process. In the early years of their relationship, he single-mindedly pursued his career in much the way he did when unattached. The summer following their engagement, he spent playing cricket. He returned from their honeymoon alone in order to play cricket. In a poignant passage in her second book, Grace notes how she gave up the chance of a career on marriage to support her husband, as most women did in the 1950s. 'I did that willingly', she writes. It reflected her evangelical upbringing, but also a belief in their shared mission. David, on the other hand, 'continued with his work much as before, and the main difference for him was that he ceased to live alone.'[89] Sheppard once admitted comparing his working life with Worlock's during their early years in Liverpool. 'Yet he is called to be celibate', Sheppard wrote, 'I am called to be married . . . private and family needs are not naturally to be switched off during working days.'[90]

---

87 Sheppard, *Steps along Hope Street*, pp. 73, 97.

88 'It's Great to Be Home', *Liverpool Diocesan News*, 154, October 1981. In *Steps along Hope Street* (p. 201), Sheppard says 'I kept weekdays clear for writing the book.'

89 Sheppard, G., *Pits and Pedestals: A Journey towards Self-Respect*, London: Darton, Longman & Todd, 1995, p. 68

90 Study Weekend, October 1980', p. 6; cf. Sheppard and Worlock, *Better Together*, pp. 257–9.

A turning point came in the mid 1980s when Grace began to have counselling to address her agoraphobia. For three years she visited a clinical psychologist, Hanna McCluskey, in London. She found the sessions transformative: '[Hanna] helped me to understand that I had the power to make decisions concerning my own life, and needed to exercise it,' Grace later wrote. 'You are a free agent', she would say. 'She helped me to re-engage with my will, my life force, and to use it without feeling that "I want to" was always selfish.'[91]

This was a huge shift for Grace. For years she had doubted her worthiness to be her husband's wife, and worried constantly that her illnesses were holding him back. Her agoraphobia, and the trauma of losing her ability to have further children at the age of 30, did her self-image great harm. Now she could be an equal in the partnership, and move outside of her husband's shadow. She would carve out her own space and pursue her own career. Her first book was published in 1989, to wide acclaim, and she developed as a speaker, broadcaster and writer. The counselling also encouraged a new assertiveness. In the early stages, her husband, and other family members found it a challenge to adapt as she declared new personal boundaries. But in time, it led to Grace discovering a new-found confidence and great creativity, which Sheppard wholeheartedly embraced. He would often say how proud he was as her new career blossomed, and their shared sense of mission, and devotion to each other, survived intact. These were a constant across their 50 years together.

Sheppard typically gives little away when describing this period. Reflecting generally on the culture shift which saw women begin to pursue their own callings, he notes how 'the rightness of assertiveness in its proper place challenged some of the attitudes that had forbidden clergy spouses to speak up for their own needs.' 'In a marriage', he continued, 'this inevitably leads to changed priorities and redistributing some responsibilities.'[92] As the dynamic of their marriage changed, Grace insisted on some of the 'modest adjustments to the timetable' her

---

91 Sheppard, G., *An Aspect of Fear: A journey from anxiety to peace*, London: Darton, Longman & Todd, 1989, p. 28; Sheppard, G., *Living with Dying*, London: Darton, Longman & Todd, 2010, p. 26.

92 Sheppard, *Steps along Hope Street*, p. 206.

husband had been slow to adopt. One was a veto on his getting up at 5.00 am.

Sheppard once heard some bishops' wives discussing their lives. 'You know we all hate it!', one said. His own wife was pushed on this question by her psychologist. 'Do I want David to be strong & successful or not?' Grace was asked. 'Do I want him to be a bishop & archbishop?' She surprised herself by answering 'no' to the second question, more than a decade after David was appointed to Woolwich. 'This is very disturbing stuff', she wrote in her diary that evening. 'I am married to a bishop. I don't like it – but I love the man inside the role.'[93]

*

Sheppard's long hours were partly a factor of his method of working. He would never attend an appointment without being as fully briefed as possible. He wanted nothing to take him by surprise or force him into a spontaneous reaction he would later regret.

Part of this process involved finding the people to help him achieve his goal. 'Who are our allies?' he would say when a situation arose. They would often be from outside the church and might only agree with him on one issue. Tracking them down was demanding and time-consuming, but Sheppard saw it as vital. Since his time in Islington he worked assiduously to build relationships with bodies in the community, from businesses to schools, local authorities to voluntary groups. 'One of my favourite words, for many years, has been allies', he told a gathering of carers in 1998. 'None of us . . . can meet all the needs of individuals or community by ourselves. We need allies in a war against a care-less society.'[94] Grace thought his appreciation of the value of contact with institutions beyond the church stemmed from his having a foot in the cricket world from the earliest days of his conversion.[95]

This commitment to thorough preparation, and reducing the risk of failure, had parallels with his approach to cricket. He had made himself a

93 Sheppard, *Steps along Hope Street*, p. 206; Grace Sheppard diaries, 3–4 October 1986.

94 'Help for Carers', typescript of talk, 8 June 1998: SHP, 26.2; cf. Sheppard, *Built as a City*, p. 277.

95 Grace Sheppard interview with Eliza Filby, 27 July 2006.

top-class batsman by sheer hard graft under the supervision of mentors. Clearly, he could not have played his finest innings without an instinctive sense of timing. He could not have been a top-class fielder without sharp reactions and superb hand–eye coordination. He had a degree of natural talent. Yet it was the hours spent in the school gym, and hitting a ball against the coal-shed door, that transformed him from a good player into an exceptional one. As a bishop he also knew his limitations and would seek the advice of others. He was always looking to learn new skills, whether formally or from friends, and these included preaching, leadership and what he called 'bishoping'. 'He didn't have the right moves in cricket and as a bishop', a close colleague once said of him. 'He had to learn them in both cases.'

Sheppard once described his journey as 'not that of a natural-born cricketer, nor of a ready-made bishop'. His life and work were the result of his 'determination'.[96] 'I really did make the most of my talents', he said of his cricket career. Listing the qualities that cricket had given him, he put 'powers of concentration', 'determination to succeed' and 'application' at the top. 'I have certainly found myself able to focus for long periods on a task', he said. His friend Eric James told him he 'did not notice interruptions', a skill he thought came from his batting.[97] Ironically, it was only cricket which upset his powers of concentration as a bishop. During his 1981 sabbatical he switched on the television during the 'Botham/Willis' Test at Headingley and lost a day-and-half he had planned for writing. On another occasion, he allowed a government minister to side-track him into discussing cricket, using much of the time she had allocated for their meeting.

Sheppard displayed a 'determination to succeed' in all aspects of his life. He would always want to win, whether at squash with a friend, beach cricket on a Mayflower holiday, or Monopoly with the family. There was something in his personality that made him competitive, whatever the context. His Sussex and Cambridge teammate Robin Marlar once said

---

96 Dawson, P., 'David Sheppard – A short biography', January 1995. I am grateful to Canon Dawson for giving me a copy of this document which was prepared for the award of the Freedom of the City and approved by Sheppard. Dawson was Sheppard's chaplain at the time.

97 Private interview, March 2005; Sheppard, *Steps along Hope Street*, pp. 13–14.

that nobody came near to Sheppard in his attitude to the game: 'He told me . . . that every time he'd gone through the gate to bat he expected to make 100.' Marlar considered Sheppard 'absolutely the best player of his generation.'[98]

Sheppard's seriousness led many to think he lacked a sense of humour. In fact, he had a fund of amusing stories, many related to cricket, and some against himself. He could also be spontaneously funny. During the 1950–1 MCC tour of Australia he was heckled by spectators for scoring too slowly. At one point he walked down the wicket and offered his bat to a loud-voiced critic in the stands. He had 'in-jokes' with close friends and would convulse with laughter. 'He did have a sense of humour,' says his close friend and colleague Nicholas Frayling, 'but you had to know him well to really appreciate and dig it out.'

Another skill Sheppard gained as a cricketer and used as a bishop was handling the press. From his earliest days as a player he was a media darling. His charm, film-star looks and potential to say something different made him a magnet for reporters. His ordination, marriage and other life events were front-page news. With cricket still widely covered, he was a celebrity of the day. He was also always prepared to meet the press when others chose to avoid them. 'They were going to write about you, whether you liked it or not,' he would say. 'And if you went to meet them, and tried, there was a much better chance that they might get it about right than if you didn't.'[99] As we have seen, two mass-market publications, the *Daily Mail* and *Woman's Own*, signed him up to write regular columns.

His relationship with the media was double-edged, however, and there were times when he was 'angered and hurt by slanted and dishonest reporting'. At his first public meeting in Islington he spoke entirely about his faith, save for a passing reference to his support for the National Playing Fields Association. The report in the paper confined itself to saying he was 'very interested in the National Playing Fields Association'.[100] Newspapers would refuse him a right of reply to critical

---

98 Test Match Special tribute to DSS, May 2005.
99 Interview with Barry Norman, BBC Five Live, 3 June 1996.
100 Sheppard, *Steps along Hope Street*, p. 32.

pieces about him or a fellow bishop. As both a cricketer and bishop he was treated roughly by sections of the press. He was deeply embarrassed as a young curate when the *Daily Mail* sent copies of his first guest column to every priest in the country, and described his six months writing for the paper as 'the biggest pain and grief of my life'. Sections would be cut from his text without discussion, and misleading headlines added.[101] Aware that Grace had contracted chickenpox on honeymoon, the *Daily Mail* reported she had caught it from her sister, Evelyn, who had been a bridesmaid. They even printed a photo of Evelyn at the wedding, with a large arrow pointing to a spot they had superimposed on to her face.[102]

As Sheppard became more outspoken on issues such as apartheid, unemployment and housing, so he was targeted by sections of the media unsympathetic to his concerns. In 1979 the *Sunday Express* ran a gossip column item suggesting he would inherit a large estate in Scotland belonging to his late father's cousin. The story appeared after Sheppard spoke out against a pay rise for bishops and called on unions to show restraint. It was easy to take a pay cut when you were heir to a £2,000,000 estate, the *Sunday Express* claimed.[103] This was news to Sheppard. Acutely embarrassed, he wrote apologetically to his cousin saying he had no interest in inheriting the estate. Following a complaint, the *Express* wrote with a full apology. Although Sheppard had formally disclaimed his interest in the estate, the story reappeared in the *Mail on Sunday* in 1983. They printed an apology. Astonishingly the story reappeared in the London *Evening Standard* in 1985, forcing Sheppard to issue a statement.

Sheppard did not court publicity as a bishop, but he saw the media's potential to further a cause. He would never be seduced into making an unguarded comment, and his response to a media approach was always, 'I'll get back to you.' In the way that they managed the media, and employed press officers, both Sheppard and Worlock were ahead of their time.

Sheppard was also disciplined about the areas on which he would publicly comment, limiting himself to those with which he was familiar

---

101 Letter dated 12 July 1995, SHP, 8.10.
102 'The SPOTS that spoiled a honeymoon', *Daily Mail*, 9 July 1957; cf. Grace's account in *Living with Dying*, p. 12.
103 This amount was 'grossly exaggerated', Sheppard's cousin told him.

and for which he felt a passion. The 'clean up TV' campaigner Mary Whitehouse once asked him to speak out against 'moral pollution' as he did urban deprivation. Sheppard said that, although 'frequently pressed' to make statements about subjects he believed to be extremely important, he tried always to speak only about subjects on which he could be 'properly briefed' and which he could sustain. 'The great urban issues of unemployment, housing, health, race relations are wide enough in all conscience', he told her. He was unhappy when people put 'an emphasis all the time on standards' and condemned 'those who failed to live up to them', he said. 'Jesus . . . made people know that they were valued . . . [and] . . .once their self confidence started to grow, he presented the challenge of responsible living very strongly. That is the route that I believe we should try to take.'[104]

He took a similar line when invited to speak at the first public rally of the Nationwide Festival of Light in 1971, another Christian movement against obscenity. 'I wanted to fight for the strengthening of family life', he said, 'but the Festival of Light seemed to identify Christian faith with a moralistic stance that was set over against society.'[105] When asked to speak against the Monty Python film, *The Life of Brian*, he said Christians needed to think about the kind of witness they were giving to Jesus Christ if they only spoke in public when their own feelings were hurt. 'I believe that the times when it is right for Christians to speak up are much more when another group of people who have no power to speak for themselves is being hurt.'[106] Yet in 1967 Sheppard supported an attempt to censor the novel *Last Exit to Brooklyn* under the Obscene Publications Act. The initiator of the case was Sir Cyril Black, a Conservative MP and leading figure in the Festival of Light. Sheppard appeared as witness for the prosecution. 'Though censorship should be a weapon sparingly used, there were times when it made for health', he later wrote.[107] Grace thought her husband chose not to speak about a broad range of issues because he feared that 'the whole of the inner cities thing would then

---

104 Letters to Mary Whitehouse, 27 May 1987, 24 June 1987: SHP, 9.7.
105 Sheppard, *Steps along Hope Street*, p. 138.
106 Letter dated 10 April 1980: SHP, 9.7.
107 Sheppard, *Steps along Hope Street*, pp. 137–8.

drop to the bottom of the pile.'[108] One of the strengths of Sheppard's partnership with Worlock, writes Pat Jones, 'was that across many years and challenges, they pursued a consistent set of themes.'[109]

*

Sheppard listed 'leadership in a team' as another facility that cricket had helped him to develop. To some, its effect on him in the church was palpable. Bishop Michael Bourke remembers the process of appointing the members of the Sponsoring Body for the *Unemployment and the Future of Work* enquiry, of which he was part. 'One could see the cricketer in David Sheppard, in the proactive relish with which he led the team-building process. It was an exhilarating experience,' Bourke has said.

For many Sheppard was a natural leader. He had an aura which led them instinctively to put him in charge. This was partly due to his celebrity, but other less palpable factors were at work. 'He had that extraordinarily old-fashioned concept called "presence",' Mark Hedley recalls. 'It's indefinable, but hugely important. When David was there, you knew it. Not because of anything he did. But just because he physically tended to dominate a gathering.'

Sheppard's career was a succession of leadership positions. Head of his house at school, captain of Cambridge, Sussex and England, 'skipper' at the Mayflower, a bishop in the church. In addition to being invited to chair established bodies, almost every group or network he joined asked him to be its chair.[110] 'He was a team man, and welcomed strong team members but in the end he was always clearly the leader,' Grace said of her husband.[111] Many would attest to his skill at chairing meetings. He would expect others to be as well-prepared as he was, but would make everyone feel valued and that their contribution mattered.

---

108 Grace Sheppard interview with Eliza Filby, 27 July 2006.

109 Jones, P., 'Sharp compassion: Derek Worlock's journey', September 2013, p. 5. Accessible at http://togetherforthecommongood.co.uk/viewpoints/opinion-pieces/articles/pat-jones-cbe.html. Pat Jones CBE was a friend and close colleague of Archbishop Worlock for many years.

110 Sheppard lists examples in *Steps along Hope Street*, including his unit cricket team in the army (16), a local branch of Eclectics (70), the Peckham Settlement (106), the Martin Luther King Foundation (136) and the Michaelmas Group (225).

111 Grace Sheppard interview with Eliza Filby, 27 July 2006.

Sheppard's leadership was a vital factor in the transformation of Merseyside. 'At a time when the city had no confidence', says former vice-chancellor of Liverpool John Moores University, Peter Toyne,

> Sheppard arrives with a vision about what could be done. Others who'd been there too long, and could only see the end of the wall, might say, "Who's he to start telling us what's what?" But thank heavens he did, in my view! That's leadership.

Someone once said that, with Sheppard, 'Liverpool had got the bishop it deserved'. Sheppard always regarded that as a personal compliment.

*

Sheppard inspired many, in cricket as well as in public life. As captain of Sussex in 1953 he provided an example many strove to emulate. The team 'were all deeply impressed by Sheppard's high personal standards and . . . were all equally determined to live up to them,' one player recalled.[112] The wicketkeeper that season, Rupert Webb, said that if he 'could have been anybody in this life', he would 'have liked to have been David Sheppard.'[113] Sheppard did much to encourage young people in the game, and would always respond enthusiastically when asked about his favourite match or best innings, and take young relatives to matches and introduce them to players.[114] He once set aside an evening to talk to the son of a colleague before nominating him for membership of MCC. His old school magazine said that 'if ever there was a worthy role-model for the 21st-century Shirburnian it is David Stuart Sheppard.'[115] A generation of young Christians was inspired by the spiritual and sporting message of his first book, *Parson's Pitch*.[116]

His decision to step back from first-class cricket while still in his

---

112 Marshall, J., *Sussex Cricket: A History*, London: Heinemann, 1959, p. 214.
113 Chalke, S., *The Way It Was: Glimpses of English cricket's past*, Bath: Fairfield Books, 2008, p. 50.
114 His cousin Jim Gratton recalls Sheppard often taking him and his brothers to Hove in his Morris Minor convertible, including during the season he captained Sussex.
115 *The Shirburnian*, 2005, p. 20.
116 Sheppard, D. S., *Parson's Pitch*, London: Hodder & Stoughton, 1964.

prime denied him a place among the 'greats', but his records for Cambridge University will almost certainly never be beaten. He is still considered one of the best players ever to have played varsity and county cricket. In 2017, *The Cricketer* chose him as 'captain' of its 'Best Oxbridge XI' of all time, and the distinguished cricket writer Christopher Martin-Jenkins had Sheppard batting at no. 2. in his 'Sussex dream team' spanning nearly two centuries.[117] On the wider stage, Sheppard's contribution to the collapse of apartheid is still remembered, especially in South Africa itself. His stand against the cricket establishment was courageous and costly, but events in the 1990s suggest his policy of isolation rather than continued engagement was sound.

*

Sheppard's memory is honoured in many ways. A blue plaque adorns his house in Peckham, a chapel is named in his memory at St Mary's Islington, as is a room at Trinity Hall, Cambridge. The Bishop David Sheppard school in Southport promotes the Christian values for which its patron will be remembered, including friendship, compassion and fairness, while the Bishop David Sheppard Anniversary Trust, established after he had completed ten years in Liverpool, make grants to adults who missed the opportunity to pursue a qualification the first time around. This was a cause close to his and Grace's heart. The Sheppard-Worlock Library is at the heart of Liverpool Hope University, and Bishop Sheppard Court acknowledges his support for the Eldonians. The Sussex ground at Hove has a cabinet displaying his blazer, bat and other memorabilia, and Brighton and Hove City Council even named a bus in his honour.

Most striking of all is a monument in memory of Sheppard and Worlock in Hope Street, halfway between the two cathedrals.[118] The two bishops, in almost life-sized form, stand before two 15-foot bronze 'doors', decorated with symbols and newspaper headlines from their lives and ministry.

---

117 Coyne, J., 'University challenge', *The Cricketer*, 14:8, May 2017, p. 63; Martin-Jenkins, C., 'Sussex dream team', *The Times*, 24 August 2007.

118 Designed by Stephen Broadbent, it was unveiled in 2008 during a walk of witness.

A cricket ball lies at Sheppard's feet. The symbolism is strong. The bishops stand side by side on the street, not on a plinth and out of reach. Looking north and south through the doors, the viewer can see the two cathedrals, or can walk or stand between the two figures, which are set in circles. The doors 'speak of welcome', Grace wrote after the unveiling.

> They are always open to all who will come. There is a third circle which is empty except for the words Better Together and We meet in Hope. This circle invites each of us to step inside and join the company . . . [It] could, however, be imagined to contain the figure of Christ – unseen, yet ever present in their lives and partnership . . . The Sculpture speaks volumes of God's ever open arms.[119]

The memorial was commissioned by the *Liverpool Echo*, and paid for by public subscription, strong pointers to the affection in which the bishops were held in their adopted city.

Sheppard lives on beyond Liverpool. Initiatives he helped to establish, including the Church Urban Fund, continue to flourish. The political edge to CUF's work, reflecting its roots in *Faith in the City*, changed over time, and the Church Commissioners withdrew their funding in the 1990s. Since 2011 central government has funded part of CUF's work. Yet the impact of the Fund on the parishes and projects in which it has invested has been enormous. The role of *Faith in the City* itself in transforming the Church's approach to the inner cities is another of Sheppard's legacies. The report was, 'after Temple's *Christianity and Social Order* . . . the most important British contribution to the development of a better society', suggested three respected scholars in 2011.[120] Sheppard also helped to stake out the Church's claim to have a public voice, however uncomfortable that might be for government and the Church itself.

Sheppard's work at the Mayflower lives on through its diaspora. Many who attended its clubs trace the origins of their faith to that experience.

---

119 Liverpool Cathedral *Life* magazine, 58, 22 June 2008.
120 Atherton, J., Baker, C., and Reader, J., *Christianity and the New Social Order: A manifesto for a fairer future*, London: SPCK, 2011, p. 42.

Some became leaders, or involved themselves in urban mission. Many would attest that Sheppard and Burton's work shaped them more than anything else into the people they became.[121] Others who worked there as residents took their new insights into inner-city culture into future roles. Many Christian groups and churches were inspired by this model of inner-city mission.

The Church of England continues to be a presence among poor communities in many areas across the country, although in some sparsely populated rural areas, the 'presence' can be a bit thin in practice. In recent years, its priority has been on growing numbers, and 'church plants' have generally been prioritized in metropolitan city centres where rapid growth is most likely. Churches in outer estates, where the most disadvantaged communities now tend to be found, have been under-supported financially and in terms of human resources, as the likelihood of growth there was thought to be low. As some in the Church have called for a return to a bias to the poor, a shift in priorities is occurring.

Bishop Philip North, chair of the Archbishops' Estates Evangelism Task Group, traces the Church's renewed mission to outer estates back to Sheppard. When training for ordination in the late 1980s, North and his peers competed to be sent to inner-city parishes as curates. 'The urban was absolutely the place to be,' North recalled. 'That was very much to do with David Sheppard and his work.'

*

Sheppard's commitment to Liverpool is dramatically captured in the memorial above his ashes in the south aisle of the Anglican cathedral. Featuring a white Portland stone set into a crater carved directly into the sandstone wall, it signifies the lasting effect Sheppard made on the city. Around it, two overlapping forms are etched into the wall, depicting his passion for reconciliation. A verse from Scripture expresses what

---

121 Correspondence in Sheppard's papers. Former Mayflower people maintained a network for keeping in touch and meeting up six decades after Sheppard, and they, left the centre. The Mayflower continued in Sheppard's wake and since 2003 the River Christian Centre has occupied the site.

Sheppard sought to do in the place to which God had called him. 'Seek the welfare of the city where I have sent you . . . and pray to the Lord on its behalf.'[122]

---

122 Jeremiah 29.7. The memorial was designed by Stephen Broadbent and created by Adrian White. The text was suggested by a long-time friend of the Sheppards, Bishop Michael Whinney. Grace's ashes were interred alongside her husband's in 2011, attended by family and Archbishop Desmond Tutu. Grace's engagement ring was buried with her ashes, and David's bishop's ring with his.

Appendix 1
Chronology

1922   December – marriage of Barbara Shepherd and Stuart Morton Winter Sheppard, DSS's parents

1923   September 28 – birth of Mary Sheppard, DSS's sister

1929   March 6 – DSS born Reigate, Surrey

1935   March 4 – birth of Eleanor Grace Isaac, DSS's wife

1937   November – death of Stuart Sheppard, DSS's father

1938   March – starts at Northcliffe House School, Bognor Regis

1942   May – starts at Sherborne School

1946   May – debut for Sherborne First XI

December – gains Exhibition to Trinity Hall, Cambridge

1947   August – first class debut for Sussex

October – begins National Service

1949   September – discharged from the Army

October – goes up to Trinity Hall, Cambridge

November – conversion during Christian Union mission, Cambridge

1950   July – awarded Blue for cricket

August – Test debut versus West Indies at The Oval

September – sails to Australia with MCC tour party

1951   April – returns from MCC tour of Australia and New Zealand

1953   March – goes down from Cambridge

Captains Sussex to second place in the Championship

October – starts ordination training at Ridley Hall, Cambridge

1954   July – captains England in two Tests versus Pakistan

1955   September 29 – ordained a deacon in St Paul's Cathedral

October – begins curacy at St Mary's, Islington

1956   March – engagement to Grace Isaac announced

	July – scores century in the 'Laker' Test at Old Trafford
	September 29 – ordained to the priesthood in St Paul's Cathedral
1957	June 19 – marriage to Grace Isaac at Lindfield, Sussex
1958	January – licensed as Warden of the Mayflower Family Centre, Canning Town
1962	March – birth of Jenny
	September – leaves for Australia with MCC tour party
1963	March – end of MCC tour – stays on in Sydney with Grace and Jenny until July
1964	June – publication of *Parson's Pitch*
1965	October – Grace has surgery for cancer
1968	December – MCC Special General Meeting to discuss the 'D'Oliveira issue'
1969	October – consecrated Bishop of Woolwich in Southwark Cathedral
1974	January – publication of *Built as a City*
1975	June – installation as Bishop of Liverpool
1976	January – Michael Henshall consecrated Bishop of Warrington
	February – Derek Worlock consecrated RC Archbishop of Liverpool
1980	December – introduced to House of Lords as a Lord Spiritual
1981	July – rioting breaks out in Toxteth
1982	May – visit of Pope John Paul II to Liverpool
1983	January – publication of *Bias to the Poor*
	March – death of Barbara Sheppard, DSS's mother
	April–May – visit to Argentina and Peru
1984	April – delivers BBC Dimbleby Lecture
	September – forms Michaelmas Group with Archbishop Worlock
1985	May – tragedy at Heysel Stadium
	December – publication of *Faith in the City*
1988	January – publication of *Better Together*
	September – marriage of Jenny to Donald Sinclair
1989	begins 4-year term as chair of Central Religious Advisory Committee (CRAC)
	April – tragedy at Hillsborough Stadium
	May – visit to South Africa with Grace and Archbishop Worlock

1991	begins 5-year term as chair of the Board for Social Responsibility (BSR)
1995	January – awarded Freedom of the City of Liverpool (with Derek Worlock)
1996	February – death of Archbishop Worlock
	Retirement of Bishop Michael Henshall
1997	April – publication of *Unemployment and the Future of Work*
	October – retirement
1998	January – life peerage announced in New Year's Honours List
	September – birth of elder grandson, Stuart Sinclair
2000	June – birth of younger grandson, Gilles Sinclair
2002	September – publication of *Steps along Hope Street*
2005	March 5 – death, aged 75
2008	May – unveiling of statue in Hope Street
2010	November 11 – death of Grace Sheppard, aged 75
2011	May – dedication of memorial in Liverpool Cathedral
2017	April – death of Mary Maxwell, DSS's sister

Appendix 2
The cricket career of
David Sheppard

TEST CRICKET

BATTING AND FIELDING

Year	M	I	NO	Runs	HS	Ave	100	50	Ct
1950 *(WI)*	1	2	-	40	29	20.00	-	-	-
1950/1 (Aus)	2	3	-	51	41	17.00	-	-	-
1950/1 (NZ)	1	2	1	7	4*	7.00	-	-	1
1952 (Ind)	2	2	-	153	119	76.50	1	-	1
1954 (Pak)	2	2	-	50	37	25.00	-	-	4
1956 (Aus)	2	3	-	199	113	66.33	1	1	-
1957 (WI)	2	2	-	108	68	54.00	-	1	2
1962 (Pak)	2	3	1	149	83	74.50	-	2	-
1962/3 (Aus)	5	10	-	330	113	33.00	1	2	2
1962/3 (NZ)	3	4	-	85	42	21.25	-	-	2
Total	**22**	**33**	**2**	**1172**	**119**	**37.80**	**3**	**6**	**12**

CENTURIES

119	India	The Oval	1952
113	Australia	Old Trafford	1956
113	Australia	Melbourne	1963

CAPTAINCY

He captained England against Pakistan at Trent Bridge and Old Trafford in 1954.
England won by an innings at Trent Bridge and had a comanding first-innings lead in a rain-ruined draw at Old Trafford.

BOWLING

He did not bowl in Test cricket.

FIRST-CLASS CRICKET

BATTING AND FIELDING
HOME

Year	M	I	NO	Runs	HS	Ave	100	50	Ct
1947	3	6	1	48	20*	9.60	-	-	-
1948	2	3	-	35	19	11.66	-	-	1
1949	11	21	-	913	204	43.47	3	3	7
1950	26	44	2	1887	227	44.92	5	10	10
1951	23	43	3	2104	183	52.60	7	9	32
1952	23	39	4	2262	239*	64.62	10	7	21
1953	35	57	7	2270	186*	45.40	7	9	43
1954	21	37	4	1398	120	42.36	3	8	25
1955	10	18	1	637	104	37.47	1	6	11
1956	11	17	1	670	113	41.87	1	4	4
1957	12	18	2	490	117	30.62	1	3	12
1958	3	5	1	172	102	43.00	1	-	2
1959	1	2	-	151	124	75.50	1	-	1
1960	6	11	-	297	100	27.00	1	1	5
1962	14	26	3	1017	112	44.21	3	5	5
Total	**201**	**347**	**29**	**14351**	**239***	**44.70**	**44**	**65**	**179**

OVERSEAS

Year	M	I	NO	Runs	HS	Ave	100	50	Ct
1950/1 *(A/NZ)*	13	20	2	415	75	23.05	-	2	4
1962/3 *(A/NZ)*	16	28	-	1074	113	38.35	1	9	11
Total	**29**	**48**	**2**	**1489**	**113**	**32.36**	**1**	**11**	**15**

HOME AND OVERSEAS

	M	I	NO	Runs	HS	Ave	100	50	Ct
Total	**230**	**395**	**31**	**15840**	**239***	**43.51**	**45**	**76**	**194**

DOUBLE CENTURIES
For Cambridge University
227	West Indians	Fenner's	1950
239*	Worcestershire	Worcester	1952

For Sussex
204	Glamorgan	Eastbourne	1949

CAPTAINCY

He captained Cambridge University in 1952, scoring 127 in the Varsity match at Lord's.

He captained Sussex in 1953, when the county finished second in the county championship.

BOWLING

He bowled 20 overs in first-class cricket and took two wickets for 88 runs.

Appendix 2

M	matches	100	centuries
I	innings	50	scores between 50 and 99
NO	not out innings	Ct	catches
HS	highest score	*	not out
Ave	average runs per completed innings		

Sources

Interviews

Lord (David) Alton: 2 May 2019

Revd Dr Andrew Atherstone: 3 July 2017

Nicholas Barber CBE: 19 June 2018

Rt Revd Michael Baughen: 27 April 2018

Canon Neville Black MBE: 15 September 2017

Peter Bounds CBE: 27 November 2017

Revd Peter Brain: 3 July 2018

Sheila Brain: 3 July 2018

Mike Brearley OBE: 14 March 2018

Elizabeth Bridger: 2 January 2017

Canon Gordon Bridger: 2 January 2017

Roger Broadbent: 7 November 2018

Lucie Broadbent Smith: 7 November 2018

Revd Dr Malcolm Brown: 13 September 2018

Wally Brown CBE: 28 November 2017

Canon Godfrey Butland: 26 July 2018

Lord (Robin) Butler: 5 July 2018

Fr John Catlin: 17 May 2016

Keith Cawdron: 2 October 2018

Canon Peter Challen: 2 April 2018

Jennet Christie: 2 September 2016

Patrick Coldstream CBE: 17 August 2018

Preb. John Collins: 18 August 2015

Canon Henry Corbett: 15 September 2017

Cllr Jane Corbett: 15 September 2017

John Crathorne: 5 May 2017

Professor Grace Davie (by Skype): 7 December 2018

Canon Myles Davies: 19 September 2017

Canon Paul Dawson: 24 November 2016

the late Hubert Doggart OBE: 3 September 2015

Rt Revd Timothy Dudley-Smith OBE: 16 March 2016

Robert Ebdon: 27 July 2016

Canon Dr John Elford: 28 June 2018

George Evans: 7 August 2018

Jon Filby: 30 October 2014

Very Revd Nicholas Frayling: 14 December 2016 and 18 June 2018

Mgr John Furnival: 19 September 2017

Pastor Dave Gill: 16 June 2016

Revd Jim Gosling: 20 September 2016

Revd Roger Grassham: 16 June 2016

Mary Gray: 25 May 2016

the late James Gray: 25 May 2016

Revd Stephen Gray: 13 April 2016

Lord (Brian) Griffiths: 25 October 2017 and 25 April 2019

Hugh Griffiths: 9 June 2016

Canon Anthony Hawley: 16 March 2016 and 31 August 2018

Rosemary Hawley MBE: 16 March 2016 and 31 August 2018

Sir Mark Hedley: 5 August 2018

Revd Chris Idle: 30 January 2018

Evelyn Isaac: 31 August 2018

Kumar Jacob MBE: 17 August 2018

Martin Kenyon: 26 April 2018

Robin Knight: 14 March 2018

Canon Bob Lewis: 10 August 2018

Enid Lodge: 3 October 2018

Philip Lodge: 3 October 2018

Canon Brian McConnell: 31 August 2018

Ruth McCurry: 5 July 2018

Tony McGann OBE: 7 August 2018

Revd Dr Colin Marchant: 15 March 2018

Sir Philip Mawer: 24 May 2018

the late Mary Maxwell: 21 July 2014

Dr Sarah Maxwell: 16 September 2018

Ken Medlock OBE: 24 January 2015

Roger Morris OBE: 25 February 2018

Revd Stuart Munns OBE: 8 October 2018

Rachel Newton: 23 April 2016 and 17 May 2017

Brian O'Gorman: 15 July 2017

Rt Revd John Packer: 20 July 2018

Dr John Parker: 12 September 2016

Professor Michael Parkinson: 6 August 2018

Jim Parks: 22 June 2016

Betty Parr: 19 October 2016

Canon Henry Pearson: 2 September 2016

Judith Pearson: 2 September 2016

the late Irene Perry: 24 June 2016

Revd John Perry: 24 June 2016

Roger Phillips: 14 September 2017

the late Professor John Pickering: 8 June 2018

Revd Michael Plunkett MBE: 2 October 2018

Liz Pope: 7 November 2018

Fr Nicholas Postlethwaite: 21 November 2017

Alan Rayment: 1 August 2016

John Roberts: 21 March 2017

Professor Hilary Russell: 3 May 2018

Robin Sheldon: 4 April 2017

Jenny Sinclair: 5 July 2018 and 17 August 2018

David Skidmore: 4 September 2018

Dr Pat Starkey: 18 September 2017

Max Steinberg CBE: 11 July 2018

Mary Sugden: 18 January 2019

Revd Robert Torrens: 29 March 2017

Angela Toyne: 22 February 2018

Professor Peter Toyne CBE: 22 February 2018

Susan Wates MBE: 4 September 2018

the late Rupert Webb: 15 July 2016

Lord (Charles) Williams: 2 June 2017

Canon Dick Williams: 17 September 2017 and 1 May 2018

the late Su Williams: 17 September 2017 and 1 May 2018

Rachel Wing: 25 May 2016

Canon Michael Wolfe: 18 September 2017

Rt Revd Wilfred Wood KA: 21 March 2017

John Woodcock OBE: 10 August 2016

Telephone calls and correspondence

Colin Abbiss; Janet Abbiss; Revd Eric Allen; Revd Bob Andrews; Lord (Kenneth) Baker; Peter Ballantine; Johnny Barclay; Charles Barr; Caroline Basil-Jones; Rt Revd Gordon Bates; Rt Hon. John Battle; Canon Chris Beales; Revd Dr Stephen Bellamy; Diana Benge-Abbott; Iona Birchall; Alan Bleasdale; Lord (David) Blunkett; Daphne Boddington; Brian Booth MBE; Professor Philip Booth; Anne Booth-Clibborn; Rt Revd Michael Bourke; Rt Revd Ronnie Bowlby; Very Revd Mark Boyling; Peter Bradhurst; Ven. Peter Bradley; Canon Andrew Britton; Lord (Clive) Brooke; Andrew Brown; Rt Hon. Gordon Brown; Rt Revd Colin Buchanan; Hon. Dr Meredith Burgmann; Michael Bushby; Rt Revd Tom Butler; Rt Revd Lord (George) Carey; the late John Carlisle; Professor Bill Chambers; Juliet Chaplin; Rt Revd Alan Chesters; Dr James Chubb; the late Revd

Sources

Graham Cook; Wendy Couzens; the late Revd John Cross; Preb. Patrick Dearnley; Revd Bob Dew; Shirley Dewes; Ted Dexter CBE; Matthew Dieppe; Liz Dodds; Claire Dove OBE; Alan Dowding; Rt Revd Chris Edmondson; Ian Elliott; Robert Ely; Canon George Farran; Rt Hon. Frank Field MP; Julian Filochowski OBE CMG; Revd Rosemary Finch; Revd David Fletcher; Rt Revd Peter Forster; Jim Gratton; Preb. Alan Green; Rt Revd Laurie Green; the late Canon Michael Green; Hester Greenstock; Lord (Leslie) Griffiths; Michael Griffiths; Judy Grimes; Barry Grinham; Canon Christopher Hall; Anne Hanson; Dr Brian Hanson; Stephen Hanvey; Canon Giles Harcourt; Ven. Peter Harrison; Very Revd Nicholas Henshall; Lord (Michael) Heseltine; Sylvia Hetherington; Revd Garth Hewitt; Rt Revd Rupert Hoare; Dr Janet Hollinshead; Richard Holman; Rt Revd Lord (David) Hope; Archie Hunter; Canon John Hunter; Peter Hunter; John Isaac; Derek Jay; Winifred Jordan; Ian Keast; Fr Kevin Kelly; Jane Kennedy; Lord (Neil) Kinnock; Brian Lamming; Canon Myrtle Langley; Les Lenham; Jim Lethbridge; Revd Malcolm Lorimer; Rt Revd Stephen Lowe; Canon Ted Lyons; Revd Bill MacDougall; Canon David MacInnes; Patrick Mackie; Shelagh McNerney; Rt Revd Vincent Malone; Judy Martin-Jenkins; Dr Damian Mawer; the late Revd George May; Canon John Maybury; Rt Revd Christopher Mayfield; Revd Jean Mayland; Barbara Mead; the late Vic Mead; Nigel Mellor; Revd Nicholas Mercer; Hazel Miller; Revd Randell Moll; Fr Peter Morgan; Revd Hugh Mumford; Douglas Murray; Canon Eddie Neale MBE; Revd Norma Nelson; Rosemary Nelson; Cardinal Vincent Nichols; John Nicholson; William Nicholson OBE; Revd Bob Nind; Rt Revd Philip North; Michael Oram; Revd Colin Oxenforth; Rt Revd Geoff Pearson; Lord (Tom) Pendry; Margaret Pinniger; Tim Pinniger; Sir Desmond Pitcher; Rt Revd Stephen Platten; Gill Potter; Lord (David) Puttnam; Barbara Quantrill; Jane Reed CBE; Henry Reid; Canon Dr Bob Reiss; George Reiss; Susan Ripley; Pat Robb; Audrey Roberts; Canon Roger Royle; Janet Ruddick; Lord (Jonathan) Sacks; Rt Revd Roger Sainsbury; Graeme Sanders; Rt Revd Mark Santer; Marion Seaman; John Segal; Rt Revd Peter Selby; Derek Semmence; Dr Ian Sharp; David Sherman; Diana Silk; Martin Slatter; Shirley Slatter; Ven. Richard Sledge; Alan C. Smith CBE; Hazel Sweetnam; Dame Mary Tanner; Canon Alan Taylor; Revd Dr John Taylor; Lord (Norman) Tebbit; Caroline Tetley; Ian Thomson; Sara Thomson; Dr Sally Thompson; Canon Barry Thorley; Rt Hon. Stephen Timms MP; Revd Linda Tomkinson; Revd Michael Toogood; Dr Protasia Torkington; Professor Ian Tracey; Archbishop Desmond Tutu; Revd Dr John Vincent; Canon Dave Wade; Revd J. M. Waters; Peter Watherston; Alison Webster; Margy Weir; Canon Richard Wheeler; Ann Whitaker; Canon Max Wigley; Revd Bob Wilkes; Francis Witts; Brenda Wolfe; Andrew Wood; Ven. David Woodhouse; Revd Jeremy Wordsworth; Chris Wright; the late Christopher Zealley.

Select bibliography

Books by David Sheppard

Parson's Pitch, London: Hodder & Stoughton, 1964
Built as a City, London: Hodder & Stoughton, 1974
Black People and Employment: The 1975 Martin Luther King Memorial Lecture, London: The
    Martin Luther King Foundation, 1975
Bias to the Poor, London: Hodder & Stoughton, 1983
The Other Britain (the 1984 Dimbleby Lecture), London: BBC, 1984
Steps along Hope Street, London: Hodder & Stoughton, 2002

Books by David Sheppard and Derek Worlock

Better Together: Christian partnership in a hurt city, London: Hodder and Stoughton, 1988
With Christ in the Wilderness, London: The Bible Reading Fellowship, 1990
With Hope in Our Hearts, London: Hodder & Stoughton, 1994

Books by Grace Sheppard

An Aspect of Fear: A journey from anxiety to peace, London: Darton, Longman & Todd, 1989
Pits and Pedestals: A journey towards self-respect, London: Darton, Longman & Todd, 1995
Living with Dying, London: Darton, Longman & Todd, 2010

Reports

*Faith in the City: A Call for Action by Church and Nation. The Report of the Archbishop of
    Canterbury's Commission on Urban Priority Areas*, London: Church House Publishing,
    1985
Unemployment and the Future of Work: An Enquiry for the Churches, London: CCBI, 1997

Secondary sources

Anderson, D., ed., *The Kindness that Kills: The churches' simplistic response to complex social
    issues*, London: SPCK, 1984
Botting, M., *Fanning the Flame: The story of Ridley Hall, volume 3, 1951–2001*, Cambridge:
    Ridley Hall, 2006
Brearley, M., *On Cricket*, London: Constable, 2018
Brown, M., and Sedgwick, P., eds, *Putting Theology to Work: A theological symposium on
    'Unemployment and the Future of Work'*, London and Manchester: CCBI and William
    Temple Foundation, 1998
Burton, G., *People Matter More Than Things*, London: Hodder & Stoughton, 1965
Chalke, S., *The Way It Was: Glimpses of English cricket's past*, Bath: Fairfield Books, 2008
Clark, H., *The Church under Thatcher*, London: SPCK, 1993

334

Select bibliography

Elford, R. J., ed., *The Foundation of Hope: Turning dreams into reality*, Liverpool: Liverpool University Press, 2003

Filby, E., *God and Mrs Thatcher*, London: Biteback, 2015

Furnival, J., and Knowles, A., *Archbishop Derek Worlock: His personal journey*, London: Geoffrey Chapman, 1998

Hewitt, D. and J., *George Burton: A study in contradictions*, London: Hodder & Stoughton, 1969

Hunter, J., *A Touch of Class: Issues of urban mission*, Sheffield: EUTP, 1995

Living Faith in the City: A Progress Report by the Archbishop of Canterbury's Advisory Group on Urban Priority Areas, London: General Synod of the Church of England, 1990

Marshall, J., *Sussex Cricket: A History*, London: Heinemann, 1959

Marshall, M., *Gentlemen and Players: Conversations with cricketers*, London: Grafton Books, 1987

Oborne, P., *Basil D'Oliveira: Cricket and conspiracy – the untold story*, London: Sphere, 2004

Quicke, A., and Quicke, J., *Hidden Agendas: The politics of religious broadcasting in Britain 1987–1991*, Virginia Beach: Dominion Kings Grant, 1992

Steen, R., *This Sporting Life: Cricket*, Newton Abbot: David & Charles, 1999

Ward, P., *Growing Up Evangelical: Youth work and the making of a subculture*, London: SPCK, 1996

Watherston, P., *A Different Kind of Church: The Mayflower Family Centre story*, London: Marshall Pickering, 1994

Photograph acknowledgements

Page 3
Top Central Press/Getty Images
Bottom left Courtesy of Brian Booth
Bottom right S&G/PA Images

Page 4
Top left Daily Herald Archive/National Science and Media Museum/ Science and Society Picture Library
Top right Daily Herald Archive/National Science and Media Museum/ Science and Society Picture Library
Bottom right Liverpool Echo

Page 5
Bottom Stephen Shakeshaft/*Liverpool Echo*

Page 6
Bottom right Dave Williams/Open Eye

Page 7
Top Liverpool Echo
Bottom right Stephen Shakeshaft/Liverpool Echo

Page 8
Top right Stephen Shakeshaft/Liverpool Echo
Bottom Jason Roberts/Liverpool Echo

All other photographs
From the private collection of Jenny Sinclair, with her kind permission.

Index